Exploring Cyber Criminals and Data Privacy Measures

Nuno Mateus-Coelho
Lapi2s, Copelabs, Lusófona University, Portugal

Manuela Cruz-Cunha
Polytechnic Institute of Cavado and Ave, Portugal

A volume in the Advances in Digital Crime, Forensics, and Cyber Terrorism (ADCFCT) Book Series

Published in the United States of America by
IGI Global
Information Science Reference (an imprint of IGI Global)
701 E. Chocolate Avenue
Hershey PA, USA 17033
Tel: 717-533-8845
Fax: 717-533-8661
E-mail: cust@igi-global.com
Web site: http://www.igi-global.com

Library of Congress Cataloging-in-Publication Data

Names: Mateus-Coelho, Nuno Ricardo, 1981- editor. | Cruz-Cunha, Maria
  Manuela, 1964- editor.
Title: Exploring cyber criminals and data privacy measures / edited
  by Nuno Mateus-Coelho and Manuela Cruz-Cunha.
Description: Hershey, PA : Information Science Reference, [2023] | Includes
  bibliographical references and index. | Summary: "The Handbook of
  Research on Cyber Criminals and Data Privacy Measures collects
  cutting-edge research on information security, cybercriminals, and data
  privacy. It proposes unique strategies for safeguarding and preserving
  digital information using realistic examples and case studies. Covering
  key topics such as crime detection, surveillance technologies, and
  organizational privacy, this major reference work is ideal for
  cybersecurity professionals, researchers, developers, practitioners,
  programmers, computer scientists, academicians, security analysts,
  educators, and students"-- Provided by publisher.
Identifiers: LCCN 2023014921 (print) | LCCN 2023014922 (ebook) | ISBN
  9781668484227 (hardcover) | ISBN 9781668484241 (ebook)
Subjects: LCSH: Computer crimes. | Computer security. | Privacy, Right of.
Classification: LCC HV6773 .H3747 2023 (print) | LCC HV6773 (ebook) | DDC
  364.16/8--dc23/eng/20230420
LC record available at https://lccn.loc.gov/2023014921
LC ebook record available at https://lccn.loc.gov/2023014922

This book is published in the IGI Global book series Advances in Digital Crime, Forensics, and Cyber Terrorism (ADCF-CT) (ISSN: 2327-0381; eISSN: 2327-0373)

British Cataloguing in Publication Data
A Cataloguing in Publication record for this book is available from the British Library.

For electronic access to this publication, please contact: eresources@igi-global.com.

Advances in Digital Crime, Forensics, and Cyber Terrorism (ADCFCT) Book Series

Bryan Christiansen
Southern New Hampshire University, USA
Agnieszka Piekarz
Independent Researcher, Poland

ISSN:2327-0381
EISSN:2327-0373

MISSION

The digital revolution has allowed for greater global connectivity and has improved the way we share and present information. With this new ease of communication and access also come many new challenges and threats as cyber crime and digital perpetrators are constantly developing new ways to attack systems and gain access to private information.

The **Advances in Digital Crime, Forensics, and Cyber Terrorism (ADCFCT) Book Series** seeks to publish the latest research in diverse fields pertaining to crime, warfare, terrorism and forensics in the digital sphere. By advancing research available in these fields, the **ADCFCT** aims to present researchers, academicians, and students with the most current available knowledge and assist security and law enforcement professionals with a better understanding of the current tools, applications, and methodologies being implemented and discussed in the field.

COVERAGE

- Hacking
- Cryptography
- Telecommunications Fraud
- Database Forensics
- Encryption
- Watermarking
- Network Forensics
- Data Protection
- Mobile Device Forensics
- Vulnerability

IGI Global is currently accepting manuscripts for publication within this series. To submit a proposal for a volume in this series, please contact our Acquisition Editors at Acquisitions@igi-global.com or visit: http://www.igi-global.com/publish/.

Titles in this Series

For a list of additional titles in this series, please visit: http://www.igi-global.com/book-series/advances-digital-crime-forensics-cyber/73676

Modeling and Simulation of Functional Nanomaterials for Forensic Investigation
Allah Rakha (Department of Forensic Medicine/Medical Jurisprudence, University of Health Sciences, Pakistan)
Anam Munawar (Department of Forensic Medicine/Medical Jurisprudence, University of Health Sciences, Pakistan) Virat Khanna (Department of Mechanical Engineering, Maharaja Agrasen University, India) and Suneev Anil
Bansal (Department of Mechanical Engineering, Bharat Institute of Engineering and Technolog, India)
Information Science Reference • © 2023 • 378pp • H/C (ISBN: 9781668483251) • US $250.00

Handbook of Research on War Policies, Strategies, and Cyber Wars
Fahri Özsungur (Mersin University, Turkey)
Information Science Reference • © 2023 • 463pp • H/C (ISBN: 9781668467411) • US $315.00

Global Perspectives on the Psychology of Terrorism
Nika Chitadze (International Black Sea University, Georgia)
Information Science Reference • © 2023 • 330pp • H/C (ISBN: 9781668453117) • US $215.00

Aiding Forensic Investigation Through Deep Learning and Machine Learning Frameworks
Alex Noel Joseph Raj (Shantou University, China) Vijayalakshmi G. V. Mahesh (BMS Institute of Technology
and Management, India) Ruban Nerssison (Vellore Institute of Technology, India) Ang Yu (Carolina University,
USA) and Jennifer Gentry (Carolina University, USA)
Information Science Reference • © 2022 • 273pp • H/C (ISBN: 9781668445587) • US $250.00

Dark Web Pattern Recognition and Crime Analysis Using Machine Intelligence
Romil Rawat (Shri Vaishnav Vidyapeeth Vishwavidyalaya, India) Shrikant Telang (Shri Vaishnav Vidyapeeth
Vishwavidyalaya, India) P. William (Sanjivani College of Engineering, Savitribai Phule Pune University, India)
Upinder Kaur (Akal University, Talwandi Sabo, India) and Om Kumar C.U. (School of Computer Science and
Engineering (SCOPE),Vellore Institute of Technology, India)
Information Science Reference • © 2022 • 281pp • H/C (ISBN: 9781668439425) • US $250.00

Using Computational Intelligence for the Dark Web and Illicit Behavior Detection
Romil Rawat (Shri Vaishnav Vidyapeeth Vishwavidyalaya, India) Upinder Kaur (Akal University, Talwandi Sabo,
India) Shadab Pasha Khan (Oriental Institute of Science and Technology, Bhopal, India) Ranjana Sikarwar (Amity
University, Gwalior, India) and K. Sakthidasan Sankaran (Hindustan Institute of Technology and Science, India)
Information Science Reference • © 2022 • 336pp • H/C (ISBN: 9781668464441) • US $250.00

701 East Chocolate Avenue, Hershey, PA 17033, USA
Tel: 717-533-8845 x100 • Fax: 717-533-8661
E-Mail: cust@igi-global.com • www.igi-global.com

Table of Contents

Detailed Table of Contents

Chapter 1
  Daniel Jorge Ferreira, University of Trás-os-Montes and Alto Douro, Portugal
  Nuno Mateus-Coelho, Lusófona University, Portugal

According to existing data, the frequency of cyberattacks on hospitals and healthcare systems more than doubled from 2016 to 2021, and the incidents exposed the protected health information of nearly 42 million patients. The global picture and the risks of being hit combine a series of issues—loss of access to critical health data, high costs of responding and preventing cyber-attacks, and threats to patient safety—that has largely shifted the focus towards infrastructure defense, of health. The groups that perpetrate such attacks are generally aggressive and their attacks directed at critical infrastructure in hospitals and healthcare organizations can disrupt operations and patient access for weeks or even months.

Chapter 2
  Ana Galvão, Instituto Politécnico de Bragança, Portugal
  Isabel Chumbo, Instituto Politécnico de Bragança, Portugal
  Eugénia Anes, Instituto Politécnico de Bragança, Portugal & CECC, Universidade Católica
    Portuguesa, Portugal

More than 99% of cybercriminal attacks exploit human characteristics and behaviour (people's vulnerabilities) rather than vulnerabilities in computer systems. When it comes to cybersecurity, it is crucial to consider human behaviour on the part of the user. Cognitive aspects such as attention, memory, and reasoning can be affected by conditions such as fatigue, illness, or injury and are pointed out as human characteristics that are at the origin of several incidents. Users' stress and anxiety may be correlated with making mistakes that compromise cybersecurity. Thus, behavioural psychology should be used to develop effective educational strategies and encourage safe and conscious behaviour in relation to cybersecurity. By understanding how users interact and respond to AI, more effective and aware cybersecurity systems can be created. This chapter's overall objective is to map the literature regarding the psychology of behaviour towards AI in cybersecurity, using a scoping review methodology to provide input into the behavioural psychology aspects regarding AI and cybersecurity.

Chapter 3

Vineeta Singh, GLA University, Mathura, India
Vandana Dixit Kaushik, Harcourt Butler Technical University, Kanpur, India

The vulnerability of wireless communication systems and technologies to various cyberattacks has been made public in recent years via different researchers; these cyberattacks not only impact private businesses but also government institutions. Sensitive and private data safety is a major challenge because of hackers since they are always trying to find loopholes in security models with different strong tactics and tools for cracking any sized keys. For minimizing such invasions, various developments have been made. This chapter carries out an in-depth study of several standard cyber security strategies currently in practice and the difficulties to be faced in cyber security practices. The modern efficient key systems are also shown, and the latest generation vulnerabilities are well described and reported. The advantages of quantum cryptography are highlighted along with its potential in the future. It presents a summarized glimpse in different aspects for novice researchers to educate themselves with recent developments in the cyber security field.

Chapter 4

Joshua Ojo Nehinbe, Federal University, Oye-Ekiti, Nigeria
Jimmy Benson Adebesin, NHS England, UK

Interdisciplinary studies on cybercrimes against some outpatient adolescents with psychiatric emergencies have identified critical concerns and new debates on the instances whereby law enforcement agents are largely compelled to use the instrument of force. The adolescents may unexpectedly harm themselves or vulnerable people. Psychiatric emergencies can lead to lawlessness like premeditated crimes and constructive vandalism. This research adopts a quantitative review of IDS logs, interviews, and virtual meeting apps. Thematic analysis suggests the limits of non-violent methods of investigating cybercrimes and further classifies clinical use of force on the need to use and suggestive circumstances that combine empathy, mutual dialogue, and compassionate care with non-toxic, refraining, harmless, and inoffensive interventions. New legal concepts on the instrument of force like proxy witness, evocative criminal liability, implicit and explicit jurisdictions, surrogated and virtual complainants were suggested to safeguard the above adolescents from cyber criminals.

Phishing is a cybercrime in active growth that could cause several damages for its victims, such as identity theft. Specifically, in the last years, cybercrime has been of particular concern due to several attacks developed against society in general. In this sense, understanding this phenomenon and the factors that may explain the susceptibility to this is essential. But it is also essential to know which of the traditional methods are used to study phishing susceptibility and the innovative ones. This chapter presents a complete study in this field, providing a theoretical and practical approach, by using a perspective that is simple and accessible to everyone. In the end, individuals, in general, will know more about the subject, and, academically, this provides important insights to better-developed studies in the phishing susceptibility field.

Cybersecurity is growing in importance, with recent cyberattacks showing an exceptional level of impact in organizations. This chapter presents a cybersecurity capability building proposal for organizations that the authors designate cybersecurity learning framework (CyberLearn). The chapter discusses cybersec initiatives in Portugal, in the European Union, in the North Atlantic Treaty Organization, and the United States of America, introducing the NICE framework as a basis to develop the CyberLearn framework and the concept representation considering functions, roles, and work roles and the knowledge units related to each role area. This framework has been applied in Portugal by Técnico to meet business needs on this domain.

This chapter investigates previous research themes and trending topics related to ChatGPT through a comprehensive analysis of the literature. An automated technique (web-scraping) was deployed to retrieve and compile all existing journal papers, conference proceedings, and book chapters from major publisher databases in the related fields, and the abstracts of the selected articles were quantitatively analysed using a probabilistic topic modeling procedure – the latent Dirichlet allocation (LDA) approach. Based on the topics identified by the LDA model utilizing their most representative terms, 10 research themes and corresponding keywords have emerged in the results. The overall findings indicate that research efforts in this field have primarily focused on performance, user disposition, application practices, and ethical and privacy concerns. A conceptual framework that delineated the relationships between the research issues and opportunities for future research on ChatGPT is also introduced.

Chapter 8

Ana Ferreira, CINTESIS@RISE, FMUP-MEDCIDS, Porto, Portugal
Tiago Morais, Department of Information Technology, Unidade Local de Saúde de Matosinhos, Portugal
José Castanheira, Department of Information Technology, Unidade Local de Saúde de Matosinhos, Portugal
Tiago Taveira-Gomes, Department of Community Medicine, Faculdade de Medicina da Universidade do Porto, Portugal & Faculty of Health Sciences, Fernando Pessoa University, Portugal & MTG Research and Development Lab, Portugal

Privacy is a fundamental human right, and the need for information security to guarantee patients' privacy is essential. In today's world, where technology and connected devices are increasingly prevalent, cyber-attacks on critical infrastructures have grown significantly. The implementation of proactive privacy and security procedures and techniques is essential to protect data privacy, prevent information leakage, and mitigate cyber risks. This chapter focuses on innovative techniques for privacy by design and by default in the practice of accessing secondary health data for research. It presents a case study of a secure computation process and technology, which includes an architectural approach to provisioning a zero-trust research environment. By adopting a zero-trust research environment, healthcare institutions can mitigate the risks of cyber-attacks and data breaches while increasing data security for the benefit of patients. Ultimately, this chapter emphasizes the importance of implementing proactive privacy and security measures to protect sensitive data in healthcare.

Chapter 9

Esteban Payares, Universidad Tecnologica de Bolivar, Colombia
Juan Carlos Martinez-Santos, Universidad Tecnologica de Bolivar, Colombia

This chapter provides a comprehensive overview of the recent developments in quantum machine learning for intrusion detection systems. The authors review the state of the art based on the published work "Quantum Machine Learning for Intrusion Detection of Distributed Denial of Service Attacks: A Comparative View" and its relevant citations. The chapter discusses three quantum models, including quantum support vector machines, hybrid quantum-classical neural networks, and a two-circuit ensemble model, which run parallel on two quantum processing units. The authors compare the performance of these models in terms of accuracy and computational resource consumption. Their work demonstrates the effectiveness of quantum models in supporting current and future cybersecurity systems, achieving close to 100% accuracy, with 96% being the worst-case scenario. The chapter concludes with future research directions for this promising field.

Chapter 10

Antoine Toni Trad, IBISTM, France

The implementation of organizational transformation projects (simply project) in the contexts of complex and dynamic businesses (or other application domains), need an optimal transformation framework and a holistic RoGCSC. The RoGCSC uses measurable cybersecurity and governance security risk (secRisk) critical factors, which are mitigated and tuned, to ensure project's successful evolution and predict/block cyber (or classical) crimes/misdeeds. The actual exponential rise of cybercrimes has become a major concern for countries, enterprises, and citizens; and that obliges projects to integrate polymathic-holistic security strategies. Actual cyberspace's resilience, control, and security concepts are siloed, insufficient, chaotic, and concentrate only on platforms' infrastructural aspects. Actual concepts focus on isolated hackers, where financial predators are the ones behind major cybercrimes. Global cybercrimes are closely related to global events and phenomena, like financial greediness, insecurity, conflicts, terrorism, pandemics, and societal crisis.

Chapter 11

Miloslava Plachkinova, Kennesaw State University, USA

The current study investigates the dark side of using gaming chat applications for illegal activities like selling credentials, stolen credit cards, private data, sexual exploitation, and organizing groups on white supremacy. With the shutdown of many Darknet websites and illegal marketplaces, criminals are now switching to chat platforms that allow them to resume their operations easily and quickly. In addition, such communities can be utilized for recruitment and for providing instructions on how to commit crimes to individuals anywhere in the world. The study is grounded in social learning theory, as it explains how crime is learned through interactions on these applications. The goal of the current work is to explore further these platforms and to provide law enforcement with guidance and recommendations on how to integrate digital forensic tools more effectively and efficiently for investigating data generated on gaming chat platforms and preventing future crimes facilitated through these platforms.

Chapter 12

Rodrigo Martinez-Bejar, University of Murcia, Spain
María S. García-González, University of Murcia, Spain
Lorenzo Scalera, University of Udine, Italy
Alessandro Gasparetto, University of Udine, Italy

Safety issues are relevant in the interaction of human and robotic systems, as these might be a risk for humans' physical integrity. Robotic systems in the armies are a good example of such risk, since these systems are highly dependent on the software integrity that governs their behaviour. But in civil society there are examples of such issues as well. Also, medical applications are usually designed to be very accurate/precise, for instance, in surgery. If that accuracy/precision is threatened due to a cyberattack— as some of those robots are connected to communication networks—the patient could even die. In this chapter, the authors describe a modelling approach that categorizes the most relevant cybersecurity threats to robots from different analytical viewpoints. To illustrate the usefulness of this model, the main characteristics of a model addressing the cybersecurity threats to manufacturing robotic systems is shown in this work. Such a model has been implemented into machine-understandable software by using standard knowledge representation methods.

The goal is to initiate a discussion over the measures to protect the victims, whom unfortunately, in Brazil, composes 30% of elderly people (older than 60 years old). The case report portrays the scam through spoofing, programs that change the caller's identification in a communication, together with Social Engineering, to trick the victim into carrying out operations in the bank's application, thus encouraging transfers to the scammer's account. The victim ended up following these guidelines and made appointments to send money to the scammer, however, he ended up suspecting the situation, decided to interrupt that communication and seek the bank branch for clarification, thus managing to cancel the appointments and reverse the transfer amounts. Actions need to be taken, urgently, because the predictions show a gigantic increase of this type of fraud.

This chapter intends to discuss cybercrime and cybersecurity laws in their current and future contexts. The initial part of this chapter discusses terms and issues related to the cyber world. This portion has touched areas where the requirement of cyber laws is increasing with the advancement of time, technology, and types of cybercrimes. The later section of this chapter will look at existing and widely used cybersecurity laws from around the world. We have emphasized on Cyber Security Laws in India, the US, and the UK. The reason for focusing on these countries is that there are many multinational organizations that have offices spread across these regions. However, it should be noted that cybercrime is not limited by national or geographical boundaries and once committed, is dealt with under international law and in accordance with the trade agreements between the countries involved. The authors have included two famous trans boundary cyber cases that were brought to justice.

Preface

The entire foundation of what it means to be human in our modern era, which is defined by the unrelenting march of technological progress, has undergone a fundamental transformation. The digital realm, which was formerly relegated to the margins of human existence, has quickly expanded to encompass every facet of our personal connections, business dealings, and public interactions. As the physical and digital worlds continue to become more intertwined in today's world, there is an ever-increasing demand for more emphasis on the prioritisation of cybersecurity measures and the protection of data confidentiality. The individual chapters that make up this book offer a comprehensive analysis of the challenges that arise in the modern digital world. They also include helpful viewpoints and solutions, both of which are necessary for successfully navigating this complex sphere.

In the first chapter, which is headed "Cybersecurity Risks in Health Data and Measures to Take: Cybersecurity Risks in Health" the primary focus is on the healthcare business, which is a sector in which the protection of patient confidentiality is of the highest importance. This chapter focuses on the need of installing robust cybersecurity measures to protect the integrity of medical records and maintain patient confidence. These precautions are also necessary to preserve patient confidentiality. It accomplishes this by undertaking an exhaustive investigation of the threats that are posed to health data and proposing several strategies that may be used to reduce or eliminate these dangers.

An insightful and thought-provoking analysis on the potential advantages of combining insights from human behaviour into cybersecurity methods can be found in Chapter 2 of the report, which is titled "Behavioral Psychology Towards Artificial Intelligence in Cybersecurity". This chapter is part of a larger study that was conducted. The intersection of behavioural psychology and artificial intelligence provides a unique viewpoint on user interactions. This makes it easier to develop AI systems that are able to adapt to shifting threat contexts while also successfully integrating with human decision-making procedures.

In the third chapter, we go deeper into the investigation of recent developments in the field of cybersecurity strategies and procedures, beginning with an investigation of the fascinating topic of quantum cryptography. This chapter will provide you with "A Brief Overview of Cyber Security Advances and Techniques Along with A Glimpse on Quantum Cryptography: Cyber Security Practices, Advances and Challenges". This chapter provides an overview of the dynamic and ever-changing environment of cybersecurity, with a special focus on the possible advantages and hurdles associated with quantum computing. The environment of cybersecurity is characterised as dynamic and ever-changing. The field of quantum computing is one that not only has the potential to bring forth ground-breaking innovations, but also faces difficult challenges in the area of information security.

The fourth chapter of the study is titled "Classifications of the Instrument of Force Required to Investigate Suspects of Cybercrimes Against Outpatients' Adolescents with Psychiatric Emergency" This chapter delves into the specific field of investigating cybercrimes, with a particular emphasis on those that target individuals who are more susceptible to being harmed. This chapter presents a methodological framework that tries to identify the means of force necessary for the arrest of cybercriminals, with the ultimate goal of gaining justice for persons whose lives have been negatively touched by these acts.

Phishing is an issue that has to be addressed since it continues to exist in the digital sphere. In Chapter 5, under the heading "Phishing: A Theoretical Approach and the Innovative Tools," an in-depth investigation of this dishonest tactic is presented. Individuals are able to obtain a comprehensive understanding of phishing methods and become familiar with state-of-the-art ways for preventing this kind of cyber threat if they make use of a theoretical framework and use sophisticated methodologies. This is possible for them to do so because of the fact that they are able to do so.

In the following chapters, an extensive variety of points of view are presented to the reader. Among these are an examination of user-centered insights in the context of the ChatGPT, as presented in the systematic review titled "A Systematic Review of Research on the ChatGPT - The User Perspective" (Chapter 7), as well as an investigation of organisational capability building through the framework known as "Cyberlearn, an Integrated Framework for Organizational Capability Building". As discussed in Chapter 8's "Privacy and Security by Design: A Case Study on Innovative Techniques for Secure Healthcare Data Research", the intricate nature of cybersecurity concerns becomes apparent in the meticulous design and strategic planning that is required to ensure the security of healthcare data research. These are two of the techniques that are essential to ensuring the safety of such research.

In Chapter 9, which is headed "Advancements in Quantum Machine Learning for Intrusion Detection, a Comprehensive Overview", the inquiry into the use of quantum machine learning as a method for detecting intrusions is discussed in depth. This chapter highlights the confluence of quantum computing with machine learning, which brings unique potential in the field of cyber threat identification. These innovative prospects are discussed in more detail later in the chapter.

The interconnectedness of cybersecurity and organisational change is investigated in Chapter 10 of the book, which is titled "Organisational Transformation Projects: The Role of Global Cyber Security and Crimes (RoGCSC)". This chapter highlights the crucial significance of strong cybersecurity measures in the context of transformative endeavours.

It is becoming increasingly clear, as the digital environment continues to expand at a rapid rate, that even platforms that at first glance may appear to be safe might possibly act as conduits for malicious objectives. The writers investigate the risks that are commonly neglected that are present inside gaming chat platforms in Chapter 11 of the book, which is headed "Examining the Negative Aspects of Gaming Chat Applications", and they emphasise how important it is to maintain a careful attitude in all facets of the digital sphere.

The focus of discussion in Chapter 12, "A Modelling Approach to Privacy and Safety Issues in Cyber-Physical Systems," is on the complex dynamic that exists between privacy and safety in the setting of cyber-physical systems. The necessity of guaranteeing the safety of the interconnected systems that power our increasingly digital world is brought into sharp relief in this chapter.

The chapter 13 is named " Detailing a Case of Cyber Fraud Through Telephone in Brazil – From the Choice of Elderly Victims, Spoofing Until Social Engineering Manipulation" provides a troubling tale that is distinguished by manipulation, dishonesty, and the victimisation of elderly folks. This story is a powerful illustration of how cybercrimes may have real-world implications, and it should serve as a reminder of this fact.

And to conclude the book, another quality research is available as the Chapter 14, which is headed "Cybercrime and Cybersecurity Laws in Current and Future Contexts with Evolving Crimes Across National Boundaries", where the author investigates the legal issues of cybersecurity. It examines the intricate link between the ever-shifting environment of cybercrime and the respective legal frameworks that try to handle it, particularly in the context of international law enforcement. Specifically, it focuses on how these issues are addressed locally and globally.

In conclusion, the necessity of cultivating a digital future that is free from vulnerabilities is of the highest significance. We are able to successfully face the difficulties that are provided by the continuously shifting digital world if we equip individuals and organisations with the knowledge and tools that are essential. We are able to assure the security of sensitive information through the coordination of efforts and the making of strategic investments.

As we move forward through the different chapters, a consistent theme starts to emerge, which is that the complexity that are involved with data privacy and cybersecurity are reflective of the multifaceted structure of the digital domain. The investigation of each subject reveals a tremendous degree of complexity across a varied range of sectors, including healthcare, quantum computing, behavioural psychology, and cyber laws. This highlights the essential demand for both attention and imaginative thinking.

This publication, which includes insightful contributions from well-known academics, has shed light on the comprehensive nature of the challenges that we face in terms of cybersecurity and data privacy. The preceding statement emphasises the great efforts of scholars, practitioners, and researchers who are working carefully to develop a digital environment that is both secure and resilient. These efforts are highlighted in this statement.

This literary work serves as a powerful appeal for proactive participation in an era that is distinguished by the practical ramifications of data breaches and cybercrimes. The author encourages readers to take an active role in safeguarding sensitive data, promoting the moral use of artificial intelligence, and advocating for comprehensive regulatory frameworks by adopting a proactive stance in these areas. The goal of the writers of these chapters is to encourage a communal commitment to the preservation of our digital future, with a particular emphasis on making the most of the limitless potential of technology for the benefit of society while simultaneously safeguarding our irreplaceable assets, including our data and privacy.

The editors hope you enjoy this book,
With our best regards

Nuno Mateus-Coelho
Lapi2s, Copelabs, Lusófona University, Portugal

Manuela Cruz-Cunha
Polytechnic Institute of Cavado and Ave, Portugal

Chapter 1
Cybersecurity Risks in Health Data and Measures to Take

Daniel Jorge Ferreira

 https://orcid.org/0000-0002-6155-5443
University of Trás-os-Montes and Alto Douro, Portugal

Nuno Mateus-Coelho

 https://orcid.org/0000-0001-5517-9181
Lusófona University, Portugal

ABSTRACT

According to existing data, the frequency of cyberattacks on hospitals and healthcare systems more than doubled from 2016 to 2021, and the incidents exposed the protected health information of nearly 42 million patients. The global picture and the risks of being hit combine a series of issues—loss of access to critical health data, high costs of responding and preventing cyber-attacks, and threats to patient safety—that has largely shifted the focus towards infrastructure defense, of health. The groups that perpetrate such attacks are generally aggressive and their attacks directed at critical infrastructure in hospitals and healthcare organizations can disrupt operations and patient access for weeks or even months.

INTRODUCTION

Because of the rapid growth of technology, information security has become an increasingly vital concern for businesses. This is especially true in the medical field, where maintaining the confidentiality of patient information is of the utmost significance. Data breaches in cybersecurity and health hazards can have a negative impact on the integrity of medical records, and in some instances, patients' physical health may be put in jeopardy as a result of these incidents. As a result, it is of the utmost importance that healthcare organisations have the resources necessary to manage these types of circumstances and reduce the negative impact they have.

However, the scientific literature indicates that the healthcare sector is one of the most vulnerable to assault. There are some disturbing figures regarding the challenges that cybersecurity will face in

DOI: 10.4018/978-1-6684-8422-7.ch001

this industry, which is both an attractive target and a lucrative supply of data. As a result of this, and in accordance with some of the literature that currently exists, adopting a risk management plan that is well-defined is an effective way to counteract cyber risks in this market.

A cyberattack that was launched on a hospital in Ontario, Canada, in April 2023 caused scheduling issues as well as delays in the treatment of patients whose conditions were not life-threatening. On Tuesday of the previous week, the hospital in question made public that it had experienced "network issues," which it later discovered were the result of a cyberattack on the institution.

Following the meeting between Ukrainian Prime Minister Denys Shmyhal and Canadian Prime Minister Justin Trudeau the previous week, a cyberattack was carried out against the Canadian government. From this point forward, it is safe to presume that this "war" also enters the political arena and that it is not just about whether or not medical units are able to understand the vulnerabilities they have and the hazards that they represent.

CONSIDERATIONS ON THE MANAGEMENT OF CYBERSECURITY INCIDENTS AND HEALTH RISKS

The process of managing cybersecurity incidents and health concerns involves a number of stages, including the assessment of threats, the implementation of security measures, and the creation of action plans. The following are some essential considerations that need to be given your attention:

The identification and evaluation of potential dangers are two of the most important preventative actions that may be taken in the management of health problems and cybersecurity incidents (Department of Health and Human Services, 2018). It is necessary to conduct an assessment of the information systems' susceptibility to attack, to identify any potential dangers that may exist, and to take into account the potential impact those dangers could have on the facility as well as the patients (Predicting Cybersecurity Risk, n.d.).

Specialists in information security are required for this task since they are able to conduct a comprehensive examination of the systems and identify potential vulnerabilities. In addition to this, it is necessary to take into consideration the most recent legislation and regulations regarding information security in the healthcare industry (Buckley & Muggleton, 2019; Health Care Industry Cybersecurity Task Force Report, 2017; Le Bris & El Asri, 2017).

Vulnerabilities in information technology and cybersecurity that place personal information of residents as well as health care systems in jeopardy (National Institute of Standards and Technology, 2018; Palmaers, 2013; Predicting Cybersecurity Risk, n.d.).

Cybersecurity and information system threats have a substantial impact on how safe and private citizen data and health systems are. As a result, the integrity of the system, sensitive data, and the privacy of individual user records are all put in jeopardy. Concerns relating to cybersecurity that could potentially have an effect on healthcare systems include the following:

1. Attacks using ransomware can compromise the availability and integrity of information systems, making it impossible for medical workers to access data that is necessary for the provision of treatment. Theft of sensitive data is a possibility whenever hackers hold data and systems hostage and demand a ransom in exchange for returning access to those systems and data.

2. Phishing: Using phishing assaults, users of information systems might have their passwords and other credentials used to get in to the system taken from them. Criminals may assume the identity of medical staff or businesses associated with the medical field in order to fool unsuspecting victims into divulging sensitive information.
3. Fraud in Electronic Form: Examples of electronic fraud in the healthcare systems include identity theft, the creation of bogus accounts, and the counterfeiting of prescription pharmaceuticals. This type of fraud is becoming a greater cause for concern as technology continues to advance. This could lead to an increase in healthcare costs, in addition to putting the health and safety of patients and the quality of treatment provided at risk.
4. Assaults that restrict access to essential information or data.
5. Assaults that prohibit access to essential information or data have the potential to reduce the availability of information systems, so preventing access to crucial information or data that is necessary for healthcare.

A number of different cybersecurity measures, including the utilization of strong authentication, data encryption, routine backups of essential data, threat monitoring and detection, and routine security software and system updates, are need to be put into place in order to secure data and health systems. User education and awareness are also essential components in putting a halt to phishing scams and other types of threats that can be found online. Implementing cybersecurity policies and ensuring legal compliance are necessary steps towards ensuring users' safety and privacy. These steps must be taken in tandem (Agencies Need to Address Aging Legacy Systems, n.d.; Ahmad et al., 2021; Arora & Kuriakose, 2019; Buckley & Muggleton, 2019; Kruse et al., 2017; Palmaers, 2013; Tejero & de la Torre, 2012).

ATTACKS ON HOSPITALS ARE CONTINUOUS AND MORE AND MORE FREQUENT

According to the technical series on primary health care published by the World Health Organization (WHO) (World Health Organisation on Primary Health Care, n.d.; World Health Organization, 2018), information and communication technology (ICT) is becoming more and more widespread with the arrival of smart phones, tablets, and laptop computers (Jannetti, 2014; Williams & Woodward, 2015; Wright et al., 2016). There are a variety of ways in which advancements in digital health technologies are reshaping the delivery and management of health care services (Jannetti, 2014; Le Bris & El Asri, 2017). These innovations range from technology that gives individuals a greater degree of control over their own health to technology that makes it possible to monitor the effects that policies have on the health of populations to technological advances that improve the ability to diagnose illnesses (Cooper & Fuchs, 2013; Liu et al., 2015; United States Government Accountability Office, 2019). One of the most significant barriers to the implementation of digital transformation projects is the proliferation of cybercrime, which exploits vulnerabilities not only in computer systems but also in human beings.

The surge in the number of cybersecurity events poses a growing risk to the healthcare industry as a whole, and to hospitals in particular (Health Care Industry Cybersecurity Task Force Report, 2017; Jalali & Kaiser, 2018). Despite the fact that the healthcare industry is not the only one affected by cybersecurity, coordinated measures to protect stakeholder data have lagged behind or been nonexistent (New Report Connects Privileged Account Exploitation to Advanced Cyber Attacks, 2013; Wikina, 2014).

In order to reduce the negative impacts of cyberattacks of this kind, some organisations have created governance techniques to encourage best practises for securing the electronic infrastructure of hospitals and other clinical contexts (Arora & Kuriakose, 2019; Department of Health and Human Services, 2018; Health Care Industry Cybersecurity Task Force Report, 2017; Jalali & Kaiser, 2018). There is growing evidence that hospital administration is investing in the improvement of the information and communications technology (ICT) infrastructure, despite the common financial challenges that healthcare organisations confront when providing healthcare services.

In April of the previous year, a cyberattack on the Illinois Hospital caused the hospital to be compelled to cease the operation of its computer system for the management of human resources. It was then that they realised their time had come. The Sarah D. Culbertson Memorial facility in Illinois is the most recent facility to be obliged to adopt shutdown procedures for electronic health records as a result of a cyberattack. This was the case since the facility was the most recent victim of a breach. As a result of the cyberattack, "access to most functions was rendered virtually impossible." (NBC News, n.d.)

After this, Antoni Castells, MD, the Medical Director of the Hospital Clinic of Barcelona, came forward to state that the disturbances that were encountered in March were brought on by a RansomHouse cyberattack (SC Magazine, n.d.). This incident had an effect on the hospital's emergency departments, labs, and clinics in addition to other areas of the facility.

There were around 3,000 medical consultations and 150 non-emergency procedures that were delayed at one of the city's major hospitals. Additionally, pharmacies at three big facilities and smaller outpatient clinics were also impacted by the outage.

Damages in the healthcare business can vary anywhere from $1 million to $2 million for each day that a network outage is caused by a cyberattack. The most recent occurrence occurred after Commonc Spirit Health was subjected to a cyberattack that caused the system to become inaccessible for a period of one month. As a direct result of the security breach, the company experienced $150 million worth of missed sales and recovery expenses, as stated in its financial report.

Cyberattacks on hospitals, in contrast to those launched against other businesses, do more damage than just to the institutions' cash and reputations. Because of disruptions in patient care caused by network outages, the morbidity rate of patients tends to increase.

Data was taken by hackers prior to the cyberattack that was launched on Tallahassee Memorial HealthCare.

Twenty-three hundred seventy-six individuals recently received notification from Tallahassee Memorial HealthCare that their personal health information had been compromised prior to a cyberattack that took place on February 3 (HIPAA Journal, n.d.).

The hospital decided to stop utilising its EHR in February after a "cybersecurity issue" was found to exist in the system. As a result of technical issues, all non-emergency patient appointments had to be postponed, and all non-emergency surgical and outpatient operations had to be cancelled.

IMPLEMENTATION OF SECURITY MEASURES

As device interconnectivity and ubiquitous computing continues to proliferate healthcare, the Medical Internet of Things (MIoT), also well known as the, Internet of Medical Things (IoMT) or the Internet of Healthcare Things (IoHT), is certain to play a major role in the health, and well-being of billions of people across the globe. When it comes to issues of cybersecurity risks and threats connected to the

IoT in all of its various flavors the emphasis has been on technical challenges and technical solution. However, especially in the area of healthcare there is another substantial and potentially grave challenge. It is the challenge of thoroughly and accurately communicating the nature and extent of cybersecurity risks and threats to patients who are reliant upon these interconnected healthcare technologies to improve and even preserve their lives (Jannetti, 2014; Medical Device Safety Action Plan, 2018; Strategies to Mitigate Cyber Security Incidents: Mitigation Details, 2017; The CIS Critical security controls for effective cyber defense, 2016)

Based on the risk analysis, it is necessary to implement security measures that can minimize the impact of possible cyber attacks. This includes installing firewalls, antivirus and other security tools, as well as adopting information access and use policies that ensure patient privacy.

In addition, it is essential to invest in training for health professionals, so that they are aware of the risks and know how to deal with possible cybersecurity incidents (ISO/IEC 27001, 2022; National Institute of Standards and Technology, 2018; The CIS Critical security controls for effective cyber defense, 2016).

Administrative safeguards were addressed by constructing extensive education and security plans, employing a Chief Information Security Officer, and adopting comprehensive education and security plans. Technical safeguards can be attained through the use of firewalls, encryption, and decryption, while technical safeguards can also be attained through the use of encryption and decryption (ISO/IEC 27001, 2022; National Institute of Standards and Technology, 2018; The CIS Critical security controls for effective cyber defense, 2016). According to Wikina (2014), administrative protections included having a manager sign off on the transfer of paper data that contained patient information and providing training sessions on how to handle incidents of missing records. On the other side, installing security cameras was required for physical safeguards.

As a result of the progression of modern technology, healthcare institutions are increasingly becoming the targets of attempts to circumvent their security measures. It is essential for organisations to remain current on threats and new technologies, and a great number of organisations, such as the Healthcare Information and Management Systems Society (Healthcare Information and Management Systems Society (HIMSS), 2018; Medical Device Safety Action Plan, 2018), the American College of Clinical Engineering, and the Clinical Engineering Information Technology Community, have taken risk management very seriously. The risk assessment and management methods, as well as the engagement of the named organisations, guarantee that the healthcare organisation is making progress in securing patient information included in electronic health records (Jannetti, 2014; Joint Commission, 2018; Medical Device Safety Action Plan, 2018). In addition, the involvement of the named organisations is a prerequisite for this. More and more healthcare companies are becoming aware of the benefits of security and privacy as a result of the implementation of RFID technology. Two examples of RFID strategies include storing data within RFID tags itself and implementing access controls for RFID tags. By restricting access to the information to only a select few individuals who are authorised to view it, these technologies have improved both the safety of the data and its level of privacy (Jalali & Kaiser, 2018; Tejero & de la Torre, 2012; Wang & Huang, 2013). Controlling and coordinating all of the security methods and activities for electronic health records can be made easier by making efficient use of a Chief Information Security Officer.

The utilization of a level gateway constitutes the third grouping of firewalls. When the IP web page of the organisation is being inspected for any dangers prior to passing the web page on to the end users, they perform the function of gatekeeping for the network of the organisation. Because the gateway allows access to the external network connections of status inspection firewalls, the organisation is able to restrict the entry of networks from the outside world into its internal network. Submission equal gates have proven to be effective at securing electronic health records. This is because they prevent hackers from directly entering the system and gaining access to protected health information.

The use of cryptography as a method for securing and protecting patients' electronic health records is now being implemented. When it comes to the process of transferring health information, the utilization of encryption has contributed to an increase in the level of safety afforded to electronic health data. When encryptions are either enabled or disabled, organisations are typically required to make a recording of the method for exchanging health information. The process of sharing health information has got specifications to be followed through criteria that normally need organisations to record the procedure for exchanging health information when the encryptions are either enabled or disabled. The Health Insurance Portability and Accountability Act (HIPAA) (Department of Health and Human Services, 2018; Palmaers, 2013; United States Government Accountability Office, 2019; Wang & Huang, 2013), established many methods by which cryptography might be utilized to ensure the confidentiality of health information. In 2003, the Concluding Rule was formulated by the United States Department of Health and Human Services, which resulted in a broadening of the HIPAA's criteria on the subject of data security. The Concluding Rule made it possible for HIPAA to broaden the ways in which organisations can generate protected health information (PHI), as well as receive it, store it, and distribute it.

WHAT MEASURES SHOULD HEALTH SYSTEMS ADOPT TO PROTECT CITIZENS' DATA?

The implementation of stringent information security protocols is required by health systems in order to ensure the confidentiality of patients' personal information. There are a number of different activities that can be taken, including the following (ISO/IEC 27001, 2022; Joint Commission, 2018; Le Bris & El Asri, 2017; National Institute of Standards and Technology, 2018; The CIS Critical security controls for effective cyber defense, 2016; Wang & Huang, 2013):

1. Encryption is a method of data security that involves converting data into a format that is unintelligible to anyone who is not entitled to access it. The protection of confidential information, such as medical data and information that could be used to identify an individual, is possible through the use of this method.
2. Strong Authentication: Two-factor authentication is a sort of strong authentication that can be used as an additional security measure to defend patient data from unauthorised access. This type of strong authentication is also known as multi-factor authentication. In this context, the use of safe passwords and other authentication methods, such as security tokens, biometric authentication, and other authentication methods, are all possible.
3. Access Control: Access control is a security strategy that limits usage to authorised individuals for the purpose of protecting systems and data. This can be accomplished by the utilisation of user profiles, access rights limits, and various other forms of security controls.
4. Threat Monitoring and Detection: As an important component of a comprehensive security strategy, threat monitoring and detection can assist in the localization of potential cybersecurity threats prior to the time when those vulnerabilities could become a problem. The deployment of cybersecurity

tools such as firewalls, intrusion detection systems, and other forms of security technology may be considered to fall under this category.

5. Employee training: Cybersecurity training that is provided by employers is an essential safety measure that can assist in warding off cyberattacks. It's possible that training in cybersecurity awareness, as well as more specialised training in information security laws and procedures, could fit under this category.

6. rules Regarding Cybersecurity and Regulatory Compliance It is absolutely necessary to put in place rules regarding cybersecurity and regulatory compliance in order to ensure the safety of patient data as well as the privacy of healthcare systems. In the context of cybersecurity policies, determining information security practises and processes, in addition to the essential compliance measures to comply with important laws and regulations, should be included as part of the process.

Through the implementation of these security measures, healthcare systems can significantly reduce their vulnerability to cyberattacks while also protecting the confidentiality and authenticity of patient data.

TO ENSURE THE AVAILABILITY OF HEALTH SERVICES, WHAT MEASURES SHOULD HOSPITALS ADOPT?

The following are some of the measures that hospitals can take to ensure that patients have access to necessary medical care (ISO/IEC 27001, 2022; National Institute of Standards and Technology, 2018; The CIS Critical security controls for effective cyber defense, 2016):

1. Contingency plans: Contingency plans are action schedules that describe the procedures to be done in the event of unplanned occurrences such as natural disasters, cyberattacks, or power outages. These types of events can have a negative impact on a business's ability to function normally. Regular testing and revisions of these plans are required in order to guarantee that they are always ready to be put into action whenever this course of action is deemed necessary.

2. Data Backup and Recovery: Hospitals need to establish procedures for data backup and recovery in order to ensure that vital data and systems can be retrieved in the event of a malfunction. These backups need to be stored in secure areas that are not a part of the main building where the hospital is located.

3. Continuous Monitoring Systems: In order for hospitals to identify potential problems before they interfere with patient care, these monitoring systems should be put into place in hospitals. The monitoring of different types of systems, including hardware, software, and networks, can all be included in this category.

4. Preventive maintenance: In order to guarantee that essential components of a hospital's infrastructure are in proper working order, preventive maintenance should be performed on a regular basis. This may include cleaning and maintaining the hardware, keeping the software up to date, and completing any number of other maintenance duties.

5. The ability to scale up: In order to keep up with the growing demand for healthcare services, hospitals need the ability to expand their facilities. In this aspect, there may be access to more people, physical space, and information technology resources.

6. Training for Staff The staff at the hospital should receive training in emergency preparedness and crisis management. They need to be able to acquire backup plans, put those plans into action, and work together in order to guarantee the uninterrupted operation of emergency services.

It is recommended that healthcare systems make use of the following metrics to control risk within their systems:

1. The amount of time, on average, that it takes for hospital security personnel to recognise and respond to a security event is the first factor that is measured by this metric.
2. The average recovery time is a measurement of how long it takes the healthcare facility to restore its systems and data following a breach of security.
3. A good indicator of how well the hospital's systems function is the percentage of times that backup and recovery operations are successful.
4. The level of software update and patching is a measurement of how well the medical facility maintains its systems and software by bringing it in line with the most recent security updates.
5. Level of Regulatory Compliance: This determines the level to which the hospital complies with relevant information security legislation, such as HIPAA in the United States or GDPR in the European Union. In the United States, HIPAA is the law that governs the protection of patient health information.
6. Number of Security events is the sixth category on the list, and it is where you can keep track of the total number of safety incidents that have occurred at the medical facility over a given period of time.
7. Staff Awareness Level: This evaluates the level of understanding that the hospital staff has regarding information security and how they may contribute to the safeguarding of patient data.

These indicators can be of use to healthcare organisations in evaluating their information security posture, identifying potential risks, and determining how to reinforce their security procedures and policies.

ESTABLISHMENT OF ACTION PROTOCOLS

The development of action procedures that can guarantee a rapid and effective response in the event of an attack is another essential component of managing cybersecurity events and health hazards. These protocols should be able to assure a prompt and effective response in the event of an attack. In order to accomplish this goal, it is required to identify roles, develop backup plans, and simulate assaults in order to evaluate the efficiency of previously created protocols.

Models that could assist organisations in managing health risks and challenges pertaining to cybersecurity.

Several different methods can be implemented in order to provide assistance to businesses in the management of health problems and cybersecurity incidents. These are some of the most well-known and important models available, presented in alphabetical order:

INFORMATION SECURITY RISK MANAGEMENT MODEL (MGRSI)

The Medical Group Risk and Security Initiative (MGRSI) is a risk management framework for information security that is also applicable to the healthcare business. This process is comprised of a total of six processes, the first of which is the identification of information assets. The remaining steps are the identification of hazards, the evaluation of risks, the definition and implementation of security measures, and the ongoing monitoring of risks.

INCIDENT MANAGEMENT LIFECYCLE MODEL (CVGI)

The CVGI paradigm, which is currently utilised to address information security concerns, is amenable to adaptation so that it may be put to use in the healthcare sector. There are four steps to this process: preparation, detection and analysis, containment, eradication and recovery, and lessons learned. Each stage builds upon the previous one.

LAYERED SECURITY MODEL (MSL)

The Multi-Layer Security Architecture, more commonly abbreviated as MSL, is a security model that safeguards information systems by utilising many levels of protection that cooperate with one another. Measures of protection for users, networks, operating systems, applications, and operating systems themselves are included in these layers of security.

HEALTH INFORMATICS SECURITY MATURITY MODEL (SMIH)

In order to assess the overall health of the organisation as well as the degree to which it has progressed in terms of its computer security, a model known as the SMIH is utilised. It is broken down into these five stages: initial, managed, defined, quantitatively managed, and optimised.

APPARENT GAPS IN MANAGING CYBERSECURITY INCIDENTS AND HEALTH RISKS

In spite of the models and factors that have been provided, it is clear that there are still holes in the management of cybersecurity incidents and health concerns. The following are some of the more significant omissions:

LACK OF INVESTMENT IN INFORMATION SECURITY

Many hospitals and other medical facilities still do not invest nearly enough in information security, which leaves them open to the possibility of being targeted by hackers. This includes the lack of resources to hire people who specialise in information security, the lack of investment in security systems, and the absence of proper training for health workers among other things.

LACK OF WELL-DEFINED ACTION PROTOCOLS

There is still a widespread lack of clearly defined action mechanisms at many organisations to deal with potential cybersecurity issues. This may result in a reaction that is inadequate or delayed in the event of an attack, which may amplify the impact of the occurrence.

LACK OF COLLABORATION BETWEEN INSTITUTIONS

It might be challenging to manage cybersecurity events and health hazards when there is insufficient collaboration amongst healthcare facilities. This includes the failure of institutions to share information with one another and to collaborate on the development of best practises, both of which might make the institutions susceptible to potential cyberattacks.

THE PURPOSE OF COLLECTING DATA FROM INFORMATION SYSTEMS IN RISK MANAGEMENT

The ability of organisations to identify and analyse risks that are associated with their information systems is made possible by the data that is gathered from information systems. This makes the data a critical component of risk management. The purpose of data collecting is to achieve the objective of gathering information on how an organization's information systems are currently performing, which enables the organisation to examine the risks that are associated with these systems and put in place the required controls.

Data collected from information systems may contain information that is relevant to system vulnerabilities, threats that are well-known, security incidents that have already occurred, and security measures that are currently in place. On the basis of this information, businesses are able to conduct an assessment of the dangers that are associated with their information systems and then take measures to reduce the likelihood that these dangers may actually manifest.

Because of the collection of data, businesses now have the ability to continuously monitor their information systems for potential vulnerabilities and to respond appropriately to mitigate the negative effects of those vulnerabilities.

In conclusion, the purpose of data gathering from information systems for the purpose of risk management is to aid organisations in recognising, analysing, and managing the risks that are associated to their information systems, with the goal of ensuring that their information systems remain secure and trustworthy.

HOW CAN THIS DATA HELP IDENTIFY POTENTIAL SECURITY INCIDENTS?

There are a variety of methods that may be applied to the data of information systems in order to assist in the detection of potential security breaches. The following is a list of some of the more common applications for this data:

1. The Detection of Anomalies The examination of the data collected by information systems can be used to assist in the detection of anomalies, such as unusual or suspicious activities that may indicate a potential security breach.
2. Detection of known threats: Data from information systems can be compared with databases of known threats to identify harmful behaviour such as attempts to gain unauthorised access or exploit vulnerabilities. This is accomplished through the process of "detection of known threats."
3. Monitoring of logs: An analysis of the logs produced by an information system can identify patterns of erroneous activity or efforts to gain unauthorised access.
4. An analysis of previous incidents Conducting an analysis of previous security incidents can help in the process of discovering the underlying causes of events and in the deployment of preventative measures to stop them from happening again.
5. The use of security tools The utilisation of security tools, such as intrusion detection systems and log analysis, can assist in the identification of potential security incidents and notify security staff so that they can take the appropriate action.

In conclusion, the data from information systems may be used in a number of different ways to identify probable security risks. This can aid security teams in recognising and responding to incidents as soon as they occur in order to limit the amount of damage caused by the occurrences.

GUIDELINES FOR SAFE USE OF THE INTERNET

The Administration of Fixes and Security Flaws

As part of the process of managing exposure and vulnerabilities, IT vulnerabilities need to be located, evaluated, and mitigated. It is predicated mostly on threat-monitoring processes, but it also incorporates all of the identification steps, such as risk assessment, correction or mitigation, and reevaluation. During the process of addressing, investigating, and remediating attacks and post-infection concerns, it is important to make use of Endpoint Detection and Response (EDR) solutions. In most cases, the risk assessment will be of a very difficult kind. Patch management is one of the steps towards rehabilitation or mitigation that might become hard because of the requirement that a health facility stay open around the clock, every day of the year. The risk analysis that is the foundation of patch processes takes into account the sensitive nature of the data that is stored on the server as well as the significant operations or assets that are most susceptible to being targeted by an attack within an organisation.

Businesses need to actively hunt for vulnerabilities in their systems and keep up with vulnerability management and testing on a continuous basis. Early identification of a potential security vulnerability can help in mitigating the risk. After the vulnerability has been identified, either the configuration hardening or patching techniques should be used, and an excessive amount of focus should not be placed on zero-day vulnerabilities. According to recent research conducted by researchers at Gartner, 99% of exploits are built on vulnerabilities that security and IT professionals have been aware of for more than six months. When determining the order of priority for fixing specific vulnerabilities, organisations ought to take into account information of this kind.

Configuration management has the advantage of making it easier to assess vulnerabilities. This is because it allows for the running of risk assessments, analyses needed for patch processes, and risk assessments thanks to a broader understanding of the facilities' IT infrastructure. This is important to keep in mind when discussing the significance of maintaining a high-quality IT infrastructure. Patches need to be applied to all configuration systems, which includes the operating system and any third-party applications, and changes need to be managed and tracked using change management.

Administrative Privileges as Well as Authentication via Many Factors for the Administrative Domain

The assumption of administrative responsibilities by patients within healthcare facilities is fraught with a large level of risk. According to the findings of CyberSheath's research on Advanced Persistent Threats Exploiting Privileged Accounts (APT Privileged Account Exploitation), the vast majority of critical damage- and expense-producing large-scale attacks were initiated by the compromise of a privileged account, such as that of a service provider. This was the scenario that played out during the incident that took place at Hancock Regional Hospital in January of 2018, when the login credentials for an account that belonged to a vendor was stolen.

Giving administrative powers in a regulated and restrictive manner should be done by health entities. This will help keep the number of these accounts at a level that can be managed on an enterprise-wide basis. It is vital to take an inventory of these accounts, keep an eye out for suspicious activity, and check for log entries all at the same time. In order to prevent hostile insider assaults, the health entity should assess its privileged access restrictions and impose local password policies in addition to user screening. According to the findings of a survey, dissatisfied employees are responsible for seventy percent of computer-related crimes. When client and user certificates are no longer required, such as in the case of deactivated user accounts, they should be revoked. Because of this, enterprises will have an easier time lowering the risk associated with such risks. Additionally, end users who require administrative capabilities should have two accounts: one with permissions restricted to local workstations, and the other without permissions, which can be used for basic tasks such as browsing the internet and checking email. When it is necessary, direct internet access on essential devices must to be blocked, or else the utilization of encapsulated browsers ought to be mandated.

Users who have been granted administrative or privileged accounts should receive additional training on the risks associated with having such capabilities so that they can be equipped with the essential safety precautions. One of the most essential safety measures is the implementation of multifactor authentication for all administrative and privileged users and, ideally, for all users. This should be done whenever possible. According to the Critical Security Controls for Effective Cyber Defence published by the Centre for Internet Security (CIS), the use of smart cards, One Time Passwords, or biometrics are some of the ways that can be implemented in order to successfully complete this essential stage.

Contingency Plan in the Event of Occurrences

In light of the fact that the frequency and severity of cyberattacks have been on the rise in recent years, health facilities ought to work on developing an incident response and business continuity strategy. It is advised that these solutions undergo consistent testing and practise, as well as offline archiving. Plans must to incorporate both a predetermined way of operation and the selection of the appropriate stakeholders. Even if the company does not have a CISO, it is still extremely important to have a clearly defined team as well as a leader for cybersecurity. There ought to be a distinct separation of labour between the many tasks and responsibilities that each member of the team is responsible for. In addition, there must be agreement among the organisations concerning the kinds of incidents that must be reported and the points at which the situation must be taken to a higher level. It is imperative that preventative training be incorporated into the plans.

The activities that are conducted after incidents should be supported by the plans for responding to incidents. After an attack, this may involve ordering all employees to change their passwords, executing a factory reset, and, if necessary, replacing compromised hardware and software. However, it is necessary to have a plan for reorganizing and implementing changes within the organisation. After that, the IT and cybersecurity system as well as its management should be updated to suit the newly revealed demands and requirements (including patching and other measures), which were made evident by the incident.

A notification procedure ought to be set up between the healthcare facility and the manufacturers. There is a process that may be put in place so that employees of the company, such as those working in information technology, business administrators, and clinicians, can report incidents to the people who produce the products. This particular form of sharing is mandated under the most recent 510(k) pre-market registration criteria established by the FDA.

By Correlating Temporal Events, It Is Possible to Define a Pattern for a Potential Attack, Minimizing the Risk of Being Attacked

Temporal event correlation can help define a pattern for a probable attack, which enables security teams to locate potential weak points and take precautionary measures to reduce the risk of being attacked.

By examining the sequence of occurrences across time, it is possible to detect suspicious activity that may be related to an approaching attack. For instance, if a security system notes multiple attempts at unauthorised access coming from the same IP address in a relatively short period of time, this may be an indication that an attack is going to be launched in the near future. By combining this activity with additional data, such as the types of data accessed, the times when access attempts occurred, and user conduct, it is possible to develop a behaviour profile that may be used to predict and anticipate prospective attacks. This profile can be used to recognise potential threats and protect against them.

By making use of this information, security teams are able to take preventative measures to lower the likelihood of an attack occurring. For instance, they might be able to block the suspected IP address, strengthen up the security measures of the system, or carefully monitor the machine in issue to keep an eye out for any additional strange behaviour. By recognising patterns of potentially dangerous behaviour and taking measures to mitigate the associated risks, security professionals can lessen the likelihood that their organisation will be the target of an attack.

How Can We Use AI to Prevent Cybersecurity Incidents?

Artificial intelligence (AI) has the potential to play an essential part in preventing breaches in cybersecurity by increasing the capabilities of detection, automating security activities, and reducing the amount of time needed to respond to threats. The following is a list of the various applications for artificial intelligence (AI) that can be used to prevent events relating to cybersecurity:

The term "artificial intelligence" (AI) refers to computer programmes that are able to simulate human intelligence and analyse large amounts of data in order to identify patterns, abnormalities, and other red flags that may indicate the presence of potential threats. Machine learning algorithms may be trained on vast datasets in order to recognise well-known attack patterns and identify new or emerging hazards. This allows the algorithms to spot both known and unknown threats.

Intrusion detection and prevention are both capabilities offered by systems that use artificial intelligence (AI). These systems are able to monitor network traffic in real time and identify suspicious activity. AI is able to recognise and prevent prospective intrusions before they do damage by studying network behaviour and comparing it to known attack signatures. This is done in order to stop potential intrusions before they cause damage.

Artificial intelligence (AI) may watch user behaviour in order to identify any abnormalities that may hint to dishonest behaviour. This can be accomplished via analysing user behaviour. By establishing baselines for the behaviours of typically approved users, AI systems are able to recognise anomalous patterns, such as efforts to access data without authorization or the exfiltration of data.

Phishing detection is possible thanks to artificial intelligence, which can be trained to recognise the telltale signs of phishing emails, websites, or attempts at social engineering. By analysing the text of emails, the links in those emails, and user behaviour, artificial intelligence algorithms are able to identify the possibility of phishing attacks and issue a warning to users.

Artificial intelligence can utilise machine learning techniques to analyse file behaviour and discover viral signatures, which enables it to detect malicious software. This can be helpful in detecting potentially hazardous files or processes and putting a stop to them before they have a chance to infect the system.

The management of vulnerabilities can be assisted by artificial intelligence (AI), which can assist in the scanning of systems, networks, and software in addition to the detection of vulnerabilities. Automating vulnerability analyses, which can help in quickly prioritising and addressing problems, can reduce the risk of exploitation and make it possible to address them more quickly.

AI's ability to automate the discovery, analysis, and containment of threats enables it to assist a rapid response to any security issues that may arise. For instance, AI systems can automatically isolate attacked systems, block suspicious IP addresses, and deploy security patches.

Analytics that anticipate future events: Artificial intelligence is capable of analysing historical data to discover patterns and threats in the field of cybersecurity. AI can assist firms in proactively improving their security posture and putting in place the appropriate preventative measures by recognising patterns and correlations in the data.

It is essential to keep in mind that artificial intelligence is not a silver bullet, despite the fact that it has the potential to greatly strengthen cybersecurity defences. For efficient cybersecurity, it is vital to implement best practises and security frameworks, perform frequent upgrades, train staff, and take a multilayered approach. The use of AI as a supplementary instrument is something that should be incorporated into every comprehensive cybersecurity plan.

We Can Therefore Think About How Models Based on AI Can Help Minimize These Risks in Order to Understand How Traditional Risk Governance Adapts to the New Digital Reality of Organizations

Artificial intelligence (AI) has the potential to lend a significant assisting hand to organisations in their efforts to cut down on the amount of cybersecurity threats they are exposed to. The use of models driven by artificial intelligence (AI), which can identify and eliminate possible security threats, can assist to make security operations more effective and efficient. This is because the AI models can identify and eliminate potential security threats.

Security

For instance, methods from the field of machine learning can be utilised to undertake an in-depth study of a significant quantity of data relevant to security in order to identify patterns that may suggest an impending attack. This can be done in order to prevent an attack from occurring. In addition, neural networks can be used to identify anomalies in activity that may point to questionable behaviour, such as efforts to gain unauthorised access to a system or to carry out phishing schemes. This capability allows neural networks to be exploited in the prevention of fraudulent activities.

Additionally, artificial intelligence can be utilised to enhance the effectiveness of pre-existing security mechanisms, such as firewalls and intrusion detection systems, which can be a significant benefit. As an illustration, AI-based models can be utilised to develop rules for threat detection that are not only more accurate but also more adaptive, which increases a system's reaction to threats.

In conclusion, artificial intelligence (AI) may be able to assist businesses in overcoming cybersecurity challenges by enabling them to more rapidly and effectively identify threats and take appropriate means to counter them, thereby increasing the security of their assets and data. AI may also assist businesses in overcoming cybersecurity challenges by enabling them to more quickly and effectively identify threats and take appropriate actions to counter them. AI can also help organisations reduce the expenses connected with cybersecurity by lowering the amount of time and effort required to conduct cybersecurity tasks. This helps businesses reduce the costs associated with cybersecurity. It is necessary to keep in mind, however, that traditional risk governance is still essential for ensuring that AI is deployed safely and responsibly, taking into consideration the ethical and legal ramifications that are inherent in the situation. It is essential to keep in mind that traditional risk governance is still essential.

CONCLUSION

The ability of healthcare organisations to effectively manage cybersecurity incidents and the associated health hazards is an issue of fundamental importance. It is absolutely necessary for them to make investments in information security, to have action processes that are well defined, and to work together in order to cut down on the potential dangers posed by potential cyber assaults. The models that are described in this article, such as the MGRSI, CVGI, MSL, and SMIH, have the potential to be useful for institutions in the process of risk management. Nevertheless, it is essential to emphasise that there are still gaps in the management of cybersecurity incidents and health risks. These gaps include a lack of investment in information security, a lack of well-defined action protocols, and a lack of communication between institutions. As a consequence of this, it is imperative for organisations to continue to modernise and enhance the information security plans they have in place in order to guarantee the safety of patient data and the uninterrupted provision of medical services.

After the models that have been provided have been elaborated upon and validated, subsequent study can be conducted on how these models can be integrated into the risk management procedures that are carried out within organisations.

It is imperative that this risk management be in complete congruence with both the governance model and the goals of the organisation.

For this, it will be useful to deepen the research in integration with:

1. Frameworks to proactively manage the implementation of risk analysis according to existing standards.
2. Frameworks to efficiently continue risk management and that allow the integration of the PCSRA as a model to be used and of reference for proactive risk management, after the implementation of the PCSRA, answering the questions: is it possible to foresee a new risk and that way to avoid possible impacts on the organization? If so, what structure can be used to lead and manage this risk management program?
3. Frameworks for designing risk management strategy and making an RBS.

Finally, a scorecard should be developed to give visibility to the information produced in order to measure the success of the PCSRA implementation.

REFERENCES

Agencies Need to Address Aging Legacy Systems. (n.d.). Retrieved from https://www.gao.gov/assets/gao-19-491.pdf

Ahmad, A., Maynard, S. B., Desouza, K. C., Kotsias, J., Whitty, M. T., & Baskerville, R. L. (2021). How can organizations develop situation awareness for incident response: A case study of management practice. *Computers & Security*, *101*, 102122. doi:10.1016/j.cose.2020.102122

Alami, H., Gagnon, M. P., Ahmed, M. A. A., Fortin, J. P., Alami, H., Gagnon, M. P., Ahmed, M. A. A., & Fortin, J. P. (2019). Digital health: Cybersecurity is a value creation lever, not only a source of expenditure. *Health Policy and Technology*, *8*(4), 319–321. doi:10.1016/j.hlpt.2019.09.002

Arora, N., & Kuriakose, D. (2019). Cybersecurity in healthcare: A review. *Journal of Healthcare Information Management*, *33*(3), 139–146.

Buckley, P., & Muggleton, S. (2019). A survey of healthcare cybersecurity incident response. *Journal of Healthcare Information Management*, *33*(4), 168–173.

Cooper, T., & Fuchs, K. (2013). Technology risk assessment in healthcare facilities. *Biomedical Instrumentation & Technology*, *47*(3), 202–207. doi:10.2345/0899-8205-47.3.202 PMID:23692102

Department of Health and Human Services. (2018). *Health Industry Cybersecurity Practices: Managing Threats and Protecting Patients*. Retrieved from https://www.phe.gov/Preparedness/planning/405d/Pages/hic-practices.aspx

Harries, D., & Yellowlees, P. M. (2013). Cyberterrorism: Is the U.S. healthcare system safe? *Telemedicine Journal and e-Health, 19*(1), 61–66. doi:10.1089/tmj.2012.0022 PMID:23113795

Health Care Industry Cybersecurity Task Force Report on Improving Cybersecurity in the Health Care Industry. (2017). Department of Health and Human Service.

Healthcare Information and Management Systems Society (HIMSS). (2018). *2018 HIMSS Cybersecurity Survey*. Retrieved from https://www.himss.org/2018-himss-cybersecurity-survey

HIPAA Journal. (n.d.). https://www.hipaajournal.com/tallahassee-memorial-healthcare-patient-data-stolen-in-cyberattack/

ISO/IEC 27001:2022 – Information Security Management Systems

Jalali, M. S., & Kaiser, J. P. (2018). Cybersecurity in Hospitals: A Systematic, Organizational Perspective. *Journal of Medical Internet Research, 20*(5), e10059. doi:10.2196/10059 PMID:29807882

Jannetti, M. C. (2014). Safeguarding patient information in electronic health records. *AORN Journal, 100*(3), C7–C8. doi:10.1016/S0001-2092(14)00873-4 PMID:24730081

Joint Commission. (2018). *Improving the Safety of Health Information Technology*. Retrieved from https://www.jointcommission.org/-/media/tjc/documents/resources/patient-safety-topics/improving_safety_of_health_information_technology_5_22_18_final.pdf

Kruse, C. S., Frederick, B., Jacobson, T., & Monticone, D. K. (2017). Cybersecurity in healthcare: A systematic review of modern threats and trends. *Technology and Health Care, 25*(1), 1–10. doi:10.3233/THC-161263 PMID:27689562

Le Bris, A., & El Asri, W. (2017). State of Cybersecurity & Cyber Threats in healthcare organizations: applied Cybersecurity strategy for managers. Cergy: ESSEC Bus Sch.

Liu, Musen, & Chou. (2015). Data breaches of protected health information in the United States. *J Am Med Assoc, 313*(14), 1471-1473. doi:10.1001/jama.2015.2252

Medical Device Safety Action Plan. (2018). 2017 HIMSS Cybersecurity survey. Chicago: HIMSS.

National Institute of Standards and Technology. (2018). *Framework for Improving Critical Infrastructure Cybersecurity*. Retrieved from https://www.nist.gov/publications/framework-improving-critical-infrastructure-cybersecurity

NBC News. (n.d.). https://www.nbcnews.com/tech/security/illinois-hospital-links-closure-ransomware-attack-rcna85983

New Report Connects Privileged Account Exploitation to Advanced Cyber Attacks. (2013). CyberArk. https://www.cyberark.com/press/new-report-connects-privileged-account-exploitation-advanced-cyber-attacks/

Palmaers, T. (2013). *Implementing a vulnerability management process*. SANS Inst Inf Secur Read Room.

Predicting Cybersecurity Risk: A Methodology for Assessments. (n.d.). https://aris-journal.com/aris/index.php/journal/article/view/23

Rochford, O., Young, G., & Lawson, C. (2016). *Predicts 2017: Threat and vulnerability management*. Gartner.

SC Magazine. (n.d.). https://www.scmagazine.com/news/barcelona-hospital-experiencing-care-delays-after-ransomhouse-attack

Strategies to Mitigate Cyber Security Incidents. Mitigation Details. (2017). ASD Australian Signals Directorate. https://www.asd.gov.au/infosec/top-mitigations/mitigations-2017-details.htm

Tejero, A., & de la Torre, I. (2012). Advances and current state of the security and privacy in electronic health records: Survey from a social perspective. [PubMed]. *Journal of Medical Systems*, *36*(5), 3019–3027. doi:10.100710916-011-9779-x

The CIS Critical security controls for effective cyber defense. (2016). https://creativecommons.org/licenses/by-nc-nd/4.0/legalcode

United States Government Accountability Office. (2019). *Health Care Cybersecurity: Federal*. Author.

Voldal, D. (2003). *A practical methodology for implementing a patch management process*. SANS Inst Inf Secur Read Room.

Wang, C. J., & Huang, D. J. (2013). The HIPAA conundrum in the era of mobile health and communications. *Journal of the American Medical Association*, *310*(11), 1121–1122. doi:10.1001/jama.2013.219869 PMID:23978879

Wikina. (2014). What caused the breach? An examination of use of information technology and health data breaches. *Perspect Health Inf Mana*, 1-16.

Williams, P., & Woodward, A. (2015). *Cybersecurity vulnerabilities in medical devices: a complex environment and multifaceted problem*. Med Devices Evid Res. doi:10.2147/MDER.S50048

World Health Organisation on Primary Health Care. (n.d.). Available online: https://www.who.int/docs/default-source/primary-health-care-conference/digital-technologies.pdf?sfvrsn=3efc47e0_2

World Health Organization. (2018). *Global diffusion of eHealth: Making universal health coverage achievable*. Report of the third global survey on eHealth. Retrieved from https://www.who.int/goe/publications/global_diffusion/en/

Wright, A., Aaron, S., & Bates, D. W. (2016). The big phish: Cyberattacks against U.S. healthcare systems. *Journal of General Internal Medicine*, *31*(10), 1115–1118. doi:10.100711606-016-3741-z PMID:27177913

Chapter 2
Behavioural Psychology Towards Artificial Intelligence in Cybersecurity

Ana Galvão
ⓘ https://orcid.org/0000-0002-9630-2905
Instituto Politécnico de Bragança, Portugal

Isabel Chumbo
Instituto Politécnico de Bragança, Portugal

Eugénia Anes
ⓘ https://orcid.org/0000-0001-8474-3474
Instituto Politécnico de Bragança, Portugal & CECC, Universidade Católica Portuguesa, Portugal

ABSTRACT

More than 99% of cybercriminal attacks exploit human characteristics and behaviour (people's vulnerabilities) rather than vulnerabilities in computer systems. When it comes to cybersecurity, it is crucial to consider human behaviour on the part of the user. Cognitive aspects such as attention, memory, and reasoning can be affected by conditions such as fatigue, illness, or injury and are pointed out as human characteristics that are at the origin of several incidents. Users' stress and anxiety may be correlated with making mistakes that compromise cybersecurity. Thus, behavioural psychology should be used to develop effective educational strategies and encourage safe and conscious behaviour in relation to cybersecurity. By understanding how users interact and respond to AI, more effective and aware cybersecurity systems can be created. This chapter's overall objective is to map the literature regarding the psychology of behaviour towards AI in cybersecurity, using a scoping review methodology to provide input into the behavioural psychology aspects regarding AI and cybersecurity.

DOI: 10.4018/978-1-6684-8422-7.ch002

INTRODUCTION

Cybersecurity is an increasingly important topic in this digital world. With the increasing amount of information stored and shared online, it is critical to ensure that data is protected from cyber-attacks. However, often the focus is directed solely towards technological security measures such as firewalls, antivirus and encryption.

That is surely not the whole picture. That is why it is important to recognise that cybersecurity is not just limited to technologies. Definitively, human behaviour does also play a critical role in this issue and can be both a weak point and a line of defence in protecting data.

Psychological and behavioural approaches are important to understand the underlying reasons for insecure behaviour and developing strategies to raise awareness of the importance of information security. Artificial intelligence (AI) can be a valuable tool to improve cybersecurity, but it can also present challenges and risks. More than 99% of attacks exploit human characteristics and behaviours (people vulnerabilities) rather than computer system vulnerabilities, i.e. most cybercriminals focus on the human factor of cybersecurity to define their attack actions and motivations. When it comes to cybersecurity, it is crucial to take into account human behaviour on the part of the user. Cognitive aspects such as attention, memory and reasoning can be affected by conditions such as fatigue, illness or injury and have been identified as human characteristics that are at the root of several incidents. Both stress and anxiety of users may be correlated with the practice of errors that consequently compromise cybersecurity.

Lack of knowledge, although not directly considered as an intrinsic human characteristic, is at the origin of many cybersecurity incidents. Increased awareness of cybersecurity and information security will make users reduce the behaviours that jeopardise cybersecurity, provided it is well used, applied and interpreted.

Behavioural psychology should be used to develop effective educational strategies and encourage safe and aware behaviour in relation to cybersecurity. AI presents itself increasingly important in cybersecurity, but it is important that behavioural psychology is considered in the development and use of this technology. By understanding how users interact with and respond to AI, more effective and aware cybersecurity systems can be created and implemented.

A strong cybersecurity culture is one of the key solutions to mitigate cybersecurity problems originating from human behaviour.

In recent studies, such as those conducted by Hadlington (2017) and Wilding et al. (2020), the importance of considering human behaviour in cybersecurity is highlighted. These authors argue that people often become the weakest link in the security chain as they are susceptible to making mistakes, such as clicking on suspicious links or providing personal information without thinking about the consequences. Hadlington (2017) suggest that organisations need to adopt a human-centric approach to cybersecurity. This means that in addition to implementing technological measures, companies should educate employees on how to behave safely online and encourage a culture of cybersecurity throughout the organisation. The authors highlight that success in cybersecurity depends on collaboration between people, processes and technologies. Wilding et al. (2018) also emphasise that while cybersecurity technologies are important, they are not the only solution to protecting data. They argue that companies must take human behaviour into consideration when designing their security systems, identifying potential vulnerabilities and creating an environment where people are motivated to act securely.

Thus, cybersecurity is a complex issue involving technologies, processes and people. It is important that organisations recognise the importance of human behaviour in data protection and adopt a human-centred approach to cybersecurity. Only then will it be possible to protect data and ensure everyone's online safety.

Behavioural psychology can inevitably become a valuable tool in cybersecurity, helping to understand and predict human behaviour related to cybersecurity and create effective strategies to prevent and mitigate cyber-attacks.

This chapter's overall objectives are to map the literature on behavioural psychology regarding AI in Cybersecurity; to demonstrate that a human-centred approach is crucial to ensure effective and sustainable cybersecurity in the long term and to highlight the importance of collaboration among cybersecurity experts, user interface designers and human behavioural/psychological science experts to develop human-centred cybersecurity solutions.

The mission of this chapter is to provide a reflective analysis on the psychology of user behaviour in relation to cybersecurity, and of the cybercriminal in the wake of AI applied to cybersecurity.

As a methodology a search in SCOPUS and Web of Science was performed as well as a consultation of the bibliographic references of the included articles. The data extraction tool will be based on the model recommended by the renowned Joanna Briggs Institute.

BACKGROUND

Behavioural psychology can play an important role in cybersecurity when combined with AI. Cybersecurity involves protecting information systems from cyber-attacks and malicious intrusions. AI can be used to detect and prevent these attacks, but behavioural psychology can help identify patterns and trends that AI may not detect.

Cybersecurity is a rather complex problem because most research focuses on the technical aspects of cybersecurity rather than on the psychological issues of users. However, evidence has been identified of the relationship between psychological factors and cybersecurity, including user perceptions, attitudes and behaviour. For this reason, psychological factors may be as important as technical factors in preventing cyber threats, and effective cybersecurity strategies need to be developed. To this end, it is necessary to understand how users perceive, evaluate and respond to cyber risks and threats. In the literature consulted, the importance of cybersecurity education and user awareness is discussed to improve internet security. Relevance is given to the need for personalised approaches to cyber safety education, taking into consideration individual differences concerning psychological factors affecting cyber safety. In this regard, a more holistic approach, which includes psychological, technical and social factors, is essential to help improve cybersecurity and reduce the risks of cyber threats.

Psychological and behavioural approaches can be useful in using AI to enhance cybersecurity.

PSYCHOLOGICAL APPROACHES REGARDING USERS AND CYBERSECURITY

There are several psychological approaches that can be attributed to users in the face of cybersecurity, of which we highlight the following:

- Behavioural approach: This approach focuses on changing specific user behaviours, such as ensuring that they create strong passwords, avoid clicking on suspicious links in emails and follow good cybersecurity practices. This approach can include training specific skills, such as recognising phishing attacks. AI can be programmed to recognise suspicious user behaviour, such as unauthorised access attempts or transfer of sensitive data, and based on these behaviours, AI can intervene to prevent the cybersecurity breach;

- Cognitive approach: This approach focuses on changing the way people think about cybersecurity. This can involve teaching basic concepts of cybersecurity and developing critical thinking, such as assessing the veracity of online information. AI can be programmed to understand the psychology of cybercriminals' behaviour by analysing their behaviours and thought patterns. With this understanding, AI can be used to develop more effective defence strategies against hacker attacks;

- Motivational approach: This approach seeks to increase users' motivation to follow proper cybersecurity practices. AI can be programmed to encourage users to follow proper cybersecurity practices by providing rewards or punishments based on their behaviour. This can help encourage users to take proper cybersecurity measures and reduce the likelihood of eventual security breaches.

- Humanistic approach: This approach focuses on understanding the underlying needs and motivations of cybersecurity users. This may include understanding what motivates people to click on suspicious links or share personal information online and consequently intervening to meet those needs more securely. In other words, AI can be programmed to understand these needs and motivations of users in relation to cybersecurity, and consequently provide personalised information and support to help them make safe decisions.

- Psychodynamic approach: This approach explores the unconscious emotions and experiences that may lead users to engage in inappropriate cybersecurity behaviours. AI can be used to analyse users' cybersecurity behaviour patterns, and to identify psychological and emotional factors that may lead to insecure behaviour. Based on this information, AI can be utilised to develop therapeutic strategies to help users overcome their insecurities, fears and anxieties about cybersecurity.

Psychological and behavioural approaches can therefore be used to improve cybersecurity through the use of AI. As a matter of fact, understanding the psychology and behavioural patterns of users can help develop more effective AI systems to protect against cybersecurity breaches.

Users are often viewed as the weakest link in cybersecurity and, as such, literature identifies some vulnerabilities of users regarding cybersecurity.

USER VULNERABILITIES REGARDING CYBERSECURITY

In the study by Welukar and Bajoria (2021) we are provided with a comprehensive review of the use of AI in cybersecurity, focusing on the latest and most advanced techniques. This work discusses the application of AI and neural network techniques to solve various cybersecurity challenges such as threat detection, user authentication, fraud detection and vulnerability analysis, among other mentioned at this point:

Weak passwords: Weak passwords are one of the major vulnerabilities in cybersecurity. Many users choose passwords that are easy to guess or reuse them across multiple accounts, making it easy for hackers to break into their accounts.

Lack of awareness about phishing: Phishing attacks are one of the main ways hackers gain access to users' accounts. Users often do not know how to identify phishing emails and click on malicious links or provide personal information to hackers. Users can be tricked by phishing emails that appear legitimate but are actually designed to steal personal information or login credentials.

Lack of software updates: The lack of software updates is another common vulnerability. Users often ignore security updates, leaving their systems vulnerable to attacks.

Poor security hygiene: Poor security hygiene includes behaviours such as sharing passwords with others, leaving devices unlocked or often connecting to public Wi-Fi networks that are not secure, thus exposing their information and activities to potential attacks.

Social networks: Users may expose sensitive information on social networks such as their location, workplace and personal information, which can be used by hackers to perform social engineering attacks.

Downloads from untrusted sources: Users may download software from untrusted or unknown sources, which may contain malware or viruses that can damage their systems and data.

Das and Sandhane (2021) analysed the use of AI in cybersecurity and discuss the advantages and disadvantages of using AI in various areas of cybersecurity such as threat detection, risk analysis, vulnerability identification and incident management. The authors discuss the main AI techniques used in cybersecurity, including neural networks, genetic algorithms and fuzzy logic (it is a type of multivariate logic that deals with uncertainty and imprecision in a system, it deals with situations where variables are vague or imprecise). They further discuss about the challenges faced in implementing AI in cybersecurity, such as the lack of sufficient training data and the need to protect users' privacy. This study concludes that AI can be a valuable tool to improve cybersecurity, but emphasises the need for a careful and ethical approach in implementing it, highlighting the importance of collaboration between cybersecurity experts and AI specialists to develop more effective and secure solutions.

To mitigate these vulnerabilities, users should be educated in cybersecurity best practices, such as choosing strong passwords, keeping software updated, avoiding downloads from unknown sources and taking precautions when using public networks. Organisations should also implement cybersecurity measures i.e. an organisational culture that includes cybersecurity, to protect their users and systems from potential cyber threats.

ORGANIZATIONAL CULTURE IN CYBERSECURITY

A solid cybersecurity culture is pointed out as one of the main solutions to mitigate cybersecurity problems originating from human behaviour. European Union Agency for Cybersecurity ENISA (2018) defines cybersecurity culture in organisations as the set of "knowledge, beliefs, perceptions, attitudes, assumptions, norms and values of people regarding cybersecurity and how they manifest in people's behaviour with information technologies". With regard to cybersecurity, it is essential to take into account human characteristics and behaviours (Gonçalves & Nunes, 2019).

Currently, social engineering is increasingly effective and widespread, so it should be a major concern for organisations (Proofpoint, 2019). The goal of social engineering in the cyber world is to convince the victim to provide sensitive information or perform a specific action, such as clicking on a malicious link or downloading an infected file.

To avoid becoming a victim of this kind of social engineering, it is important that people are aware of the risks and take measures to protect themselves, such as not sharing personal information with strangers and keeping security software updated on their devices.

- The human factor in cybersecurity

The Human Aspects of Information Security Questionnaire (HAIS-Q) is a recently developed scale to explore the information security of individuals (Parsons et al., 2017). The HAIS-Q is composed of a variety of items that assesses three key elements in the context of cybersecurity: knowledge, attitude and behaviour. The underlying structure of the HAIS-Q examines these constructs in five main areas, including password management, email use, internet use, social media, incident reporting, mobile computing and information manipulation (Parsons et al., 2014). Higher scores on the HAIS-Q indicate good information security awareness, while lower scores demonstrate a lack of knowledge and a propensity to engage in potentially risky activities, such as sharing passwords.

The work of Warrington et al. (2021) included an exploration of how personality traits and a measure of risk taking were associated with scores on the HAIS-Q. The study used the five-factor personality model, with the most frequently cited version being that of John and Srivastava (1999), noted in Table 1.

Table 1. The five-factor model of personality as taken from John and Srivastava (1999)

Factor Name	Description
Extroversion	An energetic approach to the social and material world and incudes traits such as sociability, activity, assertiveness, and positive emotionality.
Agreeableness	Contrasts a prosocial and communal orientation towards others with antagonism and includes traits such as altruism, tender-mindedness, trust and modesty.
Conscientiousness	Socially prescribed impulse control that facilitates task and goal oriented behavior, such as thinking before acting, delaying gratification, following norms and rules, and planning, organizing, and prioritizing tasks.
Neuroticism	Contrasts emotional stability and even-temperedness with negative emotionality, such as feeling anxious, nervous, sad, and tense.
Openness	In contrast to closed-mindedness, describes the breadth, depth, originality, and complexity of an individual's mental and experiential life.

In this research a significant and positive relationship was observed between the personality traits of friendliness, openness and conscientiousness with the scores on HAIS-Q. A negative correlation was also observed between risk taking and scores on the HAIS-Q, with those less likely to engage in risky behaviour showing higher scores overall.

There appears to be some similarity in the results that examined self-reported cybersecurity knowledge, attitudes and behaviours. Predominantly, individual differences in aspects of personality have the potential to predict at what level that individual will engage in information security behaviours. It appears that those who are more conscientious, open-minded, agreeable, risk-averse and rational are more likely to engage positively in effective cybersecurity behaviours. In addition to these personality traits, it appears that age and gender also serve as important moderators of active information security behaviour.

- Cybersecurity awareness

Cybersecurity awareness is an integral part of cybersecurity culture (ENISA, 2018). Thus, awareness aims to make people aware of, and ideally committed to, the organisation's security objectives (Siponen, 2000).

Increased awareness regarding cybersecurity and information security will make employees reduce the practice of behaviours that jeopardise cybersecurity, if it is well used, applied and interpreted. Therefore, it is important to identify, quantify and understand the mistakes previously made by the organisation's employees, always bearing in mind that it is a continuous process that requires repetition (Organization of American States, 2020; Siponen, 2000). It can essentially be considered as a preventive measure that aims to establish cybersecurity principles and procedures in the minds of all employees, alerting them to existing security problems and their possible consequences.

- Training and Education

Raising awareness, training and educating employees on appropriate behaviours for cybersecurity culture is the basis for making organisations more resilient (Gonçalves & Nunes, 2019).

Cybersecurity education is a process of teaching and training skills and using tools that has the main objective of creating relevant and necessary security skills in all employees.

Education, besides the fundamental concepts that are transmitted, also allows the understanding of tools, techniques and technologies related to cybersecurity. Cybersecurity education is characterised by being a long-term formal study, comprising a duration of months or years (Organization of American States, 2020).

To design successful awareness and training actions, one should identify the individual and collective skills that should be developed in employees.

MULTIDISCIPLINARY TEAM

The importance of a multidisciplinary approach to these issues is often highlighted in articles and academic publications on the subject. For example, researchers such as Zhang and Zhang (2023) argue that collaboration between different disciplines is essential to understand the ethical and security challenges of AI. Also, authors such as Wilding et al. (2020) emphasise the importance of considering human behaviour in cybersecurity. Therefore, the idea of integrating psychologists into the AI and cybersecurity study team is a proposal that emerges from a practical need and is widely supported by a variety of experts and researchers in these fields.

The integration of psychologists into the AI and cybersecurity study team can be beneficial for several reasons:

Understanding human behaviour: Psychologists have a deep understanding of human behaviour, which can be applied to the development of more effective and secure AI systems. They can help understand how users interact with systems and how security decisions are made.

Cyber threat analysis: Psychologists can contribute in analysing cyber threats from a behavioural and psychological perspective, identifying possible attack vectors and vulnerabilities in terms of human behaviour.

Promotion of a security culture: Psychologists can help create a security culture in the organisation by increasing users' awareness and motivation to adopt secure behaviour.

Development of effective trainings: Psychologists can contribute to the development of more effective cybersecurity trainings, taking into consideration the users' needs and the best way to convey security information.

Risk assessment: Psychologists can assist in assessing cybersecurity risks by identifying behavioural factors that may increase or reduce risks.

Moreover, integrating psychologists into the AI and cybersecurity study team can promote a multidisciplinary approach to these issues, combining technical expertise with behavioural and psychological knowledge.

In the research conducted we found recent studies on behavioural psychology and how it can be used favourably in the production of solutions that will enhance cybersecurity.

In the following section we present the methodological aspects that guided the scoping review carried out to build this chapter.

METHODOLOGY

Given its standardisation, the preparation of a scoping review (Munn et al., 2018; Noble & Smith, 2018) presupposes rigour and transparency. To carry out this study, we followed Arksey and O'Malley's (2005) guidelines. Similarly, the writing of this chapter was organised to meet the PRISMA-ScR checklist, developed by Page et al. (2021) for reporting scoping reviews. According to Arksey and O'Malley (2005), the recommended steps for conducting a scoping review are: (1) to identify the research question(s); (2) to search for relevant studies; (3) to select the studies; (4) to analyse the results; and (5) to group, summarise and present the results.

The conduct of this scoping review aimed to answer the following research questions: Does human behaviour impact cybersecurity? Does artificial intelligence enable the identification of human behaviours that increase cybersecurity risks?

Search for Relevant Studies

Prior to the identification of potentially relevant studies, the search terms were determined according to the research questions. In this follow-up, the search was conducted in the Web of Science Core Collection and Scopus using the following search terms, Boolean operators and inclusion criteria:

- Search terms: "human behaviour" AND cybersecurity AND "artificial intelligence"
- Years included: all
- Type of access: all
- Type of documents: articles and publications in scientific congress proceedings
- Type of studies: all
- Languages: documents in English, Portuguese, Spanish, French and German

Data extraction was performed in February 2023.

Selection of Studies

In this review, primary studies (original investigations) and published studies were considered. Quantitative, qualitative, and mixed-methods paradigm studies, as well as systematic and unstructured literature reviews were also considered. Likewise, observational studies (with descriptive, exploratory and analytical designs) and experimental studies, as well as cross-sectional and longitudinal studies. The PCC (Participants, Concept and Context) methodology was applied to better filter the documents to be included, as presented in Table 2.

Table 2. Participants, concept, and context

Participants	Adults (aged 18 years or older) or articles, in the case of literature reviews
Concept	Relationship among human behavior, cybersecurity and artificAll intelligence
Context	No limitations in context

The evidence search and selection process is summarised in the flowchart for scoping reviews according to PRISMA-ScR (Figure 1).

Figure 1. Document selection flowchart

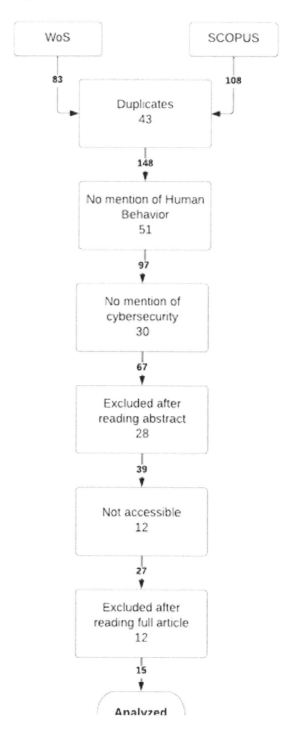

As the aim of a scoping review is to cover as much of the available literature as possible (Arksey & O'Malley, 2005), the main criterion for the selection of the documents included in the study was the relevance to answer the research questions, with the assessment of methodological quality taking second place.

Analysis of Results

The analysis of the title, abstract and full text was always performed by two or more independent researchers of the research team, who selected the articles to be considered for review based on the inclusion and exclusion criteria. Data extraction was performed by three of the researchers, basing the instrument developed around the objectives and research questions, defined for the study, on the Joanna Briggs Institute model (Jordan et al., 2019).

Presentation of the Results

The research findings were organised according to the SPIDER model, an acronym for Sample, Phenomenon of Interest, Design, Evaluation and Research type and summarise the results in an organised and easily interpretable table (Cooke et al., 2012).

RESULTS

Table 3 presents the results of the research according to the SPIDER model.

Table 3. Documents included in the scoping review

Authors and Year	Sample	Phenomenon of Interest	Drawing	Evaluation	Type of research
Burns (2020)	413 employees of national security agencies	Can artificial intelligence (AI) predict human behavior, such as insider threats?	Case study	The prevalence and success of adversarial attacks on AI systems indicate the clear need to conduct quantitative risk and threat assessments for companies and agencies beginning to implement AI and *machine learning* tools, but have not necessarily considered security implications.	Quantitative
Al-Amri et al. (2021)	27 scientific articles relevant to the topic under study	Can AI predict and reduce human errors that lead to cybersecurity risks?	Unstructured literature review	Artificial intelligence has evolved over the years and has been increasingly applied to cybersecurity and the detection of human error.	Literature review
Sharma (2019)	24 articles relevant to the topic under study	Study the impact of using AI to help people change their cybersecurity habits	Unstructured literature review	Popular visions of AI often focus on robots and the dystopian future they will create for humanity, but to understand the true impact of AI, its sceptics and detractors must look to the future of cybersecurity.	Literature review
Bone (2016)	17 articles relevant to the topic under study	Study two of the most common storylines in cyber warfare: the rise of the "hacker" as an industry and the "cybersecurity paradox," i.e., why billions spent on cybersecurity fail to deal with semantic cyberattacks	Unstructured literature review	The Cognitive Risk Framework for Cybersecurity revolves around five pillars: Design of Intentional Controls, Cognitive Computer Security, Cognitive Risk Governance, Cybersecurity Intelligence and Active Defense Strategies, and legal considerations on "Best Efforts" in Cyberspace.	Literature review
Goethals and Yodo (2019)	31 articles relevant to the topic under study	Study possible methods to prevent cyberattacks from within organizations	Unstructured literature review	A more holistic assessment of the individual and their surroundings, grounded in industrial engineering techniques, can give an organization a greater general awareness of its internal attack risk.	Literature review
Dennis and Minas (2018)	31 articles relevant to the topic under study	The risks that System 1 cognition can impose on cybersecurity	Unstructured literature review	One of the reasons cybersecurity is such an important issue in organizations, and why existing training programs seem to have little effect, is because we have failed to focus on the second locus of control: System 1.	Literature review
Ngambeki et al. (2021)	N.A.	Implement a social engineering course	Review of existing best practices, adapting and conjuncting them in order to meet the identified needs	It was possible to implement the course, based on the social constructivism approach to learning, where students first develop an understanding of the individual and social context of social engineering. It uniquely combines the psychology of human behavior, legal precepts, and computer science to identify how psychological principles are applied in cyberspace to explore individuals.	Case study
Alqahtani and Kavakli-Thorne (2020)	33 articles relevant to the topic under study	Explore the possibility of applying gamification techniques to educate users with the aim of increasing general awareness about cybersecurity by developing a game based on augmented reality techniques as an Android application called CybAR	Literature review and analysis of technical possibilities	Its conclusion is a lack of studies examining user behaviour in relation to cybersecurity risk behaviours that can be reduced using augmented reality.	Exploratory study
Kalhoro et al. (2022)	16 articles relevant to the topic under study	Study the relationship between psychological aspects, endpoint cyberattacks, personality traits, high and low scores of employee behaviours, and risky behaviour	Systematic review	High openness and extraversion were associated with lower susceptibility to phishing. Openness and conscientiousness significantly impacted a given behaviour more than other characteristics. Women demonstrate much lower security behaviour in terms of password development, updating, andactive awareness than men.	Systematic review
Qashqari et al. (2020)	13 articles relevant to the topic under study	Study the threats derived from the human factor in the world of cybersecurity, which is affected by an individual's personality, background, gender, age, and experience.	Unstructured literature review	Personality traits have an impact on cybersecurity risk.	Literature review
López-Aguilar and Solanas (2021)	38 articles relevant to the topic under study	Study the impact of the five major personality traits on cybersecurity	Systematic review	There is no well-established psychological theory that explains the role of neuroticism in the context of phishing. We maintain that non-representative samples and the lack of homogeneity between studies may be to blame for this lack of consensus on the role of neuroticism in phishing susceptibility.	Systematic review

Continued on following page

Table 3. Continued

Authors and Year	Sample	Phenomenon of Interest	Drawing	Evaluation	Type of research
Gillam and Foster (2020)	184 working adults in the United States	Study whether risky cybersecurity behaviour is predicted by cybersecurity avoidance behaviour factors related to cybersecurity	This is an exploratory, descriptive and correlational study, in a cross-sectional plan, through a self-report questionnaire	Hierarchical regression observed significant predictive associations between various factors preventing technological threats and self-reported risky cybersecurity behaviour: perceived susceptibility (p = 0.027), perceived cost (p = 0.003), and self-efficacy (p = 0.043). Combined, these variables explained 9.4% of the adjusted variance in levels of risky cybersecurity behavior (p = 0.001). Calculations of the effect size revealed low- to medium-range predictive impacts. Age was also confirmed as a confounding covariate (p = 0.045).	Quantitative
Eftimie et al. (2022)	235 employees of a computer consulting company	Study the psychological aspects of socAIl engineering by analyzing personality traits in the context of spear-phishing attacks	. Phishing emails were built by leveraging multiple vulnerable personality traits to maximize the success of an attack. The emails were then used to test various hypotheses about phishing susceptibility.	The results show that personality traits correlate with phishing susceptibility in certain circumstances and pave the way for new methods of protecting individuals from phishing attacks.	Quantitative study
Xiao et al. (2022)	N.A.	Study security behaviour in cyberspace and in the research question of how to provide assistance for this	Exploratory and theoretical study, from the techno-psychological and techno-economic perspectives	Human security behaviours in cyberspace will be affected by more factors in different environments, as they occur in parallel in the two spaces.	Exploratory study
Hakami and Alshaikh (2022)	100 articles relevant to the topic under study	Study the impact of the human factor on cybersecurity	Systematic review	Scholars consistently argue the importance of safety awareness to prevent incidents caused by human behavior	Systematic review

DISCUSSION

Human behavioural factors are fundamental to understand, detect and mitigate insider threats, but to date, they are insufficiently represented in a formal ontology.

(Burns (2020) study examines the applications of AI in cybersecurity, including the prediction of human behaviour. The author highlights that AI can be used to analyse large amounts of data in real time, identify potential threats and mitigate cybersecurity risks. The study also discusses other applications of AI in cybersecurity, such as malware detection and system vulnerability analysis. In addition, the author addresses ethical and privacy issues related to the use of AI in cybersecurity. Overall, he concludes that AI has the potential to significantly improve cybersecurity, but also emphasises the importance of ensuring transparency and accountability in the development and use of these technologies.

In the study conducted by (Al-Amri et al., 2021), two of the main components of the cybersecurity infrastructure, the human element and AI, are discussed. The risks associated with current cybersecurity are taken into consideration and an analysis of the role of AI in future cybersecurity is discussed. An in-depth analysis of the human factor in the field of cybersecurity is made. Different models to recognise and calculate the variants in employee reaction to Information Security Awareness (ISA) are discussed with there being agreement that the human element represents one of the main weaknesses threatening software security. In the gender-based analysis, it was determined that older individuals are less likely to be attacked by vulnerable attacks compared to people aged 18-35. Human behaviour towards cybersecurity is analysed and it is determined that human behaviour towards cybersecurity is based on different intentions and outcomes and that there are also weaknesses that threaten software security. Although AI has shown great promise in improving security, it is not a perfect solution and human input and supervision are still crucial. Therefore, the challenge will be to find the right balance between human expertise and AI capabilities to maximise the effectiveness of information security. In addition, there are ethical and legal implications that must be considered when implementing AI in security measures, such as privacy concerns and potential discrimination. Overall, while AI can be a valuable tool in improving information security, it is important to approach it with a critical and thoughtful mindset to ensure that its benefits are maximised and potential risks are mitigated. Besides, in another study by Rajwar et al. (2020), they discuss the importance of user behaviour analysis in cybersecurity and how behavioural psychology can be used to improve security. The authors argue that behaviour analysis can be used to identify suspicious or malicious activity, even when an attacker is adopting the user's legitimate credentials. In addition, the study discusses the application of AI techniques to analyse and detect anomalies in user behaviour. The authors state that behaviour analysis is a rapidly developing field in cybersecurity and has the potential to be used to significantly improve the effectiveness of cybersecurity systems. However, they also note that there are significant challenges to be faced in implementing these techniques, including privacy and ethical issues.

The study conducted by Sharma (2019) finds that in today's technical world, the word AI itself is significant for its functionality, work efficiency, etc. It has completely changed human lifestyle, work processing, thinking skills, competition, behavioural change, etc. It is used to help people overcome their habits, it is a clinically effective and economical tool by automating reminders for practices. It is considered for the future as a great promise for hybrid systems. However, there is no formula for intuition, which means that not every aspect can be replicated by an algorithm, but "Augmented Intelligence" has been introduced, which better combines human and artificial intelligence to change human behaviour. Despite popular visions of AI often focusing on robots and a dystopian future they will create for humanity, it would be important to look into the future of cybersecurity to understand the true positive impact of AI.

Bone (2016) study addresses the creation of a Cognitive Risk Framework (CRFC) to help companies manage cybersecurity risks. The Cognitive Risk Framework for Cybersecurity revolves around five pillars: Intentional Design Controls, Cognitive IT Security, Cognitive Risk Governance, Cybersecurity Intelligence, and Active Defence Strategies and Legal "Best Efforts" Considerations in Cyberspace.

Semantic cyber-attacks, also known as social engineering, manipulate human users' perceptions and interpretations of computer-generated data to obtain confidential non-public data. The cyber battlefield has shifted from attacking physical assets to a much softer target: the human mind. If human behaviour is the new and ultimate 'weakest link' in the cybersecurity armour, is it possible to build cognitive defences at the intersection of human-machine interactions? The answer is yes, but the necessary change requires a new way of thinking about security, data governance and strategy. The concepts referenced in the Cognitive Risk Framework for Cybersecurity come from a large body of research on multidisciplinary topics. Cognitive risk management is a close discipline of a parallel body of science called Cognitive Computing Security or CogSec. It is also important to note that as the creator of the CRFC, the principles and practices prescribed in the study are borrowed from cognitive computing security, machine learning, AI, and behavioural and cognitive science, among just a few that are still evolving.

Goethals and Yodo (2019) note that human behaviour, in practice and theory, can have a tremendous impact on the effectiveness of a system's security. In the field of cybersecurity, its effects can be particularly damaging. The email phishing attack, the unintentional release of malware and the deliberate theft of confidential information are examples of events where individual activities are of primary interest.

The complexity or difficulty in predicting various aspects of human behaviour, however, is undeniable. This research provides a brief review of recent notable models in the literature and proposes a candidate framework for further research in measuring insider attack risk. It interlinks principles from psychology with industrial and systems engineering techniques to provide viable tools for quantifying human behaviour.

Dennis and Minas (2018) state that most current theories of information systems security assume that a rational actor makes deliberate decisions, however, recent research in psychology suggests that such deliberate thinking is not as common as we expect. Much of human behaviour is controlled by automatic, non-conscious cognition (called System 1 cognition). Rational, deliberate System 2 cognition is triggered when System 1 detects something that is not normal; otherwise, we often operate on autopilot. When we engage System 2 cognition, it is influenced by the System 1 cognition that preceded it. This paper, presents an alternative theoretical approach to information security, based on non-conscious automatic System 1 cognition. In a System 1 world, cognition is a sub-second process of pattern matching a stimulus to an existing person-context heuristic. These person-context heuristics are influenced by personality traits and a lifetime of experiences in context. Thus, System 1 theories are closely linked to individuals and the specific security context of interest. Methods for improving safety compliance take a very new form; traditional safety education and training approaches that provide guidelines and ways of thinking about safety have no effect when behaviour is controlled by System 1, because System 1 cognition is instantaneous pattern matching, not deliberative. Therefore, in a System 1 world, we improve safety by changing the heuristics used by System 1 pattern matching and/or changing what System 1 sees as "normal" to trigger System 2 deliberative cognition. As suggestions further research is needed to develop theories of System 1 cognition in the cybersecurity literature.

The article by Ngambeki et al. (2021) is on Innovative Practice, describing the implementation of a Social Engineering(SE) course. SE is the process of gaining unauthorised access to systems by exploiting humans, which has been highlighted by the FBI and the US banking industry as a threat to national security. According to a McAfee report, the global cost of cybercrime has exceeded 1 trillion since 2018, and an additional 145 billion has been spent on cybersecurity by 2020 (Gann, 2020). The research showed that 97% of cyber-attacks employ some element of Social Engineering. This Innovative Practice paper presents an effective and practical course designed to introduce students to Social Engineering penetration testing. The course is based on a social-constructivism approach to learning, where students first develop an understanding of the individual and social context of Social Engineering. It combines the psychology of human behaviour, legal precepts and computer science to identify how psychological principles are applied in cyberspace to exploit individuals and how the same principles can be applied during SE penetration testing to detect vulnerabilities.

Alqahtani and Kavakli-Thorne (2020), based on the idea that human behaviour is considered the weakest link in the cybersecurity field, and that despite the development of a wide range of Augmented Reality (AR) applications in various fields, no AR application is available to educate users and raise their awareness about cybersecurity issues, developed a game based on AR techniques as an Android application called CybAR. As there are few acceptance studies in the AR field, it was especially important to identify the factors affecting user acceptance of AR technology. Technology acceptance studies generally predict behavioural adoption by investigating the relationship between attitudes and intentions, although intention may not be the best predictor of actual behaviour. Personality constructs and cultural difference dimensions have recently been found to further explain variance in behaviour and provide insights into user behaviour. The aim of this study was to identify the personality traits that affect users' acceptance of CybAR and increase their cybersecurity awareness. The study also aimed to identify the cultural factors that influence CybAR acceptance by comparing users from Saudi Arabia and Australia according to Hofstede's cultural value dimensions (Hofstede, 1980). Thus, potential predictors of CybAR app usage were derived from the unified extended theory of technology acceptance and use (UTAUT2), personality traits and cultural moderators. They concluded that there is a paucity of studies examining user behaviour in relation to cybersecurity risk behaviours that can be reduced using augmented reality and that personality traits have an impact on cybersecurity risk.

Kalhoro et al. (2022), consider that human behaviour is considered the main risk in small businesses. Attackers aim to achieve their destructive goals by exploiting end-user flaws and prefer to attack people rather than systems. As a result, human vulnerabilities endanger electronic systems, data confidentiality and reliability. Due to their recognised susceptibility to cybersecurity, cyber attackers are increasingly targeting small and medium-sized enterprises (SMEs) rather than large organisations. Previous studies have shown that employees are the weakest point in cybersecurity. For successful cybersecurity practices in enterprises, security risks and employee decision-making processes must be considered more closely. Personality is one of the most important psychological traits that influence human behaviour. Personality traits influence people's decision-making processes and drive the performance of employee behaviours. These authors discuss psychological aspects, cyber-attacks on endpoints, personality traits, high and low scores of employee behaviours and risk-taking behaviour. High openness and extroversion were associated with lower susceptibility to phishing. Openness and conscientiousness significantly impacted a given behaviour more than other traits. Women demonstrate much lower security behaviour in terms of password development, updating and active conscientiousness than men.

Qashqari et al. (2020), consider that information security is not only limited to technology and systems, but also includes the humans and processes that use and depend on it. Even with strong information security policies, humans are the weakest link in information security. Even if people are aware of the policies, they may not act accordingly, thus leading to mistakes. This article illustrates how human factors affect cybersecurity and explains the demographic characteristics, such as gender, age, personality and cultural background, which are key determinants of an individual's attitude and behaviour towards cybersecurity. It discusses the concept of insider threat and how its potential impact on cybersecurity policies, proposing the importance of ensuring cybersecurity training and intervention programmes. The study indicates that attitudes towards technological, regulatory and strategic aspects of IS management are positively correlated with certain personality traits, for the trait "conscientiousness".

Individual human factors reflect behaviours, attitudes, personal, sociocultural or ideological issues and various biographical factors that may indicate increased risk. The individual level also differentiates psychological traits from dynamic states.

López-Aguilar and Solanas (2021) report that the COVID-19 pandemic situation has opened up a wide range of opportunities for cybercriminals, who take advantage of the anxiety generated and the time spent on the Internet to carry out mass phishing campaigns. Although companies are adopting protective measures, the psychological traits of victims are still considered from a very general perspective. The literature determines that the proposed model of the five major personality traits (Openness, Conscientiousness, Extroversion, Agreeableness and Neuroticism) may play an important role in human behaviour to combat cybercrime. However, the results do not provide unanimity regarding the correlation between phishing susceptibility and neuroticism. The results of this study show that there is no well-established psychological theory that explains the role of neuroticism in the context of phishing. Supporting that non-representative samples and the lack of homogeneity between studies may be responsible for this lack of consensus on the role of neuroticism in phishing susceptibility.

The behavioural determinants of cybersecurity have gained increased attention among information technology experts in recent years. However, the factors that drive risky cybersecurity behaviours have not been widely studied. (Gillam and Foster (2020) conducted an exploratory study that examines the extent to which risky cybersecurity behaviour is predicted by avoidance behaviour factors related to cybersecurity. Self-reported cybersecurity risk behaviour was examined in light of technological threat avoidance factors in a sample of 184 working adults in the United States. Hierarchical regression observed significant predictive associations between several technology threat avoidance factors and self-reported risky cybersecurity behaviour: perceived susceptibility ($p = 0.027$), perceived cost ($p = 0.003$) and self-efficacy ($p = 0.043$). Combined, these variables explained 9.4% of the adjusted variance in levels of risky cybersecurity behaviour ($p = 0.001$). Effect size calculations revealed low- to mid-range predictive impacts. Age was also confirmed as a confounding covariate ($p = 0.045$). The results found are distinct from previous studies. The evidence also suggests that training in protective behaviours can mitigate a significant portion of risky cybersecurity behaviour.

Eftimie et al. (2022) conducted a study that examines the psychological aspects of social engineering by analysing personality traits in the context of spear-phishing attacks. Phishing emails were constructed by leveraging multiple vulnerable personality traits to maximise the success of an attack. The emails were then used to test various hypotheses about phishing susceptibility by simulating a series of spear-phishing campaigns within a software development company. The company's employees underwent a standard Big Five personality test, four different phishing emails over four weeks and cybersecurity training. Results were aggregated before and after the cybersecurity course, and binary logistic regression analyses were performed at each stage of the phishing attack. The results show that personality traits correlate with susceptibility to phishing in certain circumstances and pave the way for new methods to protect individuals from phishing attacks.

With the development of human-computer interaction technology, the concept of space is constantly being further extended. As technology continues to be incorporated into daily life, the boundaries between the physical world and cyberspace are becoming increasingly blurred. Human security behaviours in cyber-physical space will be affected by more factors in different environments as they occur in parallel in both spaces. Therefore, in this new socio-technical system, we need to reconsider how to guide and assist human security behaviour. Xiao et al. (2022), in their paper, focus on security behaviour in cyber-physical space and the research question of how to provide assistance for this. On the one hand, they consider the characteristics of the environment, i.e. cyber-physical space as the product of technological development. On the other hand, as human behaviour is affected by psychological characteristics and bounded rationality, therefore the behavioural characteristics of the subject are also considered. Starting from techno-psychological and techno-economic perspectives, they propose changing motivation, changing ability, providing appropriate triggers or using people's status quo bias, regression aversion bias, social influence to assist human security behaviour based on persuasive technology and push theory.

The evidence reviewed here reflectively is unanimous that the human factor poses a very big challenge to organisations and is responsible for many cybersecurity incidents due to lack of compliance with the organisation's security policies. In their study Hakami and Alshaikh (2022) identified strategies to address the human factor and concluded that security awareness, training and education programme is the main security awareness strategy to prevent incidents caused by human behaviour.

The Cybersecurity Observatory of the National Centre for Cybersecurity has released the 2020 edition of the report Cybersecurity in Portugal – Society (Centro Nacional de Cibersegurança [CNCS], 2021). The document presents indicators on the human factor linked to cybersecurity, namely the attitudes, behaviours and education and awareness of individuals and organisations, in Portugal. It analyses the updated figures on these matters, establishing an overview on the strengths and weaknesses of individuals and organisations regarding good cybersecurity practices.

CONCLUSION

Holistic cybersecurity risk assessment is a complex multi-component, multi-level problem that involves hardware, software, environmental, and human factors. As part of an ongoing effort to develop a holistic and predictive model for cybersecurity risk assessment, human factors characterisation, which includes human behaviour, is necessary to understand how the actions of users, defenders and attackers affect cybersecurity risk. In cybersecurity, the study of human factors explores how humans interact with computers. Studies prove that inherent personality traits have a great effect on an individual's behaviours and attitudes towards cybersecurity. People's perceptions, attitudes and actions towards information cybersecurity are affected by personality traits. Evidence suggests that personality may be a better predictor of cybersecurity behaviour than an individual's stated intentions. However, people often behave in ways that are at odds with what they intend. Assuming that most people intend to comply with secure practices, it is still not surprising that they violate policies and put confidential data at risk on a regular basis.

New technologies (social media, communication channels, etc.) are changing the way we think, work, play and communicate on a global scale. These same technologies have created risks that were not imagined at their conception. As more advanced cognitive solutions become available in the near future, cybersecurity professionals need a transition plan and framework to manage this new environment in a sustainable and adaptive way as new solutions are introduced. If the consensus is that the human is the "weakest link", then we need tools to strengthen this vulnerability. The Cognitive Risk Framework for Cybersecurity is an approach to ease the transition to a more intuitive security program through its "guiding principles" and the "Five Pillars".

As it has become obvious that the human aspects of cybersecurity pose as many risks as the technological aspects, it is important to continue to develop studies to better understand the various human factors that impact cybersecurity. Combining behavioural psychology with artificial intelligence could be an effective approach to strengthen cybersecurity.

REFERENCES

Al-Amri, B. O., Alsuwat, H., & Alsuwat, E. (2021). Human Factor & Artificial Intelligence: For future software security to be invincible, a confronting comprehensive survey. *International Journal of Computer Science and Network Security*, 21(6), 245–251.

Alqahtani, H., & Kavakli-Thorne, M. (2020). Exploring Factors Affecting User's Cybersecurity Behaviour by Using Mobile Augmented Reality App (CybAR). *ACM International Conference Proceeding Series*, 129–135. 10.1145/3384613.3384629

Arksey, H., & O'Malley, L. (2005). Scoping studies: Towards a methodological framework. *International Journal of Social Research Methodology: Theory and Practice*, *8*(1), 19–32. doi:10.1080/1364557032000119616

Bone, J. (2016). The Five Pillars of a Cognitive Risk Framework—Part II. *Edpacs*, *54*(6), 1–16. doi:10.1080/07366981.2016.1257219

Burns, D. (2020). Applications of artificial intelligence in cybersecurity. In *Software Engineering* (pp. 21–48). Artificial Intelligence, Compliance, and Security. doi:10.1201/9781003147176-1

Centro Nacional de Cibersegurança. (2021). *Cibersegurança em portugal*. Author.

Cooke, A., Smith, D., & Booth, A. (2012). Beyond PICO: The SPIDER tool for qualitative evidence synthesis. *Qualitative Health Research*, *22*(10), 1435–1443. doi:10.1177/1049732312452938 PMID:22829486

Das, R., & Sandhane, R. (2021). Artificial Intelligence in Cyber Security. *Journal of Physics: Conference Series*, *1964*(4), 042072. Advance online publication. doi:10.1088/1742-6596/1964/4/042072

Dennis, A. R., & Minas, R. K. (2018). Security on autopilot: Why current security theories hijack our thinking and lead us astray. *The Data Base for Advances in Information Systems*, *49*(SI, s1), 15–37. doi:10.1145/3210530.3210533

Eftimie, S., Moinescu, R., & Racuciu, C. (2022). Spear-Phishing Susceptibility Stemming From Personality Traits. *IEEE Access : Practical Innovations, Open Solutions*, *10*, 73548–73561. doi:10.1109/ACCESS.2022.3190009

ENISA. (2018). Behavioural Aspects of Cybersecurity Culture. In *European Union Agency for Network and Information Security*. Issue December., doi:10.2824/324042

Gann, T. (2020). *The hidden cost of cybercrime on government*. https://www.mcafee.com/blogs/other-blogs/executive-perspectives/the-hidden-costs-of-cybercrime-on-government/

Gillam, A. R., & Foster, W. T. (2020). Factors affecting risky cybersecurity behaviors by U.S. workers: An exploratory study. *Computers in Human Behavior*, *108*(February), 106319. doi:10.1016/j.chb.2020.106319

Goethals, P. L., & Yodo, N. (2019). Insider attack metrics for cybersecurity: investigating various research options. *IISE Annual Conference and Expo 2019*, 1578–1584.

Gonçalves, R. S., & Nunes, S. (2019). *O fator humano da cibersegurança nas organizações*. Cybersecurity in the XXI Century. doi:10.33965/ciawi2019_201914L007

Hadlington, L. (2017). Human factors in cybersecurity; examining the link between Internet addiction, impulsivity, attitudes towards cybersecurity, and risky cybersecurity behaviours. *Heliyon*, *3*(7), e00346. doi:10.1016/j.heliyon.2017.e00346 PMID:28725870

Hakami, M., & Alshaikh, M. (2022). Identifying Strategies to Address Human Cybersecurity Behavior: A Review Study. *International Journal of Computer Science & Network Security*, *22*(4), 299–309. doi:10.22937/IJCSNS.2022.22.4.37

Hofstede, G. (1980). Motivation. Leadership and Organization. In Do American Theories Apply Abroad (pp. 42–63). Academic Press.

John, O., & Srivastava, S. (1999). The Big Five trait taxonomy: History, measurement, and theoretical perspectives. *Handbook of Personality: Theory and Research, 2*(510), 102–138.

Jordan, Z., Lockwood, C., Munn, Z., & Aromataris, E. (2019). The updated Joanna Briggs Institute Model of Evidence-Based Healthcare. *International Journal of Evidence-Based Healthcare, 17*(1), 58–71. doi:10.1097/XEB.0000000000000155 PMID:30256247

Kalhoro, S., Ayyasamy, R. K., Jebna, A. K. K., Kalhoro, A., Krishnan, K., & Nodeson, S. (2022). How Personality Traits Impacts on Cyber Security Behaviors of SMEs Employees. *2022 International Conference on Innovation and Intelligence for Informatics, Computing, and Technologies, 3ICT 2022*, 635–641. 10.1109/3ICT56508.2022.9990621

López-Aguilar, P., & Solanas, A. (2021). Human susceptibility to phishing attacks based on personality traits: The role of neuroticism. *Proceedings - 2021 IEEE 45th Annual Computers, Software, and Applications Conference, COMPSAC 2021*, 1363–1368. 10.1109/COMPSAC51774.2021.00192

Munn, Z., Peters, M. D. J., Stern, C., Tufanaru, C., McArthur, A., & Aromataris, E. (2018). Systematic review or scoping review? Guidance for authors when choosing between a systematic or scoping review approach. *BMC Medical Research Methodology, 18*(1), 1–7. doi:10.118612874-018-0611-x PMID:30453902

Ngambeki, I., Ahluwalia, G., Ansari, S., Li, M., & Arul, G. L. R. (2021). Developing a Social-Engineering Course. *Frontiers in Education Conference, FIE*, 1–8.

Noble, H., & Smith, J. (2018). Reviewing the literature: Choosing a review design. *Evidence-Based Nursing, 21*(2), 39–41. doi:10.1136/eb-2018-102895 PMID:29535117

Organization of American States. (2020). *Cybersecurity Education: planning for the future through workforce development*. Author.

Page, M. J., McKenzie, J. E., Bossuyt, P. M., Boutron, I., Hoffmann, T. C., Mulrow, C. D., Shamseer, L., Tetzlaff, J. M., Akl, E. A., Brennan, S. E., Chou, R., Glanville, J., Grimshaw, J. M., Hróbjartsson, A., Lalu, M. M., Li, T., Loder, E. W., Mayo-Wilson, E., McDonald, S., ... Moher, D. (2021). The PRISMA 2020 statement: An updated guideline for reporting systematic reviews. *BMJ (Clinical Research Ed.), 372*(71), 1–9. doi:10.1136/bmj.n71 PMID:33782057

Parsons, K., Calic, D., Pattinson, M., Butavicius, M., McCormac, A., & Zwaans, T. (2017). The Human Aspects of Information Security Questionnaire (HAIS-Q): Two further validation studies. *Computers & Security, 66*, 40–51. doi:10.1016/j.cose.2017.01.004

Proofpoint. (2019). *Human Factor Report*. Author.

Qashqari, A. A., Munshi, A. M., Alturkstani, H. A., Ghwati, H. T., & Alhebshi, D. H. (2020). The Human Factors and Cybersecurity Policy. *International Journal of Computer Science and Network Security, 20*(4), 1–5.

Rajwar, A., Kharbanda, S., Chandrasekaran, A. R., Gupta, S., & Bhatia, D. (2020). Designer, Programmable 3D DNA Nanodevices to Probe Biological Systems. *ACS Applied Bio Materials, 3*(11), 7265–7277. doi:10.1021/acsabm.0c00916 PMID:35019470

Sharma, M. (2019). Augmented Intelligence: A Way for Helping Universities to Make Smarter Decisions. *Advances in Intelligent Systems and Computing, 841*, 89–95. doi:10.1007/978-981-13-2285-3_11

Siponen, M. T. (2000). Conceptual foundation for organizational information security awareness. *Information Management & Computer Security, 8*(1), 31–41. doi:10.1108/09685220010371394

Warrington, C., Syed, J., & Tappin, R. M. (2021). Personality and Employees' Information Security Behavior among Generational Cohorts. *Computer and Information Science, 14*(1), 44. doi:10.5539/cis.v14n1p44

Welukar, J. N., & Bajoria, G. P. (2021). Artificial Intelligence in Cyber Security - A Review. *International Journal of Scientific Research in Science and Technology, 488–491*, 488–491. Advance online publication. doi:10.32628/IJSRST218675

Wilding, S., Walker, P., Clinton, S., Williams, D., & Olszewska, J. I. (2020). Safe Human-Computer Interface Based on Efficient Image Processing Algorithm. *20th IEEE International Symposium on Computational Intelligence and Informatics, CINTI 2020 - Proceedings, 1*, 65–70. 10.1109/CINTI51262.2020.9305821

Xiao, R., Qu, L., & Shi, W. (2022). Human Security Behavior Assistance in the Cyber-Physical Space. In *Communications in Computer and Information Science* (Vol. 1680, pp. 28–43). CCIS. doi:10.1007/978-981-19-7769-5_3

Zhang, J., & Zhang, Z. (2023). Ethics and governance of trustworthy medical artificial intelligence. *BMC Medical Informatics and Decision Making, 23*(1), 1–15. doi:10.118612911-023-02103-9 PMID:36639799

40

Chapter 3
A Brief Overview of Cyber Security Advances and Techniques Along With a Glimpse on Quantum Cryptography:
Cyber Security Practices, Advances and Challenges

Vineeta Singh
https://orcid.org/0000-0003-1084-279X
GLA University, Mathura, India

Vandana Dixit Kaushik
Harcourt Butler Technical University, Kanpur, India

ABSTRACT

The vulnerability of wireless communication systems and technologies to various cyberattacks has been made public in recent years via different researchers; these cyberattacks not only impact private businesses but also government institutions. Sensitive and private data safety is a major challenge because of hackers since they are always trying to find loopholes in security models with different strong tactics and tools for cracking any sized keys. For minimizing such invasions, various developments have been made. This chapter carries out an in-depth study of several standard cyber security strategies currently in practice and the difficulties to be faced in cyber security practices. The modern efficient key systems are also shown, and the latest generation vulnerabilities are well described and reported. The advantages of quantum cryptography are highlighted along with its potential in the future. It presents a summarized glimpse in different aspects for novice researchers to educate themselves with recent developments in the cyber security field.

DOI: 10.4018/978-1-6684-8422-7.ch003

Copyright © 2023, IGI Global. Copying or distributing in print or electronic forms without written permission of IGI Global is prohibited.

1 INTRODUCTION

Nowadays, most of a person's time is spent in virtual environments which facilitate varying social networks as well as private and public services. These environments must therefore be secured against online criminals who might take data or interfere with systems. In order to maintain the productivity of communication systems as well as electronic information, ensure the privacy as well as confidentiality of personal data, and shield users from intrusions as well as threats; organizational, technical as well as executive measures collectively termed as cyber security. Subsequently, this article examines artificial intelligence's role in this field while also examining cyber security procedures that shield computer systems from attacks, hacking and data theft. This piece also provides a summary of the key academic studies examining the functions and impacts of deep learning and machine learning in cyber security. Results demonstrated for deep learning as well as machine learning strategies playing essential roles in preventing unauthorized access to computer systems as well as for managing system intrusion via recognising and understanding the activity and behaviour of harmful software. Subsequently, this article examines artificial intelligence's role in this field while also examining cyber security procedures that shield computer systems from attacks, hacking and data theft. This piece also provides a summary of the key academic studies examining the functions and impacts of deep learning and machine learning in cyber security. The world became like a tiny village with people exchanging information along with culture, because of internet, which has made many things in our lives easier. Networks are the basis of the Internet, computers as well as mobile phones. Such gadgets lose almost all of their value without the Internet. Computers are connected via networks that transmit data, information as well as apps over radio waves as well as cables. Personal information-containing data is the most crucial data sent over networks. Networks labour to safeguard these data which could be used by hackers for stealing identities as well as creating fake accounts on social networking sites (Bhalaji, 2020).

Digital transactions with little to no human touch have become common place in many places since the COVID-19 pandemic broke out (Budd et al., 2020) (Leung et al., 2021). This is done to stop the virus from spreading. Many organizations and businesses adopted computerized transactions following the COVID-19 pandemic, which they later realized was much better and more convenient for all customers. Facebook and other applications that promote and facilitate the selling of goods have seen an increase in online shopping, and universities and other institutions shifted mostly their educational along with training programmes online. Internet evolution facilitated towards remote employment gaining popularity in public as well as commercial fields (Shrestha et al., 2022) (Ssenyonga, (2021).

Despite the fact that employees are now not confined to just one place to finish their job duties, the widespread use of online working ambiances has forced security experts to assess the enterprise hazards that come with telecommuting as well as stop individuals other than businesses from eavesdropping or utilizing environments like these (Saleous et al., 2022) (Lallie et al., 2021). No matter how many sophisticated technological security measures are implemented by organizations to fight cyber threats, Given that it is the poorest connection throughout the chain, the human factor—more especially, employee skills—deserves special attention. Such staff members also need to be aware of any possible eavesdropping efforts or malicious programs that could take or destroy their personal information lacking their awareness. Organizations should implement a number of technical measures in addition to organizing awareness activities, like trainings and seminars, for staff members who lack a lot of cyber security knowledge. Employees leaving their workstations unlocked, leaving their devices unattended in public areas, and disobeying business policies, such as those pertaining to password security, are just a few examples of the behaviours that put information security at risk. Therefore, more research into the risks associated with remote employment is required. Techniques for artificial intelligence are regarded as some of the most sophisticated and useful in recent years. As a result, these methods have a big impact on many industries, such as information security as well as cyber security (Li, 2018) (Zhang, 2022).

Devices, computers, mobile devices, apps, software, or video game systems with artificial intelligence have the ability to recognize, recall and comprehend information as well as utilize data in such a manner that is comparable to how the human brain works and makes decisions (Mijwil, 2021). These methods gather data from trials and then put them to use (Singh and Kaushik, 2022). In other words, artificially intelligent gadgets have electronic brains that can process information and carry out necessary tasks. The term "cyber security" has only lately become popular because of widespread utilization of Internet networks as well as accessibility of them, particularly with the introduction of 5G technology (Cáceres-Hidalgo and Avila-Pesantez, 2021). Computers along with different electronic gadgets are vulnerable to loss as well as unauthorized access via people that wish to carry out various electronic crimes. Organizations hope to create systems based on AI that can foresee hacking attempts, attacks, even computer invasions in the manner described above. These methods can more effectively determine whether users entering the network are authorized to view the information therein than can experts. Due to their high capacity for learning, remembering, and completing assignments rapidly, experts also benefit greatly from these techniques in terms of time and effort savings. Repetitive patterns can also be preserved using artificial intelligence methods (Ghosh et al., 2021; Adadi et al., 2022). The habits and actions of every person that joins a network can be saved using this function in terms of cyber security (Singh and Kaushik, 2023). In other words, using artificial intelligence techniques, it is possible to forecast whether malicious software will infiltrate a system or behave in an abnormal manner by analyzing user behaviours and practices (Abdullahi et al., 2022; Kilincer et al., 2021).

This article makes a significant contribution by examining the main function of machine learning as well as deep learning strategies in cyber security, highlighting their use in various cyber applications, and illustrating how they help decrease computer intrusions and attacks. The primary areas of cyber security research which utilized deep learning as well as machine learning approaches are also briefly reviewed in this piece, along with the findings and how they affect decision-making. For saving time along with effort for interested researchers in this cyber security field, this book chapter comprises of different sources data taken from news websites as well as different literature. Information as well as service disruption, degradation, denial, and corruption are the main goals of cyber attacks on the host machine. The different defence mechanisms used to thwart such attacks are referred to as cyber security. "Cyber forensics" is a research field of data retrieval along with intrusion detection after a hacking incident. Conventional security software spends a lot of time and energy identifying and classifying establishing these classifications of potential/new vulnerabilities allows researchers to recognise attacks similar to this in subsequent years. It may be possible to speed up this laborious process by using machine learning methods. To more quickly and accurately identify assaults, different machine learning techniques were developed (Ahmed, 2015).

Because of the widespread use and quick growth of computer systems and internet capabilities, cyber security and forensics are serious issues in all industries and sectors. These dangers are appearing more frequently in higher schooling as well. Universities have reportedly experienced data breaches as a consequence of cyber attacks. Users of higher education use portable devices that enable them to be very flexible. These tools help students get used to networking by letting them join unprotected with any device, at any moment, over networks. Higher educational institutions have an especially difficult time implementing cyber security because of the openness and ease of access to data and information (Ramim & Levy 2006). Because of the risks involved with inadequate cyber security and the abundance of academic research data, educational organisations have become a popular target for cybercriminals (Chabrow, 2015). This suggests that institutions of higher education, like colleges, are now exposed to cyber security risks (Nakhodchi and Dehghantanha, 2020).

Figure 1. Cyber security definition

They become more vulnerable because the majority of schools support open access and a culture of information sharing. Higher education should be concerned about this situation because cyber threats like cyber attacks could disrupt classes. Hackers disseminate valuable information from colleges, since data is now a commodity, they can easily sell this knowledge. Online systems at universities could be a target for cyber security issues like malware. This is so because university networks are rich in ideas of intellectual property produced via academics as well as private information about teachers, students as well as staff that is sensitive. The culture of open communication and cooperation within the university community, which includes students, staff members, teachers and research groups increases the system's vulnerability to problems (Miskiewicz, 2020; Rouzbahani et al., 2020). Some of the most crucial areas of data science are data security and forensics which continue to gain significance as more and more businesses, big and small, collect enormous amounts of pertinent data (Mohammadi et al., 2019). The sensitive information of administrations, military organizations, corporations, security organizations, banks, insurance companies, businesses, farms and plenty more is the target of cybercrime (Grooby at al., 2019). A major focus is also on the data that well-known companies like Microsoft and Google use to better understand the connections between current and emerging technologies and to get views for their decision-making (Azmoodeh, 2019).

1.1 Basics of Cyber Security and Cyber Attacks

On a personal computer or smartphone, typical safety violations including intrusions involve obtaining unauthorized entry, deleting or altering content with the purpose of harming the system, to mention a few. Potential hazards are used to describe all of the aforementioned security infringements, potential risk and hazard as well as attacks is used to describe such attempts to commit a violation (Sikder et al., 2021). There are many ways to describe Cyber Security (Please refer Figure 1). Definition from Kaspersky's for cyber security involves protecting PCs, data on a computer network, servers as well as mobile devices from malicious attacks. Further Kaspersky categorized cyber security as following: such as information security, network security as well as other categories (Lewis, 2014). All key categories outlined via Kaspersky as well as the International Organization for Standardization coincide to the topic of cyber security. It is widely acknowledged that attackers adopt as well as develop different new approaches more quickly compared to do the defences that identify and stop those infringements, intrusions as well as attacks (Cheung and Bell, 2021).

Approximately 50% of cyber attacks resulted in at least $500 million in damage, based on Cisco's 2018 financial statement (Cisco, 2018). Cyber security works to prevent unauthorised access, wrongful utilisation and malicious manipulation of private and public data as well as corporate reports. Additionally, cyber security includes safeguarding along with assuring the confidentiality as well as information integrity being protected from numerous risks and attacks and safeguarding tools, software as well as hardware (Fischer, 2005). The most serious threats are thought to be phishing as well as malware (Özgür & Erdem 2016). Brand spoofing is another name of spoofing and it is the technique of gaining control over private information for disruption or abuse while posing as an authorised user. One instance of phishing is when websites pose as trustworthy websites while acting deceitfully to obtain confidential data (Purkait, 2012; Jagatic et al., 2007; Mohammad et al., 2015). Trojan horses, worms as well as viruses make up the three primary classifications of malware. A virus is a piece of software which, without awareness of user, adversely impacts the operation of their computer. Both the computer's operating system and its files can be harmed by viruses. Elk Cloner, which first circulated using a floppy disc in 1981, was the very first computer virus (Spafford, 1994). A programme known as a "worm" frequently duplicates itself and uses up computer or network resources as an outcome. A Trojan horse, which is unlike a worm or viruses, disguises it as another normal programme and is activated in response to a specific action or operation (Shelly & Vermaat, 2010; Shelly et al., 2007). Spam emails that are undesired as well as unwanted are another danger to safety online. Such emails demand a long processing time and tangle up the mailbox, moreover they additionally serve as the basis to execute Java applets whenever an email is accessed. Spam calls, texts including video messages are all examples of spam that may be found in smart phones including mobile networks (Drucker & Vapnik 1999; Jindal & Liu 2007; Shafi'I et al. 2017; Arifin & Bijaksana, 2016).

Spammers use YouTube as well as Twitter to propagate their messages as text as well as videos, respectively. A defence mechanism like antivirus software, firewalls along with detection systems for intrusions, is a component of any network safety framework. An intrusion detection system aids in tracking down and recognising any unauthorised access or unlawful infiltration that has malicious motives. There are three basic categories for network assessment for intrusion detection system: signature-driven approach is usually utilised for recognising known breaches while minimising the number of false alarm rates; an anomaly-based approach is typically utilised to spot unusual network along with system behaviour; as well as a hybrid approach combines aforementioned both approach to lower the false alarm rate for unidentified breaches. The attacks have been divided by others into four main types (Raiyn, 2014).

When a cybercriminal conducts a denial of service (DOS) attack, the network system becomes overloaded or has insufficient memory resources, preventing an authorised individual from getting access as requested. A distant attacker attempts to get local control through a network via taking advantage of its weaknesses that make it remote to local attack. A user to root attack occurs when an authorised individual with restricted network access attempts to become a root user. The term "probing" refers to a type of cyber attack where a cybercriminal scans a network or computer system identifying vulnerabilities and weaknesses that could be exploited in future attacks. Since a little alteration in a hacking behaviour can readily defeat signature-driven intrusion detection systems, machine learning-based solutions outperformed the traditional signature-based method.

But machine learning driven algorithms pick up on traffic patterns. They are adept at spotting attack varieties. Furthermore, because machine learning driven frameworks lack the ability to assess every signature throughout the database, their range in terms of CPU demands ranges from moderate to moderate. While collecting and revealing the intricate aspects of attack behaviour, machine learning driven algorithms also demonstrate greater effectiveness with regard to speed and as well as accuracy. Other sorts of attacks along with dangers include those involving SQL injection, password attacks, drive-by attacks, authentication attacks, man-in-the-middle attacks, web shells, wrapping attacks as well as watering hole attacks (Thangavel et al., 2022; Ganapathi, 2020). Through this article researchers have mainly elucidated about intrusion detection (ID), spam detection as well as malware detection further here it also has been illustrated about machine learning strategies have been imposing for enhancing cyber security to protect mobile devices and computer machines from such attacks.

Kotapati et al. (2005) categorized cyber attacks as interception, modification, fabrication, denial of service as well as disruption in terms of the 3G network's physical access. Chris et al. (2009) categorized the attacks relied over the nature of attacks, involving informational and operational impact, attack vector, defense as well as attack target. Moreover, the devised taxonomy didn't involve physical as well as defense techniques. Narwal *et al.* (2019) cyberattacks have been classified according to the type of application they target, like online, industrial and mobile as well as computer operating systems and so on. Kotapati et al. (2005) and Sari and Atasoy (2019) categorized the attacks further as passive attacks as well as active attacks. A comprehensive description of several attack categories by researchers Pitropakis et al. (2019) and Somani et al. (2017) may be referred for detailed understanding.

1.2. Cyber Security Practices

Electronics and technology have expanded significantly in recent years, becoming a vital component of people's lives without which they would be unable to carry out their tasks and businesses. Modern devices require a number of security precautions to guard against intrusions, hacking, attacks and unauthorised entries in order to function. These applications must service humanity. Many businesses and organisations are very concerned about data theft and hacking (Kuipers & Schonheit, 2022; Rawindaran et al., 2021).

Businesses across a variety of industries are starting to pay attention to cyber security as they become more aware of the value of their data. Cyber security can refer to a number of things, like the measures required to safeguard communications networks, data including unprocessed information; operating system-related virtual including physical elements; secure and safe apps which are required to function inside the framework but are limited to utilize via particular individuals (Quayyum et al., 2021; Formosa et al., 2021; Sarker et al., 2021). Cyber security has also been defined as a collection of techniques and procedures that can be used to safeguard a computer system's data and thwart the installation of harmful software (Fosch-Villaronga & Mahler 2021). There are different elements of cyber security (Please refer Figure 3). The various forms of cyber security and how they help to safeguard computer networks are listed in Table 1. Three elements make up cyber security. First, secrecy shields data in a computer system from unauthorised access and manipulation. In Second, integrity ensures for data not to be altered or removed in an unauthorised/malicious manner. Thirdly, Accessibility ensures that messages, data as well as information arrive at the desired receiver unaltered or decoded via an uninvited party. A cyber attack can have catastrophic results for a business, its customers and its workers regardless of where it occurs. Employees must understand the internet security policies of their companies and how to reduce risk. Some significant instances of cyber attacks are shown in Table 2.

Table 1. Cyber security types along with their roles

Type of Role	Illustration
Application Security	Carry out complex operations to protect and encrypt data in a manner that is challenging to decipher (Sharma et al., 2021)
Infrastructure Security	Protect infrastructures, including data centers and electricity networks and make sure there are no gaps (Hale & Bartlett, 2019).
Information Security	Defend data against unauthorized entry and alterations (Rehman et al., 2019).
User Education	Plan a number of beneficial workshops and seminars for staff members and cyber security professionals (Broo et al., 2021).
Network Security	Protect networks from breaches by using solutions such as remote access management, two-factor authentication i.e. 2FA, as well as working firewall (Wang et al., 2022).

Table 2. Types of cyber security attacks

S.No.	Security Attack Type	Definition
1	Malware	a group of malicious programmes that aim to compromise networks and steal data (Mijwil, 2020)
2	Phishing	a type of cyber attack and common method of social engineering that tricks people into posting confidential information online or engaging in other risky behavior (AL-Otaibi & Alsuwat, 2020)
3	Ransomware	a malicious programme that locks down systems, encrypts data and prevents authorized users from reaching these systems (Urooj et al., 2022)
4	DDoSA	hinders users from getting network resources and disables systems, harming a company's or organization's finances or reputation (Narote et al., 2022).
5	Zero-Day Exploit	A newly found security hole exploited by a network of hackers who target computer systems. When a system administrator uses this phrase, it means they have just realized the system's flaws but don't have enough time to fix them or halt the attack. (Singh et al., 2019)
6	SQL Injection	Web security flaw that enables unauthorized individuals to view, take, altering or removing information in a website rendering this website inoperable (Bedeković et al., 2022)
7	DNS Tunneling	an advanced, hard-to-detect attack that encrypts framework information as well as applications (Wang et al., 2021)
8	Social Engineering	an art of convincing people to divulge their passwords to the attacker through manipulation and deception, enabling the latter to gain entry to data, steal data or introduce harmful programs (Salahdine & Kaabouch, 2019)
9	XSS Attacks	Creates the appearance of a safe browser script while injecting malware into reputable websites (Zhou & Wang 2019)

The first malicious programme to destroy computer data called Creeper, first appeared in the 1970s. "I'm a creeper, catch me if you can!" is written on the screen of a computer that has been infected. Reaper, the first antivirus program, was launched in reaction to this threat. Nevil Maskelyne was the first hacker in history. He intercepted the first wireless telegraph message in 1903 and exposed the flaws in Marconi's system. In the meantime, John Draper, the first cybercriminal, found that he could make free calls by tricking telephone exchange signals with an item that was included in Cap'n Crunch cereal boxes: a whistle.

1.3 Motivation, Objective and Importance of the Study

The presented study is motivated by the desire to offer in-depth and insightful perspectives on the most important researchers and partnerships in the areas of cyber forensics as well as cyber security over the past ten years as well as to highlight the most significant study fields, historical patterns in topical groups, key phrases including scientific papers. The basic objective of this study is to offer recommendations for future research in this quickly developing area based on the aforementioned analyses. The significance of this research is demonstrated by how crucial cyber forensics as well as cyber security are in making sure the security and dependability of whole digital data along with transactions. Compromising here at any level could result in confidential information or functionality breaches, which would result in catastrophic losses. This study is important because it contributes to the discipline of cyber security as well as cyber forensics as an entire field using bibliometric evaluation. The scientific research community as a whole will greatly benefit from the acknowledgment of the most influential scholars, institutions, countries, journals along with their multi-disciplinary collaborations. Second, the researchers can focus their research on specialised and understudied areas thanks to the temporal evolution of research ideas, subjects as well as key terms over the past ten years. This study highlights some crucial emerging and future areas that will be useful to this field's up-and-coming scholars.

1.4 Background of Work

Reviewing scholarly developments in a given area of study may be accompanied in different different ways (Jiang et al., 2019). The major subcategories of these methods are relational and evaluative reviews (Borgman & Furner, 2002). The quantitatively analyzing the absolute research influences of research articles, writers, organizations along with nations is done through the use of evaluative reviews. This study takes into account a number of productivity factors involving several journals, year wise publications, citations and so on (Jamal et al., 2008). It is also possible to conduct qualitative evaluation reviews using expert opinions on research impact indicators in a specific area (Benckendorff, 2009). The relational review methods, on the other hand, focus on how the aforementioned evaluative measures interact with one another. To quantify and describe these inter-relationships, the amount of collaborative outputs, collaborative links and related link strengths are used. Other beneficial relational measures involve connections relied over citations, co-occurrences as well as analyses based on citations (Benckendorff & Zehrer, 2013). The existence of links between co-authors is an essential sign of information flow between different study groups (Hu & Racherla, 2008). Evaluation of reference linkages is necessary to comprehend research connections between eminent authors and organisations (White & McCain, 1998). Connection strengths also influence the scope of partnerships and co-citations across geographical boundaries (Baggio et al., 2008).

2 DIFFERENT TYPES OF CYBER ATTACKS: AN OVERVIEW

2.1. Attacks Category

This section presents a wide variety of attack types in various areas, which are further categorised (Please refer Figure 2), it involves various form of cyber attacks (Please refer Figure 4).

2.1.1. Cryptographic Attack

Attack of this kind recovers plain text without the secret by using pragmatism to break encryption (Singh & Dubey 2015a; Singh & Dubey 2015b) as well as locate a vulnerability in a protocol, code, or cipher that is too complicated.

2.1.2. Access Attack

Such kind of attack includes getting control and reach ability to the host's machine without authorization with the aim of manipulating information. Attackers are gaining access to databases, private information, e-accounts through the breach of file transfer services as well as web application services.

2.1.3. Reconnaissance Attack

It is a kind of hacking attempt where the attacker maps with the intended targets' computers to look for possible security holes with the target's hardware and collect information. This kind of situation is comparable to theft, for instance, in a home where weak locks, doors, and joined windows are easily broken.

2.1.4. Active Attack

A cyber attack causes significant harm when data transfer modifies the content and interferes with operations.

2.1.5. Passive Attack

The intruder does not access or modify the database; instead, they merely keep track of the target to access the data while it is being transmitted. In simple terms, the attacker's primary goal is to gather information by using various methods to listen in on a discussion between hosts.

2.1.6. Phishing Attack

A practice of disseminating false information through various channels, such as emails, text messages, and pretending that it is coming from a reliable source in order to trick users and acquire private information like card numbers and login passwords.

2.1.7. Malware Attack

A cyber attack, in which the attacker installed malicious software on the target's machine with the intention of spreading it further.

Figure 2. Different types of cyber attacks

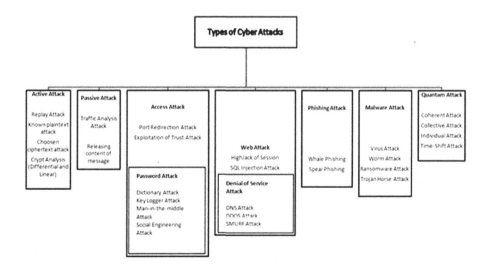

Table 3. Different types of techniques along with their attacks and limitations

S.No.	Techniques (Authors)	Secure From Attacks	Limitations
1.	Ciphering including variable key length (Lawnik & Kapczyński, 2019)	Resistant towards different attacks like chosen plain text attack, related key attack, side channel attacks	Space as well as time taken for execution very high.
2.	Relied on public key encryption along with a binary string and apt length (Fujisaki, 2018)	Reduces possibility of Man –in the middle attack	Denial-of –Service attack vulnerability.
3.	factoring issue resolved utilizing two party distributed (Hazay et al., 2019)	Robust against malicious attacks were reduced	Space as well as time taken for execution very high
4.	key agreement strategy utilized for generating session keys (Chien, 2018)	Robust to active as well as passive attacks	Vulnerability for Third-Party attack.
5.	modified ECC utilized to secure session keys (Thangarasu & Selvakumar 2019)	Possibility of Intruder attacks reduced	Vulnerable towards traditional Attacks
6.	Developed novel key sizes utilizing NFS variant (Barbulescu & Duquesne 2019).	Mitigate dos, replay attacks as well as impersonation attacks	No access to multi-server environment
7.	For RSA factoring problem Generic Ring Strategy Used (Aggarwal & Maurer 2016)	factoring issue of RSA was reduced	Vulnerability towards different cryptanalytic attacks.
8.	Pairless cryptography relied over Certificate-based encryption (Le et al., 2016)	Possibility of Chosen Cipher text Attack reduced	Denial-of –Service attack vulnerability, ineffective given a small bandwidth
9.	RSA was integrated to DES (Mohit & Biswas, 2016)	Possibility of different attacks reduced	Vulnerability towards brute force attack as well as known-cipher text attack

Figure 3. Cyber security components

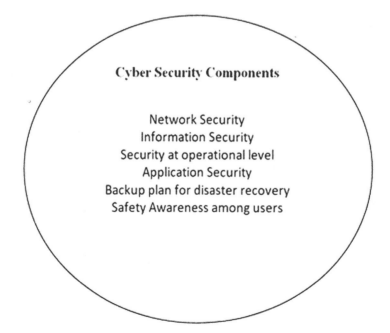

Figure 4. Various cyber attacks

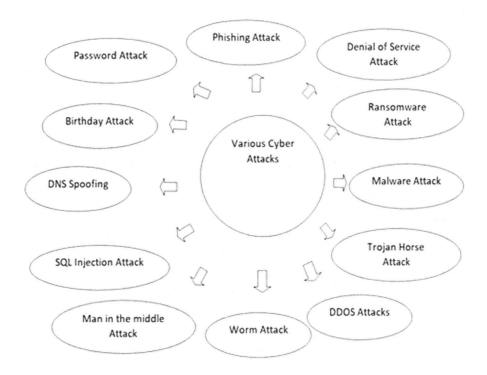

3 DEEP LEARNING IN CYBER SECURITY

Different approaches are used to address complex issues in cyber security depending on particular factors like issue sensitivity, data volume, issue type as well as decision bear ability in the solution. Parallel processing-based deep learning methods are very useful for big data and call for intricate procedures (Ahmed et al., 2022; Faieq & Mijwil, 2022; Mijwil, et al., 2022). This part analyses the research on the use of deep learning techniques for malware, intrusion and attack detection. In order to guarantee confidentiality, integrity of data along with reliability as well as to make sure that no unauthorised people may access the computer/network, the deep learning architectures are configured over server-based computers as compared to local based computers. A deep learning model must go through two phases in order to function properly in cyber security. The first step is to encrypt the local environment region where data is transferred to the server. The second step entails sending these data to the computer, where they will be processed, classified, and given a type in order to decrypt the encrypted data. For instance, the first stage of character recognition from images entails the encoding along with transmitting characters, whereas the second stage included obtained data processing as well as determining possibility of a man-in-the-middle attack between local system as well as server—which is crucial for classifying data—existed. Subsequently ensuring users receive their information securely and prevents unauthorised users from accessing the system. Users can obtain and receive data through networks. Networked systems must therefore be located in locations where the businesses in charge of the mandate take the necessary security precautions for ensuring secure transmission, archival as well as storage of data. As per the network's size along with activity, many breach types may occur. Specifically, there will be large amount of data flowing onto the network that requires to be handled the bigger, busier and more effective the network is. Given their high speed as well as accuracy, deep learning strategies and parallel processing are favoured when processing these data. Malware detection has also recently benefited from the use of deep learning methods (Shaukat et al., 2020; Chen et al., 2021; Muhammad & Ghafory, 2022). Malicious programmes can influence systems by changing their data thanks to a variety of traits. The convolutional neural network has been employed by many researchers to categorise data, identify required features, extract genetic sequences from malicious applications and then send those sequences to the network to get trained. Deep learning methods may be utilized also for recognising a user's voice or image, identify biological features like a PIN and password and identify other behaviour-based licences. At this point, the long-short-term memory and RNN-derived gated recurrent unit methods are used, when a face along with fingerprint recognition model is developed. Another crucial aspect of internet security is device security. More interactions between people and the electronic environment may result from better security. Data, systems and applications maintenance require deep learning methods. Due to these techniques' excellent results in tests using 2D and 3D media data as well as different big data, they have been used in image and video processing. To determine which set of data is obtained, whether it will suit supervised or unsupervised strategies and whether previous knowledge affects subsequent knowledge, deep learning in cyber security aims to answer these questions. However, whether the examples are one-dimensional or multi-dimensional, deep learning evaluates how well systems work in solving a problem. Researchers are constantly looking for answers to a variety of problems through deep learning strategies in cyber security research field (Krishnan et al., 2021; Salem et al., 2022; Rasheed et al., 2021).

4 PRESENT CHALLENGES OF MACHINES LEARNING TECHNIQUES IN CYBER SECURITY

Approaches for machine learning are frequently employed in cyber security field, although it has a number of obstacles in this path. While building the models, ML approaches require a sizable amount of outstanding performance data as well as resources. Multiple GPUs can be used as a solution; however this is neither a cost-effective nor a power-efficient approach. Additionally, methods relied over machine learning are not intended for identifying cybercrimes. Traditional ML algorithms did not place much emphasis on cyber security. Reliable and efficient machine learning strategies that are designed specifically for handling unfavourable inputs as well as combating security risks are required. It needs to be mentioned that one ML model cannot reliably identify various security issues. A relevant ML (machine learning) strategy needs to be developed to deal with a certain type of cyber attack.

Another challenging assignment involves earlier prevention of attacks. These real-time as well as zero-day threats require being quickly detected using machine learning approaches. Machine learning algorithms have been used for taking decisions in health care or for terrorist activity identification. Forecasting shouldn't be relied blindly in such circumstances to prevent disastrous outcomes (Ribeiro et al., 2016).

It is essential to make sure that machine learning approaches offer certain high-level accuracy assurances rather than accuracy as well as speed whenever they are employed in mission-critical or life critical applications (like cyber security, autonomous vehicles, as well as surgical robotics) (Ghosh et al., 2017). The safe application of machine learning methodologies on the web is referred to as trustworthy machine learning. Classifier dependability may be described as following: (a) believing a prediction or if an end user will rely on a given prediction model to perform a certain action as well as (b) trusting a model or whether a user will rely on a model used like a tool in a reasonable manner.

When a framework was trained as well as evaluated using several datasets. Quionero-Candela et al., (2009) looked into the issue of dataset shift. Additionally, researchers here recommended that the leaked data may be removed or the training data might be altered so that it can prevent the dataset shift. Finding out exactly what has to be done to transform an unreliable framework into a reliable one is helpful. Traditional linear or shallow learning is typically more dependable though less efficient or slower. Despite a theory that is continually evolving, deep learning is comparatively complex as well as challenging. Pandemic control as well as forensic science has chances to determine the location data of specific moving objects, because of the development of global positioning system as well as cell phones. However, preserving the specific object's credibility is a difficult operation considering the likelihood to inaccuracies or tampered information on mobile devices.

A method for assessing the degree of similarity between data received from various sources regarding the position of a specific object has been developed out by Chenyun (Dai et al., 2009). There is always a chance of ambiguity when determining how reliable location information derived through the trajectories of objects in motion is. Due to network delays and object movement, this uncertainty exists (Trajcevski et al., 2004). Researchers Zhu & Jin (2009) proposed a trust ontology method for assisting service providers and customers in having reliable interactions within an online web based platform. The reliability is additionally employed in natural language processing to classify text, particularly when a communication is sent during missions that are life-or-death. For gettting the optimum reliability detection outcome, it is obvious that the reliability needs to be taken into account when the text content is evaluated considering both semantic as well as practical aspects (Su et al., 2010) a metric framework has been developed by researchers (Tao & Chen 2009) for assessing the software reliability. Power-aware methods have been developed using machine; learning strategies for cutting down on the amount of power used by businesses and data centres (Berral et al., 2010). Automatically turning off an idle machine can lower total power utilisation. If the idle machine prediction is accurate, energy use will undoubtedly go down. When planning which machines to turn off, the prediction model's reliability is absolutely essential. Alarm fatigue refers to the sensitivity of an alarm's detection that causes a higher false alarm rate. Security personnel have been negatively impacted by the increasing frequency of false alarms, which has led to missed crucial alarms or slow response times. A difficult research problem in cyber security is such phenomenon (Wang et al., 2015; Eerikäinen et al., 2015).

5 INTRODUCTION TO QUANTUM CRYPTOGRAPHY

Quantum 2.0, also referred to as the second quantum revolution, is the quick development of novel disruptive frameworks relied over the most potent features as well as techniques of quantum mechanics, including o-cloning theorem, quantum entanglement as well as teleportation. Due to the indulgement of multinational companies vying to develop powerful quantum computers, quantum computing (Nielsen & Computation, 2000) has gained a lot of momentum, these days Josephson junctions (Schoelkopf & Girvin, 2008) based supercomputing chips are scaling qubits number in a rapid manner subsequently may initiate factorizing nontrivial integers via utilizing Shor's model (Shor, 1994)(Shor, 1997). While quantum computing poses a threat to the Rivest-Shamir-Adleman (RSA) protocol (Rivest et al., 1978) and other public key cryptosystems, there is additionally a chance that number theory will progress to the point during which an effective factorization algorithm for traditional Turing machines could be developed. For instance, the Agrawal-Kayal-Saxena algorithm (Agrawal et al., 2004) had already completed the test of primality into a polynomial in 2004. There is a crucial distinction to be made between the prospective harm posed by the present-day vulnerability of conventional cryptosystems as well as the more significant and imminent threat they provide for the future. Hackers can now intercept encrypted messages that they cannot decrypt at present but when a sufficiently large quantum computing device is developed, they might keep these encrypted secret messages waiting for their decryption (or a new standard strategy is developed). This shows that the confidentiality of communications might only be temporary. Two strategies are currently being thought about to transition to quantum-safe cryptography: Postquantum cryptography (PQC) as well as quantum key distribution (QKD). Starting with the latter, a subset of traditional cryptography, let's move on. It takes advantage of cryptosystems whose security depends on traditionally challenging computational issues that are distinct from those which quantum computers have been proven to tackle effectively. (For example: factoring or discrete log). This is undoubtedly a possible remedy, however it does not entirely address the issue because new quantum (or maybe conventional) algorithms could sporadically compromise security. By using quantum systems to create hidden correlations, QKD claims to provide the ideal cybersecurity alternative. Confidentiality in this situation is based on unbreakable natural laws, including the concept of uncertainty or the monogamy of interconnectedness. Even while a perfect QKD implementation would completely encrypt a channel of communication, in reality QKD protocol implementations leave gaps that lead to challenges at the level of hardware machines utilised locally via the remote participants (such as detectors and modulators). Such could be the target of numerous side-channel attacks including attempts to hack them. The strongest implementation in this instance would be completely device-independent (DI) QKD algorithms (Mayers & Yao, 1998; Barrett et al., 2005); moreover their exceptionally great degree of safety is attained at the cost of comparatively less secret key rates. While On the other side, much productive QKD techniques rely on a certain amount of device trust. By doing this, they can obtain acceptable key rates, however at the expense of reduced security (Pirandola et al., 2020).

Here a brief discussion has been taken about fundamental ideas and recent developments in the area of quantum cryptography through this study. The majority of the conversation has been on QKD; however we additionally addressed several advancements that extend outside the parameters of conventional key distribution. Although quantum cryptography is without a doubt the most advanced application of quantum technology so far, its practical and theoretical advancement continue to encounter many challenges and unresolved issues. There is still a demand for more dependable QKD protocols which are capable of operating over wide areas at respectable rates. The effectiveness of trusted node QKD networks might therefore be enhanced by integrating these types of protocols. The establishment of a QKD network which is both expandable as well as end-to-end, allowing the middle nodes to be any number while being additionally unreliable, would result in an even better outcome. A development of effective quantum repeaters for entanglement distilling as well as distribution might theoretically lead to the realisation of this network. In reality, we would like to use less costly designs, such as unreliable QKD repeaters that just rely on measurement procedures. But at the moment, this solution cannot be scaled. From a strictly theoretical perspective, work is being done to show the efficacy of several QKD techniques, both in CV as well as DV circumstances have completely composable finite-size security. Determining the secret key capacity of a number of important quantum channels enabling quantum communications, including the amplitude damping channel as well as the thermal-loss channel, is an open challenge at this point. The two-way aided capabilities associated with such channels could require the implementation of an entirely new as well as distinct strategy, despite the fact that the most recent methods of simulation have proven effective in numerous circumstances. A number of topics are being pursued in present research, including satellite quantum communications, PICs, more secure point-to-point protocols, qubit-based strategies, trusted node quantum networks, larger dimensions, along with CV frameworks. Extended wavelengths like THz as well as microwaves might have non-trivial short-range uses, however optical and telecom frequencies are probably far more conducive to quantum communications. A number of gaps need to be thoroughly investigated before QKD can be recognised as a truly secure quantum technology. Side-channel hacking attempts are a serious threat, and solutions are at present being researched and developed for some of the most serious quantum hacks. Vulnerability could be caused by problems such as RNG or detector defects. As a result, quantum hacking and its solutions are a vital and developing topic. In order to implement QKD as well as quantum cryptography technologically, we will generally require to take into account how they will integrate with the existing conventional structures while creating additional layers of security, based on the level of privacy we want to achieve, depending on the stakeholders as well as the kind of business associated. Bounded-memory and QDL-based protocols offer a transiently less level of quantum security which would be appropriate for private, one-on-one conversations. Higher levels of security are offered by standard QKD protocols, which might be appropriate for financial operations. Different secret key rates may be taken into account within QKD, for example, in reference to single, grouped, or highly cohesive invasions. Choosing one of such rates could additionally be related to the requirement for a specific level of security. For applications like making political or strategic decisions, higher degrees of security, such as DI-QKD, that is much resistant to side-channel and standard attacks, may be used. As quantum cryptography gradually spreads as a technology, these elements will become more and more obvious.

6 CONCLUSION

As we know due to globalization and increasing use of internet in every walk of life, on one side, we have ease of access of information and finishing various tasks online, while on the other hand, it also increased the cyber security risks, but with certain preventive measures and safety awareness information a person and organization may help themselves to be safe up to some extent from cyber fraud and risks. The practises that safeguard against cyber attacks, security risks as well as data breaches are referred to as cyber security. There are numerous unanswered concerns surrounding the phrase "cyber security" including what type of challenges as well as risks organisations are now facing. How can we prevent such invasions? Who is particularly at risk? What steps are required to decrease the risks and cyber attacks? Moreover, yet many unanswered questions are still there, that needs to be addressed. Throughout this study researchers have discussed about basics of cyber security, its need at present time, how modern workstations, persons and companies can be at risk of cyber attacks and possible remedies to make them secure and safe. Awareness is essential among people and organizations to be safe from cyber threats. Different types of cyber attacks have been discussed herewith also. Machine learning models are also helping up to some extent for specific kind of cyber attack prediction with a limitation of a specific type of model is applicable only a specific type of cyber attack. Evolution of quantum cryptography and its' effects in present conventional cryptosystem has been also presented. Quantum computing also poses a threat to present RSA algorithm and other public key cryptosystems.

Table 4. List of abbreviations

PQC	Post quantum cryptography
QKD	Quantum key distribution
DI (QKD)	Device independent QKD algorithms
PIC	Photonic integrated circuits
CV systems	Continuous-variable systems
RNGs	Random number generators
RSA	Rivest-Shamir-Adleman
DV	Discrete variable
QDL protocols	Quantam data locking protocols

REFERENCES

Abdulhamid, S. I. M., Abd Latiff, M. S., Chiroma, H., Osho, O., Abdul-Salaam, G., Abubakar, A. I., & Herawan, T.Shafi'I. (2017). A review on mobile SMS spam filtering techniques. *IEEE Access : Practical Innovations, Open Solutions*, 5, 15650–15666. doi:10.1109/ACCESS.2017.2666785

Abdullahi, M., Baashar, Y., Alhussian, H., Alwadain, A., Aziz, N., Capretz, L. F., & Abdulkadir, S. J. (2022). Detecting cybersecurity attacks in internet of things using artificial intelligence methods: A systematic literature review. *Electronics (Basel)*, 11(2), 198. doi:10.3390/electronics11020198

Adadi, A., Lahmer, M., & Nasiri, S. (2022). Artificial Intelligence and COVID-19: A Systematic umbrella review and roads ahead. *Journal of King Saud University-Computer and Information Sciences*, 34(8), 5898–5920. doi:10.1016/j.jksuci.2021.07.010 PMID:37520766

Aggarwal, D., & Maurer, U. (2016). Breaking RSA generically is equivalent to factoring. *IEEE Transactions on Information Theory*, 62(11), 6251–6259. doi:10.1109/TIT.2016.2594197

Agrawal, M., Kayal, N., & Saxena, N. (2004). PRIMES is in P. *Annals of Mathematics*, 160(2), 781–793. doi:10.4007/annals.2004.160.781

Ahmed, S., Abbood, Z. A., Farhan, H. M., Yasen, B. T., Ahmed, M. R., & Duru, A. D. (2022). Speaker Identification Model Based on Deep Neural Networks. *Iraqi Journal For Computer Science and Mathematics*, 3(1), 108–114. doi:10.52866/ijcsm.2022.01.01.012

Ahmed, U., Raza, I., Hussain, S. A., Ali, A., Iqbal, M., & Wang, X. (2015). Modelling cyber security for software-defined networks those grow strong when exposed to threats: Analysis and propositions. *Journal of Reliable Intelligent Environments*, 1(2-4), 123–146. doi:10.100740860-015-0008-0

Al-Otaibi, A. F., & Alsuwat, E. S. (2020). A study on social engineering attacks: Phishing attack. *Int. J. Recent Adv. Multidiscip. Res*, 7(11), 6374–6380.

Arifin, D. D., & Bijaksana, M. A. (2016, September). Enhancing spam detection on mobile phone Short Message Service (SMS) performance using FP-growth and Naive Bayes Classifier. In *2016 IEEE Asia Pacific Conference on Wireless and Mobile (APWiMob)* (pp. 80-84). IEEE.

Azmoodeh, A., Dehghantanha, A., & Choo, K. K. R. (2019). Big data and internet of things security and forensics: Challenges and opportunities. Handbook of Big Data and IoT Security, 1-4.

Baggio, R., Scott, N., & Arcodia, C. (2008). Collaboration in the events literature: a co-authorship network study. *Proceedings of the EUTO*, 1-16.

Barbulescu, R., & Duquesne, S. (2019). Updating key size estimations for pairings. *Journal of Cryptology, 32*(4), 1298–1336. doi:10.100700145-018-9280-5

Barrett, J., Hardy, L., & Kent, A. (2005). No signaling and quantum key distribution. *Physical Review Letters, 95*(1), 010503. doi:10.1103/PhysRevLett.95.010503 PMID:16090597

Bedeković, N., Havaš, L., Horvat, T., & Crčić, D. (2022). The Importance of Developing Preventive Techniques for SQL Injection Attacks. *Tehnički glasnik, 16*(4), 523-529. doi:10.31803/tg-20211203090618

Benckendorff, P. (2009). Themes and trends in Australian and New Zealand tourism research: A social network analysis of citations in two leading journals (1994–2007). *Journal of Hospitality and Tourism Management, 16*(1), 1–15. doi:10.1375/jhtm.16.1.1

Benckendorff, P., & Zehrer, A. (2013). A network analysis of tourism research. *Annals of Tourism Research, 43*, 121–149. doi:10.1016/j.annals.2013.04.005

Berral, J. L., Goiri, I., Nou, R., Julià, F., Guitart, J., Gavaldà, R., & Torres, J. (2010). Towards energy-aware scheduling in data centers using machine learning. *Proc. 1st Int. Conf. Energy-Efficient Comput. Netw. (E-Energy)*, 215–224.

Bhalaji, N. (2020). Reliable data transmission with heightened confidentiality and integrity in IOT empowered mobile networks. *Journal of ISMAC, 2*(2), 106–117. doi:10.36548/jismac.2020.2.004

Borgman, C. L., & Furner, J. (2002). Scholarly communication and bibliometrics. *Annual Review of Information Science & Technology, 36*(1), 1–53.

Broo, D. G., Boman, U., & Törngren, M. (2021). Cyber-physical systems research and education in 2030: Scenarios and strategies. *Journal of Industrial Information Integration, 21*, 100192. doi:10.1016/j.jii.2020.100192

Budd, J., Miller, B. S., Manning, E. M., Lampos, V., Zhuang, M., Edelstein, M., Rees, G., Emery, V. C., Stevens, M. M., Keegan, N., Short, M. J., Pillay, D., Manley, E., Cox, I. J., Heymann, D., Johnson, A. M., & McKendry, R. A. (2020). Digital technologies in the public-health response to COVID-19. *Nature Medicine, 26*(8), 1183–1192. doi:10.103841591-020-1011-4 PMID:32770165

Cáceres-Hidalgo, J., & Avila-Pesantez, D. (2021, October). Cybersecurity Study in 5G Network Slicing Technology: A Systematic Mapping Review. In *2021 IEEE Fifth Ecuador Technical Chapters Meeting (ETCM)* (pp. 1-6). IEEE. Doi: 10.1109/ETCM53643.2021.9590742

Chabrow, E. (2015). China blamed for Penn State breach: Hackers remained undetected for more than two years. *Data Breach Today, 1*.

Chen, D., Wawrzynski, P., & Lv, Z. (2021). Cyber security in smart cities: A review of deep learning-based applications and case studies. *Sustainable Cities and Society, 66*, 102655. doi:10.1016/j.scs.2020.102655

Cheung, K. F., & Bell, M. G. (2021). Attacker–defender model against quantal response adversaries for cyber security in logistics management: An introductory study. *European Journal of Operational Research, 291*(2), 471–481. doi:10.1016/j.ejor.2019.10.019

Chien, H. Y. (2018). Using the Modified Diffie–Hellman Problem to Enhance Client Computational Performance in a Three-Party Authenticated Key Agreement. *Arabian Journal for Science and Engineering, 43*(2), 637–644. doi:10.100713369-017-2725-6

Cisco, A. C. R. (2018). Accessed: Feb, 2023 Online. Available: https://www.cisco.com/c/m/en_au/products/security/offers/annual-cybersecurity-report2018.html

Dai, C., Lim, H. S., Bertino, E., & Moon, Y. S. (2009, November). Assessing the trustworthiness of location data based on provenance. In *Proceedings of the 17th ACM SIGSPATIAL International Conference on Advances in Geographic Information Systems* (pp. 276-285). 10.1145/1653771.1653810

Drucker, H., Wu, D., & Vapnik, V. N. (1999). Support vector machines for spam categorization. *IEEE Transactions on Neural Networks, 10*(5), 1048–1054. doi:10.1109/72.788645 PMID:18252607

Eerikäinen, L. M., Vanschoren, J., Rooijakkers, M. J., Vullings, R., & Aarts, R. M. (2015, September). Decreasing the false alarm rate of arrhythmias in intensive care using a machine learning approach. In *2015 Computing in Cardiology Conference (CinC)* (pp. 293-296). IEEE. 10.1109/CIC.2015.7408644

Faieq, A. K., & Mijwil, M. M. (2022). Prediction of heart diseases utilising support vector machine and artificial neural network. *Indonesian Journal of Electrical Engineering and Computer Science, 26*(1), 374–380. doi:10.11591/ijeecs.v26.i1.pp374-380

Fischer, E. A. (2005, February). *Creating a national framework for cybersecurity: An analysis of issues and options*. Library of Congress.

Formosa, P., Wilson, M., & Richards, D. (2021). A principlist framework for cybersecurity ethics. *Computers & Security, 109*, 102382. doi:10.1016/j.cose.2021.102382

Fosch-Villaronga, E., & Mahler, T. (2021). Cybersecurity, safety and robots: Strengthening the link between cybersecurity and safety in the context of care robots. *Computer Law & Security Review, 41*, 105528. doi:10.1016/j.clsr.2021.105528

Fujisaki, E. (2018). All-but-many encryption. *Journal of Cryptology, 31*(1), 226–275. doi:10.100700145-017-9256-x

Ganapathi, P. (2020). A review of machine learning methods applied for handling zero-day attacks in the cloud environment. Handbook of Research on Machine and Deep Learning Applications for Cyber Security, 364-387.

Ghosh, S., Lincoln, P., Tiwari, A., & Zhu, X. (2017, March). Trusted machine learning: Model repair and data repair for probabilistic models. In *Workshops at the Thirty-First AAAI Conference on Artificial Intelligence*. AAAI.

Ghosh, T., Al Banna, M. H., Rahman, M. S., Kaiser, M. S., Mahmud, M., Hosen, A. S., & Cho, G. H. (2021). Artificial intelligence and internet of things in screening and management of autism spectrum disorder. *Sustainable Cities and Society, 74*, 103189. doi:10.1016/j.scs.2021.103189

Grooby, S., Dargahi, T., & Dehghantanha, A. (2019). A bibliometric analysis of authentication and access control in IoT devices. Handbook of big data and IoT security, 25-51. doi:10.1007/978-3-030-10543-3_3

Hale, G., & Bartlett, C. (2019). Managing the regulatory tangle: Critical infrastructure security and distributed governance in Alberta's major traded sectors. *Journal of Borderlands Studies*, *34*(2), 257–279. doi:10.1080/08865655.2017.1367710

Hazay, C., Mikkelsen, G. L., Rabin, T., Toft, T., & Nicolosi, A. A. (2019). Efficient RSA key generation and threshold paillier in the two-party setting. *Journal of Cryptology*, *32*(2), 265–323. doi:10.100700145-017-9275-7

Hu, C., & Racherla, P. (2008). Visual representation of knowledge networks: A social network analysis of hospitality research domain. *International Journal of Hospitality Management*, *27*(2), 302–312. doi:10.1016/j.ijhm.2007.01.002

Jagatic, T. N., Johnson, N. A., Jakobsson, M., & Menczer, F. (2007). Social phishing. *Communications of the ACM*, *50*(10), 94–100. doi:10.1145/1290958.1290968

Jamal, T., Smith, B., & Watson, E. (2008). Ranking, rating and scoring of tourism journals: Interdisciplinary challenges and innovations. *Tourism Management*, *29*(1), 66–78. doi:10.1016/j.tourman.2007.04.001

Jiang, Y., Ritchie, B. W., & Benckendorff, P. (2019). Bibliometric visualisation: An application in tourism crisis and disaster management research. *Current Issues in Tourism*, *22*(16), 1925–1957. doi:10.1080/13683500.2017.1408574

Jindal, N., & Liu, B. (2007). Review spam detection. *Proc. 16th Int. Conf. World Wide Web*, 1189–1190. 10.1145/1242572.1242759

Kilincer, I. F., Ertam, F., & Sengur, A. (2021). Machine learning methods for cyber security intrusion detection: Datasets and comparative study. *Computer Networks*, *188*, 107840. doi:10.1016/j.comnet.2021.107840

Kotapati, K., Liu, P., Sun, Y., & LaPorta, T. F. (2005). A taxonomy of cyber attacks on 3G networks. In Intelligence and Security Informatics: IEEE *International Conference on Intelligence and Security Informatics, ISI 2005, Atlanta, GA, USA, May 19-20, 2005 Proceedings*, *3*, 631–633.

Krishnan, S. A., Sabu, A. N., Sajan, P. P., & Sreedeep, A. L. (2021). *SQL injection detection using machine learning*. doi:10.58496/MJCS/2022/002

Kuipers, S., & Schonheit, M. (2022). Data breaches and effective crisis communication: A comparative analysis of corporate reputational crises. *Corporate Reputation Review*, *25*(3), 176–197. doi:10.105741299-021-00121-9

Lallie, H. S., Shepherd, L. A., Nurse, J. R., Erola, A., Epiphaniou, G., Maple, C., & Bellekens, X. (2021). Cyber security in the age of COVID-19: A timeline and analysis of cyber-crime and cyber-attacks during the pandemic. *Computers & Security*, *105*, 102248. doi:10.1016/j.cose.2021.102248 PMID:36540648

Lawnik, M., & Kapczyński, A. (2019). Application of modified Chebyshev polynomials in asymmetric cryptography. *Computer Science*, *20*(3), 289–303. doi:10.7494/csci.2019.20.3.3307

Le, M. H., Kim, I., & Hwang, S. O. (2016). Efficient certificate-based encryption schemes without pairing. *Security and Communication Networks*, *9*(18), 5376–5391. doi:10.1002ec.1703

Leung, K., Wu, J. T., & Leung, G. M. (2021). Real-time tracking and prediction of COVID-19 infection using digital proxies of population mobility and mixing. *Nature Communications*, *12*(1), 1501. doi:10.103841467-021-21776-2 PMID:33686075

Lewis, J. A. (2014). National perceptions of cyber threats. *Strategic Analysis*, *38*(4), 566–576. doi:10.1080/09700161.2014.918445

Li, J. H. (2018). Cyber security meets artificial intelligence: A survey. *Frontiers of Information Technology & Electronic Engineering*, *19*(12), 1462–1474. doi:10.1631/FITEE.1800573

Martínez Torres, J., Iglesias Comesaña, C., & García-Nieto, P. J. (2019). Machine learning techniques applied to cybersecurity. *International Journal of Machine Learning and Cybernetics*, *10*(10), 2823–2836. doi:10.100713042-018-00906-1

Mayers, D., & Yao, A. (1998, November). Quantum cryptography with imperfect apparatus. In *Proceedings 39th Annual Symposium on Foundations of Computer Science* (Cat. No. 98CB36280) (pp. 503-509). IEEE. 10.1109/SFCS.1998.743501

Mijwil, M. M. (2020). Malware Detection in Android OS Using Machine Learning Techniques. *Data Science and Applications*, *3*(2), 5–9.

Mijwil, M. M. (2021). Implementation of Machine Learning Techniques for the Classification of Lung X-Ray Images Used to Detect COVID-19 in Humans. *Iraqi Journal of Science*, 2099-2109. doi:10.24996/ijs.2021.62.6.35

Mijwil, M. M., Abttan, R. A., & Alkhazraji, A. (2022). Artificial intelligence for COVID-19: A short article. *Artificial Intelligence*, *10*(1). Advance online publication. doi:10.24203/ajpnms.v10i1.6961

Miskiewicz, R. (2020). *Internet of things in marketing: Bibliometric analysis.* Academic Press.

Mohammad, R. M., Thabtah, F., & McCluskey, L. (2015). Tutorial and critical analysis of phishing websites methods. *Computer Science Review*, *17*, 1–24. doi:10.1016/j.cosrev.2015.04.001

Mohammadi, S., Mirvaziri, H., Ghazizadeh-Ahsaee, M., & Karimipour, H. (2019). Cyber intrusion detection by combined feature selection algorithm. *Journal of Information Security and Applications*, *44*, 80-88.

Mohit, P., & Biswas, G. P. (2016, March). Modification of symmetric-key DES into efficient asymmetric-key DES using RSA. In *Proceedings of the Second International Conference on Information and Communication Technology for Competitive Strategies* (pp. 1-5). 10.1145/2905055.2905352

Muhammad, T., & Ghafory, H. (2022). SQL Injection Attack Detection Using Machine Learning Algorithm. *Mesopotamian Journal of Cybersecurity*, 5-17. doi:10.1016/B978-0-323-85209-8.00007-9

Nakhodchi, S., & Dehghantanha, A. (2020). A bibliometric analysis on the application of deep learning in cybersecurity. *Security of Cyber-Physical Systems: Vulnerability and Impact*, 203-221.

Narote, A., Zutshi, V., Potdar, A., & Vichare, R. (2022). Detection of DDoS Attacks using Concepts of Machine Learning. *International Journal for Research in Applied Science and Engineering Technology*, *10*(6), 390–403. doi:10.22214/ijraset.2022.43723

Narwal, B., Mohapatra, A. K., & Usmani, K. A. (2019). Towards a taxonomy of cyber threats against target applications. *Journal of Statistics and Management Systems*, *22*(2), 301–325. doi:10.1080/0972 0510.2019.1580907

Nielsen, M. A., & Computation, I. C. Q. (2000). *Quantum Information. Cambridge University Press.*

Özgür, A., & Erdem, H. (2016). *A review of KDD99 dataset usage in intrusion detection and machine learning between 2010 and 2015.* Academic Press.

Pirandola, S., Andersen, U. L., Banchi, L., Berta, M., Bunandar, D., Colbeck, R., Englund, D., Gehring, T., Lupo, C., Ottaviani, C., Pereira, J. L., Razavi, M., Shamsul Shaari, J., Tomamichel, M., Usenko, V. C., Vallone, G., Villoresi, P., & Wallden, P. (2020). Advances in quantum cryptography. *Advances in Optics and Photonics*, *12*(4), 1012–1236. doi:10.1364/AOP.361502

Pitropakis, N., Panaousis, E., Giannetsos, T., Anastasiadis, E., & Loukas, G. (2019). A taxonomy and survey of attacks against machine learning. *Computer Science Review*, *34*, 100199. doi:10.1016/j.cosrev.2019.100199

Purkait, S. (2012). Phishing counter measures and their effectiveness–literature review. *Information Management & Computer Security*, *20*(5), 382–420. doi:10.1108/09685221211286548

Quayyum, F., Cruzes, D. S., & Jaccheri, L. (2021). Cybersecurity awareness for children: A systematic literature review. *International Journal of Child-Computer Interaction*, *30*, 100343. doi:10.1016/j.ijcci.2021.100343

Quionero-Candela, J., Sugiyama, M., Schwaighofer, A., & Lawrence, N. D. (2009). Dataset Shift in Machine Learning. MIT Press.

Radmand, P., Talevski, A., Petersen, S., & Carlsen, S. (2010, April). Taxonomy of wireless sensor network cyber security attacks in the oil and gas industries. In *2010 24th IEEE International Conference on Advanced Information Networking and Applications* (pp. 949-957). IEEE. 10.1109/AINA.2010.175

Raiyn, J. (2014). A survey of cyber attack detection strategies. *International Journal of Security and Its Applications*, *8*(1), 247–256. doi:10.14257/ijsia.2014.8.1.23

Ramim, M., & Levy, Y. (2006). Securing e-learning systems: A case of insider cyber attacks and novice IT management in a small university. *Journal of Cases on Information Technology*, *8*(4), 24–34. doi:10.4018/jcit.2006100103

Rasheed, R. T., Niu, Y., & Abd, S. N. (2021). Harmony search for security enhancement. *Mesopotamian Journal of CyberSecurity*, *5-8*, 5–8. Advance online publication. doi:10.58496/MJCS/2021/002

Rawindaran, N., Jayal, A., Prakash, E., & Hewage, C. (2021). Cost benefits of using machine learning features in NIDS for cyber security in UK small medium enterprises (SME). *Future Internet*, *13*(8), 186. doi:10.3390/fi13080186

Rehman, A., Saba, T., Mahmood, T., Mehmood, Z., Shah, M., & Anjum, A. (2019). Data hiding technique in steganography for information security using number theory. *Journal of Information Science*, *45*(6), 767–778. doi:10.1177/0165551518816303

Ribeiro, M. T., Singh, S., & Guestrin, C. (2016, August). "Why should i trust you?" Explaining the predictions of any classifier. In *Proceedings of the 22nd ACM SIGKDD international conference on knowledge discovery and data mining* (pp. 1135-1144). 10.1145/2939672.2939778

Rivest, R., Shamir, A., & Adleman, L. (1978). A method for obtaining digital signatures and public-key cryptosystems. *Communications of the ACM*, *21*(2), 120–126. doi:10.1145/359340.359342

Rouzbahani, H. M., Karimipour, H., Dehghantanha, A., & Parizi, R. M. (2020). Blockchain applications in power systems: A bibliometric analysis. *Blockchain Cybersecurity, Trust and Privacy*, 129-145.

Salahdine, F., & Kaabouch, N. (2019). Social engineering attacks: A survey. *Future Internet*, *11*(4), 89. doi:10.3390/fi11040089

Salem, I. E., Mijwil, M., Abdulqader, A. W., Ismaeel, M. M., Alkhazraji, A., & Alaabdin, A. M. Z. (2022). Introduction to The Data Mining Techniques in Cybersecurity. *Mesopotamian Journal of Cybersecurity*, *2022*, 28–37. doi:10.58496/MJCS/2022/004

Saleous, H., Ismail, M., AlDaajeh, S. H., Madathil, N., Alrabaee, S., Choo, K. K. R., & Al-Qirim, N. (2022). *COVID-19 pandemic and the cyberthreat landscape: Research challenges and opportunities*. Digital Communications and Networks. doi:10.1016/j.dcan.2022.06.005

Sari, A., & Atasoy, U. C. (2019). Taxonomy of Cyber Attack Weapons, Defense Strategies, and Cyber War Incidents. In Applying Methods of Scientific Inquiry Into Intelligence, Security, and Counterterrorism (pp. 1-45). IGI Global.

Sarker, I. H., Furhad, M. H., & Nowrozy, R. (2021). Ai-driven cybersecurity: An overview, security intelligence modeling and research directions. *SN Computer Science*, *2*(3), 1–18. doi:10.100742979-021-00557-0

Schoelkopf, R. J., & Girvin, S. M. (2008). Wiring up quantum systems. *Nature*, *451*(7179), 664–669. doi:10.1038/451664a PMID:18256662

Sharma, P., Jain, S., Gupta, S., & Chamola, V. (2021). Role of machine learning and deep learning in securing 5G-driven industrial IoT applications. *Ad Hoc Networks*, *123*, 102685. doi:10.1016/j.adhoc.2021.102685

Shaukat, K., Luo, S., Varadharajan, V., Hameed, I. A., Chen, S., Liu, D., & Li, J. (2020). Performance comparison and current challenges of using machine learning techniques in cybersecurity. *Energies*, *13*(10), 2509. doi:10.3390/en13102509

Shelly, G. B., Cashman, T. J., & Vermaat, M. E. (2007). *Discovering Computers 2008: Study Guide*. Course Technology Press.

Shelly, G. B., & Vermaat, M. E. (2010). *Discovering Computers-Fundamentals 2011 Edition*. https://dl.acm.org/doi/book/10.5555/1841059

Shor, P. W. (1997). Polynomial-time algorithms for prime factorization and discrete logarithms on a quantum computer. *SIAM Journal on Computing*, *26*(5), 1484–1509. doi:10.1137/S0097539795293172

Shor, P. W. (1994). Polynomial-time algorithms for prime factorization and discrete logarithms on a quantum computer. *Proceedings of the 35th Annual Symposium on Foundations of Computer Science.*

Shrestha, S., Haque, S., Dawadi, S., & Giri, R. A. (2022). Preparations for and practices of online education during the Covid-19 pandemic: A study of Bangladesh and Nepal. *Education and Information Technologies*, *27*(1), 1–23. doi:10.100710639-021-10659-0 PMID:34341654

Sikder, A. K., Petracca, G., Aksu, H., Jaeger, T., & Uluagac, A. S. (2021). A survey on sensor-based threats and attacks to smart devices and applications. *IEEE Communications Surveys and Tutorials*, *23*(2), 1125–1159. doi:10.1109/COMST.2021.3064507

Simmons, C., Ellis, C., Shiva, S., Dasgupta, D., & Wu, Q. (2009). *AVOIDIT: A cyber attack taxonomy*. University of Memphis, Technical Report CS-09-003.

Singh, U. K., Joshi, C., & Kanellopoulos, D. (2019). A framework for zero-day vulnerabilities detection and prioritization. *Journal of Information Security and Applications*, *46*, 164–172. doi:10.1016/j.jisa.2019.03.011

Singh, V., & Kaushik, V. D. (2023). A State-of-the-Art Review Covering Security Attack Analysis and Intelligent Cloud Computing. In *Security and Risk Analysis for Intelligent Cloud Computing: Methods, Applications, and Preventions*. CRC Press, Taylor and Francis Group. (in production)

Singh, V., & Dubey, V. (2015). A two level image security based on Arnold transform and chaotic logistic mapping. *International Journal of Advanced Research in Computer Science and Software Engineering*, *5*(2), 883–887.

Singh, V., & Dubey, V. (2015). An Entropy based color image encryption based on Arnold Transform and Pixel chaotic shuffling method. *International Journal of Advanced Research in Computer Science and Software Engineering*, *5*(2), 888–892.

Singh, V., & Kaushik, V. D. (2022). Concepts of Data Mining and Process Mining. In *Process Mining Techniques for Pattern Recognition* (pp. 1–17). CRC Press. doi:10.1201/9781003169550-1

Somani, G., Gaur, M. S., Sanghi, D., Conti, M., & Buyya, R. (2017). DDoS attacks in cloud computing: Issues, taxonomy, and future directions. *Computer Communications*, *107*, 30–48. doi:10.1016/j.comcom.2017.03.010

Spafford, E. H. (1994). Computer viruses as artificial life. *Artificial Life*, *1*(3), 249–265. doi:10.1162/artl.1994.1.3.249

Ssenyonga, M. (2021). Imperatives for post COVID-19 recovery of Indonesia's education, labor, and SME sectors. *Cogent Economics & Finance, 9*(1), 1911439. doi:10.1080/23322039.2021.1911439

Su, Q., Huang, C. R., & Chen, H. K. (2010, July). Evidentiality for text trustworthiness detection. In *Proceedings of the 2010 Workshop on NLP and Linguistics: Finding the Common Ground* (pp. 10-17). Academic Press.

Tao, H., & Chen, Y. (2009, September). A metric model for trustworthiness of softwares. In *2009 IEEE/WIC/ACM International Joint Conference on Web Intelligence and Intelligent Agent Technology* (Vol. 3, pp. 69-72). IEEE. 10.1109/WI-IAT.2009.233

Thangarasu, N., & Selvakumar, A. A. L. (2019). Improved elliptical curve cryptography and Abelian group theory to resolve linear system problem in sensor-cloud cluster computing. *Cluster Computing*, *22*(S6), 13185–13194. doi:10.100710586-017-1573-1

Thangavel, M., TGR, A. S., Priyadharshini, P., & Saranya, T. (2022). Review on machine and deep learning applications for cyber security. In Research Anthology on Machine Learning Techniques, Methods, and Applications (pp. 1143-1164). IGI Global.

Trajcevski, G., Wolfson, O., Hinrichs, K., & Chamberlain, S. (2004). Managing uncertainty in moving objects databases. *ACM Transactions on Database Systems (TODS), 29*(3), 463-507.

Urooj, U., Al-rimy, B. A. S., Zainal, A., Ghaleb, F. A., & Rassam, M. A. (2022). Ransomware detection using the dynamic analysis and machine learning: A survey and research directions. *Applied Sciences (Basel, Switzerland), 12*(1), 172. doi:10.3390/app12010172

Wang, X., Gao, Y., Lin, J., Rangwala, H., & Mittu, R. (2015). A machine learning approach to false alarm detection for critical arrhythmia alarms. In *Proc. IEEE 14th Int. Conf. Mach. Learn. Appl. (ICMLA)* (pp. 202–207). IEEE.

Wang, Y., Smahi, A., Zhang, H., & Li, H. (2022). Towards double defense network security based on multi-identifier network architecture. *Sensors (Basel), 22*(3), 747. doi:10.339022030747 PMID:35161493

Wang, Y., Zhou, A., Liao, S., Zheng, R., Hu, R., & Zhang, L. (2021). A comprehensive survey on DNS tunnel detection. *Computer Networks, 197*, 108322. doi:10.1016/j.comnet.2021.108322

What is Cyber-Security? (n.d.). Available: https://www.kaspersky.com.au/resource-center/definitions/what-iscyber-security

White, H. D., & McCain, K. W. (1998). Visualizing a discipline: An author co-citation analysis of information science, 1972–1995. *Journal of the American Society for Information Science, 49*(4), 327–355.

Zhang, Z., Ning, H., Shi, F., Farha, F., Xu, Y., Xu, J., Zhang, F., & Choo, K. K. R. (2022). Artificial intelligence in cyber security: Research advances, challenges, and opportunities. *Artificial Intelligence Review, 55*(2), 1–25. doi:10.100710462-021-09976-0

Zhou, Y., & Wang, P. (2019). An ensemble learning approach for XSS attack detection with domain knowledge and threat intelligence. *Computers & Security, 82*, 261–269. doi:10.1016/j.cose.2018.12.016

Chapter 4
Classifications of the Instrument of Force Required to Investigate Suspects of Cybercrimes Against Outpatients' Adolescents With Psychiatric Emergencies

Joshua Ojo Nehinbe
https://orcid.org/0000-0002-0098-7437
Federal University, Oye-Ekiti, Nigeria

Jimmy Benson Adebesin
NHS England, UK

ABSTRACT

Interdisciplinary studies on cybercrimes against some outpatient adolescents with psychiatric emergencies have identified critical concerns and new debates on the instances whereby law enforcement agents are largely compelled to use the instrument of force. The adolescents may unexpectedly harm themselves or vulnerable people. Psychiatric emergencies can lead to lawlessness like premeditated crimes and constructive vandalism. This research adopts a quantitative review of IDS logs, interviews, and virtual meeting apps. Thematic analysis suggests the limits of non-violent methods of investigating cybercrimes and further classifies clinical use of force on the need to use and suggestive circumstances that combine empathy, mutual dialogue, and compassionate care with non-toxic, refraining, harmless, and inoffensive interventions. New legal concepts on the instrument of force like proxy witness, evocative criminal liability, implicit and explicit jurisdictions, surrogated and virtual complainants were suggested to safeguard the above adolescents from cyber criminals.

DOI: 10.4018/978-1-6684-8422-7.ch004

1. INTRODUCTION

Interdisciplinary studies have shown that cybercrime can occur against outpatients' adolescents with psychiatric emergency but they are not attracting the kind of research attention that is expected from the global society even if its impacts and the numbers of victims suddenly increase (Michael et al, 2002; MoH, 2018). There are numerous dilemmas that correlate to the above issues. Firstly, several suspects and complainants may not habitually assist law enforcement agents in the standard ways of recording and investigating crime scenes. Hence, the generic circumstances at which statutory laws have empowered law enforcement agencies to minimally apply instrument of force to arrest suspects in the above crime scenes have raised critical concerns in recent time because they are less clinical (ICRC, 2015). Psychiatric emergence is a form of psychiatric disorder that is treated in psychiatric hospitals (AACAP, 2018). Children that exhibit such disorder must be considered in terms of their plight (or health challenges), environmental conditions and capacity to critically assess their circumstances and convincingly speak to police.

Studies have also shown that some cybercrimes on the adolescents in the above setting can subject them into three interrelated traumas such that they will always require suitable diagnosis and effective therapeutic treatments of their mental disorders so that they can cope and recover. They could feel like having access to smooth channels for reporting infringements to the law enforcement agents so that detectives can adequately investigate and bring the perpetrators of cybercrime against them to justice. Such adolescents could require succour, succourers, well-wishers or assistance from someone to whom private matters can be confided and would always available for them. Such confidants should be able to relate their concerns and cyber infringements against them to the police when the need arises. Nonetheless, there are several dilemmas that associate with the issues that involve the need for person(s) to stand-in for complainant(s) in law courts.

Legal issues on outpatients' adolescents with psychiatric emergency often require creative combination of multiple academic disciplines to resolve (Sudarsanan et al, 2004). Some outpatients' adolescents with psychiatric emergency are students and extremely young children that attend hospitals for treatments on behavioral disorders without necessarily staying there overnight (Kenneth et al, 2022). Significant numbers of them are victims of various forms of cybercrimes. Some of the above adolescents can be offended, misbehaved and annoyed especially if specific people repeatedly ask some questions from them (Paus et al, 2008). However, the proportions of cybercrime and the totality of vulnerable adolescents that are troubled or annoyed with persistent requests and malicious interruptions over Internet across the globe are largely unknown till date. These have raised several doubts about planning, investigation and administrative aspects of interventions for them since their geographic and demographic disparities are largely unknown. Another central issue is that international bodies often advise States to enact and review legal and administrative benchmarks to address the above critical issues in the society (ICRC, 2022). Unfortunately, the trauma experienced by some of the above children may unexpectedly made them to harm themselves unintentionally and they can suddenly endanger a number of vulnerable people living in their environment especially if they are neglected or unseen over time.

Another trouble is that psychiatric emergency itself can lead to premeditated crimes. It can cause Sudden and Unnatural Death (SUD) (e.g. suicide), constructive vandalism and other forms of lawlessness like gang-raping and substance abuse (e.g. alcoholism) in the society (AACAP, 2018, MoH, 2018). Investigators can encounter a wide range of unrelated crimes scenes that involve the above setting. For these reasons, Human Rights' issues involving the above group of adolescents, the need to respect human dignity and the applicability of some international laws and domestic laws may conflict with the standard norms and proven discretionary strategies (Yermek et al, 2020). Sometimes, suitable legislations that stakeholders can invoke to safeguard victims and vulnerable children in the above category may require supervisory input of numerous virtual professionals in far jurisdictions and professionals that can be contacted. However, these tradeoffs must be ethically handled to avoid infringement of law (ICRC, 2015).

Another dilemma is that the alerts of Intrusion Detection Systems (IDSs) such as Snort that should assist investigators of crimes do not obviously indicate potential crimes against victims of cybercrime. The reason is that such alerts are primarily designed to indicate potential security violations in the networks or device(s) under surveillance. So, some detectives would still require some resources before they can completely convert all of them to useful criminal evidence. Therefore, minors in the above setting should require therapeutic methodology and calculated amount of force to reasonably compel them and extract useful information that can assist law enforcement agencies to arrest and investigate the perpetrators of cybercrimes against them. Similarly, detectives may need to also apply instrument of force to compel the defendants to defend themselves on the allegations that complainants have levied against them. Feelers have suggested the necessities of involving confidant(s) that can stand-in for such complainants during criminal investigations deserve critical examination. These notions have obviously elicited contentions on the legality of the third party to stand-in for complainants and how some law enforcement agencies will conclude investigations of cybercrime against outpatients' adolescents with the above health condition given the restrictive applicability of the instrument of force in carrying out their duties across the globe.

Furthermore, the objectives of this chapter are divided into two significant points. The chapter seeks to critically explore whether detectives and courts can admit criminal evidence from complainant(s) that 'voluntarily acquire(s)' and 'voluntarily seek(s)' criminal action(s) to be taken against defendant(s) of cybercrime against outpatients' adolescents with psychiatric emergency. The second objective of the chapter is that it intends to investigate whether criminal law can permit an interchange of suspect, witness and proven suspect on cybercrime against that above setting in certain circumstance(s). This research adopts quantitative review of IDS logs, qualitative interviews and virtual meeting apps to conduct 3 brainstorming sessions on the above issues. Data gathering was spread across 6 months intervals. Each section engages 3 undergraduate students; 5 mental healthcare, 2 social healthcare, 2 legal and 3 digital forensic experts and thematic breakdown of the above datasets were thoroughly carries out. The contributions of the chapter are as follows. The chapter suggests the limits of non-violent methods of gathering statements from complainants and defendants of cybercrime in the above setting and further classifies the use of instrument of force on the basis of "needs to use" and "suggestive circumstances". The chapter subsequently recommends new legal concepts and how governments can extend the existing laws on instrument of force to cover implicit jurisdictions (jurisdictions that are not well-understood), explicit jurisdictions (jurisdictions that are well-understood); surrogated complainants, virtual complainants and witness by proxy in other to effectively safeguard outpatients' adolescents from cyber criminals. The remainders of this chapter are as follows: section 2 discusses definitions of important terminologies in this chapter. Section 3 discusses criminal liability. Section 4 discusses the methodology; section 5 enumerates the results while section 6 concludes the chapter.

2. DEFINITIONS AND TERMINOLOGIES

Psychiatric emergence is a form of psychiatric disorder that is treated in psychiatric hospitals.

Cybercrime is an act of using computer and Internet to perpetrate offence that is considered unlawful in the society. The penalties for cybercrimes are spelt out in cyber Act, criminal law, etc.

Complainant is a person that reports criminal allegation to the police or courts of competent jurisdictions. Complainant is synonymous to an accuser, plaintiff, petitioner; applicant and claimant.

Defendant is a suspect of criminal allegation. Defendant is synonymous to an accused, appellant, litigant and respondent.

Criminal liability is the state of being lawfully accountable, guilty or responsible to specific criminal charge(s).

Criminal court is a court that have competent jurisdiction to preside over criminal cases.

Criminal law is a body of statutory law that states each crime and its respective punishment in a jurisdiction.

Criminal suit is a lawsuit against defendant in other to allege violations of criminal law.

Third party is someone other than the principal actor (i.e. defendant) or actual complainant (ie. main victim) in a criminal allegation.

Surrogated complainant is a person that can take the place of a complainant (or appointed to represent a complainant) in a criminal allegation. *Surrogated defendant is a person* that can take the place of a defendant (or appointed to represent a defendant) in a criminal allegation.

3. PRECEDENCE OF CRIMINAL LIABILITY

Criminal liability is the consideration for determining the potential and actual conditions through which a person can be held legally responsible for committing a crime (Faure and Partain, 2019). Mental element or physical element can present or absent in some allegations of cybercrime. Some cybercrime may possess of mental element or physical element, or combinations of both elements (Gaevskaja, 2016). Fundamentally, studies have shown that the above elements can be adjudged on the basis of cyber act (or action) that depicts "commission" and "omission". Commission is applicable to cyber action that is due to command, instruction or order that originates from superior person(s) to the subordinate(s) staff. Omission is applicable to cyber action that is due to the oversight of responsibility of an employee (or a set of employees) such as failure of employee to observe preventive procedure, or failure due to negligence on duty, or failure fur to mistake and ignorance of law.

Nehinbe (2022) raises new legal debates on specific circumstance whereby employers of labour, organizational culture and procedures at workplace may compel employees to inevitably perform obligations that turn out to be unlawful dealings. Thus, the scholar believes that the issues of compelling liability (i.e. act of "compulsion") and obligated liability (i.e. "duty-bound necessities") with respect to cybercrime deserve global review.

The premise of this chapter is that criminal liability can correlate to specific precedence order especially if instrument of force that can be used to achieve the needed results seems to be less clinically oriented in nature. Investigators of the crime scenes that relate to cybercrimes in such scenario may need to expend more resources before they can detect and prevent the agony of the complainants, suspects or witnesses that may be covertly affected by non-clinical segments of the principles designed to control violence and injustice in the society. The search for evidence that indicates criminal liability in cybercrime on outpatients' adolescents with psychiatric emergency usually congregates diverse opinions together. Investigations can indicate the possibility of switching seemingly equivalent criminal liabilities. This means that certain charges are supplants and some criminal liabilities will supersede two or many closely related criminal liabilities in certain cybercrime scenes. The displaced criminal liabilities are said to therefore have low precedence order.

With different legal jurisdictions, the question is that can detectives and court honour complainants that acquire and bring criminal action(s) against complainants in the above setting as his/her own and by free choice (Spapens, 2017)? Should law permit interchange of suspect(s) or prisoner(s) in circumstance(s) of psychiatric emergency especially in the above scenario? The fact is that reciprocal transfers of equivalent criminal liability and considering the status of the mental health of different complainants, there are a number of possibilities and legal implications for both the complainants and defendants of cybercrime in the above situation. The challenge is that some witnesses may not be within reach. Similarly, it may be difficult to forcibly arrest and interrogate some defendants with the motive of absolving or indicting them especially if the complainants are visibly known with the above mental disorder in the society.

4. METHODOLOGY

We conducted direct interviews of social workers that have worked with adolescents with psychiatric emergency and we adopted virtual meeting apps to conduct virtual brainstorming for three separate sessions. Each section engaged 3 undergraduate students, 3 mental healthcare nurses, 3 social healthcare workers, 2 legal officers and 4 digital forensic experts to deeply explore and reflect on the criticality of the above issues.

Quantitatively, the message descriptions of specific rules that relate to web servers, html, http, ftp, tcp, udp, gtp, dns, icmp, ip and ftp client in the logger modules of Snort-IDS were modified and duplicated. These enabled us to generate and broadly discuss two concurrent categories of alerts from Snort-IDS. The first category of the alerts was the "default warnings" that signified potential security violations while the second category of alerts converted each of the default warnings from the IDS to "explicitly alert" that may be indicative of cybercrime. Thereafter, the toolkit was used to analyze trace files that were extracted from the spanning mode of the gateway into Software laboratory in a University. The conventional alerts from Snort-IDS and the newly modified alerts were compared and discussed with the participants. The data gathering process was spread across 6 months intervals. Thereafter, we thematically deconstruct and breakdown the responses obtained from the participants into distinctive and comparable themes. The most informative of the results obtained from the study are discussed below.

5. RESULTS AND ANALYSIS

The results in Figure 1 to Figure 4 are classified into the prevalence of cybercrime against adolescents with psychiatric emergence, factors that may influence the attitudes of adolescents with psychiatric emergence, new classification of instrument of force and potential factors that may promote the coping and recovery of the above category of adolescents in the society. Figure 1 show potential cybercrimes that perpetrators can carry out against some adolescents with psychiatric emergence. The statistics suggest that it is possible that about 70% of the above adolescent may be frightened by means of Internet apps, 84% of them may be victims of online molestation, 65% of the may be victims of continuous pestering of victims with unsolicited Internet calls and 55% of the may likely be victims of lascivious behavior via Internet resources. Similarly, the study argues that the circumstances of adolescents with psychiatric emergence make them disposed to trick. Thus, we observe that it is possible to have about 69% of them that may probably be victims of online extortion that uses mind games to trick them in some societal settings.

Figure 1. Prevalence of cybercrime against

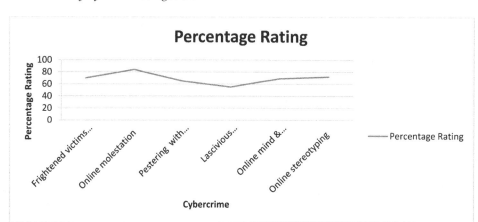

Figure 2. Factors that may influence attitudes of adolescents with psychiatric emergency

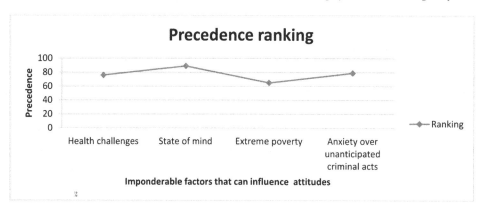

Figure 2 suggests that possible attitudes of the adolescents with psychiatric emergency. Accordingly, such teenagers may be influenced by imponderable factors like health challenges, state of mind and indigence (or extreme poverty). It was also revealed that fear and anxiety over unanticipated criminal acts can increase the level of apprehension of the adolescents with psychiatric emergency.

Figure 3. Classification of instrument of force

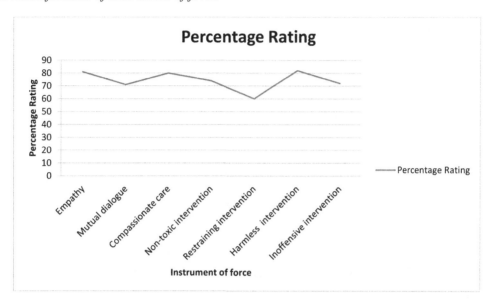

Figure 3 classifies instrument of force require to investigate complainants and defendants in the above setting on the basis of "needs to use" and "suggestive circumstances". Respondents argue that suggestive circumstances that warrant the administration of instrument of force connote combined strategies whereby the investigators of cybercrime in the above scenario decide to use suite of empathy, mutual dialogue and compassionate care together with non-toxic intervention, mild, serene and refraining interventions that produce harmless and inoffensive intercessions on defendants and complainants. In other words, instrument of force must be harmless to the investigators, complainants, defendants and witness of cybercrime. The outcomes of such combined interventions must not lead to grievance, pain and impairment to any of the parties to the allegations of cybercrime in the above setting. Further still, the results corroborate well- established and the conventional usage of instrument of force that usually conforms to the principle of needs to use basis.

Figure 4 suggests three core factors that can enable the adolescents with psychiatric emergency to cope and promote their recovery. Accordingly, the concept of sensitivity to emotional feelings, sensitivity to therapies and improved surveillance are imperative pointers to indicate the level at which the required teenagers are coping and recovering from their health issues. The study articulates that society must understand adolescents with psychiatric emergency because they are not always sensitive to themselves and they are insensitive to the difficulty of others. It is also argued that such adolescents that are coping and showing recovery would be sensitive to their circumstances and the emotional feelings of people around them.

Figure 4. Coping and recovery factor

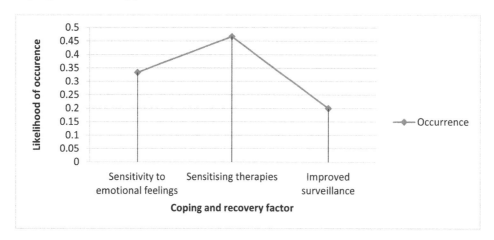

The above findings have called for new data privacy measures that can assist the effective fulfillment of law enforcement objectives and protection of the above children. Detectives can subject electronic devices of vulnerable teenagers to strict surveillance. Hence, there is need to promulgate new legislations in the form of teenagers mental health protection capacity Act to empower detective to monitor the devices of adolescents with psychiatric emergency without infringement to their privacy life. Investigators of cybercrime should aware that such adolescents can occasionally alter distorted statements. They can also be delusional and elicit attitudes that relate to hallucination, chimera, false impression and misconception (or misapprehension) of simple questions that require them to narrate their ordeal in the hands of the suspects of cybercrime. The concept of sensitizing therapies depict that the above group of adolescents require mental health interventions that would enable them to acquire the ability they would need to actively respond to emotive changes in their interpersonal and social surroundings. The notion of improved (or advanced) surveillance entails that police investigations should be accompanied with close observations of people and social groups in the communities where cases of psychiatric emergence have been reported and communities where they are yet to be reported.

Participants that evaluated two categories of the alerts that we extracted from Snort-IDS declared that the alerting mechanisms of most Intrusion Detection Systems (IDSs) must be upgraded to reflect the desires and duties of security and law enforcement professionals. The argument is that experts in computer and network security need alerts from IDSs to enable them monitor and assess the level of protection of computers, networks and their peripherals in their organizations so that they can state, examine, assess and mitigate the impacts of intrusions and intruders on them. They also need alerts to enable them identifying the root causes of intrusions and improve business continuity plans in the corporations. Contrarily, detectives would need alerts from IDSs to identify malicious actors that are responsible for the allegations of cybercrime (or computer crimes) that occur under their jurisdictions, collect the evidence, document them, conduct arrest and charge the culprits of the act to the courts of competent jurisdictions.

The participants in the research subsequently advocate that instrument of force should be clinical to be effectively useful for investigating the above kind of cybercrime. The participants further recommends new legal concepts and how governments can extend the existing laws on instrument of force to cover implicit and explicit jurisdictions, surrogated complainants, virtual complainants, evocative criminal liability and witness by proxy in other to effectively safeguard outpatients' adolescents from cyber criminals. Accordingly, cybercrime against the above setting may enable detectives to directly or indirectly work in unfamiliar (implicit) jurisdictions or familiar (explicit) jurisdictions. Local knowledge is instrumental to the success of detective works. Hence, we argue that explicit jurisdictions and implicit jurisdictions are indicative of jurisdictions whereby detectives may (or may not) have the needed local knowledge that should enable them to perform their responsibilities due to some exigencies required to protect adolescents with psychiatric emergency. It was rigorously buttressed that such investigations can compel stakeholders to permit surrogated complainants (i.e. someone to legally represent the complainants), virtual complainants (i.e. someone that's can legally provide evidence via conference apps) and witness by proxy (i.e. someone who got useful evidence from main witness) that can furnish needed information to assist detectives, social workers and mental healthcare managers. We argue that evocative criminal liability is a kind of criminal liability that makes a person guilty for causing emotional damage to his/her fellow human being. Respondents further advocated that stereotyping and stigmatization are potential offences that can make adolescents with psychiatric emergency who are at the threshold of recuperating to suddenly think and breakdown whenever perpetrators make them unsecure about their past health life.

The above findings have many implications in policing, parenting and mental health management and practices. For instance, criminal liability that is based on hallucination is an unfounded claim that is inadmissible in courts of competent jurisdictions. The fact that complainants hear or feel they are victims of cybercrimes does not necessarily point out that they are realistic accusations. Similarly, the study believes that criminal liability that is based on misconception is of low precedent. Adolescents with psychiatric emergency can display attitudes that connote mistake of identity due to their lack of capability to correctly recognize events at all time. Finally, the argument is that criminal liability that is based on delusions should high precedence. The implication is that the actions or accusations of criminality that adolescents with psychiatric emergency believe and want the detectives to accept as infringements of their fundamental human rights should not be discarded as vague claims. Such allegations require in-depth investigations because they may be indicative of insightful evidence to the police.

6. CONCLUSION

Cybercrimes against adolescents with psychiatric emergence do not often attract attention in most settings due to the circumstances that surround their mental health. Several infringements against them by perpetrators of cybercrimes are not even reported to the appropriate law enforcement agencies for proper investigations. Some societies treat their allegations with levity even whenever there are obvious needs to intimate detectives. Research further says that the above group of teenagers has unstable emotional traits. They can be moody, hushed, whispering and decline to open up when they needed to assist detectives.

Their erratic attitudes often make it difficult to take down their statements, arrest appropriate suspects and summon suitable witnesses to give useful evidence that can assist investigators, mental health nurses and social workers on the allegations of cybercrimes against them. The technicality and legality of the above issues have raised novel deliberations in criminology in recent time. Feelers begin to ponder concerning the possibility of the society to have unintentionally ignored countless numbers of innocent victims with their plight and horrible experience by erroneously allowing their abusers to go scot-free in the long run.

Suitable mental and social healthcare interventions that can appease to the voices of survivors are newly separated concerns in mental health management given the low level of global awareness on the constraints that are facing law enforcement agencies whenever they want to perform their duties of assisting and protecting vulnerable teenagers. However, some selective voices argue that ignoring the above teenagers can be tantamount to the act of cruelty, discrimination, injustice and intolerance to human care. Experts also proffer that attempt to declare the abusers in the above circumstances blameless or exonerate them by not allowing them to accept responsibility, criticisms and punishment for the crimes they have committed is related to insensitivity to the predicament faced by sick children in the general public. This chapter has investigated the above issues. We argue that some investigations may eventually indicate the chances of switching seemingly equivalent criminal liabilities to protect teenagers and vulnerable adolescents in the above setting. We then proposed suggestive circumstances to actuate the legality and necessity to adopt customized instrument of force in the investigation of cybercrime in the above setting. We believe this notion would raise new legal debates across the globe on the prospect of surrogate complainant, surrogate defendant, surrogated liability and proxy witness. Hence, the forefront of the chapter itemizes that above paradigms would require comprehensive deliberations involving criminologist, law enforcement, legal, clinicians, social and mental healthcare professional to converse them without usurping any segment of Human Rights.

Finally, the chapter catalogues critical cybercrimes against the above adolescents as online harassment, mind games, bugging games, online stereotyping, pestering with unsolicited Internet services, online molestations, covert recording of conversations by the use of Internet-enabled digital devices, etc. We recommend new data privacy measures that can assist the effective fulfillment of law enforcement objectives and protection of the above children. We also recommend clinically-based instrument of force. We believe that such therapeutic methodology can include a suite of empathy, mutual dialogue and compassionate care together with non-toxic intervention, mild, serene and refraining interventions. These must be able to produce harmless and inoffensive instrument of force on the defendants and complainants as well as assisting law enforcement agencies to detect and prevent cybercrimes against the above group of adolescents or assist them in case of emergencies. Nonetheless, the above research findings did not investigate crimes against outpatients' adolescents that can co-occur together with cybercrime. The research has not also explored juvenile crimes that perpetrators carried out with the use of Artificial Intelligence (A.I.) against the above setting. We hope to critically explore the above two research domains in future time.

REFERENCES

AACAP. (2018). *What is a Psychiatric Emergency?* American Academy of Child and Adolescent Psychiatry. Available at: https://www.aacap.org/AACAP/Families_ and_ Youth/Facts_ for_ Families/FFFGuide/What_is_a_Psychiatric_Emergency_126.aspx

Faure, M., & Partain, R. (2019). Environmental crime. In Environmental Law and Economics: Theory and Practice (pp. 211-232). Cambridge University Press. doi:10.1017/9781108554916.011

Gaevskaja, E. J. (2016). On the issue of criminal law impact on environmental crime. *Bulletin of the Omsk Law Academy*, *3*(32), 40–45.

International Committee of the Red Cross (ICRC). (2015). *International rules and standards for policing*. Available at: https://www.icrc.org/en/doc/assets/files/other/icrc-002-0809 .pdf

International Committee of the Red Cross (ICRC). (2022). *The use of force in law enforcement operations*. ICRC.

Jennifer, M. P., Abigail, L. D., Lawrence, P., & Laura, M. P. (2010). Emergency Psychiatry. In Massachusetts General Hospital Handbook of General Hospital Psychiatry (6th ed.). Academic Press. doi:10.1176/appi.ajp.21060614

Kenneth, S. K., Kathryn, T., & John, W. (2022). The Emergence of Psychiatry: 1650–1850. American Journal of Psychiatry. doi:10.1176/appi.ajp.21060614

Michael, H. A., Peter, F., Joseph, Z., & Glenn, C. (2002). *Report and Recommendations Regarding Psychiatric Emergency and Crisis Services: A Review and Model Program Descriptions*. APA Task Force on Psychiatric Emergency Services.

Ministry of Health (MoH). (2018). *Clinical orientation manual: psychiatric emergencies; emergency medical services division, Bhutan*. Available at: https://www.moh.gov.bt/wp-content/uploads/moh-files/2017/10/ Chapter-16-Psychiatric-Emerfgencies.pdf

Nehinbe, J. (2023). Classification Models for Preventing Juvenile Crimes Committed with Malware Apps. *Malware - Detection and Defense*, doi:10.5772/intechopen.107188

Paus, T., Keshavan, M., & Giedd, J. (2008). Why do many psychiatric disorders emerge during adolescence? *Nature Reviews. Neuroscience*, 9(12), 947–957. doi:10.1038/nrn2513 PMID:19002191

Spapens, T. (2017). Cross-border police cooperation in tackling environmental crime. Transnational Environmental Crime, 505-518. doi:10.4324/9781315084589-30

Sudarsanan, S., Chaudhury, S., Pawar, A. A., Salujha, S. K., & Srivastava, K. (2004). Psychiatric Emergencies. *Medical Journal, Armed Forces India*, 60(1), 59–62. doi:10.1016/S0377-1237(04)80162-X PMID:27407580

Yermek, A. B., Zhanna, A. K., Canzada, S., & Nurlan, Zh. A. (2020). Legislative Regulation of Criminal Liability for Environmental Crimes. *Journal of Environmental Accounting and Management*, 8(4), 323–334. doi:10.5890/JEAM.2020.12.002

Chapter 5
Phishing:
A Theoretical Approach and the Innovative Tools

Liliana Queirós Ribeiro
University of Porto, Portugal

Inês Guedes
Faculty of Law, University of Porto, Portugal

Carla Cardoso
Faculty of Law, University of Porto, Portugal

ABSTRACT

Phishing is a cybercrime in active growth that could cause several damages for its victims, such as identity theft. Specifically, in the last years, cybercrime has been of particular concern due to several attacks developed against society in general. In this sense, understanding this phenomenon and the factors that may explain the susceptibility to this is essential. But it is also essential to know which of the traditional methods are used to study phishing susceptibility and the innovative ones. This chapter presents a complete study in this field, providing a theoretical and practical approach, by using a perspective that is simple and accessible to everyone. In the end, individuals, in general, will know more about the subject, and, academically, this provides important insights to better-developed studies in the phishing susceptibility field.

INTRODUCTION

Nowadays, with the growth of Internet use, several online threats are emerging. Phishing is a cybercrime that has existed since 1996 when attacks against America On-Line (AOL) were developed. But, in recent years, this cybercrime has grown, attracting increasingly more attention. For example, according to the Anti-Phishing Working Group (2022), the last quarter of 2022, registered 1.270.883 phishing attacks, marking it as the worst period in 2022. In the form of social engineering, offenders deceive individuals

DOI: 10.4018/978-1-6684-8422-7.ch005

through phishing attempts to steal their personal information, causing damage to both individuals and organizations (Dhamija & Tygar, 2005; Tembe et al., 2013).

In fact, phishing is marked by its complexity, particularly because it can be executed through different means and techniques to align with the various motivations of offenders. One of the most common methods to launch phishing attacks involves sending fraudulent emails (Verma et al., 2012; Salloum et al., 2021). Effectively, the majority of studies focus on phishing emails as a means for launching these attempts and understanding phishing susceptibility (e.g., Sheng et al., 2010; Canfield et al., 2016; Pfeffel et al., 2019; McAlaney & Hills, 2020).

The present chapter intends to provide significant insights into phishing and the factors that predict individual susceptibility to this cybercrime. Additionally, it aims to offer insights into the methodologies applied to study phishing susceptibility, with a focus on an innovative method – the Eye Tracker. Thus, the chapter begins with the theoretical conceptualization of phishing and its typologies, processes, and techniques. Subsequently, we will delve into explanatory theories for understanding phishing susceptibility from different perspectives (such as information processing). Furthermore, we will focus on individual and contextual factors that can predict phishing susceptibility, namely sociodemographic and technology competencies. Finally, we will present both traditional and innovative methods in the study of phishing susceptibly.

To summarize, by the end of this chapter, readers will gain knowledge about (1) the definitions of phishing, its typologies, and techniques; (2) the factors that predict phishing susceptibility (individual and contextual factors); (3) the principal theoretical models to understand phishing susceptibility; and (4) the traditional and innovative methods employed in phishing susceptibility study.

Theoretical Knowledge

Concept and Typologies of Phishing

There are several definitions of the term "phishing", and some authors have noted that this is still developing (e.g., Kumaraguru et al., 2007; 2010; Hong, 2012; Lastdrager, 2014).

In scientific literature of recent decades, numerous authors formulated their own definitions of phishing, and only recently have efforts to standardize the term emerged. One point of consensus is that phishing is a fraudulent attempt, in a social engineering form, that utilizes technological and communication means (Welk et al., 2015; Barraclough et al., 2021; Ghanzi-Tehrani & Pontell, 2021; Govaparam et al., 2021). However, if initially phishing term was understood as a misleading way that leads individuals to share their personal data on Web pages (Whittaker et al., 2010), other authors complexify it. Hong (2012) studied state phishing attacks and claimed that:

"Phishing attacks initially targeted general consumers, aiming to steal identity and credit-card information, but evolved to also include high-profile targets, aiming to steal intellectual property, corporate secrets, and sensitive information concerning national security." (p.1).

Khonji and colleagues (2013) added to the definition, describing phishing as "a type of computer attack that communicates socially engineered messages to humans via electronic communication channels to persuade them to perform certain actions for the attacker's benefit." (p. 2092).

Given the diverse definitions of phishing, Lastdrager (2014) developed a systematic review, identifying 113 different definitions. Thus, the author concluded that five words are more used: user, information, website, email, and personal. These terms could be grouped into three categories: (1) actors – victims, users, attackers, businesses, banks; (2) assets – email, website, information, password, user name, count, credit card; (3) activities – social engineering, identity theft, attack, spoofing. In fact, expressions such as "social engineering" are being increasingly used in recent publications, as seen in Ghanzi-Tehrani and Pontell's study (2021): "Phishing is an automated form of social engineering whereby criminals use the Internet to fraudulently extract sensitive information from businesses and individuals, often by impersonating legitimate web o." (p.316). However, Lastdrager (2014) argues that phishing definitions should incorporate the words 'information', 'target', 'scalability', 'deception', and 'impersonation', proposing the definition: "phishing is a scalable act of deception whereby impersonation is used to obtain information from a target" (p. 8). This abstract definition of phishing encompasses various actions and, in the author's view, different types of phishing (*idem*).

In this sense, concerning phishing typologies, Alabdan (2020) built upon previous assumptions by Parmar (2012 to identify three components of phishing: (1) the medium – referring to the means through which attacks are communicated to the victims (e.g., SMS, MMS, Internet); (2) the vector – limited by the medium and indicating the avenue through which a phisher attacks; and (3) the technical approach – indicating the implementation methods during the attack, which can use social engineering to increase the success of phishing attempt (Alabdan, 2020).

Taking into consideration the three components of phishing, five types of phishing stand out: (1) *Vishing* – developed through voice methods, where the call number is forged, leading individuals to believe that the source is legitimate; (2) *Smishing* – utilizing SMS and MMS means; for instance, a message can be sent posing as a legitimate entity (e.g., a Bank). This message alerts individuals about a problem with their personal account and directs them to a site where they unwittingly provide data to resolve the issue. Simultaneously, the phisher collects this data for future use; (3) *Spear Phishing* – an attack directed at individuals or organizations, often through an email that appears to be from a known entity or person. The appearance is tailored to the potential victim's interests (e.g., addressing the recipient by name), and may request the opening of a link or file containing malware; (4) *Whaling* – targeting higher-status employees or senior individuals, using vectors such as eFax or email, with the aim of installing malware and gaining access to system information; and (5) *Business Email Compromise (BEC)* – a subtype of *Spear Phishing*, aimed at non-profit, commercial, and governmental organizations to inflict primarily financial harm.

Furthermore, four principal motivations to practice phishing attacks are referred to: (1) financial benefits; (2) identity theft; (3) industrial espionage; and (4) malware distribution. However, motivations can also include a desire for fame, ambition, and visibility within peer groups (Yu et al., 2008).

Finally, phishing is a highly complex and adaptable attack that misleads and damages individuals, companies, organizations, and governments alike (Hong, 2012). As a result, in the present chapter, we adopt the following phishing definition (developed by researchers from the School of Criminology, Faculty of Law of the University of Porto, and a criminal investigator):

"phishing is a fraudulent method of obtaining personal data (username and respectively password), through e-mail messages, writing messages (SMS or WhatsApp), or telephonic messages. By rule, criminals pose as credible institutions such as Banks, Online Service Providers, etc. with the threat that individuals

must take urgent action and upload a link. Thus, misleadingly, individuals provide their personal data, believing that they are inserting it on the website of the real entity." (Neves, 2022)

The Process and Techniques of Phishing

Following the discussion of phishing conceptualization, the debate about its taxonomy and techniques exists, in the scientific literature.

Aleroud and Zhou (2017) developed an extensive systematic review to define the phases of phishing attacks and, consequently, to define its taxonomy. The referred authors established three key phases, based on the previous studies of Wetzel (2005), and Jakobsson and Myers (2006). Specifically, Wetzel (2005) identified five phases (attack planning, attack configuration, attack execution, spoofing, and post-attack phases), while Jakobsson and Myers (2006) included detailed phases such as 'attack preparing', 'sending of a specific attack', 'compromise of data', 'information transfer to the phisher', etc. Consequently, the three key phases identified are (1) preparation; (2) execution; and (3) exploitation of results; each comprising subphases (Aleroud & Zhou, 2017). In the first phase – preparation – cybercriminals select communication means, with email being the most common, but others such as voice and mobile applications can be considered. Also at this phase, devices (e.g., mobile) and attack techniques are selected, and cybercriminals prepare the necessary materials. The second phase – execution – starts with the material distribution to one or more targets, who then interact with the material, enabling cybercriminals to collect information and, finally, to access the target's resources. The last phase – exploitation of results – includes the utilization of previously collected information for different purposes (*idem*).

During this process, three different attack techniques are distinguished: (1) attack initialization; (2) data collection; and (3) system penetration. The first occurs during the preparation phase and encompasses activities like creating spoofed emails and/or sites, as well as interactions on social media networks. Moreover, attack initialization techniques can be further divided into 'technical category' (e.g., crafting fake URLs to send phishing emails) and 'behavioral category' (e.g., employing social engineering used to coax individuals into revealing personal information). Regarding data collection techniques, occurring during or after victims interact with the attack material, it can be manual – resulting from human error –, or automatic – utilizing spoofed surveys that gather personal data (e.g., surveys for job positions on social media networks) or online information readily available (Aleroud & Zhou, 2017). Finally, system penetration techniques are used to explore the system resources, facilitating phishing attacks (Jakobsson & Myers, 2006; Aleroud & Zhou, 2017).

Explicative Models and Factors of Phishing Susceptibility

The increase in phishing attempts prompts an exploitation of factors and/or reasons to explain why certain individuals are more susceptible to phishing than others. Concretely, phishing susceptibility is understood as the detection failure of phishing attempts, namely phishing emails (e.g., Moody et al., 2017; Vishwanath et al., 2018; Gopavaram et al., 2021).

Therefore, this section presents four explanatory models of phishing susceptibility which focus on different strands: (1) the opportunity to perpetrate the crime – Routine Activity Theory (RAT; Cohen & Felson, 1979); and (2) the information processing perspective – Heuristic-Systematic Model (HSM; Chaiken, 1980) and Suspicion, Cognition, and Automaticity Model (SCAM; Vishwanath et al., 2018).

Routine Activity Theory (RAT; Cohen & Felson, 1979)

RAT, a situational theory, is the most tested "traditional" theory in the cybercrime field (Yar, 2005; Leukfeldt, 2015; Leukfeldt & Yar, 2016; Ghanzi-Tehrani & Pontell, 2021; Kigerl, 2021), specifically in phishing studies (Ghanzi-Tehrani & Pontell, 2021).

This theory advocates that crime occurs in daily routine when three elements concurrently exist in time and space – namely, a suitable target, a motivated offender, and the absence of a capable guardian (Cohen & Felson, 1979). A motivated offender refers to an individual inclined to commit a crime (e.g., phishing or identity theft). A capable guardian embodies protective measures in place (e.g., spam filter guarding against phishing attempts). A suitable target refers to something that can increase the motivation of the offender to the crime practice (e.g., credit card numbers) (Kigerl, 2021). The determination of the last element relies on its Value, Inertia, Visibility, and Access (VIVA) (Leukfeldt, 2014). Considering the phenomenon in exploration, the 'Value' can refer to the potential victim's income, specifically individuals with higher income will have a higher risk of receiving phishing e-mails (Graham & Triplett, 2017). Moreover, 'Visibility' can be raised through the Internet, which can cause an increase in offender motivation (Yar, 2005), namely because of online victims' presence, and 'Inertia' applies to the people or objects' characteristics (e.g., an attachment is downloaded with a virus) (Leukfeldt & Yar, 2016). Finally, 'Access' can be limited by the potential victims, employing security measures like passwords or dual authentication.

Although certain challenges arise in applying this theory to cybercrime, such as the absence of the simultaneous convergence of all three elements (Yar, 2005) in both time and space, some authors propose a broader interpretation of convergence. For instance, temporal contact between email phishing and the victim could be considered as convergence, rather than focusing on victim-offender proximity (e.g., Ghanzi-Tehrani & Pontell, 2021). Thus, phishing susceptibility is diminished when one element is removed – such as a 'suitable target' being less exposed on the Internet or employing cyber security mechanisms as an updated Internet browser.

Heuristic-Systematic Model (HSM; Chaiken, 1980)

The Heuristic-Systematic Model, a sociocognitive perspective, was created by Chaiken (1980). As the HSM distinguishes two modes of information processing – systematic and heuristic – it can also be categorized as a 'double process theory'. Systematic processing, also known as deliberate processing, involves a broad and analytical treatment of received information, demanding a higher ability and cognitive skills (Chaiken, 1980; Chen & Chaiken, 1999; Luo et al., 2013). In turn, heuristic processing involves minimal utilization of cognitive abilities, and a heavier reliance on readily identifiable cues, such as format, subject, and message source in e-mail. Therefore, individuals use cognitive shortcuts that can lead to quick decisions based on immediate emotions – which will be distorted decisions through rapid processing (Chaiken, 1980; Chen & Chaiken, 1999). Empirical evidence shows that individuals used both processing modes, yet there is a prevalence of heuristic processing over systematic processing (Chen & Chaiken, 1999; Vishwanath et al., 2011). Hence, the information processing model is not random, but it is adjusted for contextual factors such as authority figures' involvement (e.g., Bank employees, school administrators), social and/or temporal pressures, and individual capabilities. Whenever these contextual factors arise, the inclination for swift action heightens, prompting individuals to lean towards heuristic processing (Chaiken, 1987). Specifically, in the specific context of detecting phishing emails, the susceptibility to fail in correct detection is expected to increase when individuals use heuristic processing. This is because the rapid analysis facilitated by cognitive shortcuts limits the identification of cues within these emails.

Suspicion, Cognition, and Automaticity Model (SCAM; Vishwanath et al., 2018)

Vishwanath and colleagues with the intent to explain phishing susceptibility, developed the *Suspicion, Cognition, and Automaticity Model* (SCAM). This model introduces a novel perspective on the phenomenon, based on previous assumptions. In the SCAM, 'suspicion' is understood as the principal endogenous predictor of an individual's susceptibility to phishing emails (Vishwanath et al., 2018). This is a unidimensional construct characterized by "the degree of uncertainty one has when interacting with a particular stimulus" (Lyons et al., 2011, p. 220). This construct emerges within a contextual environment, generating a dissonance between an individual's perceived reality – obtained in a context that influences the evaluation mode and cognitive processing of information – and expected reality – contextually reflecting the individual beliefs of what is plausible (Lyons et al., 2011). Thus, SCAM reaches both cognition factors, processing modes, and cyber-risk beliefs. Based on HSM, the SCAM postulates that a higher level of heuristic processing will decrease the suspicion of individuals about email phishing, while systematic processing will increase the suspicion of individuals given the legitimacy of the same type of email (Vishwanath et al., 2018). In turn, cyber-risk beliefs are related to the individuals' perceptions of risks associated with online behavior. These beliefs bridge the gap between individuals' experiences, their efficacy in managing risks, and their level of knowledge (*idem*).

Thus, it is advocated that the higher the cyber-risk beliefs, the lower the heuristic processing and the higher the systematic processing. Moreover, these beliefs will influence the suspicion of the legitimacy of a phishing email (Vishwanath et al., 2018). If an individual regards the probability of encountering cyber-risks as high, they will meticulously scrutinize email information using systematic processing, fostering a sense of doubt in its legitimacy. This, in turn, reduces their susceptibility to falling victim to phishing emails. Researchers have shown that individuals' overconfidence in the correct detection of phishing has a negative relationship with effective correct detection of phishing (Hong et al., 2013; Wang et al., 2016).

EMPIRICAL STUDIES

The increasing frequency and prominence of phishing attacks have promoted the study of factors that can predict phishing susceptibility (Williams et al., 2017). This section is subdivided into 'individual factors' and 'contextual factors', where studies and results of predictors of phishing susceptibility will be presented.

Individual Factors

Gender, age, education, and technology competencies

Gender and age are two individual factors that have been extensively studied to understand their influence on phishing susceptibility. However, both factors have demonstrated mixed results when explored for their influence on the phenomenon.

Concerning the relationship between gender and phishing susceptibility, some authors found gender differences (Sheng et al., 2010; Hong et al., 2013; Abroshan et al., 2021), while others have not (Canfield et al., 2016; Sarno et al., 2017; Gopavaram et al., 2021). Sheng and colleagues (2010) in order to explore the relationship between sociodemographic variables and phishing susceptibility, using a sample of 1001 participants, concluded that women are more susceptible than men because they fail more in phishing email detection. This conclusion is supported by another study involving 53 university students, where women presented a lower likelihood of correctly identifying phishing attempts compared to men (Hong et al., 2013). More recently, Abroshan and colleagues (2021), in a study with 135 university students, researchers, and graduates found that gender predicts clicking on links in phishing emails. Specifically, their results suggest that women are more susceptible to phishing than men. Nonetheless, the majority of studies assert that gender is not a predictor of phishing susceptibility, regardless of the methodology approach employed. For example, Albladi and Weir (2018), in an experimental study that included 43 security experts, found no differences between the responses of women and men. In Florida, Sarno and colleagues (2017) had already found the same evidence when developed a study in which the sample was composed of 101 university students. Moreover, one Australian study (Parsons et al., 2019) and a transnational study (Gopavaram et al., 2021) have long proven that gender does not influence phishing susceptibility. Other noteworthy evidence comes from Tjosthein and Waterworth (2020), who discovered in a comprehensive sample of nearly 3000 participants that men are more susceptible to phishing than women.

Accordingly, the relationship between age and phishing susceptibility has yielded mixed results as well. While some studies argue that age is not a predictor of phishing susceptibility (e.g., Flores et al., 2015; Sun et al., 2016; Moody et al., 2017; Sarno et al., 2017), others have found age to be a significant factor (Darwish et al., 2013). Recent studies, such as from Goparavam and colleagues (2021), found a negative relation between age and phishing susceptibility. In other words, older individuals fail more in phishing email detection than younger ones, but they also fail more in legitimate email identification. Moreover, evidence suggests that older individuals exhibit higher susceptibility to phishing and lower awareness (Lin et al., 2019). In turn, O'Connor and colleagues (2021) through a sample of Ontario (Canada) support that older individuals are more prone to be victims of fraudulent attempts, including phishing, than younger ones. One possible explanation could be that advancing age leads to a maladaptive shift in the overall perception of security (Grilli et al., 2021). Effectively, in a study developed with 65 individuals aged 50 or more, without cognitive problems, it was found that age was related to considerable difficulty distinguishing between phishing and legitimate emails, while not being associated with a general perception of emails as secure. This lack of security perception contributed to their susceptibility to phishing victimization.

However, studies like Sheng and colleagues' research (2010) argue that individuals aged 18 to 25 are more susceptible to phishing victimization than other age groups. This result supports previous evidence from Kumaraguru and colleagues' study (2009), which revealed that 62.6% of individuals aged

18 to 25 fell into phishing attacks and 41.1% aged 26 or more fell into the same attacks. The adoption of risky behavior by younger individuals could explain to their increased susceptibility to phishing (Hassandoust et al., 2020). In addition, another study from the United States suggests that older individuals tend to possess greater knowledge of phishing and, then, exhibit lower susceptibility to the phenomenon (Gavett et al., 2017).

Besides, some authors seek to understand how phishing susceptibility is influenced by the integration of age and gender variables. The evidence has shown that older women report higher phishing susceptibility since women present lower knowledge and lower computer and Internet experience than men (Lin et al., 2019). This demonstrates that computer knowledge allows to individuals identify correctly phishing emails (Gopavaram et al., 2021). Education appears to be a crucial factor in this domain (Jakobsson & Menczer, 2007; Albladi et al., 2018), with some researchers advocating it as the best way to shield individuals from phishing attempts (Wright & Marett, 2010; Miyamoto et al., 2014; Ghanzi-Therani & Pontell, 2021). Research has revealed a negative relationship between education and phishing susceptibility, suggesting that more educated tend to be less susceptible to phishing (Moody et al., 2017). Additionally, a negative association between increased Internet use and phishing susceptibility has been identified, which can be attributed to an individual's willingness to click on links in emails (*idem*).

Perceived consequences and trust

Phishing is one of the fastest-growing cybercrimes, causing various forms of damage, namely financial damage and information-related consequences (CNCS, 2022b; CNCS, 2022a).

Concerning damage caused by phishing, identity theft stands out as the most frequently identified consequence within the scientific community (Abad, 2005; Brody et al., 2007; Butler, 2007). Furthermore, it is consensual to victims that identity theft is one consequence of a successful phishing attack (Tembe et al., 2013), being personal information, several times, compromised (Butler & Butler, 2018). And when their personal information is stolen other consequences, such as purchases with their bank cards exist (Butler, 2007). Money loss is an outcome of phishing victimization (Hardee et al., 2006; Butler, 2007; Tembe et al., 2013), as well as time loss to solve the problem (Dhamija & Tygar, 2005; Hardee et al., 2006; Butler, 2007). In addition to these negative outcomes stemming from phishing victimization, individuals may experience a decline in their trust in utilizing the Internet (Dhamija & Tygar, 2005; Butler, 2007; Tembe et al., 2013), feelings of humiliation (Butler, 2007), shame and decreased of self-esteem (Tembe et al., 2013), stress (Dhamija & Tygar, 2005; Butler, 2007), frustration and anger (Butler, 2007). Among these consequences, the loss of personal information or services tends to be of higher concern among individuals (Hardee et al., 2006).

In response to these concerns, efforts to identify phishing attempts are influenced by a perceived threat (Arachchilage & Love, 2013). The scientific community argues that a high perceived threat leads individuals to search for information about phishing and adopt better protective measures (Williams & Joinson, 2020). Effectively, the perception of emails as potential phishing attempts; a high perception of severity is associated with lower susceptibility to phishing (Canfield et al., 2016). In this sense, the concept of trust has been defined by several authors (e.g., Blomqvist, 1997; Das & Teng, 2004) in different ways, depending on the scope of the study (Thielmann & Hilbig, 2015). A widely agreed-upon definition of trust originates from Mayer and colleagues (1995), who define trust as the willingness of an individual to rely on another, based on a degree of risk and uncertainty, due to the lack of control by the thrusting party. Moreover, those who trust believe that the other party will act in a way that respects mutual interests. Thus, those who trust accept their vulnerability in the probability of being betrayed (Thielmann & Hillbig, 2015).

In phishing studies, two types of trust are distinguished: prospective trust – the belief in one's ability to accurately perform a task – and retrospective trust – the degree to which individuals believe they mastered what is asked of them (Busey et al., 2000). Among these, retrospective trust is the most used in studies of phishing (Wang et al., 2016).

Researches have shown that individuals' overconfidence in the correct detection of phishing has a negative relationship with effective correct detection of phishing (Hong et al., 2013; Wang et al., 2016). Moreover, when individuals believe that are not susceptible to phishing, but also, they have lower confidence in themselves and consider that phishing is a cyberattack with severe consequences the probability of identifying correctly phishing decreases (Perrault, 2017). Therefore, there has been an incompatibility between the degree of confidence and the accuracy of phishing identification (Dhamija et al., 2006). Furthermore, it should be noted that trust in the cyber community is pointed out by Albladi and colleagues (2018) as a construct that can lead to misperceptions of the judgment of phishing emails and thus increase susceptibility to phishing.

Trust also plays a crucial role in recognizing the consequences of phishing. Greater mistrust leads individuals to consider emails less frequently as legitimate, as they also realize the severity of phishing consequences (Canfield et al., 2016). Therefore, individuals make efforts to accurately detect phishing attempts, depending on the perceived threat that leads individuals to adopt protective behaviors. In turn, perceived threat depends on individuals' perceptions of both the severity of the threat and their susceptibility to susceptibility (Arachchilage & Love, 2013). It is argued that a greater perception of the severity of the threat will lead to the search for information about the phenomenon, and the search for an effective response (Williams & Joinson, 2020). This supports the positive relationship between awareness of the severity of phishing and the adoption of protective measures (Hassandoust et al., 2020).

Previous Experience of Phishing Victimization

Studies focusing on the influence of previous phishing victimization on phishing susceptibility are relatively scarce. Besides that, when previous phishing victimization is studied two perspectives exist: some authors focus on specific instance of victimization, while others focus on known phishing susceptibility across different situations. In the latter scenario, it is argued that victims learn from previous victimization experiences, thereby reducing their phishing susceptibility (Chen et al., 2020).

Although previous experience of victimization assumes essential importance in decreasing phishing susceptibility (Chen et al., 2020), it is argued in a minority of studies that this is not always the case. For example, Hong and colleagues (2013) verified that 89% of their study's sample had encountered at least one phishing attack, and 92% of these victims were susceptible to phishing. Thus, the success in previous detection can lead to an indirect increase in phishing susceptibility (Chen et al., 2020). In a sample of 53 university students from North Carolina found, it was found that when a monetary loss derives from an email response, without a total refund amount, individuals tend to adopt more cautions behavior in the future (Welk et al., 2015). In 2006, Downs and colleagues, through roleplay with 20 participants, observed that previous knowledge of phishing emails was determinant of not being a victim. Therefore, previous experience of phishing victimization serve as an enabler for the adoption of security behaviors (Hassandoust et al., 2020), enabling individuals to accurately identify phishing attempts (Wang et al., 2012; O'Connor et al., 2021).

Contextual Factors

Construction and Load of Emails

A phishing attack can succeed due to human factor, but various other factors also enhance the probability of a successful attack.

A set of principles comes into play when a phisher constructs illegitimate emails to make individuals perceived them as legitimate and provide their personal information. Based on Cialdini's assumptions (2007), Lin and colleagues (2019) list six principles: (1) authority – the sender's email looks like a credible entity (e.g., police, teacher, doctor, lawyer); (2) commitment – if an individual has previously taken a stance, like supporting animal rights, they may click in an email soliciting their collaboration; (3) liking – the receipt of an email with a product or service that individual normally share and like will increase the success of phishing attack; (4) reciprocation – usually, when a document is attached on the email the human tendency is opening that, and when it is opened malware is installed; (5) scarcity – normally occur through a message/email to inform that product or service is scarce which create pressure to do one specific action (e.g., click on the link in the email to book); and (6) social proof – individuals tend to avoid mistakes and act according what society is doing, so an phishing attempt can be well succeed when an email announce that is providing an unique opportunity to get one service that only the top 10 of companies have. Additionally, the author introduces a seventh principle – perceptual contrast – which refers to "the way people perceive the relative difference between two things that are present in tandem." (Lin et al., 2019, p. 6).

Studies have shown that when individuals have a relationship with the email's topic increases the probability of opening links within emails (Zielinska et al., 2016: Hassandoust et al., 2020). Familiarity with the email's source (e.g., Bank employee) can give a sense of security and lead individuals to respond, even when facing a phishing email (Harrison et al., 2015; Chen et al., 2020). Specifically, topics related to authority and legal issues increase phishing susceptibility (Lin et al., 2019), as well as the presence of urgency and threat elements (Vishwanath et al., 2011). Furthermore, when email represents the possibility of losing something individuals tend to click on links (Williams & Pollage, 2019).

McAlaney and Hills (2020) explore how individuals process and judge phishing emails, based on a set of common elements, and create four types of phishing emails: threatening, financial, urgent, and misspelling. The authors found that misspelling emails are less judged as confinable than financial and urgent emails. Thus, the latter types increase phishing susceptibility (*idem*).

In addition, other email-related factors can influence susceptibility to phishing, such as email overload – the volume of received and sent emails on a daily or weekly basis. Higher email loads correlate with a reduced ability to correctly identify phishing attempts (Sarno & Neider, 2021), meaning individuals who send more emails and read more files are less likely to classify emails as illegitimate (Sarno et al., 2017).

Cues in Emails

Email is a commonly exploited medium for launching phishing attacks, where offenders craft messages that appear legitimate, tricking individuals into revealing their personal information. In this sense, the identification of cues in phishing emails becomes crucial in avoiding victimization (Nasser et al., 2020).

Some studies have searched for the cues that allow individuals to accurately identify phishing emails. Jakobsson (2007) highlighted grammar, spelling, and email design as the primary cues that individuals use for identification, followed by scrutiny of hyperlinks and sender email addresses. Moreover, emails containing legal issues or information concerning copyrights are swiftly recognized as phishing attempts. Also, emails that include grammatical or spelling errors are more likely to be categorized as phishing rather than legitimate, as individuals associate legitimate emails with familiar senders and more hyperlinks (Parsons et al., 2016). However, this can lead individuals to adopt wrong behaviors, processing fewer cues in emails such as security indicators and the real sender's email (Dhamija et al., 2006).

Another important cue to individuals identifying correctly (or not) emails is the personalization of email (Egelman et al., 2008; Parson et al., 2013). Specifically, when emails present personification or when the sender's email is perceived as original, individuals become more confident in interacting with them (Parsons et al., 2013). Familiarity with the sending entity, as previously mentioned in the construction of phishing emails by phishers, is another cue that captures individuals' attention. Usually, when this cue is present, individuals identify emails as legitimate (Williams et al., 2018). On the other hand, the presence of urgency cues diminishes the probability of correct management of emails (Parsons et al., 2016). Additionally, an innovative cybersecurity study utilizing Eye Tracker technology revealed that urgency and threat cues received more attention than financial cues (McAlaney & Hills, 2020).

Thus, the knowledge and the correct identification of these cues play a vital role in preventing phishing victimization, underscoring the importance of education to empower individuals against such attacks.

Methods to approach phishing susceptibility

To measure the extent and determinants of phishing susceptibility, understood as the detection failure of phishing attempts, several methods can be employed. Traditional methods, such as surveys, ask individuals if they usually answer phishing campaigns or if they have ever been victimized by phishing attacks. The retrospective character of these measures, adding issues such as social desirability or difficulties in the interpretation of the questions, led researchers to use complementary methods to understand why and how individuals fail to distinguish between legitimate and illegitimate emails or webpages.

Recently, innovative approaches have been used to better understand not only the prevalence of phishing susceptibility but also the mechanisms behind a successful phishing attack. One of these innovative approaches is the eye-tracking methodology, allowing us to explore, for instance, what are the specific cues of the e-mails or phishing websites that usually base the decision of answering these attacks.

Eye-tracking is intended to measure an individual's eye movements, thus informing the researcher what where are individuals looking at, which is generally called the *point of regard* (McAlaney & Hills, 2020). One of the most popular forms of eye-tracking techniques is the one that uses "video captured by optical devices (a camera) recording infrared light that illuminates the eyes and provides reference points for the eye-tracker" (Xiong et al., 2017, p. 642). This method can be considered non-intrusive because i) it is mounted remotely from the user and ii) does not require wearing any special device.

The eye-tracker can be used in real or controlled environments (such as a laboratory) in response to a stimulus, making it possible to achieve what are the areas of the environment where individuals fix their attention (Barreto, 2012; Bergstrom & Schall, 2014). In addition to this volume of fixations, the eye-tracker also allows obtaining measures such as the duration of fixations and in what order they are visually explored. These measures, in turn, allow us to understand the selective attention attributed to the stimulus, because it is understood that the direction of the look will reflect the orientation of attention (Hoffman & Subramanian, 1995).

As a tool of research, eye-tracker has been used in several fields such as marketing, psychology, product design and, more recently, criminology. Nevertheless, specifically to phishing susceptibility, with a few exceptions, studies that explore visual attention to phishing cues are scarce. Taking into consideration that eye-tracker provides a more direct source of data than other methods to explore decisions when responding to or judging phishing attacks, more research is needed using this technique. For instance, eye-tracker would allow us to understand how the common elements of phishing emails, such as the use of urgency, threatening language or misspellings influence how the email is processed by individuals (McAlaney & Hills, 2020). In the next lines, an overview of relevant studies will be made.

Pfeffel and colleagues (2019) used an eye-tracker to understand how users distinguished phishing emails from real ones. Moreover, it attempted to find out which features were used by individuals for making the decision process concerning the reality of the email. Using a sample of 22 subjects who had to analyze 21 emails, the authors found that subjects mainly looked at the body and the header of an email when stimuli were presented. Moreover, they found that the two most important factors that helped recognize phishing emails were knowledge about phishing emails and the processing time.

Important was also the research undertaken by McAlaney and Hills (2020) which used 32 emails that either did or did not include a phishing indicator. A sample of 22 subjects was shown the emails in a random order and the eye-tracker measured, among others, the total dwell time, mean fixation count and the number of regressions. Results suggested that participants looked more frequently at the elements related to phishing than would be expected by chance, but spent less time viewing these elements than would be expected by chance. Furthermore, it was found that phishing indicators relating to threatening language or urgency were viewed before misspellings.

A few years before, Miyamoto and colleagues (2014) built a pioneering study using an eye-tracker applied to phishing, showing that individuals with greater technical skills analyzed specific areas of the email that allowed them to correctly detect (e.g. website URL). Additionally, in 2015, Miyamoto et al., found that, although individuals justified the decision process based on the URL, when indicating whether or not a certain email was phishing, through heatmaps it was possible to observe that no one had intentionally looked at that feature. Moreover, the authors conclude that with a probability of 79.3%, it was possible to estimate the victimization of phishing attacks by analyzing their visual patterns. However, it is important to point out that individuals' behavior is conditional and the detection is imperfect, since they may know how to identify emails, but do not know when to do so (Canfield et al., 2016).

Other researchers have suggested that the time spent analyzing emails is a crucial aspect, because individuals who take longer in this process are less likely to click on the links (Canfield et al., 2016) and are more capable of identifying emails (Bayl-Smith, Sturman & Wiggins, 2020).

Even though the eye-tracker is a promising method for understanding phishing susceptibility, some limitations should be addressed. For instance, because most of the studies using eye-tracker to study phishing susceptibility take place in laboratory contexts, usually the samples are small and tend to rely on university populations (e.g., Pfeffel et al., 2019), which compromises the external validity. Moreover, due to the small sample size and consequently the lack of variability, it is difficult to understand how individual variables might interplay with phishing susceptibility.

Another limitation is concerned with the relationship between attention and the point of gaze. As Fotios (2015, p.135) points out, "fixations do not necessarily indicate attention is being directed towards the fixated object, or that the fixated object is important to the task". Therefore, precautions are needed when analyzing the data and studies should rely on mixed-methods approaches to deeply explore how stimuli is processed and judged.

CONCLUSION

Phishing is a form of social engineering where cybercriminals exploit the Internet to obtain sensitive information from individuals, such as usernames and passwords, by using fraudulent methods. This is often accomplished by impersonating legitimate websites. It is a rapidly growing phenomenon that continually evolves in its attack techniques and strategies. As discussed in this chapter, phishing attacks generally follow different phases (e.g., preparation, execution, and exploitation of results). As a result, multiple victims can answer to these phishing scams, leading to several damages.

Understanding phishing susceptibility has become a critical focus of research, with numerous studies aiming to uncover the factors that increase the likelihood of failing the detection of phishing attacks (through email, for instance).

This chapter also highlights the potential of eye-tracking technology as a promising and viable method to shed light on phishing susceptibility. By revealing how individuals visually process and assess phishing emails, eye-tracking can help identify elements that receive greater attention during the evaluation process. This, in turn, can contribute to the development of more informed strategies to mitigate phishing susceptibility. Nevertheless, it is important to note that innovative methods such as eye-tracker also come with their own set of limitations, underscoring the need for adopting mixed-methodologies approaches to comprehensively address the multifaceted phenomenon of phishing.

REFERENCES

Abad, C. (2005). The economy of phishing.

Abroshan, H., Devos, J., Poels, G., & Laermans, E. (2021). Phishing Happens Beyond Technology: The Effects of Human Behaviors and Demographics on Each Step of a *Phishing* Process. *IEEE Access : Practical Innovations, Open Solutions*, *9*, 44928–44949.

Alabdan, R. (2020). *Phishing* Attacks Survey: Types, Vectors, and Technical Approaches. *Future Internet*, *12*(10), 1–39. doi:10.3390/fi12100168

Albladi, S. M., & Weir, G. R. S. (2018). User characteristics that influence judgment of social engineering attacks in social networks. *Human-centric Computing and Information Sciences*, *8*(5), 1–24. doi:10.118613673-018-0128-7

Aleroud, A., & Zhou, L. (2017). Phishing environments, techniques, and countermeasures: A survey. *Computers & Security*, *68*, 160–196.

Arachchilage, N. A. G., & Love, S. (2013). A game design framework for avoiding Phishing attacks. *Computers in Human Behavior*, *29*(3), 706–714. doi:10.1016/j.chb.2012.12.018

Barraclough, P. A., Fehringer, G., & Woodward, J. (2021). Intelligent cyber-Phishing detection for online. *Computers & Security*, *104*, 1–17. doi:10.1016/j.cose.2020.102123

Blomqvist, K. (1997). The many faces of trust. *Scandinavian Journal of Management*, *13*(3), 271–286.

Brody, R. G., Mulig, E., & Kimball, V. (2007). PHISHING, PHARMING AND IDENTITY THEFT. Academy of Accounting & Financial Studies Journal, 11(3).

Busey, T. A., Tunnicliff, J., Loftus, G. R., & Loftus, E. F. (2000). Accounts of the confidence-accuracy relation in recognition memory. *Psychonomic Bulletin & Review*, *7*(1), 26–48. doi:10.3758/BF03210724

Butler, R. (2007). A framework of anti-phishing measures aimed at protecting the online consumer's identity. *The Electronic Library*.

Butler, R., & Butler, M. (2018). *Assessing the information quality of phishing-related content on financial institutions' websites*. Information & Computer Security.

Canfield, C. I., Fischhoff, B., & Davis, A. (2016). Quantifying Phishing Susceptibility for Detection and Behavior Decisions. *Human Factors*, *58*(8), 1158–1172. doi:10.1177/0018720816665025

Centro Nacional de Cibersegurança. (2022a). Relatório Cibersegurança em Portugal – Economia – maio de 2022. Avaliable at https://www.cncs.gov.pt/docs/relatorio-economia2022-obciber-cncs.pdf

Centro Nacional de Cibersegurança. (2022b). Relatório de Cibersegurança em Portugal: Riscos e Conflitos. Avaliable at https://www.cncs.gov.pt/docs/relatorio-riscosconflitos2022-obciber-cncs.pdf

Chaiken, S. (1980). Heuristic versus systematic information processing and the use of source versus message cues in persuasion. *Journal of Personality and Social Psychology*, *39*(5), 752.

Chaiken, S. (1987). The heuristic model of persuasion. *Hillsdale, NJ: Lawrence Erlbaum*. Symposium conducted at the meeting of the Social influence: the Ontario symposium. *5* (3-39).

Chen, R., Gaia, J., & Rao, H. R. (2020). An examination of the effect of recent Phishing encounters on *Phishing* susceptibility. *Decision Support Systems*, *133*, 1–14. doi:10.1016/j.dss.2020.113287

Chen, S., & Chaiken, S. (1999). The heuristic-systematic model in its broader context. In S. Chaiken & Y. Trope (Eds.), *Dual-process Theories in Social and Cognitive Psychology* (pp. 73–96). Guilford.

Cohen, L. E., & Felson, M. (1979). Social change and crime rate trends: A routine activity approach. *American Sociological Review*, 588–608.

Darwish, A., El Zarka, A., & Aloul, F. (2013). Towards understanding Phishing victims' profile. In *2012 International Conference on Computer Systems and Industrial Informatics* (pp. 1-5). IEEE.

Das, T. K., & Teng, B. S. (2004). The risk-based view of trust: A conceptual framework. *journal of Business and Psychology*, *19*, 85-116.

Dhamija, R., & Tygar, J. D. (2005, July). The battle against phishing: Dynamic security skins. In *Proceedings of the 2005 symposium on Usable privacy and security* (pp. 77-88).

Dhamija, R., Tygar, J. D., & Hearst, M. (2006, April). Why Phishing works. In *Proceedings of the SIGCHI conference on Human Factors in computing systems* (pp. 581-590).

Downs, J. S., Holbrook, M. B., & Cranor, L. F. (2006). Decision strategies and susceptibility to Phishing. In *Proceedings of the second symposium on Usable privacy and security* (pp. 79-90).

Downs, J. S., Holbrook, M., & Cranor, L. F. (2007). Behavioral response to Phishing risk. In *Proceedings of the anti-Phishing working groups 2nd annual eCrime researchers summit* (pp. 37-44).

Egelman, S., Cranor, L. F., & Hong, J. (2008, April). You've been warned: an empirical study of the effectiveness of web browser phishing warnings. *In Proceedings of the SIGCHI Conference on Human Factors in Computing Systems* (pp. 1065-1074).

Flores, W. R., Holm, H., Nohlberg, M., & Ekstedt, M. (2015). Investigating personal determinants of Phishing and the effect of national culture. *Information & Computer Security*, *23*(2), 178–199.

Fotios, S., Uttley, J., Cheal, C., & Hara, N. (2015). Using eye-tracking to identify pedestrians' critical visual tasks, Part 1. Dual task approach. *Lighting Research & Technology*, *47*, 133–1.

Gavett, B. E., Zhao, R., John, S. E., Bussell, C. A., Roberts, J. R., & Yue, C. (2017). Phishing suspiciousness in older and younger adults: The role of executive functioning. *PLoS One*, *12*(2), e0171620.

Ghazi-Tehrani, A. K., & Pontell, H. N. (2021). Phishing Evolves: Analyzing the Enduring Cybercrime. *Victims & Offenders*, *16*(3), 316–342. doi:10.1080/15564886.2020.1829224

Gopavaram, S., Dev, J., Grobler, M., Kim, D., Das, S., & Camp, L. J. Cross-National Study on *Phishing* Resilience. *2021 Workshop on Usable Security and Privacy (USEC), 1-11.*

Graham, R., & Triplett, R. (2017). Capable guardians in the digital environment: The role of digital literacy in reducing phishing victimization. *Deviant Behavior*, *38*(12), 1371–1382.

Grilli, M. D., McVeigh, K. S., Hakim, Z. M., Wank, A. A., Getz, S. J., Levin, B. E., ... Wilson, R. C. (2021). Is this phishing? Older age is associated with greater difficulty discriminating between safe and malicious emails. *The Journals of Gerontology: Series B*, *76*(9), 1711–1715.

Hardee, J. B., West, R., & Mayhorn, C. B. (2006). To download or not to download: an examination of computer security decision making. *interactions, 13*(3), 32-37.

Harrison, B., Vishwanath, A., Ng, Y. J., & Rao, R. (2015). Examining the impact of presence on individual Phishing victimization. *IEEE 48th Hawaii International Conference on System Sciences.* 3483-3489. Doi: 10.1109/HICSS.2015.419

Hassandoust, F., Singh, H., & Williams, J. (2020). The Role of Contextualization in Individuals' Vulnerability to Phishing Attempts. *AJIS. Australasian Journal of Information Systems*, *24*, 1–32.

Hong, J. (2012). The state of phishing attacks. *Communications of the ACM*, *55*(1), 74–81. doi:10.1145/2063176.2063197

Hong, K. W., Kelley, C. M., Tembe, R., Murphy-Hill, E., & Mayhorn, C. B. (2013). Keeping up with the Joneses: Assessing Phishing susceptibility in an email task. *Proceedings of the Human Factors and Ergonomics Society Annual Meeting*, *57*(1), 1012–1016.

Jakobsson, M., & Menczer, F. (2007). Social Phishing. *Communications of the ACM*, 1–10. doi:10.114 5/1290958.1290958.1290968

Jakobsson, M. (2007). The human factor in phishing. *Privacy & Security of Consumer Information*, *7*(1), 1–19.

Jakobsson, M., & Myers, S. (Eds.). (2006). *Phishing and countermeasures: understanding the increasing problem of electronic identity theft.* John Wiley & Sons.

Khonji, M., Iraqi, Y., & Jones, A. (2013). Phishing Detection: A Literature Survey. *IEEE Communications Surveys and Tutorials*, *15*(4). Advance online publication. doi:10.1109/SURV.2013.032213.00009

Kigerl, A. (2021). Routine activity theory and malware, fraud, and spam at the national level. *Crime, Law, and Social Change*, *76*(2), 109–130.

Kumaraguru, P., Rhee, Y., Acquisti, A., Cranor, L. F., Hong, J., & Nunge, E. (2007, April). Protecting people from phishing: the design and evaluation of an embedded training email system. In *Proceedings of the SIGCHI conference on Human factors in computing systems* (pp. 905-914).

Kumaraguru, P., Sheng, S., Acquisti, A., Cranor, L. F., & Hong, J. (2010). Teaching Johnny not to fall for phish. *ACM Transactions on Internet Technology*, *10*(2), 1–31.

Kumaraguru, P., Sheng, S., Acquisti, A., Cranor, L. F., & Hong, J. (2009). Teaching Johnny Not to Fall for Phish. *ACM Transactions on Internet Technology*, *5*, 1–30.

Lastdrager, E. E. (2014). Achieving a consensual definition of phishing based on a systematic review of the literature. *Crime Science*, *3*(1), 1–10.

Leukfeldt, E. R. (2014). Phishing for suitable targets in the Netherlands: Routine activity theory and phishing victimization. *Cyberpsychology, Behavior, and Social Networking*, *17*(8), 551–555.

Leukfeldt, E. R. (2015). Comparing victims of phishing and malware attacks: Unraveling risk factors and possibilities for situational crime prevention. *arXiv preprint arXiv:1506.00769*.

Leukfeldt, E. R., & Yar, M. (2016). Applying routine activity theory to cybercrime: A theoretical and empirical analysis. *Deviant Behavior*, *37*(3), 263–280. doi:10.1080/01639625.2015.1012409

Lin, T., Capecci, D. E., Ellis, D. M., Rocha, H. A., Dommaraju, S., Oliveira, D. S., & Ebner, N. C. (2019). Susceptibility to spear-*Phishing* emails: Effects of internet user demographics and email content. [TOCHI]. *ACM Transactions on Computer-Human Interaction*, *26*(5), 1–28. doi:10.1145/3336141

Lyons, J. B., Stokes, C. K., Eschleman, K. J., Alarcon, G. M., & Barelka, A. J. (2011). Trustworthiness and IT suspicion: An evaluation of the nomological network. *Human Factors*, *53*(3), 219–229. doi:10.1177/0018720811406726

Miyamoto, D., Iimura, T., Blanc, G., Tazaki, H., & Kadobayashi, Y. (2014). EyeBit: Eye-Tracking Approach for Enforcing *Phishing* Prevention Habits. *Third International Workshop on Building Analysis Datasets and Gathering Experience Returns for Security* (BADGERS). Doi: 10.1109/BADGERS.2014.14

Moody, G. D., Galletta, D. F., & Dunn, K. (2017). Which phish get caught? An explanatory study of individuals' susceptibility to *Phishing*. *European Journal of Information Systems*, *26*(6), 564–584. doi:10.105741303-017-0058-x

Nasser, G., Morrison, B. W., Bayl-Smith, P., Taib, R., Gayed, M., & Wiggins, M. W. (2020). The role of cue utilization and cognitive load in the recognition of phishing emails. *Frontiers in big data*, *3*, 546860.

Neves, R. A. C. (2022). Vitimação por phishing: um estudo empírico.

O'Connor, A. M., Judges, R. A., Lee, K., & Evans, A. D. (2021). Can adults discriminate between fraudulent and legitimate e-mails? Examining the role of age and prior fraud experience. *Journal of Elder Abuse & Neglect*, 1–25. doi:10.1080/08946566.2021.1934767

Parmar, B. (2012). Protecting against spear-*Phishing*. *Computer Fraud & Security*, (1), 8–11. doi:10.1016/S1361-3723(12)70007-6

Parsons, K., Butavicius, M., Delfabbro, P., & Lillie, M. (2019). Predicting susceptibility to social influence in Phishing emails. *International Journal of Human-Computer Studies*, *128*, 17–26.

Parsons, K., Butavicius, M., Pattinson, M., Calic, D., Mccormac, A., & Jerram, C. (2016). Do users focus on the correct cues to differentiate between phishing and genuine emails? *arXiv preprint arXiv:1605.04717*.

Parsons, K., McCormac, A., Pattinson, M., Butavicius, M., & Jerram, C. (2013, July). Phishing for the truth: A scenario-based experiment of users' behavioural response to emails. In *IFIP international information security conference* (pp. 366–378). Springer.

Perrault, E. K. (2017). Using an Interative Online Quiz to Recalibre College Students' Attitudes and Behavioral Intentions About *Phishing*. *Journal of Education Computing*, *0*(0), 1–14. doi:10.1177/0735633117699232

Salloum, S., Gaber, T., Vadera, S., & Shaalan, K. (2021). Phishing email detection using natural language processing techniques: A literature survey. *Procedia Computer Science*, *189*, 19–28.

Sarno, D. M., & Neider, M. B. (2021). So Many Phish, So Little Time: Exploring E-mail Task Factors and Phishing Susceptibility. *Human Factors*, *00*(0), 1–25. doi:10.1177/0018720821999174

Sarno, D. M., Lewis, J. E., Bohil, C. J., Shoss, M. K., & Neider, M. B. (2017). Who are Phishers luring?: A Demographic Analysis of Those Susceptible to Fake Emails. *Proceedings of the Human Factors and Ergonomics Society Annual Meeting*, *61*(1), 1735–1739. doi:10.1177/1541931213601915

Sheng, S., Holbrook, M., Kumaraguru, P., Cranor, L., & Downs, J. (2010). Who Falls for Phish? A Demographic Analysis of Phishing Susceptibility and Effectiveness of Interventions, *Proceedings of the 28th International Conference on Human Factors in Computing Systems*, CHI 2010, Atlanta, Georgia, USA. doi: 10.1145/1753326.1753326.1753383

Sun, J. C. Y., Yu, S. J., Lin, S. S., & Tseng, S. S. (2016). The mediating effect of anti-phishing self-efficacy between college students' internet self-efficacy and anti-phishing behavior and gender difference. *Computers in Human Behavior*, *59*, 249–257.

Tembe, R., Hong, K. W., Murphy-Hill, E., Mayhorn, C. B., & Kelley, C. M. (2013, June). American and Indian conceptualizations of phishing. In *2013 Third Workshop on Socio-Technical Aspects in Security and Trust* (pp. 37-45). IEEE.

Thielmann, I., & Hilbig, B. E. (2015). Trust: An integrative review from a person–situation perspective. *Review of General Psychology*, *19*(3), 249–277.

Tjostheim, I., & Waterworth, J. A. (2020). Predicting personal susceptibility to phishing. In *Information Technology and Systems* [Springer International Publishing.]. *Proceedings of ICITS*, *2020*, 564–575.

Verma, R., Shashidhar, N., & Hossain, N. (2012). Detecting phishing emails the natural language way. In *Computer Security–ESORICS 2012: 17th European Symposium on Research in Computer Security, Pisa, Italy, September 10-12, 2012.* [Springer Berlin Heidelberg.]. *Proceedings, 17,* 824–841.

Vishwanath, A., Harrison, B., & Ng, Y. J. (2018). Suspicion, Cognition, and Automaticity Model of Phishing Susceptibility. *Communication Research, 45*(8), 1146–1166. doi:10.1177/0093650215627483

Vishwanath, A., Herath, T., Chen, R., Wang, J., & Rao, H. R. (2011). Why do people get phished? Testing individual differences in Phishing vulnerability within an integrated, information processing model. *Decision Support Systems, 51,* 576–586. doi:10.1016/j.dss2011.03.002

Wang, J., Li, Y., & Rao, H. R. (2016). Overconfidence in Phishing email detection. *Journal of the Association for Information Systems, 17*(11), 759–783.

Wang, J., Li, Y., & Rao, H. R. (2016). Overconfidence in Phishing e-mail detection. *Journal of the Association for Information Systems, 17*(11), 759–783.

Welk, A. K., Hong, K. W., Zielinska, O. A., Tembe, R., Murphy-Hill, E., & Mayhorn, C. B. (2015). Will the "Phisher-Men" Reel You In?: Assessing individual differences in a Phishing detection task. [IJCBPL]. *International Journal of Cyber Behavior, Psychology and Learning, 5*(4), 1–17. doi:10.4018/IJCBPL.2015100101

Wetzel, R. (2005). Tackling phishing. *Business Communications Review, 35*(2), 46–49.

Whittaker, C., Ryner, B., & Nazif, M. (2010). Large-scale automatic classification of phishing pages. Conference: Proceedings of the Network and Distributed System Security Symposium, NDSS 2010, San Diego, California, USA.

Williams, E. J., & Polage, D. (2019). How persuasive is Phishing e-mail? The role of authentic design, influence and current events in e-mail judgement. *Behaviour & Information Technology, 38*(2), 184–197. doi:10.1080/0144929X.2018.1519599

Williams, E. J., Beardmore, A., & Joinson, A. N. (2017). Individual differences in susceptibility to online influence: A theoretical review. *Computers in Human Behavior,* 412–421. doi:10.1016/j.chb.2017.03.002

Williams, E. J., Hinds, J., & Joinson, A. N. (2018). Exploring susceptibility to phishing in the workplace. *International Journal of Human-Computer Studies, 120,* 1–13.

Wright, R. T., & Marett, K. (2010). The Influence of Experiential and Dispositional Factors in *Phishing*: An Empirical Investigation of the Deceived. *Journal of Management Information Systems, 27*(1), 273–303. doi:10.2753/MIS0742-1222270111

Yar, M. (2005). The Novelty of 'Cybercrime' An Assessment in Light of Routine Activity Theory. *European Journal of Criminology, 2*(4), 407-427. doi: 101177/147737080556056

Yu, W. D., Nargundkar, S., & Tiruthani, N. (2008). A *Phishing* vulnerability analysis of web based systems. *2008 Symposium on Computers and Communications,* 326-331. IEEE.

Zielinska, O. A., Welk, A. K., Mayhorn, C. B., & Murphy-Hill, E. (2016). A temporal analysis of persuasion principles in Phishing e-mails. *Proceedings of the Human Factors and Ergonomics Society Annual Meeting, 60*(1), 765–769.

Chapter 6
Cyberlearn:
An Integrated Framework for Organizational Capability Building

Carlos Páscoa
Portuguese Air Force, Portugal

José Tribolet
https://orcid.org/0000-0003-1903-4561
Instituto Superior Técnico, Portugal

Miguel Correia
Instituto Superior Técnico, Portugal

ABSTRACT

Cybersecurity is growing in importance, with recent cyberattacks showing an exceptional level of impact in organizations. This chapter presents a cybersecurity capability building proposal for organizations that the authors designate cybersecurity learning framework (CyberLearn). The chapter discusses cybersec initiatives in Portugal, in the European Union, in the North Atlantic Treaty Organization, and the United States of America, introducing the NICE framework as a basis to develop the CyberLearn framework and the concept representation considering functions, roles, and work roles and the knowledge units related to each role area. This framework has been applied in Portugal by Técnico to meet business needs on this domain.

DOI: 10.4018/978-1-6684-8422-7.ch006

INTRODUCTION

"Change is the law of life and those who look only to the past or present are certain to miss the future."
– John F. Kennedy

Cybersecurity (cybersec) is growing in importance world-wide with recent cyberattacks showing an exceptional level of impact on private and public organizations. Cybersec concepts like threat, risk, strategy, impact, attack, and vulnerability are among the top interests of governments, public administration, companies, military, and other organizations. Although much has been done in recent years, often in reaction to cyber-attacks, it is still necessary to find a path from the notion of cyber hygiene, a responsibility of every citizen, to the creation of highly specialized personnel in organizations that can detect, deter, and react in a proactive manner to cyber threats. In other words, we need to find a path for cybersec capability building for organizations.

This chapter presents a cybersecurity capability building proposal for organizations that we designate Cybersecurity Learning framework (CyberLearn). This framework aims to establish paths for education and training, from basic cyber hygiene to high specialization. The framework is firstly targeted at organizations, either public or private. However, it can also serve as the foundation for a larger-scale capability building joint venture between government, universities, the military, security institutes and companies, in a similar way to initiatives that have been appearing in the European Union (EU) and the North Atlantic Treaty Organization (NATO). The CyberLearn framework builds on the National Initiative for Cybersecurity Education (NICE) (Newhouse, 2017). The proposed framework also considers the work being developed in Europe in the cyber domain and is based on a set of requirements: i) the universe of education and training candidates includes both military and civilian professionals; ii) the program shall provide students with basic theoretical and practical knowledge in all key areas of cybersec; iii) the program should provide deep conceptual and professional, theoretical, and practical skills in cybersec; iv) the program has to be modular and adaptable to the needs of different organizations.

The *CyberLearn framework* aims to foster individual learning to progress through the following levels: security awareness, cybersec essentials, role-based training, and education and/or experience to develop the ability and vision to perform complex multi-disciplinary tasks. The highest level comprehends personal competencies and skills to counter cyber-attacks and foster comprehensive cybersec activities. The framework is generic, not targeted as a specific organization. In practice, when it is going to be applied to a specific company, it must be adapted in a process of interaction between the education provider and the target organization.

Instituto Superior Técnico (Técnico) is the engineering school of University of Lisbon, the largest in Portugal. Técnico has been deeply involved in cybersec teaching activities, from courses in programs like the master's in computer science and engineering, to full programs like the master's in information security and Cyberspace Law (a master program) or Cybersecurity for Companies (a short program for professionals). We use some of these courses and programs to show how the *CyberLearn framework* can be instantiated in practice.

This chapter is organized as follows. Chapter 2 discusses cybersec initiatives in Portugal, EU, NATO, and the US, as well as NIST's NICE cybersec education initiative. Chapter 3 introduces the NICE framework and the concept representation considering functions, roles and work roles and the knowledge units related to each role area. In Chapter 4, we use the NICE framework as a basis to develop the CyberLearn framework proposal. Chapter 5 concludes.

OBJECTIVES, QUESTIONS AND METHODOLOGY

The objective of the research was to find (or create) a cybersec framework that, with adequate adaptations, would provide a path to educate people through a grooming process that, once adapted, would provide learning content that supports career and knowledge progress.

The research questions are:

- (RQ1) is there a framework that is suited, after adaptation, to the objectives or, in turn, it is necessary to develop a new framework?
- (RQ2) after completing the adaptation or development of the framework is it possible to fill it with meaningful content that will foster cybersec leaning?

The methodology used was Action Research that precludes the involvement of the researchers in the process and activities.

BACKGROUND AND LITERATURE REVIEW

Alberts & Dorofee (2005) state that "advances in technology . . . have enabled people to link work processes together. The end result of connecting several small processes is a larger, more complex process, which includes numerous activities as well as intricate interrelationships and dependencies among those activities". The authors developed a Mission Assurance Analysis Protocol, as an approach targeting "advanced risk analysis techniques for highly complex and distributed work processes".

According to Solms & van Niekerk (2013), "Cybersecurity is the collection of tools, policies, security concepts, security safeguards, guidelines, risk management approaches, actions, training, best practices, assurance and technologies that can be used to protect the cyber environment and organization and user's assets."[1]

The International Telecommunications Union (ITU) developed an overview and a strategy for Cybersecurity (ITU, 2008; 2011).

Cheng et al. (2014) tackle the need to define and use metrics as quantitative characteristics to represent the security state of a network and measure cyber situational awareness from a defender's point of view.

Current knowledge about cybersec acknowledges that is a threat that can make a difference in the nation's interests and that investment should be made to foster specialized agents to defend the nations towards a cybersecurity safe environment. Therefore, having mechanisms to develop these specialized agents is a priority.

Next, we discuss several cybersec initiatives in Portugal, in the EU, in NATO and in the United States of America (USA) with a view on existing learning frameworks and the offers on graduation courses.

Cybersecurity in Portugal

In Portugal, in 2012, the Portuguese National Cybersecurity Centre (PNCSC) was created and placed under the National Security Cabinet (PCM, 2012). The PNCSC has the following mission "to contribute to the free, reliable and secure use of the cyberspace in Portugal, through the continuous improvement of the national cybersecurity and the international cooperation, in coordination with all the competent authorities, and the implementation of measures and instruments required for the anticipation, detection, reaction and recovery of situations that, in the imminence of occurrence of incidents or cyberattacks, may compromise national interests" (PNCSC, 2023).

A few years later, the Resolution of the Council of Ministers (RCM) no. 36/2015 of June 12 (PCM, 2015), adopted the first National Strategy for Cyberspace Security (NSCS)[2]. In 2017, the RCM 115/2017 (PCM, 2017) created the Higher Council for Cyberspace Security (HCCS) with the objective, among others, to propose the revision and elaborate a new PNSCS. The Law no. 46/2018, of 13 August (PP, 2018), established the legal regime for the cyberspace security[3].

The HCCS has the power to verify the implementation of the PNSCS, and must be heard, in PNSCS approval process. Hence, the National Strategy for the CyberSpace Security 2019-2023 (NSCS19-23) (PCM, 2019), aims to be a structuring instrument for the national qualification in this scope, are met, defining the framework, objectives, and guidelines of State action on cyberspace security, in accordance with the national interest.

The NSCS19-23 is based on three strategic objectives: maximizing resilience, promoting innovation, and generating and securing resources, translated into six intervention axes, which form lines of action aimed at strengthening the national strategic potential in cyberspace. It also determines the elaboration within 120 days of a Plan of Action for NSCS19-23.

Portugal has a set of infrastructures and has defined the jurisdictional range of action for cybersec. The PCM (2022) approves the National Strategy for Cyber defense referencing a set of regulations, for example the Strategic Concept of National Defense, and determining that the implementation of the National Strategy for Cyber defense should be monitored by the General Staff of the Armed Forces, in articulation and close cooperation with all relevant entities. forward, in the sense of keeping it permanently current and relevant. The PCM (2022a) Regulates the Legal Framework for Cyberspace Security and sets out the cybersecurity certification obligations[4].

Cybersecurity in the EU

The EU recognizes cybersec as essential to guarantee a normal citizenship. In 2013 the Cybersecurity Strategy of the European Union – An Open, Safe and Secure Cyberspace was approved. The EU vision presented in this strategy is articulated in five strategic priorities (EP, 2013):

- Achieving cyber resilience;
- Drastically reducing cybercrime;
- Developing cyberdefense policy and capabilities related to the Common Security and Defense Policy (CSDP);
- Develop the industrial and technological resources for cybersec;
- Establish a coherent international cyberspace policy for the European Union and promote core EU values.

In 2016, the European Parliament and the European Council approved the Directive 2016/1148 (EP-CEU, 2016), replaced by Directive 2022/2555 (EPCEU, 2022), concerning measures for a high common level of security of network and information systems across the Union.

The European Union Agency for Cybersecurity (ENISA), created in 2004, has the mission to actively contribute to European cybersec policy, assisting "Member States and European Union stakeholders to support a response to large-scale cyber incidents that take place across borders in cases where two or more EU Member States have been affected. It also contributes to the proper functioning of the Digital Single Market" (EPCEU, 2021). ENISA's mission and mandate have been updated recently (EPCEU, 2019; EU, 2023) and its activities comprehend:

- Recommendations on cybersec and independent advice;
- Activities that support policy making and implementation;
- "Hands on" work, collaborating directly with operational teams;
- Coordinating the response to large scale cross-border cybersec incidents
- Drawing up cybersec certification schemes.

The European Commission (EC) has given top priority to cybersec in its proposals for the next long-term EU budget for years 2021-2027, to guarantee adequate funding. Under the new Digital Europe programme, the EC proposed a budget of €7.5 billion to "strengthen investments in supercomputing, artificial intelligence, cybersecurity, advanced digital skills, and ensuring a wide use of digital capacity across the economy and society. Its goal is to boost Europe's competitiveness and the green transition towards climate neutrality by 2050 as well as ensure technological sovereignty" (EC, 2020).

Of the €7.5 billion, €1.7 billion are for cybersecurity to "strengthening cybersecurity coordination between Member States tools and data infrastructures, support the wide deployment of the cybersecurity capacities across the economy, boost Europe's capabilities in optical communications and cybersecurity through Quantum Communication Infrastructures and reinforce advanced skills and capabilities within Member States and the private sector for a uniformly high level of security of network and information systems" (EC, 2020).

In the Defense domain the EU Global Strategy (EU, 2016), called for a new strategic and shared vision and common action materialized in a Global Strategy for the European Union's Foreign and Security Policy.

Under the hat of the EUGS, The EC launched, in 2017, the Permanent Structured Cooperation (PESCO) (EU, 2023), part of the Common Security and Defense Policy (CSDP) that deals with the future EU role in global affairs. PESCO adopted 34 projects in seven areas: Space, Air System, Land, Formations & Systems, Maritime, Enabling and Joint Capabilities, Common Training & Facilities and Cyber and C4ISR[5] (UE, 2018; 2021). The PESCO holds the following projects in the Cyber domain:

- **Cyber Rapid Response Teams and Mutual Assistance in Cyber Security** (CRRT) that "will allow the member states to help each other to ensure a higher level of cyber resilience and collectively respond to cyber incidents. CRRTs could be used to assist other member states, EU Institutions, CSDP operations as well as partners. CRRTs will be equipped with commonly developed deployable cyber toolkits designed to detect, recognize, and mitigate cyber threats. Teams would be able to assist with training, vulnerability assessments and other requested support. Cyber Rapid Response Teams would operate by pooling participating member states experts";
- **Cyber and Information Domain Coordination Center**, with the objective to develop, establish and operate a multinational Cyber and Information Domain Coordination Center as a standing multinational military element, where – in line with the European resolution of 13 June 2018 on

cyber defense – the participating member states continuously contribute with national staff but decide sovereignly on case-by-case basis for which threat, incident and operation they contribute with means or information;

- **Cyber Threats and Incident Response Information Sharing Platform** (CTIRISP), to develop more active defense measures, potentially moving from firewalls to more active measures. This project aims to help mitigate these risks by focusing on the sharing of cyber threat intelligence through a networked Member State platform, with the aim of strengthening nations' cyber defense capabilities;
- Cyber Ranges Federations (CRF), with the primary objective to enhance the European Cyber Ranges capability by federating existing national Cyber Ranges into a larger cluster with more capacity and unique services. This correspondingly enables to share and pool the capabilities and improve the quality of cyber training, exercises as well as using the federation for cyber-related research and development purposes.

The European Defense Fund (EDF), created in 2017 (EU, 2021), has the objective to promote co-operation and cost savings among Member States to produce state-of-the-art defense technology and equipment. The EDF financing is composed of two parts, RESEARCH, funded directly from the EU budget (90 M€ from 2017-2020 and 500 M€/year post 2020), and DEVELOPMENT where Member States budget is at least 80% (€2 billion total from 2017-2020 and expected €4 billion/ year post 2020) and Co-financing from EU budget up to 20% (500 M€ from 2017-2020 and expected €1 billion/year post 2020).

In 2016, NATO and the EU signed a Technical Arrangement for cooperation on cyber defense, mainly in information exchange, training, research, and exercises.

Cybersecurity in NATO

NATO states that "cyber defence is part of NATO's core task of collective defence" (NATO, 2014) and, as such "Article 5 of the North Atlantic Treaty on collective self-defence can be invoked in case of a cyber-attack with effects comparable to those of a conventional armed attack" (NATO, 2014a).

Along with the cooperation with EU[6] (NATO, 2016) mentioned before, the NATO allies agreed: i) to set up a new Cyberspace Operations Centre as part of NATO's strengthened Command Structure; ii) that NATO can draw on national cyber capabilities for its missions and operations.

In 2016, NATO endorsed the Cybersecurity Reference Curriculum as a NATO Educational Reference Document (NATO, 2016a).

In the domain of related infrastructures NATO (NATO, 2019):

- Created the Computer Incident Response Capability (NCIRC) in the structure of the NATO Communications and Information Agency;
- Is setting up a new Cyber Operations Centre;
- Has the NATO Cyber Range, in Estonia, operated Estonian Defense Forces
- Operates the Cooperative Cyber Defense Centre of Excellence, in Estonia as a NATO-accredited research and training facility dealing with cyber defense education, research and development.

- Is strengthening its relationship with industry and academia through the NATO Industry Cyber Partnership, which efforts to protect networks, increase resilience and help Allies develop their cyber capabilities.

In 2023, NATO published a statement about Cyber defense identifying its policy, governance, and evolution details (NATO, 2023).

Cybersecurity in United Nations and United Kingdom

The United Nations General Assembly created "a Global Culture of Cybersecurity and taking stock of national efforts to protect Critical Information Infrastructures" (UN, 2010). The United Kingdom (UK) released its Cyber Security Strategy (UK, 2009; 2011).

Cybersecurity in the USA

In the USA, cybersec has evolved from a discipline of IT to an essential domain. In the military, the crucial importance of this domain led to the creation of the Cyber Command, which had the same value as other commands. The Core Functions each contribute to a high-level understanding of the cybersec needs of the organization:

- Identify (ID): develop the organizational understanding to manage cybersec risk to systems, assets, data, and capabilities;
- Protect (PR): develop and implement the appropriate safeguards to ensure delivery of critical infrastructure services;
- Detect (DE): develop and implement the appropriate activities to identify the occurrence of a cybersec event;
- Respond (RS): develop and implement the appropriate activities to act regarding a detected cybersec event;
- Recover (RC): develop and implement the appropriate activities to maintain plans for resilience and to restore any capabilities or services that were impaired due to a cybersec event.

The armed forces are a key player in the cyber domain and therefore, the Joint Chiefs of Staff developed a Joint Publication 3-12 (USJCS, 2018) and the USAF also developed its Air Force Doctrine Publication 3-12 (USAF, 2023) to list only two examples.

There are many other players of the cybersec domain in the USA, from IT companies, to non-IT companies, institutes like the National Institute of Standards and Technology (NIST), the National Security Agency, the Department of Homeland Security, universities.

NIST authors developed the National Initiative for Cybersecurity Education (NICE), led by the NIST in the U.S. Department of Commerce, is a partnership between government, academia, and the private sector focused on cybersec education, training, and workforce development. We consider this framework essential for capability achievement in the domain of personal and hence, the next paragraph describes this concept.

The NICE Framework

To successfully fulfill their roles within an organization, individuals must be given the right tools and training. These tools and training include a combination of basic security awareness, essential skills, cooperative learning or on-the-job training, education, experience and the knowledge, skills and ability suited to the role. The *Cybersecurity Learning Continuum* is an approach to provide all the necessary training for individuals (Wilson & Hash, 2003).

Learning Continuum

The Learning Continuum (Figure 1) is a progression of learning across the spectrum of roles within an organization. Security awareness training is provided to all users within an organization. Cybersecurity Essentials training is provided to all users involved with IT systems. Role- based training is provided to users with responsibilities relative to IT systems. Knowledge, education and/or experience are gained by IT Security Specialists and professionals. The appropriate level of cybersec awareness, training and education is determined by the role within an organization. Individuals obtain skills as they participate in role-based training with their agency.

Figure 1. Learning continuum
Source: Adapted from Wilson and Hash (2003, p. 8)

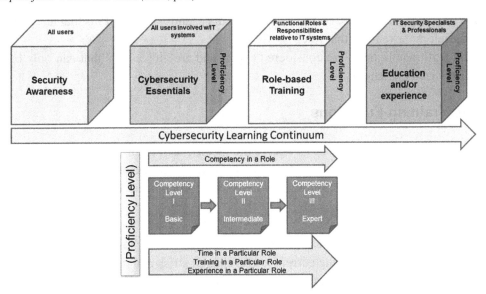

The model illustrates the following concepts (Wilson & Hash, 2003):

- **Security Awareness**: explicitly required for all individuals within the organization;
- **Cybersecurity Essentials**: needed for those involved in any way with IT systems, including contractors. Cybersecurity Essentials is the transition stage between Basic Awareness and Role-Based Training. It provides the foundation for subsequent specialized or role-based training by providing

a universal baseline of key security terms and concepts, such as: technical underpinnings of cybersec and its taxonomy, terminology and challenges; common information and computer system security vulnerabilities; common cyber-attack mechanisms, their consequences and motivation for use; different types of cryptographic algorithms; intrusion, types of intruders, techniques and motivation; firewalls and other means of intrusion prevention; vulnerabilities unique to virtual computing environments; social engineering and its implications to cybersec; and Fundamental security design principles and their role in limiting point of vulnerability;

- **Role-Based Training**: provides the knowledge and skills specific to an individual's roles and responsibilities relative to Organizational information systems;
- **Education and Experience**: develops the ability and vision to perform complex multi-disciplinary activities and the skills needed to further the IT/cybersec profession and to keep pace with threats and technology changes. This can be accomplished with experience, cooperative training such as "on the job" training or through certification and advanced education such as undergraduate and graduate studies and degrees as accepted by that Organization.

The concept comprehends the following Competency Levels (NIST, 2014):

- **Level I** skill requirements are basic and are usually obtained during the first few years in that role. Although a person may have been working in the security arena for the last 15 years, if they move into a new role requiring additional functional skills, they will need to possess more than Competency level I skills;
- **Level II** skill requirements are considered intermediate, and are those skills that have obtained and honed during more years in that role;
- **Level III** skill requirements are considered expert and are those skills that can only be obtained after many years in the role.

Role-Based Training Functions

Includes the security-related experience as well as the specific area the individual occupies. Functional perspectives are also helpful to identify and scope requirements for each role and enhance the training development and outcomes. For the purposes role- based training, the following specific functional perspectives are generically defined as follows:

- **Manage**: functions that encompass overseeing a program or technical aspect of a security program at a high level, and ensuring currency with changing risk and threat environments; including the management of any program, persons, or operations;
- **Design**: functions that encompass scoping a program or developing procedures, processes, and architectures that guide work execution at the program and/or system level; as well as the secure development of systems, networks or applications;
- **Implement**: functions that encompass putting programs, processes, or policies into action within an organization; including operation and maintenance of systems, networks, or applications;
- **Evaluate**: functions that encompass assessing the effectiveness of a program, policy, process, or security service in achieving its objectives; including the evaluation of the security state of a system, network, or application.

Cybersecurity Concepts

NIST developed the NICE Framework, which organizes cybersec and related work in terms of the following components (Newhouse, 2017):

- **Categories**: provide the overarching organizational structure of the NICE Framework. There are seven Categories that are all composed of Specialty Areas and Work Roles;
- **Specialty Areas**: groupings of cybersec work that represent an area of work of function. Each category contains a set of Specialty Areas;
- **Work Roles**: the most detailed groupings of cybersec work, which include a list of attributes required to perform that role in the form of knowledge, skills, and abilities (KSAs) and tasks performed in that role;
- **Knowledge, Skills, and Abilities** (KSAs): the attributes required to perform work roles. KSAs are demonstrated through experience, education, or training;
- **Knowledge**: a body of information applied directly to the performance of a function;
- **Skill**: an observable competence to perform a learned psychomotor act;
- **Ability**: competence to perform an observable behavior or a behavior that results in an observable product;
- **Tasks**: an activity that has the aim of achieving an objective.

Each Category is composed of Specialty Areas, each of which is composed of one or more Work Roles. Each Work Role, in turn, includes KSAs and Tasks. Figure 2 illustrates the relation concept.

Figure 2. Relationships among NICE framework components
Source: Adapted from Newhouse (2017, p. 6)

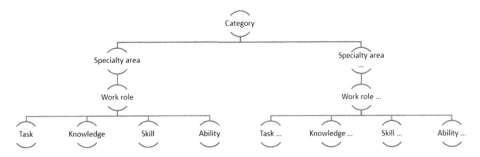

Cybersecurity Concept Representation

This section shows how to represent Functions, Roles, Role Modules, Work Roles, and Work Roles Capability indicators. The representations are central to the work development since they represent the basic comparisons between the course programs and the different components of the Framework.

Representing Categories

Table 1 provides a description of each NICE Framework Workforce Categories and correspondent Specialty Areas described by the NICE Framework and the relation to the core cybersec functions (Newhouse, 2017).

Table 1. Relationships among NICE framework components (adapted from Newhouse, 2017, p. 11)

Categories	Descriptions	Functions
Securely Provision (SP)	Conceptualizes, designs, procures, and/or builds secure information technology (IT) systems, with responsibility for aspects of system and/or network development. The associated specialty areas are: Risk Management (RSK), Software Development (DEV), Systems Architecture (ARC), Technology R&D (TRD), Test and Evaluation (TST), Systems Development (SYS)	Identify (ID), Protect (PR)
Operate and Maintain (OM)	Provides the support, administration, and maintenance necessary to ensure effective and efficient information technology (IT) system performance and security. The associated specialty areas are: Data Administration (DTA), Knowledge Management (KMG), Customer Service and Technical Support (STS), Network Services (NET), Systems Administration (ADM), Systems Analysis (ANA)	Protect (PR), Detect (DE)
Oversee and Govern (OV)	Provides leadership, management, direction, or development and advocacy so the organization may effectively conduct cybersec work. The associated specialty areas are: Training, Education, and Awareness (TEA), Cybersecurity Management (MGT), Legal Advice and Advocacy (LGA), Strategic Planning and Policy (SPP), Program/Project Management (PMA) and Acquisition, Executive Cyber Leadership (EXL)	Identify (ID), Protect (PR), Detect (DE), Recover (RC)
Protect and Defend (PR)	Identifies, analyzes, and mitigates threats to internal information technology (IT) systems and/or networks. The associated specialty areas are: Cybersecurity Defense Analysis (CDA), Cybersecurity Defense Infrastructure Support (INF), Incident Response (CIR), Vulnerability Assessment and Management (VAM)	Protect (PR), Detect (DE), Respond (RS)
Analyze (AN)	Performs highly specialized review and evaluation of incoming cybersec information to determine its usefulness for intelligence. The associated specialty areas are: All-Source Analysis (ASA), Exploitation Analysis (EXP), Targets (TGT), Threat Analysis (TWA), Language Analysis (LNG)	Identify (ID), Detect (DE), Respond (RS)
Collect and Operate (CO)	Provides specialized denial and deception operations and collection of cybersec information that may be used to develop intelligence. The associated specialty areas are: Collection Operations (CLO), Cyber Operations (OPS), Cyber Operational Planning (OPL)	Detect (DE), Protect (PR), Respond (RS)
Investigate (IN)	Investigates cybersec events or crimes related to information technology (IT) systems, networks, and digital evidence. The associated specialty areas are: Digital Forensics (FOR), Cyber Investigation (INV)	Detect (DE), Respond (RS), Recover (RC)

The NICE Framework allows understanding organizational needs and assessing the extent to which those needs are met. It can help an organization to plan, implement, and monitor a successful cybersec program through skilled workers to perform cybersec functions.

There are activities that impact on an organization's ability to develop a capable and ready workforce (Newhouse, 2017):

- "Using the common lexicon of the NICE Framework clarifies communication between cybersec educators, trainers/certifiers, employers, and employees."
- "Performing criticality analysis will identify those KSAs and tasks that are critical for successful performance with a given work role and those that are key to multiple work roles."
- "Running a proficiency analysis will inform an organization's expectation of the level (e.g., entry-level, expert) for positions, comprised often of more than one work role. The proficiency analysis should enable refinement of selection of the relevant tasks, and KSAs needed for the work roles that make up that position."

Representing Functions

The Function representation format is as follows:

- Function Area: Identifies a security function area (for example "Oversight, Management and Support");
- Roles Areas: Identifies various roles that are covered by the function (for example "Legal Advice and Advocacy"). These roles are guidelines and may exist under different names within a particular Agency;
- Definition: Provides a definition of the function (for example "Provides oversight and support so that others may effectively conduct Cybersecurity work");
- Learning Objective(s): Identifies the various outcomes that the training module should strive to meet for each of the functions and their associated roles (for example "Provide legally sound advice and recommendations to leadership and staff on a variety of relevant topics within the pertinent subject domain.").

Representing Roles

All roles should have training on the Overall Knowledge and Skills. These are the fundamental basis of knowledge/skills required for all jobs and roles.

The format is as follows:

- **Function Area**: Provides a general description of the area and the Learning Objectives for those functions (for example "Operate and Maintain");
- **Role Area**: Describes the overall role (for example "Data Administration");
- **Roles**: Identifies various roles that are covered by the function (for example "Data Security Analyst");
- **Responsibility**: Defines the activities, tasks and/or responsibilities of that particular role (for example "Develop and administer databases and/or data management systems that allow for the storage, query, and utilization of data");
- **Knowledge Unit**: Identifies the competencies associated with the role (for example "Data Security").

Representing Work Roles

All roles should have training on the Overall Knowledge and Skills. These are the fundamental basis of knowledge/skills required for all jobs and roles. The format is as follows:

- **Work Role Name**: the overall Work Role name (for example "Cyber Ops Planner");
- **Work Role Identification**: the overall Work Role Identification (for example "CO-OPL-025");
- **Specialty Area**: Provides a general description of the area and the Learning Objectives for those functions (for example "Cyber Operational Planning");
- **Category**: Category where the Work Role is inserted (for example "Collect and Operate");
- **Work Role Description**: Describes the Work Role (for example "Develops detailed plans for the conduct or support");
- Corresponding Knowledge and Skills: Provides a breakdown of the specific KSAs and Tasks to each competency.

Table 2 presents an example.

Representing Work Roles Capability Indicators

The Work Roles Capability Indicators provide the recommended Work Role scope in the following areas: Credentials/ Certifications, Continuous Learning, Education, Experiential Learning and Training. Table 2 presents an example for the work role "Cyber Ops Planner".

Table 2. Cybersecurity work roles capability indicators representation

Capability Indicators	Type	Basic	Intermediate	Advanced
Credentials/ Certifications	Recommended	Not essential	Essential	Essential
	Example Types	N/A	N/A	N/A
	Example Topics	Certifications addressing new attack vectors (…)	Certifications addressing system security, (…)	Certifications addressing security, (…)
Continuous Learning	Recommended	Essential	Essential	Essential
	Examples	40 hours annually (…)	40 hours annually (…)	40 hours annually (…)
Education	Recommended	Not essential but may be beneficial	Essential	Essential
	Example Types	Associate's	Bachelor's	Master's
	Example Topics	(…)	(…)	(…)
Experiential Learning	Recommended	(…)	(…)	(…)
	Examples	(…)	(…)	(…)
Training	Recommended	Not essential	Essential	Essential
	Example Types	(…)	(…)	(…)
	Example Topics	Joint cyber analysis, (…)	Advanced cyber warfare, (…)	Advanced cyber warfare, (…)

This section described the NICE Framework and its components. We consider that this is a mature framework and therefore proposes to use it in attaining the objective of proposing a training concept for any organization that wants to build cyber capability.

Therefore, the answer to RQ1, on whether there is a framework that is suited, after adaptation, to the objectives or, in turn, it is necessary to develop a new framework, is positive. The NICE Framework provides the necessary concepts and components to the starting point to attain the research objectives and answer to RQ2.

The next section develops the insights provided by this training concept and presents the *CyberLearn framework*.

THE CYBERLEARN FRAMEWORK

Cybersec is already part of every citizen's life, at least in Western countries, and as digitalization becomes more prevalent in daily transactions, ensuring privacy and personnel assets will become more important. Society is in the early stages of building awareness on the cybersec domain and hence construct society response to live up to the requirements needed to enjoy new digital artifacts that ease life in a protected and safe manner. As such, citizen preparation to deal with cybersec starts with understanding (and complying with) a set of concepts that begin with basic cyber hygiene and follow with proper education to eventually become a cybersec expert.

In large organizations, such as public administration, large companies, or the military, which include a complete set of transversal knowledge, normally followed by specific (and demanding) requirements in security, a clear path to achieve cybersec transformation is needed.

This paragraph presents the author's training concept to foster the organization from basic level of knowledge in the cybersec domain to achieving cybersec superiority by investing in education and training. As mentioned, we designate it the *CyberLearn framework*.

Cybersecurity "AS IS" and "TO BE"

The previous sections show that cybersec is an essential and very present theme for Portugal, the EU, NATO, and the USA. The core components are present since all the entities have legal means published, all possess cybersec official entities, and all possess cybersec dedicated centers. The EU has set a cooperation protocol with NATO that includes this discipline and the EU itself, through PESCO and the EDF included cybersec.

The discipline is also strongly related to digital transformation in a way that, as the world is becoming more and more dependent on digital artifacts to deal with everyday business transactions, the threat of intrusions is strong and therefore, a successful transition to the digital economy must be conveniently secured.

Going back to the initiatives described to affirm and establish cybersec as a societal need training and development of the cyber defense capability, in response to PESCO and EDF programs, should be inserted as one of the components that should be subject to intensive research and development to answer to the question: "How to insert cybersec in the DNA of the Portuguese/European citizens, guaranteeing the principles that everyone has its unique responsibility to safeguard digital assurance?"

The answer to that question involves:

- Building a transversal societal concept that assures that not only every citizen is capable and at least understands and practices cybersec hygiene, but also the grooming of the right people to become, in time, cybersec experts;
- Involving transversal national and European resources in order to assure the development a transversal societal concept;
- Establishing cybersec European (applicable to all countries) metrics that can determine the model network security and deliver the vulnerability risk assessment.

The U.S. Department of Commerce NIST has developed an approach to national training by creating the NICE framework. Although complex it can be applied to national environments with some adaptations. Hence, the next section introduces the NICE concept.

This section introduces the concept of *Cybersecurity Essentials Training*. Competencies are acquired when an individual gathers knowledge and skills in a certain functional area (Knowledge and Skills = Competencies). Certain roles entail certain competencies, such as a security engineer requires having analytical abilities to detect and identify network problems. This differs from proficiency, which is acquired through experience and education. Proficiencies increase as the acquired competencies, associated skills and knowledge are utilized over time.

Training Concept

For application to organizations, the work begins by identifying specific requirements, namely the Role Areas and respective Work Roles. It is assumed that the organization wants to provide training for all the chosen work roles and that this training should, to the best extent possible, encompass the best standards available in the area. It is also assumed that the NICE framework (or a subset) is the starting basis for training development.

For example, joining information from the different concepts allows establishing Knowledge Units related to each Role Area, as shown in Table 3.

Therefore, we propose to adopt the Cybersecurity Learning Continuum and Proficiency Levels layered approach and adapt it to the unique organization context in the form of a specific Cybersecurity Learning Continuum and Proficiency Levels layered Framework that is represented in Figure 3.

Table 3 (a). Knowledge units related to each role area (adapted from NIST, 2014)

	Architecture	Compliance	Computer Network Defense	Configuration Management	Cryptography and Encryption	Data Security	Database	Digital Forensics	Emerging Technologies	Enterprise Continuity
SP										
RSK		x								x
DEV	x			x		x				
ARC	x			x	x		x		x	
TRD	x	x			x			x	x	
TST	x									
SYS	x			x	x		x			
OM										
DTA	x				x	x	x	x		
KMG						x			x	
STS										
NET	x		x	x	x	x				
ADM	x			x	x			x	x	
ANA	x			x	x		x			
OV										
LGA		x			x				x	
TEA										
MGT		x								
SPP	x	x	x						x	
EXL	x	x	x		x			x		
PMA		x								
PR										
CIR	x		x					x		
INF	x		x		x			x		
VAM	x	x	x					x		
AN										
ASA	x	x	x	x	x	x		x	x	
OM										
DTA		x								
IN										
INV		x						x		
FOR	x	x	x		x	x		x		

Table 3 (b). Knowledge units related to each role area (adapted from NIST, 2014)

	Identity Management/ Privacy	Incident Management	Incident Management/ Privacy	Industrial Controls Systems	Information Assurance	Information Systems	IT Security Awareness and Training	IT Systems and Operations	Management	Modeling and Simulation
SP										
RSK		x		x						
DEV	x					x				x
ARC	x				x	x		x		x
TRD	x	x			x	x		x		x
TST	x				x	x		x		
SYS	x				x	x		x		x
OM										
DTA	x	x				x				x
KMG		x				x		x		
STS		x				x		x		
NET	x				x	x		x		
ADM	x	x				x				
ANA	x	x			x	x	x	x		
OV										
LGA										
TEA							x		x	
MGT	x				x		x		x	
SPP					x					
EXL		x			x	x				
PMA									x	
PR										
CIR		x			x	x				
INF	x	x			x	x				
VAM	x				x	x				
AN										
ASA			x			x				
OM										
DTA	x	x					x		x	
IN										
INV								x		
FOR		x			x	x		x		

Table 3 (c). Knowledge units related to each role area (adapted from NIST, 2014)

	Network and Telecommunications Security	Personnel	Personnel Security	Physical and Environmental Security	Procurement	Security Risk Management	Software	Systems and Applications Security	Web Security	Web Technology
SP										
RSK				x		x				
DEV	x		x			x	x	x	x	
ARC	x		x			x	x	x		
TRD	x		x	x	x	x	x	x		
TST	x					x	x	x		
SYS	x		x		x	x	x	x		
OM										
DTA										
KMG	x									
STS	x					x		x		
NET	x					x		x		x
ADM	x					x	x	x		
ANA	x		x		x	x	x	x		
OV										
LGA						x	x			
TEA		x								
MGT			x		x	x				
SPP				x	x	x				
EXL	x					x	x			
PMA						x				
PR										
CIR	x					x				
INF	x					x			x	
VAM	x		x		x	x	x	x		
AN										
ASA	x					x	x			
OM										
DTA			x							
IN										
INV				x		x				
FOR	x					x	x		x	

Figure 3. Proposed organization cybersecurity learning continuum and proficiency levels framework
Source: Adapted from Wilson and Hash (2003)

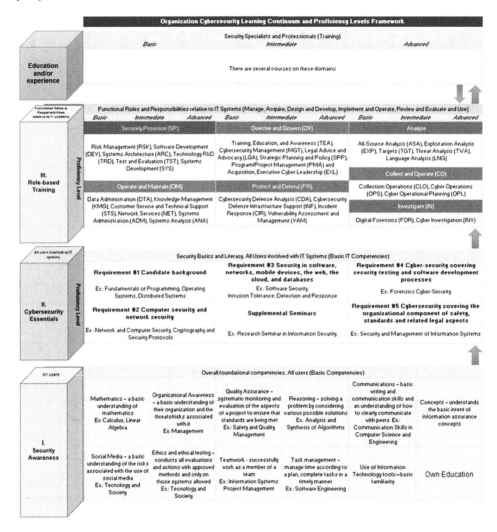

The model illustrates the following concepts, translated into tangible actions:

- **Security Awareness**: is explicitly required for all individuals within the organization. Academic degree and experience should be considered. Organizational Education should be extended to all working personnel. This can be instantiated as a preparatory course that should be given by the Organization cybersec personnel during basic preparation;

- **Cybersecurity Essentials**: needed for those, including contractors, who are involved in any way with IT systems. Cybersecurity Essentials is the transition stage between Basic Awareness and Role-Based Training. A organization-context approach should be materialized in a specialized module, comprehending different courses (example in Section 4.2) that cover IT foundations for subsequent specialized or role-based training by providing a universal baseline of key security terms and concepts, such as: technical underpinnings of cybersec and its taxonomy, terminology, and challenges; common information and computer system security vulnerabilities; common cyber-attack mechanisms, their consequences, and motivation for use; different types of cryptographic algorithms; intrusion, types of intruders, techniques and motivation; firewalls and other means of intrusion prevention; vulnerabilities unique to virtual computing environments; social engineering and its implications to cybersec; and fundamental security design principles and their role in limiting point of vulnerability;

- **Role-Based Training**: shall provide the knowledge and skills specific to an individual's roles and responsibilities; For each Work Role, taking into account the individual background and the Work Role Capability Indicators, and based on the analysis of the Role Area Knowledge;
- **Education and/or Experience**: develop the ability and vision to perform complex multi-disciplinary activities and the skills needed to further the IT/cybersec profession and to keep pace with threats and technology changes. Técnico will develop specific training scenarios in the form of exercises to foster cooperative training such as on the job training and advanced education.

The course offer can consider the Competency Levels, e.g., allowing personnel with Level III skills to act as instructors on the different Work Roles.

Cybersecurity Essentials will be typically the first module taught since it provides concept awareness in all the cybersec categories and to all work roles.

Requirement identification

Example requirements for the instantiation of the modules are the following:

- **Requirement #1**. The universe of candidates is composed of professionals with different academic and professional backgrounds, i.e., it is heterogeneous. However, candidates shall have a basic knowledge base that covers the fundamental areas of operating systems, distributed systems, mobile computing, cloud computing, and databases in the computer security area. Considering this requirement, a Propaedeutic Module provides students with knowledge in the fundamental domains of operating systems, distributed, mobile computing, cloud computing, and database, with emphasis on topics more relevant to safety. It should be noted that it is intended, through these two units' curricula, if necessary and based on the individual's background, to present the concepts underlying operating systems, distributed systems, mobile environments, or databases. Thus, this module allows ensuring that all students have uniform knowledge necessary in other modules. The two curricular units are Fundamentals of Distributed Operating Systems, and Fundamentals of Mobile and Cloud Computing;
- **Requirement #2**. The program shall provide students with basic theoretical and practical knowledge in all key areas of cybersec, covering computer security and network security; The Fundamentals Module, in response to requirement #2, develops the fundamental competences of computer security. This module can include for example two disciplines: Fundamentals of Computer Security, Fundamentals of Network Security;

- **Requirement #3**. The program should provide deep conceptual and professional, theoretical and practical skills in cyber-security covering security in software, networks, mobile devices, the web, the cloud, and databases; The Advanced Module, in response to requirement #3, develops competencies computer security in the area of software security and networking, as well as security in today's computing environments (mobile devices, cloud, data). This module can include four curricular units: Application Software Security, Network Software Security, Mobile Application Security, and Web, Cloud and Database Security;

- **Requirement #4**. The shall provide in-depth conceptual, professional, theoretical, and practical skills in cyber-security covering security testing and software development processes; The Module Development and Testing, in response to requirement #4, develops the advanced computer security skills in the testing and software. This module may include two curricular units: Software Security Testing, and Secure Software Development Processes;

- **Requirement #5**. The program shall provide in-depth theoretical and practical skills in cybersec covering the organizational component of safety, standards and related legal aspects. The Organizational Module, in response to this requirement, develops advanced computer security skills in organizational safety, as well as related standards.

Additionally, the program may provide a set of seminars to provide knowledge in recent areas considered important (e.g., ChatGPT or Web 3) or very specific to the organization (e.g., certain weapons in the case of the military).

The curricular units must be organized in such a way that the students are able to develop the projects in an environment that evolves throughout the course, resulting in an application of complete software, with all the safety aspects subjects. Thus, during the program, students shall progressively incorporate and integrate the skills learned in the different curricular units.

With this training, students have to acquire new skills and intellectual and professional on the following (example of courses in Section 4.2):

- Knowledge of security vulnerabilities in information systems;
- Knowledge of mechanisms, algorithms, and technologies to detect and resolve vulnerabilities most common security issues in local, distributed, mobile computing environments, and as well as in databases;
- Knowledge of the organizational, regulatory, and legal components of security computing in organizations;
- Practical experience of detecting security vulnerabilities and respective solutions in the development of networked systems, including cloud and databases.

Course Modules

This section comprises *examples* of the several courses that are being prepared by Técnico (see Table 4) to apply in the CyberLearn framework to specific organizations (one company and one public). Some of the courses are real examples taken from the offers already existent in other countries, which Técnico is adapting for specific contexts.

This is an initial proposal; the final course syllabus depends on specific requirements of the target organization, so the list and contents of the courses presented here can be refined.

Table 4. Course module examples

Level	Name	Overview	Proficiency Level	Framework Connections
I. Security Awareness	All users (Basic Competencies)	Present the fundamental concepts regarding network security; understand the most important vulnerabilities and the corresponding solutions in computer networks and security with a focus on the general awareness and procedures to avoid compromising the work post and network.	NONE	None, since this is a foundational course designed for all the persons in the Organization
II. Cybersecurity Essentials	Fundamentals of Network Security	Present the fundamental concepts regarding network security; understand the most important vulnerabilities and the corresponding solutions in computer networks with a with a focus on the fundamental mechanisms and algorithms for communication, malware, cryptography, digital signatures, certificates, transport-level security, wireless network security, electronic mail security, IP security, intrusion, firewalls.	NONE	Securely Provision; Protect and Defend; Analyze; Oversee and Govern.
III. Role-Based Training, Level I Basic	Monitoring, Detection and Analytics	The goal of the course is to learn about system and network security monitoring, intrusion detection, and security analytics.	Level: x – Basic	Analyze; Investigate; Operate and Maintain.
III. Role-Based Training, Level II Intermediate	Digital Forensics Techniques for Weapons Systems	Digital Forensics Techniques for Weapons Systems explores the forensic investigation of traditional workstations, embedded systems, and networks. This class is ideal for military law enforcement and IT professionals.	Level: 2 – Intermediate	Investigate
III. Role-Based Training, Level III Advanced	Embedded Security Tools and Techniques	Objective: to learn tools and techniques to identify and mitigate cyber-security threats to embedded systems. The course is a series of hands-on labs (exercises) supplemented by a relatively small amount of lecture material.	Level: 3 – Advanced	Operate and Maintain
IV. Education and/or Experience	Introduction to Penetration Testing	This lab-based course will provide students with an understanding of the threat vectors and exploitation techniques used to penetrate systems and networks.	Level: 2 – Intermediate	Operate and Maintain

We further detail two of these courses in Tables 5 and 6.

The framework can also be instantiated with short programs. For example, Técnico, periodically organizes a program called Information Security and Data Protection for Non-Technological Professionals,[7] targeted at Data Protection Officers (DPOs) and other non-tech professionals who need to better understand cybersec concepts and technology. This project was designed following an early version of the *CyberLearn framework*. It was designed by Técnico in collaboration to an association of professionals (DPOs). The program is for non-tech professionals, so it only includes courses from the first two levels: awareness and essentials. The first three courses can also be considered propaedeutic as they provide information required for understanding the rest of the program. Table 7 summarizes the program. The program had so far four editions that, jointly with a similar one with two editions, had a total of around 120 students.

Table 5. Fundamentals of network security course

Name: Fundamentals of Network Security (FNS)
Workload Theoretical classes: 15 hours Practical / lab classes: 15 hours Autonomous work: 54 hours
Objectives Present the fundamental concepts regarding network security; understand the most important vulnerabilities and the corresponding solutions in computer networks with a with a focus on the fundamental mechanisms and algorithms for communication, malware, cryptography, digital signatures, certificates, transport-level security, wireless network security, electronic mail security, IP security, intrusion, firewalls.

Competences
Upon unit completion, students will have the competencies to:
   • Understand the main concepts regarding network cyber-security;
   • Knowledge of the most important vulnerabilities in computer networks;
   • Mastering the mechanisms and algorithms used for key management (to encrypt/decrypt, sign), for transport-level security, wireless and IP security;
   • Relate the solutions studied with those used in Unix based information systems.

Requirements C and Java programming.

Program
The unit covers the following topics:
   • OSI Security Architecture,
   • cryptography (basic concepts, symmetric, asymmetric),
   • key distribution (certificates, PKI),
   • digital signatures,
   • transport-level security,
   • wireless network security,
   • electronic mail security,
   • IP security,
   • intrusion,
   • firewalls,
   • web security.

Method
   • Theoretical, practical, and lab classes;
   • Team projects.

Evaluation
The evaluation results from the following combination of components:
   • Project (50%);
   • Final exam (50%).

Bibliography Network Security Essentials Applications and Standards (5th Edition). William Stallings. 2013. Pearson

Table 6. Monitoring, detection, and analytics course

Name: Monitoring, Detection and Analytics (MDA)
Workload Theoretical classes: 15 hours Practical / lab classes: 15 hours Autonomous work: 54 hours
Objectives To learn about system & network security monitoring, intrusion detection, and security analytics.
Competences Upon unit completion, students will have the competencies to: • Understand the concepts, paradigms, and tools for system & network security monitoring, intrusion detection, and security analytics.
Requirements C and Python programming.
Program The unit covers the following topics: • Intrusion detection systems • Security Information and Event Management systems (SIEMs) • Artefact acquisition and analysis • Log search and management (ELK) • Incident management processes (CERT approach) • Threat intelligence • Security analytics
Method • Theoretical and lab classes; • Team project.
Evaluation The evaluation results from the following combination of components: • Project (50%); • Final exam (50%).
Bibliography Applied Network Security Monitoring: Collection, Detection, and Analysis. Chris Sandres, Jason Smith. 2013. Syngress Data-Driven Security: Analysis, Visualization and Dashboards. Jay Jacobs & Bob Rudis. 2014. Wiley

Cybersecurity Organization Case Study

As explained, the *CyberLearn framework* includes the notion that courses must be refined considering specific requirements provided by the target company. The framework is being applied to several businesses. This section lists some of the aspects that the applying organizations need to consider.

The organization must provide the following contents:

- **Level I. Security Awareness**: a broad instruction (Organization specific Education with proposed topics), so it is necessary that the organization will define its approach to materialize the concept, namely what would be, if considered, the training companies or academia roles on eventually help to prepare or train the course instructors, that should be intrinsic to the organization.

Table 7. Information security and data protection for non-technological professionals courses

Level	Module	Course	Overview
I. Security Awareness	1. Current Computer Systems	IT Infrastructure	Introduction - definition, evolution, technological drivers; Infrastructure components and hardware platforms; Software platforms - Linux and open source, web software, cloud; IT infrastructure management - change management, administration and governance, investment.
I. Security Awareness	1. Current Computer Systems	Databases	Problems of data management in files; Main functionalities of database management systems; Policies, management, data quality and main technologies to process large amounts of data.
I. Security Awareness	1. Current Computer Systems	Internet and networking	Introduction and network components - what is a network, main technologies; Types of networks - digital vs. analog, LAN / WAN, means and speed of transmission; Internet - addressing and architecture, services, the web. Communication protocols - client and server technologies; Wireless networks - cellular networks, Wi-Fi and Bluetooth, RFID and sensor networks.
I. Security Awareness	2. Cybersecurity	Cybersecurity - Introduction	Definition, scope of cybersecurity (technological and organizational) and introduction to information security; Types of common vulnerabilities affecting hardware, software, networks, personnel, facilities and the organization; Typical threats and the current threat landscape; Value of security.
II. Cybersecurity Essentials	2. Cybersecurity	Mechanisms and Security Controls	Cryptography, digital certificates and digital signature; Anonymization and pseudo-anonymization; Identity management, authentication and access control (RBAC, MAC, DAC); Facility and data processing center security; Peripheral and network security - firewalls, DMZs, VPNs, intrusion detection and prevention systems; Security event management (SIEM), event and operation records (logs); Terminal equipment security; Security of servers, storage and databases - integrity control and logging of operations; Role of users - training, awareness and communication of security policies, rules and good practices; Software quality and security by design of information systems.
II. Cybersecurity Essentials	2. Cybersecurity	Cybersecurity - Security Assessment and Management	Evaluation and risk management - analysis and treatment; Audits, vulnerability analysis and security tests of human and technological components of organizations; Supply chain; Outsourcing of security; Security of external services (cloud); Incident Response - incident management plans, disaster recovery and business continuity, CSIRTs and forensic analysis.
II. Cybersecurity Essentials	2. Cybersecurity	Privacy - Processing of Personal Data	The processing of personal data in professional activity in the field of data protection; Case study.

- **Level II. IT Security Awareness**: has the objective of ensuring that all students have uniform knowledge necessary in other modules it is required that the organization makes available the following information:
  ◦ Number of students;
  ◦ Individual academic, professional and experience background;
  ◦ Preference for the type of course: intensive, all days are fully dedicated to the course or, mixed, where students are available for two or three days per week and are not fully dedicated to the course.
- **Level III. Role Training**: has the objective of provide specific role training. Therefore, it is required that the organization makes available the following information:
  ◦ Work Role and Proficiency Level prioritizing;
  ◦ Number of students for each role (if the role is not fulfilled Técnico can provide advice based on the individuals' performance on the Level II course);

- ◦ Individual academic, professional and experience background, if students did not attend the Level II course (not recommended);
- ◦ Preference for the type of course: intensive, all days are fully dedicated to the course or, mixed, where students are available for two or three days per week and are not fully dedicated to the course.

- **Level IV. Education and/or Experience**: has the objective of provide specific role training. Therefore, it is required that the organization makes available the following information:
  - ◦ Work Role and Proficiency Level prioritizing;
  - ◦ Period of the year that is considered most favorable;
  - ◦ Number of students for each role;
  - ◦ Type of training (Lab hands-on specific training; virtual training; simulated real-time world scenarios; typical players within the organization; other players).

As the courses have been taken for several years and are applied to several businesses, we find that the answer to (RQ2) "after completing the adaptation or development of the framework is it possible to fill it with meaningful content that will foster cybersec leaning?" is yes as it was verified by the case study described.

CONCLUSION AND FUTURE WORK

With the growing in importance of cybersec, there is a need to find a path for capability building for organizations.

This chapter presents a cybersecurity capability building proposal for organizations: the *Cybersecurity Learning framework (CyberLearn)*. The framework is targeted at organizations, either public or private, but arguably expandable for a larger-scale capability building effort, e.g., as a joint venture between government, universities, the military, security institutes and companies. The framework is based on NIST's NICE and includes a set of guidelines on how it can be instantiated by different organizations. We also provide some instantiations with courses and programs from Instituto Superior Técnico.

Técnico developed this research using the action research methodology, which implies self-involvement in the process. The research questions were:

- (RQ1) is there a framework that is suited, after adaptation, to the objectives or, in turn, is it necessary to develop a new framework? The answer is YES since the NICE framework provided all the concepts and components needed to develop the *CyberLearn framework*.
- (RQ2) after completing the adaptation or development of the framework, is it possible to fill it with meaningful content that will foster cybersec leaning? The answer is YES since the Técnico courses were used to fill the *CyberLearn framework and provide insightful training to meet* business's needs.

Therefore, the objective of the research (find (or create) a cybersec framework that would allow, with adequate adaptations, to foster a path to educate people and allow a grooming process and, once adapted (or created) fill with the appropriate leaning content that allows career and knowledge progress) was fully attained.

Future work entails establishing a full model of lessons learned to insert meaningful experiences from the trainees into the courses and improve the quality of the *CyberLearn framework* to step up to new threats.

REFERENCES

Alberts, C., & Dorofee, A. (2005). *Mission Assurance Analysis Protocol (MAAP): Assessing Risk in Complex Environments. CMU/SEI-2005-TN-032.* Carnegie Mellon University. doi:10.21236/ADA441906

Cheng, Y., Deng, J., Li, J., DeLoach, S. A., Singhal, A., & Ou, X. (2014). Metrics of Security. In A. Kott, C. Wang, & R. Erbacher (Eds.), *Cyber Defense and Situational Awareness. Advances in Information Security* (Vol. 62). Springer.

European Commission (EC). (2020). *Digital Europe Programme 2021-2027 Fact Sheet.* https://ec.europa.eu/newsroom/dae/document.cfm?doc_id=67268

European Commission (EC). (2021). *The European Defence Fund Fact Sheet.* https://defence-industry-space.ec.europa.eu/system/files/2022-05/Factsheet%20-%20European%20Defence%20Fund.pdf

European Parliament, Council of the European Union (EPCEU). (2016). *Directive (EU) 2016/1148 of the European Parliament and of the Council of 6 July 2016 concerning measures for a high common level of security of network and information systems across the Union.* https://eur-lex.europa.eu/legal-content/EN/TXT/PDF/?uri=CELEX:32016L1148&from=EN

European Parliament, Council of the European Union (EPCEU). (2019). *Regulation (EU) 2019/881 of the European Parliament and of the Council of 17 April 2019 on ENISA (the European Union Agency for Cybersecurity) and on information and communications technology cybersecurity certification and repealing Regulation (EU) No 526/2013 (Cybersecurity Act).* https://eur-lex.europa.eu/legal-content/EN/TXT/PDF/?uri=CELEX:32019R0881&qid=1681208226017&from=EN

European Parliament, Council of the European Union (EPCEU). (2021). *Regulation (EU) 2021/887 of the European Parliament and of the Council of 20 May 2021 establishing the European Cybersecurity Industrial, Technology and Research Competence Centre and the Network of National Coordination Centres.* https://eur-lex.europa.eu/legal-content/EN/TXT/PDF/?uri=CELEX:32021R0887&qid=1681208461508&from=EN

European Parliament, Council of the European Union (EPCEU). (2022). *Directive (EU) 2022/2555 of the European Parliament and of the Council of 14 December 2022 on measures for a high common level of cybersecurity across the Union, amending Regulation (EU) No 910/2014 and Directive (EU) 2018/1972, and repealing Directive (EU) 2016/1148 (NIS 2 Directive).* https://eur-lex.europa.eu/legal-content/EN/TXT/PDF/?uri=CELEX:32022L2555&from=EN

European Parliament (EP). (2013). *European Parliament resolution of 12 September 2013 on a Cybersecurity Strategy of the European Union: An Open, Safe and Secure Cyberspace (2013/2606(RSP)).* https://eur-lex.europa.eu/legal-content/EN/TXT/PDF/?uri=CELEX:52013IP0376&qid=168121074808&from=EN

European Union (EU). (2016). *Shared Vision, Common Action: A Stronger Europe, A Global Strategy for the European Union's Foreign And Security Policy.* https://www.eeas.europa.eu/sites/default/files/eugs_review_web_0.pdf

European Union (EU). (2018). *Towards a stronger EU on security and defence.* https://eeas.europa.eu/headquarters/headquarters-homepage/35285/eu-strengthens-cooperation-security-and-defence_en

European Union (EU). (2021). *Permanent Structured Cooperation (PESCO)'s projects – Overview.* https://www.consilium.europa.eu/media/53013/20211115-pesco-projects-with-description.pdf

European Union (EU). (2021a). *PESCO Projects Fact Sheet.* https://www.eeas.europa.eu/sites/default/files/pesco_projects_15nov_002.pdf

European Union (EU). (2023). *Permanent Structured Cooperation (PESCO) Official Site.* https://www.pesco.europa.eu/

European Union (EU). (2023). *The European Union Agency for Cybersecurity.* https://www.enisa.europa.eu/about-enisa

International Telecommunications Union (ITU). (2008). ITU-T X.1205 - Overview of Cybersecurity. In *Series X: Data Networks, Open System Communications and Security - Telecommunication Security.* Telecommunication Standardization Sector of ITU (ITU-T).

International Telecommunications Union (ITU). (2011). *The ITU National Cybersecurity Strategy Guide.* Telecommunication Standardization Sector of ITU (ITU-T). https://www.itu.int/ITU-D/cyb/cybersecurity/docs/itu-national-cybersecurity-guide.pdf

Newhouse, W. (2017). *NICE Cybersecurity Workforce Framework: National Initiative for Cybersecurity Education, Special Publication (NIST SP 800-181).* National Institute of Standards and Technology. doi:10.6028/NIST.SP.800-181

North Atlantic Treaty Organization (NATO). (2014). *NATO Summit Updates Cyber Defence Policy, from NATO Cyber Defence Policy at the NATO Summit in Wales on 4-5 September 2014.* https://ccdcoe.org/incyder-articles/nato-summit-updates-cyber-defence-policy/

North Atlantic Treaty Organization (NATO). (2014a). *Wales Summit Declaration, Paragraph 72, NATO Summit Updates Cyber Defence Policy, from NATO Cyber Defence Policy at the NATO Summit in Wales on 4-5 September 2014.* https://www.nato.int/cps/en/natohq/official_texts_112964.htm

North Atlantic Treaty Organization (NATO). (2016). *Point 3. of the Joint Declaration signed by the President of the European Council, the President of the European Commission, and the Secretary General of the North Atlantic Treaty Organization, Brussels, Belgium, Dec. 2016.* https://www.nato.int/cps/en/natohq/official_texts_138829.htm

North Atlantic Treaty Organization (NATO). (2016a). *Cybersecurity Reference Curriculum, 27 Sept. 2016, Norfolk, USA.* https://www.nato.int/nato_static_fl2014/assets/pdf/pdf_2016_10/1610-cybersecurity-curriculum.pdf

North Atlantic Treaty Organization (NATO). (2019). *NATO Cyber Defence Factsheet.* https://www.nato.int/nato_static_fl2014/assets/pdf/pdf_2019_02/20190208_1902-factsheet-cyber-defence-en.pdf

North Atlantic Treaty Organization (NATO). (2023). *Cyber defence*. https://www.nato.int/cps/en/natohq/topics_78170.htm

Petersen, R., Santos, D., Wetzel, K., Smith, M., & Witte, G. (2020). *Workforce Framework for Cybersecurity (NICE Framework), Special Publication (NIST SP 800-181r1)*. National Institute of Standards and Technology. doi:10.6028/NIST.SP.800-181r1

Portuguese National Cybersecurity Centre (PNCSC). (2023). *Mission*. https://www.cncs.gov.pt/en/about-us/#missao

Portuguese Parliament (PP). (2018) *Establishes the legal framework for cyberspace security by transposing Directive (EU) 2016/1148 of the European Parliament and of the Council of 6 July 2016 on measures to ensure a high common level of network and information security across the Union, Law no. 46/2018, 13 August, Diário da República n.º 155/2018, Série I de 2018-08-13, p 4031–4037*. https://files.dre.pt/1s/2018/08/15500/0403104037.pdf

Presidency of the Council of Ministers (PCM). (2012). *Approves the organic of the National Security Office, Decree-Law n. 3/2012, of 16 January, Diário da República n. 11/2012, Série I de 2012-01-16, p. 174-177*. https://files.dre.pt/1s/2012/01/01100/0017400177.pdf

Presidency of the Council of Ministers (PCM). (2015). *Aproves the National Strategy for the CyberSpace Security, Resolution of the Council of Ministers no. 36/2015, 12 june, Diário da República n. 113/2015, Série I de 2015-06-12, p. 3738 – 3742*. https://files.dre.pt/1s/2015/06/11300/0373803742.pdf

Presidency of the Council of Ministers (PCM). (2017). *Creation of the group "Cyberspace Security Superior Council", Resolution of the Council of Ministers no. 115/2017, 24 August, Diário da República n. 163/2017, Série I de 2017-08-24, p. 5035 – 5037*. https://files.dre.pt/1s/2017/08/16300/0503505037.pdf

Presidency of the Council of Ministers (PCM). (2019). *Aproves the National Strategy for the CyberSpace Security 2019-2023, Resolution of the Council of Ministers no. 92/2019, 5 june, Diário da República, 1.ª série — N.º 108 — 5 de junho de 2019, p 2888-2895*. https://files.dre.pt/1s/2019/06/10800/0288802895.pdf

Presidency of the Council of Ministers (PCM). (2022). *Aproves the National Strategy for Cyberdefense, Resolution of the Council of Ministers no. 106/2022, 2 november, Diário da República n. 211/2022, Série I de 2022-11-02, p. 13–22*. https://files.dre.pt/1s/2022/11/21100/0001300022.pdf

Presidency of the Council of Ministers (PCM). (2022a). *Regulates the Legal Framework for Cyberspace Security and sets out the cybersecurity certification obligations under Regulation (EU) 2019/881 of the European Parliament of 17 April 2019, Decree-Law n. 65/2021, 30 june, Diário da República n.º 147/2021, Série I de 2021-07-30, p. 8 – 21*. https://files.dre.pt/1s/2021/07/14700/0000800021.pdf

United Kingdom (UK). (2009). *Cyber Security Strategy of the United Kingdom - Safety, Security and Resilience in Cyber Space, UK Office of Cyber Security and UK Cyber Security Operations Centre, Crown, Richmond, Surrey*. https://assets.publishing.service.gov.uk/government/uploads/system/uploads/attachment_data/file/228841/7642.pdf

United Kingdom (UK). (2011). *The UK Cyber Security Strategy, Cabinet Office, Crown, London*. https://assets.publishing.service.gov.uk/government/uploads/system/uploads/attachment_data/file/60961/uk-cyber-security-strategy-final.pdf

United Nations General Assembly (UN). (2010). *A/RES/64/211: Creation of a Global Culture of Cybersecurity and taking stock of national efforts to protect Critical Information Infrastructures. in Sixty Fourth Session of the United Nations (UN) General Assembly – Resolution adopted by the General Assembly, New York, United Nations.* https://digitallibrary.un.org/record/673712/files/A_RES_64_211-EN.pdf?ln=en

United States Air Force. (2023). *Air Force Doctrine Publication 3-12, Cyberspace Operations.* Available at https://www.doctrine.af.mil/Portals/61/documents/AFDP_3-12/3-12-AFDP-CYBERSPACE-OPS.pdf

United States Joint Chiefs of Staff (USJCS). (2018). *Joint Publication 3-12, Cyberspace Operations, June 8 2018.* https://nsarchive.gwu.edu/sites/default/files/documents/4560063/Joint-Chiefs-of-Staff-Joint-Publication-3-12.pdf

von Solms, R., & van Niekerk, J. (2013, October). From information security to cyber security, Elsevier Science Direct. *Computers & Security, 38*, 97–102. doi:10.1016/j.cose.2013.04.004

Wilson, M., deZafra, D., Pitcher, S., Tressler, J., & Ippolito, J. (1998). *Information Technology Security Training Requirements: A Role- and Performance-Based Model, Special Publication (NIST SP 800-16).* National Institute of Standards and Technology. doi:10.6028/NIST.SP.800-16

Wilson, M., & Hash, J. (2003). *Building an Information Technology Security Awareness and Training Program, Special Publication (NIST SP 800-50).* National Institute of Standards and Technology. https://tsapps.nist.gov/publication/get_pdf.cfm?pub_id=151287

ENDNOTES

[1]   The authors preclude that there is a clear path from information security to cybersecurity.

[2]   With the objective of *"deepen the security of networks and information systems and to promote a free, secure and efficient use of cyberspace, by all citizens and public and private entities."*

[3]   Transposing Directive no. 2016/1148 of the European Parliament and of the Council of 6 July 2016 on the same subject, comprising measures to ensure a high common level of security for networks and information systems throughout the Union.

[4]   Under Regulation (EU) 2019/881 of the European Parliament of 17 April 2019.

[5]   Command, Control, Communications, Computers, Intelligence, Surveillance and Reconnaissance.

[6]   In the Meeting of NATO Ministers of Foreign Affairs in Brussels in December 2016, implementation of the Joint Declaration signed by the President of the European Council, the President of the European Commission, and the Secretary General of the North Atlantic Treaty Organization.

[7]   https://tecnicomais.pt/cursos/protecao-e-seguranca-de-dados-para-profissionais-nao-tecnologicos/

Chapter 7
A Systematic Review of Research on ChatGPT:
The User Perspective

Chong Guan

https://orcid.org/0000-0002-7827-1498

Singapore University of Social Sciences, Singapore

Ding Ding

Singapore University of Social Sciences, Singapore

Priyanka Gupta

Singapore University of Social Sciences, Singapore

Yu-Chen Hung

https://orcid.org/0000-0001-5462-4378

Singapore University of Social Sciences, Singapore

Zhiying Jiang

https://orcid.org/0000-0001-8014-6963

Singapore University of Social Sciences, Singapore

ABSTRACT

This chapter investigates previous research themes and trending topics related to ChatGPT through a comprehensive analysis of the literature. An automated technique (web-scraping) was deployed to retrieve and compile all existing journal papers, conference proceedings, and book chapters from major publisher databases in the related fields, and the abstracts of the selected articles were quantitatively analysed using a probabilistic topic modeling procedure – the latent Dirichlet allocation (LDA) approach. Based on the topics identified by the LDA model utilizing their most representative terms, 10 research themes and corresponding keywords have emerged in the results. The overall findings indicate that research efforts in this field have primarily focused on performance, user disposition, application practices, and ethical and privacy concerns. A conceptual framework that delineated the relationships between the research issues and opportunities for future research on ChatGPT is also introduced.

DOI: 10.4018/978-1-6684-8422-7.ch007

INTRODUCTION

As a transformer-based neural network by OpenAI, ChatGPT represents state-of-the-art generative artificial intelligence (AI) that is capable of generating human-like text responses in natural language processing (NLP) tasks. The term generative AI refers to algorithms (such as ChatGPT) that can be used to generate new content such as audio, code, images, text, simulations, and videos (McKinsey & Company, 2023). It is estimated that ChatGPT reached 100 million monthly active users just months after its launch in January, making it the fastest-growing consumer application in history and setting a record for the fastest-growing user base (K. Hu, 2023).

ChatGPT has taken the world by surprise. Thousands of studies have been carried out on ChatGPT to assess its performance, capabilities, and limitations across its applications, such as content creation, virtual assistants, and conversational agents in a variety of settings. However, there has not been a systematic literature review to synthesize the key findings from the existing ChatGPT literature with a particular focus on user disposition and responses.

In this chapter, we investigate previous research themes and trending topics on ChatGPT through a comprehensive analysis of the literature. We use an automated technique (web-scraping) to retrieve and compile journal papers, conference proceedings, and book chapters from major publisher databases in the related fields, such as IEEE, Association for Computing Machinery (ACM), Springer, IGI, and Wiley. The search keywords used were "ChatGPT", "transformer-based language models", and "generative language models". Considering the rapidly evolving landscape, we have carefully curated papers from repositories of electronic preprints such as arXiv and SSRN. Industry/trade publications, policy briefs, and government white papers were excluded. The inclusion criteria were as follows: (1) the study should be related to ChatGPT, (2) the study should evaluate the performance of ChatGPT in NLP tasks from a user perspective and/or discuss the user responses to such tools, and (3) the study should be published in a peer-reviewed journal, book or conference or repository. We selected over 228 relevant studies that met our inclusion criteria, which were published between 2020 and 2022.

The abstracts of selected articles were quantitatively analysed using a probabilistic topic modeling procedure - the latent Dirichlet allocation (LDA) approach (Blei, 2012a; Blei et al., 2003a). This technique can reveal the hidden (latent) structure of the articles determining which articles address similar topics. LDA enables us to determine three components of the hidden structure: (1) a relatively small number of topics as research themes; (2) each article can be considered as a compilation of the topics discovered by the model, with the exact mix determined by how heavily each abstract is weighted toward each topic; (3) Specific words from each featured topic are assigned to the article by the model. This strategy is rooted in the notion that each article is made up of a variety of different topics, each with its own collection of words. Topic coherence (C_v), a summary measure that captures the tendency of a topic's high probability words to co-occur in the same document, or simply put, the degree of semantic similarity between top keywords in a topic (Mimno et al., 2011), is used to determine the optimal number of topics for topic extraction and conceptual evaluation.

Based on the topics identified by the LDA model utilizing their most representative terms - terms that have a substantially higher chance of occurring in articles concerning that topic than their average chance of appearing across the corpus, we derive five research themes and corresponding keywords that have emerged in the results. The overall findings indicate that research efforts in this field have primarily focused on performance, user disposition, application practices, and, ethical and privacy concerns.

One of the most important aspects of any AI language model is its performance. In the case of ChatGPT, various studies have shown its capability to perform high cognitive level tasks. In a study by (Gilson et al., 2023), ChatGPT was found to outperform other language models on a range of natural language processing tasks, including question-answering and summarization. These findings suggest that ChatGPT is an effective tool for a range of language-related tasks.

As generative AI technology advances, users' expectations for the accuracy and quality of generated content rise. As a result, understanding the user's attitude and disposition toward ChatGPT technology is critical to better evaluate its use. The functional domains — creative writing, essay writing, prompt writing, code writing, and answering questions—represent the most comprehensive possible use cases of ChatGPT based on extant studies. Users have divided attitudes about it: the convenience and relative accuracy of the technology are seen as major advantages (Tlili et al., 2023), while the potential for misuse and the lack of control over the generated content are seen as potential drawbacks, such as assessment integrity(Susnjak, 2022), ethical hazards (Mhlanga, 2023) and confidentiality concerns (Sallam, 2023).

In conclusion, a thematic synthesis of the literature on ChatGPT suggests that the tool has significant potential to be effective and satisfying for a wide range of tasks. However, there are also important considerations related to the model's potential for bias and misuse. As such, there is a need for continued research and development in this area to ensure that ChatGPT is used in a responsible and ethical manner. There is a need for research that focuses on developing strategies for mitigating the risks associated with the tool's use, as well as research that explores the potential for ChatGPT to be used for positive social impact.

LITERATURE REVIEW

The widespread popularity of ChatGPT due to its exceptional ability to produce human-like answers across diverse contexts has led to a surge of research interest in ChatGPT by researchers from various domains. A substantial body of literature has been devoted to various aspects of ChatGPT, covering a broad range of topics including technology advancements (Ce Zhou, 2023; Chien-Chang Lin, 2023; Omar et al., 2023), commercial and non-commercial applications (A. Shaji George, 2023; Luo et al., 2022; Sakib Shahriar, 2023), ethical considerations (Kasneci et al., 2023; Mhlanga, 2023; Susnjak, 2022) and etc.

Created by MIT Professor Joseph Weizenbaum (Luo et al., 2022; Weizenbaum, 1976), ELIZA was the first chatbot to simulate human conversation by asking questions and responding with scripted answers. As an early model, ELIZA, based on a pattern matching and substitution methodology could not be considered to show real understanding of what had been said by each party in a conversation. Natural language programming (NLP) is a milestone in the history of chatbot, which allows chatbot to understand and respond human queries more accurately. With key advancement in NLP (Chien-Chang Lin, 2023), chatbots are then able to complete various tasks including question answering, composing essays/reports, reading comprehension and machine translation. The building blocks of state-of-the-art generative AI models are large-language models (LLMs)(Andrei Kucharavy, 2023; Kim et al., 2021; Sezgin et al., 2022). Chatbots based on large language models are often trained over enormous amounts of data. For example, GPT-3 is trained over data from web, books, Twitters, Wikipedia, etc. LLM allows GPT-3 to learn the language structure in general. The model of GPT-3 has a staggering scale of 175 billion parameters. Such complex system was trained with a reported training resource of over 350GB memory costing $12 million backed by Microsoft (Sakib Shahriar, 2023). ChatGPT as a spinoff of

GPT-3 is capable of producing text content in a wide range of contexts with remarkable accuracy, detail and coherence. What makes ChatGPT unique is the novel technique called reinforcement learning as part of the training method. The reinforcement learning is a reward model that uses human responses as feedback to help ChatGPT understand the human intention, thus minimizing mistakes and making its responses relevant (Mitrovic et al., 2023; Yoshua Bengio, 2000). ChatGPT revolutionizes communication with the general population by providing a powerful tool that can connect easily with users in various scenarios. Its ability to understand and respond to natural language enables it to be widely applied in both commercial and non-commercial occasions.

With the prevalence of digital marketing in the last decade, chatbots have been widely used by firms and organizations to support customers 24/7 . However, the traditional chatbots that are built on question answering system (QAS) provide only factual information and does not engage the customers well resulting in low usage and satisfaction. Extent research has found that low human-likeness leads to low customer trust in the human-chatbot interaction (Jenneboer et al., 2022; Nordheim et al., 2019). Similarly, human-likeness measured as conversation style and intelligence of a chatbot remarkably impacts user's trust and satisfaction when served by a chatbot (Haugeland et al., 2022). With its capability to converse like a human, ChatGPT is poised to become a dominant prototype for customer service automation. In a study by Salah et al. (2023), a survey with a sample of 732 participants is conducted to see how chatting with ChatGPT affects a user's psychological wellbeing. It is found that users exhibit high degree trust on the responses generated by ChatGPT and have high confidence in ChatGPT's accuracy and reliability. In another recent study (Sakirin & Said, 2023), it is found that 70% of users chose ChatGPT enabled conversational tools over the traditional chatbots, citing-efficiency, convenience and personalization as the reasons. In addition to its potential as a customer service automation device, ChatGPT can also be used as a content creation tool for web pages and social media postings. It can also be used to address user views when pre-trained with company's policies (Haleem et al., 2022).

Education is an area where ChatGPT raises both promises and concerns (Baidoo-Anu & Ansah, 2023; Jurgen Rudolph, 2023; Kasneci et al., 2023; Mhlanga, 2023). Due to the constant advancement in technology, the education industry has witnessed a rapid changing landscape. One major change is the increasing adoption of teaching and learning technology, for example, the use of learning platforms such as Zoom, Google Meeting largely facilitates the delivery of education. Also, there has been a shift towards self-directed and asynchronous learning enabling students to have more autonomy in their learning process and allowing them to learn at their own pace. ChatGPT's capability to resolve complex problems offers various opportunities to facilitate self-directed and asynchronous learning. In an exploratory study by Baidoo-Anu and Ansah (2023), they proposed the following supportive roles that can be carried out by ChatGPT- personalized tutoring, language translation, interactive learning, adaptive learning and etc. Kasneci et al. (2023) also discussed several settings where ChatGPT can be applied in both learning and teaching. They propose how ChatGPT can assist learners with different background and under different learning contexts. They also suggest how ChatGPT can assist with teaching activities such as lesson planning, assessment writing and evaluation. Choi et al. (2023), Mhlanga (2023), Qadir (2022) and Khan et al. (2023) present how ChatGPT will impact educational domains such as law, lifelong learning, engineering and medical education respectively. As many great opportunities brought by ChatGPT, there arise many concerns as well. Jalil et al. (2023) and his colleagues studied ChatGPT's capability in the traditional software testing course. They found ChatGPT is able to respond to 77.5% of the questions, out of which only 55.6% are correct and balance are partially correct. This result contrasts with the result of applying ChatGPT to law and medical examination. In addition, responses from

ChatGPT were essentially constructed based on statistical rules and lack true understanding. Hence, they might have limited performance when it comes to inspiring students proactively as human teacher often does (Baidoo-Anu & Ansah, 2023). However, the largest concern over a powerful AI-tool like ChatGPT comes from its threats toward academic integrity, especially in the higher education setting. As ChatGPT is able to perform high-level cognitive tasks with indistinguishable text generated by a human, such capacity might lead to potential use as a tool for academic misconduct. To mitigate such risk, various technological strategies as well as institutional academic integrity policies should be developed or revised (King, 2023; Rudolph et al., 2023; Susnjak, 2022). Hence, ChatGPT should be used in a responsible and ethical manner to ensure safety and fairness to all the stakeholders (Baidoo-Anu & Ansah, 2023; Kasneci et al., 2023; King, 2023; Mhlanga, 2023).

While AI-technology advancement has made remarkable progress in various industries, its application in clinical care remains limited. The fact that ChatGPT managed to perform the United States Medical Licensing Exam (USMLE) with passing grade has spurred fervent discussions in its potential to assist medical research, education and clinic management (Tiffany H. Kung et al., 2023). Studies investigating ChatGPT's capability in each specific branche of medical care started to emerge. To list a few, Arya Rao et al. (2023) evaluated ChatGPT's capability for clinical decision support in radiology in breast cancer screening and breast pain. Jeblick, Schachtner, Dexl, Mittermeier, Anna, et al. (2022) explores the possibility for ChatGPT to simplify radiology reports so that ChatGPT can be applied to more downstream tasks. Duong and Solomon (2023) analysed ChatGPT's performance on answering genetics questions by comparing to human experts. Yeo et al. (2023) assessed ChatGPT's answers to 164 questions regarding cirrhosis and hepatocellular carcinoma. Their results showed that ChatGPT may be used as a complementary informational tool for patients and doctors to improve outcomes. Singh (2023) suggests that given ChatGPT's capability to produce high quality content, it may be used as a viable alternative for psychiatric diagnosis making treatment accessible and affordable. Again, concerns were raised regarding using ChatGPT in health care settings, among which the negative consequence of generating inaccurate information is the most disconcerting (Ahn, 2023; Dat Duong & Benjamin D. Solomon, 2023; Tiffany H. Kung et al., 2023). In the area of personalized medicine, lack of transparency regarding the information used to pre-train ChatGPT becomes an important issue given the heterogeneity of individual's health-related traits in a population (Sallam, 2023).

With ChatGPT's extraordinary capability to conduct high-cognitive level task and generate human-like content in a coherent and engaging manner, a large body of research emerged in the last three months in all related fields. There have been systematic literature reviews regarding research on ChatGPT in specific domains. Reviews have been conducted to summarize the technology advancement in AI-driven conversational chatbots in terms of design, methodologies, applications and etc (Ce Zhou, 2023; Chien-Chang Lin, 2023; Luo et al., 2022). Jenneboer et al. (2022) implemented a systematic literature review on the impact of chatbots on customer loyalty and a recent publication by Mariani et al. (2023) performed a systematic survey of research on AI-empowered conversational agents on customer service. Then, Sallam (2023) carried out a systematic review on ChatGPT's utility in healthcare education, research and practice. These domain specific literature review studies provide timely information on the research progression in their respective fields, shedding light on future research agenda. However, given the fast and wide adoption of ChatGPT in all user related fields and the shift to interdisciplinary research, there is a need to have a comprehensive and systematic literature review of ChatGPT from the user's perspective. Such literature review allows us to have a bird's eye view for the development of research in different sectors that are not fragmented- helping researchers and practitioners to understand the trend, key issues, opportunities and challenges pertaining to the use of ChatGPT.

METHODOLOGY

This chapter presents an in-depth investigation of the trending themes and topics in previous studies related to ChatGPT by conducting a comprehensive investigation of the academic literature. The present systematic review was carried out by utilizing an automated retrieval technique in the form of web-scraping to gather and compile scholarly articles from academic journals, conference proceedings, book chapters, and working papers with a predefined set of keywords commonly employed in the pertinent literature, specifically "ChatGPT" and "users."

The keywords were used to conduct an extensive search of leading publisher databases such as Association for Computing Machinery (ACM), Emerald, IGI, IEEE, ScienceDirect, Springer, Sage, Taylor & Francis, and Wiley. Given the constantly changing landscape in generative AI, we have carefully selected articles from reputable archives of electronic preprints in the relevant fields, including arXiv, bioRxiv, EdArXiv, TechRxiv, medRxiv, PubMed, and PsyArXiv. Each collated paper is reviewed by an expert panel to ensure its user focus on ChatGPT applications. Industry/trade publications, editorials and correspondences without abstracts, policy briefs, and government white papers were excluded. As a result, we identified a total of 228 articles for analysis.

The abstracts of selected papers were qualitatively analysed by Latent Dirichlet Allocation (LDA) (Blei et al., 2003b), one of the most popular natural language processing (NLP) techniques for Topic modelling. It uses an unsupervised Bayesian learning algorithm that extracts "topics" from the text on the basis of co-occurrence (Blei, 2012b; Blei et al., 2003b). LDA surpasses other existing techniques for extracting dimensions from textual material due to several factors. First, the LDA framework is highly efficient and is suitable for handling large-scale corpus and sparse matrices. Second, as an unsupervised (automated) machine learning technique, LDA obviates the need for researchers to create complex dictionaries for analysis. Third, it permits exploratory topic analysis of document collections. By tuning the LDA parameters, researchers can extract an optimum number of latent dimensions and resulting document clusters to fit the dataset. Last, the latent dimensions extracted can be readily interpretable as there is a direct mapping between each dimension (topic) and the attributes (words) that compose it. This automatic extraction of the candidate terms facilitates topic labelling, comprehension, and interpretation.

Previous studies have established the effectiveness of LDA in identifying dimensions and top keywords expressed in online reviews (Chong Guan et al., 2022; Tirunillai & Tellis, 2014), and to generalise research trends in literature analysis (Cheng, 2022; C. Guan et al., 2022; Wang et al., 2015).

In line with previous literature, LDA was used to analyse the words contained in abstracts and to generate a list of interpretable topics. This technique is deployed to uncover the latent structure of the papers by identifying which are the ones that address similar subjects. More specifically, LDA enables the identification of three components of the hidden structure: (1) a relatively small number of topics as research themes; (2) each paper is viewed as a combination of the themes discovered, with the exact blend determined by the weights assigned to each topic in the abstract; and (3) the model assigns specific words from each featured topic to each paper. This approach is based on the concept that each article comprises of various topics, each with its own set of words.

Preparing Text for Analysis

The textual data contained in the abstracts was cleaned and standardized for subsequent analysis. First, non-English characters, punctuation and words containing numbers that typically do not include informational content about the topics of interest were eliminated. All common English stopwords (e.g., "the," "and," "when," "is," "at," "which," "on," "in") that are used to connect grammatical elements but are not required for connotation were excluded using the predefined stopwords list by NLTK in Python. The cleansed resulting set forms the "corpus" of textual content used for analysis (Manning et al., 2008).

Dimension Extraction

LDA was extended (Blei et al., 2003) using Genism to identify an optimum number of topics and the topics were labeled based on the words representing each dimension. The model delineates the process that determines the joint probability distribution across the observed words in the abstracts and the latent topics that could be inferred from the distribution of these words.

Next, the components of the likelihood specification via the generative process and the inference of the dimensions are as follows. Each document w denotes an abstract. For each document w, a distribution over topics is denoted by $\hat{I}_,$. For each word in the document w, a topic variable z_n is specified based on $\hat{I}$. The word probabilities are parameterized using a $k \times V$ matrix β. LDA model assumes that the topic mixture θ is a k-dimensional Dirichlet random variable that is constructed as follows, where the parameter α is a k-vector with elements $\hat{I} \pm_i > 0$ and where $\Gamma(x)$ represents the gamma function.

$$P\left(\theta | \alpha\right) = \frac{\Gamma\left(\sum_{i-1}^{k} \alpha_i\right)}{\prod_{i-1}^{k} \Gamma\left(\alpha_i\right)} \theta_1^{\alpha_1 - 1} ... \theta_k^{\alpha_k - 1}$$

Across the corpus of abstracts, it is assumed that K is the total number of topics (dimensions). Here, LDA assumes that the abstracts emerge from these latent dimensions, and the abstracts exhibit a subset of these hidden dimensions in various proportions.

Given the parameters $\hat{I} \pm$ and $\hat{I}^2$, the joint distribution of a topic mixture θ, a collection of N topics z, and a collection of N words, w is given by:

$$p\left(\theta, z, w | \alpha, \beta\right) = p\left(\theta | \alpha\right) \prod_{n-1}^{N} p\left(z_n | \theta\right) p\left(w_n | z_n, \beta\right)$$

where $p(Z_n | \hat{I}_,)$ represents $\hat{I}_{,i}$ for the unique i such that $z_n^i = 1$. By integrating over θ and summing over z, the marginal distribution of a document is obtained:

$$p\left(w | \alpha, \beta\right) = \int p\left(\theta | \alpha\right) \left(\prod_{n-1}^{N} \sum_{z_n} p\left(z_n | \theta\right) p\left(w_n | z_n, \beta\right) d\theta\right)$$

Lastly, by taking the product of the marginal probabilities of all documents, the probability of a corpus D will be obtained:

$$p\left(D\,|\,\alpha, \beta\right) = \prod_{d=1}^{M} \int p\left(\theta_d\,|\,\alpha\right) \left(\prod_{n-1}^{N} \sum_{z_{dn}} p\left(z_{dn}\,|\,\theta_d\right) p\left(w_{dn}\,|\,z_{dn}, \beta\right)\right) d\theta_d$$

Both parameters, α and β serve as corpus level parameters, which are assumed to be sampled once during the process of generating a corpus. The variables $\hat{I}_{,d}$ represent document-level variables, that are assumed to be sampled once per document. Finally, the variables z_{dn} and w_{dn} assume the role of word-level variables. They are sampled once for every word in each document.

RESULTS

Selection Of The Optimum Number Of Dimensions

The selection of the optimal number of dimensions requires quantitative evaluation and selection of topic models. One way to evaluate topic extraction is to assess topic coherence(C_v), which serves as a summary measure that captures the tendency of a topic's high probability words to co-occur in the same document or simply put, the degree of semantic similarity between top keywords in a topic (Mimno et al., 2011). C_v measure is based on a sliding window one-set segmentation of the high-scoring words and an indirect confirmation measure that applies a normalised version of pointwise mutual information (PMI) criterion and the cosine similarity, which is the choice of metric for model performance comparison in this study.

To determine the optimum number of dimensions, the coherence score distribution for a varying number of dimensions was sampled. Figure 1 below outlines the coherence scores, C_v, as a function of the number of topics, with $\alpha = 0.91$ and $\beta = 0.91$. Based on the plots of the coherence scores, and the corresponding number of topics, both three and seven dimensions extracted yield relatively high coherence scores. For the purpose of this research, ten dimensions are adopted over the others as the framework extracts a relatively more parsimonious and interpretable set of latent dimensions.

Figure 1.

Coherence

LDA was then applied to extract and label the latent topics across all the abstracts. Table 1 presents the dimensions extracted and the corresponding top keywords in each dimension. These keywords with the highest weights relating to each dimension help label the topic and interpret the characteristics represented by the dimensions.

Topics	Representative Top Words
Topic 1 – Generative language models	generative, models, language, artificial, intelligence
Topic 2 – Assistive Technology	potential, applications, information, analysis, writing
Topic 3 – Human centricity	human, data, text, students, correct
Topic 4 – Large language model (LLM) and its social impacts	language, models, questions, large, llms
Topic 5 – Performance in view of social impact	technology, performance, information, diagnosis, tools
Topic 6 – Medical applications	clinical, applications, medical, reasoning, decision
Topic 7 – human-AI collaboration	gpt, work, generative, questions, answers
Topic 8 – Research and education	models, scientific, question, content, paper
Topic 9 – Use cases	medical, language, questions, education, performance
Topic 10 – Responsible systems	data, knowledge, systems, nlp, responsible

One of the limitations of the LDA method is that for certain dimensions, the automatic extraction of the candidate words by weight scores may not express the words' connotation in its entirety, when they are taken out of context. Each word typically represents partial information of the overall dimension. Such cases have resorted to manual labeling and interpretation of the dimensions through human intervention. For each extracted dimension, ten documents with high probability (from the LDA model) were randomly selected for dimension allocation. A deeper manual analysis of the review texts not only enhances the understanding of the context but also offers more insight into the cause or nature of the associated dimension.

Discussion

As shown in Table 1, ten research topics and corresponding keywords have emerged from the research articles related to ChapGPT in the past few months. We also performed manual content analysis to corroborate the findings with qualitative illustrations of emergent topics. Appendix A contains a list of representative text excerpts from the abstracts for each topic, demonstrating how the concepts in the articles are related to the research in ChatGPT. The overall findings indicate that research efforts in this field have primarily focused on the following five aspects:

- Technology used in ChatGTP and its performance
- Application use cases in different domains
- Human centricity

- Human-AI collaboration
- Pervasive social impacts and challenges across disciplines

These five areas of prominent research thrusts that have emerged throughout the literature will be discussed in the following section. A conceptual framework that delineates the relationships between research issues and opportunities for future research on ChatGTP is then introduced.

a. The technology used in ChatGPT and its performance (Topic 1, 2, &10)

The first group of literature (**Topic 1**) emerged from our LDA analysis focus on the technology behind ChatGTP, namely the Large Language Models, and its strength and limitations. In these research articles, the authors explained how generative language models work, their algorithms, functionality, and capabilities. ChatGPT is based on the GPT-3.5 architecture, which is a transformer-based neural network designed for natural language processing tasks. This advanced model is built on top of the GPT-3 architecture, which is known for its ability to generate high-quality text that is nearly indistinguishable from human-written content. The GPT-3.5 architecture is designed to learn how to understand and generate human-like language by training on massive amounts of text data. This model has over 175 billion parameters, which is significantly larger than the 13.5 billion parameters of its predecessor, GPT-3. The additional parameters enable the model to better capture the nuances of human language and improve its performance on a range of NLP tasks.

The transformer-based architecture of the GPT-3.5 model is particularly well-suited for generating high-quality text. This architecture consists of a series of transformer blocks that process input text and generate output text. Each transformer block consists of a self-attention mechanism that enables the model to learn how to attend to different parts of the input text and generate highly relevant responses. The GPT-3.5 model also incorporates a number of advanced features that enhance its performance on NLP tasks. For example, it uses a technique called dynamic prompts to improve the relevance of its responses. Dynamic prompts enable the model to adjust its responses based on the context of the conversation and the user's intent, allowing it to generate more accurate and helpful responses.

Overall, the technology behind ChatGPT represents a significant advance in the field of NLP. Its ability to generate high-quality text that is nearly indistinguishable from human-written content makes it a powerful tool for a range of applications, from chatbots to language translation. As researchers continue to refine and improve the GPT-3.5 architecture, we can expect to see even more impressive results in the years to come.

On the other hand, another group of studies (**Topic 2**) focuses more on the performance of ChatGPT as compared to human beings, and the feasibility and robustness of ChatGPT in various domains. ChatGPT has a wide range of potential use cases, including chatbots, language translation, content generation, and more. Its advanced natural language processing capabilities make it a powerful tool for automating conversations and generating high-quality text. Additionally, its ability to understand context and learn from previous interactions enables it to provide highly personalized responses and enhance user experiences. Many studies have showed that the large language models used in ChatGTP may have the potential to assist humans in a variety of areas(Kung et al., 2023) and ChatGTP shows consistent advantages on most tasks and astounding performance(Wang et al., 2023).

Despite its many benefits, there are also limitations to the technology behind ChatGPT. One key limitation is the significant computational resources required to train these models, which can have negative environmental impacts. Additionally, as with any AI model, there is a risk of generating inappropriate or offensive responses. Furthermore, ChatGPT is limited by the quality and diversity of its training data, which can impact its ability to accurately represent the full range of human language and perspectives.

Research in **Topic 10** focused on the issues related to responsible systems. The issue of responsible system regarding ChatGPT is a critical consideration, as the technology's widespread applications have the potential to influence human behaviour and decision-making in various domains. The development and use of ChatGPT must be conducted in a responsible and ethical manner, considering potential biases and limitations that could negatively impact outcomes.

One of the primary considerations regarding responsible ChatGPT development is the quality and source of training data. If the data used to train ChatGPT models is biased or flawed in some way, it could lead to discriminatory or inaccurate outcomes(Ghosal, 2023). For instance, a medical ChatGPT model trained on data that primarily represents certain populations may not be effective in identifying symptoms or suggesting treatments for other populations. As such, it is imperative to carefully scrutinize training data sources, their representativeness, and quality, and take appropriate steps to mitigate any potential biases.

Another issue pertains to the potential impact of ChatGPT on human behaviour and decision-making. For example, if ChatGPT models are used to provide personalized feedback on written assignments, there is a risk that they may reinforce biases or stereotypes(Rao et al., 2023). To mitigate such risks, it is necessary to carefully assess the potential impact of ChatGPT on human decision-making and behaviour and take appropriate steps to ensure that its use is responsible and ethical. Furthermore, privacy and data protection are also major concerns when using ChatGPT to collect and analyse sensitive information. To ensure that ChatGPT use remains responsible, it is imperative to have measures in place that protect personal data from misuse or unauthorized access.

In order to address these issues, responsible ChatGPT development requires transparency and accountability. Developers and users of ChatGPT should be transparent about the technology's workings, data sources, and outcomes. They should also take responsibility for any potential negative impacts of ChatGPT and take necessary steps to mitigate these impacts. These steps could include measures such as auditing ChatGPT models for bias, providing accurate and clear information to users regarding the technology's functionality, and establishing ethical standards and guidelines for its use. Ultimately, responsible ChatGPT development requires ongoing evaluation and improvement to ensure that it is used in a manner that is responsible, ethical, and aligned with human values.

a.   Application use cases in different domains (Topic 6, 8 & 9)

ChatGPT has the potential to revolutionize communication in a variety of domains, including medical, research, and education. Its advanced natural language processing capabilities and ability to generate high-quality text make it a powerful tool for automating conversations and improving the user experience in these fields.

Medical domain (Topic 6):
In the medical domain, ChatGPT has the potential to revolutionize patient care. For example, it could be used to automate patient communication, such as answering common questions about medications, providing guidance on managing specific health conditions, and scheduling appointments (Budler et al., 2023). ChatGPT could also be used to help healthcare providers identify symptoms and suggest appropriate treatments. For example, it could be used to identify patients at risk of developing a particular

condition and provide preventative guidance. Additionally, ChatGPT could be used to monitor patients remotely, such as tracking their symptoms or vital signs, and alerting healthcare providers to any changes that may require medical intervention.

Research and Education domain (Topic 8):

ChatGPT could also be a valuable tool in the research domain, helping to automate conversations with study participants and collect data more efficiently and accurately. For example, it could be used to administer surveys and collect responses in a standardized and automated way, reducing the potential for human error. Additionally, ChatGPT could be used to analyze large amounts of data and generate insights that could inform future research studies. For example, it could be used to analyze patient records and identify patterns or trends that could inform the development of new treatments or interventions.

In the education domain, ChatGPT could be used to enhance the learning experience for students. For example, it could be used to provide personalized feedback on written assignments, suggest resources that are relevant to specific topics, and answer common questions about course materials. Additionally, ChatGPT could be used to automate administrative tasks, such as scheduling appointments with academic advisors, registering for classes, and paying tuition fees.

Other Use cases (Topic 9)

More use cases are provided in this cluster including the causal discovery in education (Tu et al., 2023), potential disruption on hydrology(Halloran et al., 2023), rewriting a novel (Thorp, 2023), philosophical arguments (Zhavoronkov, 2022), automating repetitive and time-consuming tasks in the construction industry (Prieto et al., 2023). The use of ChatGPT varies widely depending on the industry. The use cases are accompanied by assessing its performance relative to standing industry practice and the ethical issues.

However, there are potential limitations and ethical concerns associated with the use of ChatGPT in these domains. For example, there may be privacy concerns around the use of ChatGPT to collect and analyze personal health data. Additionally, there is a risk of bias in the training data used to develop ChatGPT models, which could lead to unfair or discriminatory outcomes. For example, if the training data used to develop a medical ChatGPT model is biased toward certain populations, it may not be effective in identifying symptoms or suggesting treatments for other populations. It is important to carefully consider the potential benefits and limitations of ChatGPT in each specific domain and take appropriate steps to mitigate any potential risks.

a.   Human centricity (Topic 3)

ChatGPT has proven to be a highly advantageous resource for professionals across various fields, including librarians (Chen, 2023), medical educators (Kung et al., 2023), clinical decision-makers (Duong & Solomon, 2023), and epidemiological researchers (Sanmarchi et al., 2023). It demonstrates immense potential in enhancing patient-centered care by effectively answering memory-based questions, as opposed to those requiring critical thinking (Jeblick, Schachtner, Dexl, Mittermeier, Stüber, et al., 2022). However, it offers convincing explanations for both accurate and inaccurate answers.

Additionally, ChatGPT aids researchers in drafting articles and selecting study designs, ultimately expediting scientific advancement under careful human supervision (Macdonald et al., 2023). It also offers valuable assistance in the development and execution of epidemiological research projects (Sanmarchi et al., 2023). To optimize its benefits, close human monitoring and addressing the "hallucination problem" are essential. Implementing techniques such as chain-of-thought prompting can facilitate a qualitative understanding of the generated responses' CoTs, enabling empirical evaluations and supplying training data (Ott et al., 2023)

a.   Human-AI collaboration (Topic 7)

Studies have explored the transformative impact of generative AI on various aspects, such as human information acquisition (Sallam et al., 2023), its influence on existing workflows, and its role in training novices (Ahmad et al., 2023). The paradigm has evolved to encompass a human-AI collaborative approach in areas like research idea generation, study design, manuscript creation, and result interpretation (Adesso, 2023). This human-in-the-loop interaction with generative AI raises questions about how to meaningfully engage with it.

Case studies have begun to illuminate the human-AI collaboration. For instance, ChatGPT is used to form a partnership with a novice software architect in the analysis, synthesis, and evaluation of a service-driven software application (Ahmad et al., 2023). This collaboration demonstrates the potential for human-AI teamwork in various fields, where humans and machines are strategically placed to do what their best.

a.   Pervasive social impacts and challenges (Topic 4 & 5)

ChatGPT as a general-purpose technology is distinguished by its extensive proliferation, ongoing enhancement, and the fostering of auxiliary innovations (Eloundou et al., 2023). These technologies possess the unique ability to spread across various sectors, continuously improve over time, and generate complementary advancements that fuel further innovation. Its proliferation also gives rise to social impact and challenges pervasive across sectors.

Topic 4: LLM and its social impacts

ChatGPT has caused at least three types of social challenges. First, the misuse of ChatGPT poses a serious threat to academic rigor. For example, a significant challenge in academia is the reinforcement of editorial policies on AI-generated papers (Hu, 2023). Identifying such papers remains difficult for the human eye, and appropriate tools for policy implementation are yet to be validated. Second, language modeling decreases the time needed for tasks in certain jobs through automation. Notable occupations affected by language modeling include telemarketers, post-secondary teachers of English language and literature, foreign languages and literature, and history (Felten et al., 2023).

In addition, since AI language models, like GPT-3 (Generative Pre-trained Transformer 3), can generate vast amounts of text mimicking human language, discerning between authentic and false information becomes increasingly challenging. The pursuit of truthful AI is in high demand due to the ongoing struggle for accuracy in AI systems and their responses (Munn et al., 2023). However, the operationalization of truth raises concerns, demanding re-evaluating AI "truth-telling" as a social practice and determining the "truth statement" that society desires as listeners. Engaging in such discussions is crucial for developing "Truth Machines"- AI language models designed to produce accurate and truthful information. These models aim to tackle the issues of misinformation and fake news, which have become increasingly pervasive in the digital era.

The social impacts are not totally negative. ChatGPT has proven useful in affective computing issues to reflect public sentiments (Amin et al., 2023). It also accelerates the innovation process in online interactive collaborative design by recombining various creative ideas (Lanzi & Loiacono, 2023). Conversational AI models like ChatGPT are also instrumental in detecting and deflecting malicious activity, making them valuable for organizations seeking to improve their cybersecurity position. Future work will concentrate on various cybersecurity implications, such as host-virus detection, and data security (McKee & Noever, 2023).

Topic 5: Performance in view of social impact

Potential applications of ChatGPT in various domains are highlighted (Chatterjee & Dethlefs, 2023), including finance (Dowling & Lucey, 2023), healthcare (Nov et al., 2023), education (Shahriar & Hayawi, 2023), and library and research (Lund & Wang, 2023). Given its pervasive impacts, its implication on public affairs has attracted much attention. For example, its ability to affect public health is assessed by examining the generated contents' clinical appropriateness, concordance with guidelines (Nastasi et al., 2023), recommendation type, and consideration of social factors (Nov et al., 2023). Another dimension of impact on public affairs is its political standing, as its public response will affect democratic society's most important decision-making process: political election. After prompting ChatGPT with political statements, ChatGPT's is uncovered to be of pro-environmental, left-libertarian ideology (Hartmann et al., 2023).

Given its implication on public affairs, there is a demand surge in seeking "explainability" from AI. Explainable AI (XAI) refers to artificial intelligence systems that are designed to be transparent and understandable to humans. The primary goal of XAI is to provide clear, easily interpretable explanations for the decisions made by AI algorithms, particularly those involved in complex tasks like machine learning and deep learning.

Explainable AI is crucial for building trust between humans and AI systems, as it allows users to comprehend the reasoning behind the AI's decisions and actions. This understanding is essential in various domains, such as finance, healthcare, and law, where the consequences of AI-generated decisions can be significant. By offering insights into AI decision-making, XAI helps address ethical concerns, ensures accountability, and enables users to assess the reliability and fairness of AI systems. One example to seek better performance in explainability is the U.S. Defense Advanced Research Projects Agency (DARPA) , which sees explainability as an important factor for AI adoption, considering the needs of warfighters to effectively collaborate with AI to boost performance (Adamson, 2023).

FUTURE RESEARCH AGENDA

Given the power of generative AI and the speed with which artificially intelligent tools, such as ChatGPT are being developed and adopted across a wide range of contexts, it becomes extremely important to envisage the potential opportunities and challenges of this technology. The future research scope has been presented along four streams- ChatGPT technical limitations that warrant further research, ChatGPT application domains, human-AI collaboration and concerns surrounding the use of ChatGPT.

a.   How to deal with generative AI's technical limitations?

Using ChatGPT as an example, as it is the one, we have been able to use for ourselves, these limitations offer research opportunities:

- *Real-time automatic data update* – When generating output, ChatGPT is unable to consider real-time vents and information which is touted as one of its major shortcomings. This calls for advanced algorithms that could facilitate real-time content creation which is still a challenge for ChatGPT.
- *Dealing with imperfect information* – This is still a challenge for AI (Dwivedi et al., 2020) and is particularly true in the case of ChatGPT.
- *Transparency and accountability* – It is crucial that generative AI design elements support transparency, and accountability and behave responsibly.
- The future of generative AI should look into making it *compatible with other systems* and this integration between systems should add to its overall performance and capability.
- Having a more targeted *domain-specific AI system* rather than a generic approach can alleviate ethical concerns, copyright infringement and other similar issues.
    b.   Future research scope in different domains

Education

Generative AI is one in a line of several technologies that have disrupted the classroom experience for students in higher education. Past disruptive technologies include calculators, email, Google search, statistical packages, etc. There are numerous fruitful avenues for research related to the application of generative AI such as ChatGPT for teaching and learning. An important research question is - How do conversational technologies make teaching and learning more effective? Can ChatGPT provide an enhanced student learning experience? It is important that the instructors adopt a two-pronged approach- exploration and experimentation. Instructors can act as facilitators on the students' journey of exploring these tools.

It will be a fruitful endeavour to engage students in a dialogue and educate them about applying IT mindfulness when using generative AI for their own work. For example, the instructors can initiate the exploration process by asking students to provide a critique of an essay written by ChatGPT on a topic related to the class(Mollick & Mollick, 2022). ChatGPT should aid progressive new-age teaching-learning processes like flipped classroom learning, and blended learning and also support students with disabilities(O'Flaherty & Phillips, 2015). Future research should investigate the appropriate ways and processes to introduce tools such as ChatGPT in curriculum design and if ChatGPT can minimise rote learning and do routine jobs like scoring and checking quizzes.

Another question that needs to be answered is- How can we assess the effectiveness of ChatGPT in terms of student performance and intention to use it? How can ChatGPT be used to develop critical thinking and problem-solving skills of students and researchers? It is equally important to apprise the students of the limitations of the technology. Students should be guided to explore and use critical thinking when using technology. Researchers have already provided compelling evidence that generative AI in general and ChatGPT specifically provide biased output (Chen et al., 2023).

Research

Next, we will take this same assumption and apply it to the research process. Researchers have also raised significant concerns regarding content created by ChatGPT (Else, 2023). The following questions require further investigation- What is the long-term impact of ChatGPT on scholarly writing and research? What is the role of human creativity when ChatGPT is used in scholarly writing?

The ethical guidelines for universities and journals also need to evolve along with the application of generative AI. Some journals have already provided guidance to their authors- generative AI does not qualify for authorship but the use of the technology should be documented in the methods section. In response to authors listing ChatGPT as a contributing author (Kung et al., 2023), Nature has developed guiding principles to help authors with the use and attribution of generative AI text (Nature, 2023). Further, publishers, editors, and conference committees have a responsibility to ensure reviewers are provided with relevant training to help mitigate the threat of technologies (when used unethically) that have the potential to undermine the craft of scholarly writing and the integrity of our disciplines.

Healthcare

ChatGPT and platforms like MedPaLM would provide a boost to digital health initiatives. It would give valuable input to medical and paramedic staff in the primary healthcare centres in remote areas under the supervision of a trained physician. The augmentation of ChatGPT in healthcare training may reduce the learning cycle time for the participants.

BFSI

ChatGPT will replace routine (non-critical) jobs like customer care, basic financial analysis, and text analytics for customer sentiments in the Banking, Financial Services, and Insurance (BFSI) sector. The audit and advisory services would get a boost by accurate analysis, which would help banking executives to focus more on the insight and implications piece of the client-interface process.

Hospitality and Tourism

The service providers in hospitality and tourism can provide ChatGPT as a widget on their websites. ChatGPT would act as a round-the-clock interactive interface for the customers for providing the travel, food, vehicle, and tourist locations along with their distance. It can enhance customer experience and minimise the manpower cost for service providers.

Marketing

Future research which involves GPT-3 should focus on how generative AI technologies can benefit marketing in customer services, customer engagement and experience, content curation and development, marketing research, lead generation, commerce, and promotional activities. Important research questions include: (1) how to design, operate and continuously improve frictionless, generative AI-governed customer journeys; (2) how can this technology guide customers effectively through their journeys and how can it be designed to be customer-error tolerant and (3) to master automated service recovery when needed. For example, the chatbots currently being used are closely based on existing frequently asked questions (FAQs) cum training data. Technology like ChatGPT can help the "chatbots" to mimic the general intelligence of a human brain in the future and the responses generated could be very similar to the ones generated by today's frontline employees.

Legal Services

Legal services highly depend on written laws of the land and past judgments. ChatGPT provides advisory and support documents by text-mining legal databases in an efficient manner. This would enhance productivity multi-fold for individuals, regulators, and law firms working in this industry.

a.   Human-AI collaboration

An important research question in this area is: What are the optimal ways to combine human and AI agents in various domains to maximise the opportunities and benefits while minimising the negative impacts? Giving a good prompt is not a sufficient condition to elicit a distinctively varied and original response for higher-level activities that involve different areas of the human brain as suggested by the recent uses of generative AI for text, music and movie generation (Vargo et al., 2008). This is even more relevant for products that involve some form of emotional intelligence (Jena & Goyal, 2022). As AI platforms and the underlying technology will evolve, future research will need to investigate the role played by generative AI in triggering innovation outcomes.

Knowledge Worker

Research suggests that a lot of time and effort of a knowledge worker is spent on writing a first draft of anything – an email, a report, a blog, a business plan, a proposal, an article, or an employee review that offers little personal satisfaction and could be handled competently by others (Birkinshaw & Cohen, 2013). 'Others' has typically been thought of as another person, but could equally be a technology solution, like ChatGPT. An experimental research program can be designed to test the difference in productivity between the two conditions. Condition one would be where a research subject completes a task from start to finish, while in the second condition, a subject uses ChatGPT to create a first draft, and then completes the task using the draft as a foundation. Experiments could be conducted employing both within-subject and between-subject designs. Productivity could be measured in two ways: time to complete the task (efficiency) and quality of the output (effectiveness)

Hybrid Teams

Knowing AI can assist with various tasks in a team can also enrich the discussion about hybrid work. Hybrid work is no longer limited to the continuum of presence and virtual but also comprehends the duality of human/human vs human/AI. AI can play two kinds of roles in hybrid teams:

- Simple roles, such as text producer, language editor and research assistant
- Sophisticated roles, such as coach, innovator and software developer

As a next step, it seems reasonable to use group roles or task frameworks to identify the strengths and weaknesses of ChatGPT. Research will need to show the tasks best suited for ChatGPT (or other AI) and the challenges associated with it .

Personalization

Many issues related to the challenges and limitations of generative AI can be more effectively addressed by customising the systems at individual and organisational levels. Personalisation is an essential criterion for the successful adoption of AI tools (Duan et al., 2012). However, personalisation requires a huge amount of time, effort and resources from the end users and the organisations concerned because they need to provide reliable data and fine-tune the model to align with their needs, value, ethical principles, and relevant regulations. This is a potentially huge research area.

a. Concerns surrounding ChatGPT

Ethical

Given ChatGPT has been coined "the industry's next big disrupter", it is important for researchers and practitioners to examine the ethical concerns surrounding black-box algorithms and how multi-disciplinary research can help alleviate these concerns. ChatGPT and other advanced digital front-line technologies carry serious ethical, fairness, and privacy risks (Belk, 2021; Breidbach & Maglio, 2020; Wirtz et al., 2022). It is disconcerting that these technologies can result in customers being assessed, predicted, and nudged, all often without their consent and awareness. We will need research to understand, manage, and mitigate the risks of generative AI such as ChatGPT and other technologies that get ever closer to achieving artificial general intelligence when used in customer service. Besides concentrating on the text queries, future research should also focus on the role of pictures and arts in generative AI frameworks.

Social

Future studies may also explore the effects of AI-generated marketing-related content on society. For example, the interplay between AI-generated content and AI safety might be investigated to find the impact of misaligned AI on users consuming AI-generated content. Presently researchers perceive the future of ChatGPT based on the existing knowledge of reflective AI. With ChatGPT yet to evidence a series of developments, researchers should enhance the available knowledge in the area of IS. There will be a need in various developing countries to understand the basis of training of publicly available ChatGPT programmes, and how their own values are represented and explicated. As tools like ChatGPT are integrated into human-AI hybrid solutions (Rai et al., 2019), researchers will have to address societal questions of access asymmetries. One example is of users who cannot use English (and other languages ChatGPT can work in), as they will suffer from their inability to use the AGI tool, while their peers will be able to. Further, inequality of access will lead to asymmetry in the data used to train and refine these algorithms, where marginalised groups will not have their data represented (Chen & Wellman, 2004; Weissglass, 2022).

Responsibility

Along with abilities and skill, the agency of human-AI systems will raise questions of responsibility. Research shows that there are gradations in degrees of agency, with humans and AI systems displaying varying values on different dimensions of agency (Dattathrani & De', 2023). With the increased use of

ChatGPT, for tasks such as coding, or planning, there will be an increased focus on responsibility when things go wrong. Along with blame and accountability, there will be the problems of allocating legal and financial liability. Future research will have to identify the human vs AI agentic responsibilities for various domains and tasks.

Regulatory

Prior research has also suggested that building a regulative system (e.g., regulations to govern ChatGPT) is the first stage of institution formation, followed by the formation of normative institutions and then cognitive institutions (Hoffman, 1999). In future empirical work, scholars also need to compare and contrast ChatGPT and other major innovations in terms of the pattern of the evolution of various types of institutions. Regarding institutional evolution around generative AI, a related future research topic could be how institutional change agents theorize such changes (Kshetri & Ajami, 2008). Theorization helps provide rationales for the practices to be adopted and thus increases the chance of acceptance of the practice (Strang & Meyer, 1993). Two key elements of theorization are framing and justifying. Framing focuses on the need for change and justification is the value of the proposed changes for concerned actors (Greenwood et al., 2002; Maguire et al., 2004). Thus, researchers could look at how various institutional change agents frame and justify the need for change in institutions related to generative AI.

REFERENCES

Adamson, G. (2023). Explaining technology we don't understand. *IEEE Transactions on Technology and Society*. doi:10.1109/TTS.2023.3240107

Adesso, G. (2023). Towards The Ultimate Brain: Exploring Scientific Discovery with ChatGPT AI. In: Authorea Preprints.

Ahmad, A., Waseem, M., Liang, P., Fehmideh, M., Shamima Aktar, M., & Mikkonen, T. (2023). *Towards Human-Bot Collaborative Software Architecting with ChatGPT*. arXiv:2302.14600. doi:10.1145/3593434.3593468

Ahn, C. (2023). Exploring ChatGPT for information of cardiopulmonary resuscitation. *Resuscitation*, *185*, 109729. doi:10.1016/j.resuscitation.2023.109729 PMID:36773836

Amin, M. M., Cambria, E., & Schuller, B. W. (2023). *Will Affective Computing Emerge from Foundation Models and General AI? A First Evaluation on ChatGPT*. arXiv:2303.03186. Retrieved March 01, 2023, from https://ui.adsabs.harvard.edu/abs/2023arXiv230303186A

Andrei Kucharavy, Maŕechal, Ẅursch, Dolamic, Sabonnadiere, David, Mermoud, & Lenders. (2023). Fundamentals of Generative Large Language Modelsand Perspectives in Cyber-Defense. arXiv pre-print server.

Baidoo-Anu, D., & Ansah, L. O. (2023). *Education in the Era of Generative Artificial Intelligence (AI): Understanding the Potential Benefits of ChatGPT in Promoting Teaching and Learning*. Academic Press.

Belk, R. (2021). Ethical issues in service robotics and artificial intelligence. *Service Industries Journal*, *41*(13-14), 860–876. doi:10.1080/02642069.2020.1727892

Birkinshaw, J., & Cohen, J. (2013). Make Time for Work that Matters. *Harvard Business Review*.

Blei, D. M. (2012). Probabilistic topic models. *Communications of the ACM*, *55*(4), 77–84. doi:10.1145/2133806.2133826

Blei, D. M., Ng, A. Y., & Jordan, M. I. (2003). Latent Dirichlet Allocation. *Journal of Machine Learning Research*, *3*, 993–1022.

Breidbach, C. F., & Maglio, P. (2020). Accountable algorithms? The ethical implications of data-driven business models. *Journal of Service Management*, *31*(2), 163–185. doi:10.1108/JOSM-03-2019-0073

Budler, L. C., Gosak, L., & Stiglic, G. (2023). Review of artificial intelligence-based question-answering systems in healthcare. *WIREs Data Mining and Knowledge Discovery, 13*(2), e1487.

Chatterjee, J., & Dethlefs, N. (2023). This new conversational AI model can be your friend, philosopher, and guide ... and even your worst enemy. *Patterns, 4*(1), 100676.

Chen, W., & Wellman, B. (2004). The global digital divide–within and between countries. *ITandSociety*, *1*(7), 39–45.

Chen, X. (2023). ChatGPT and Its Possible Impact on Library Reference Services. *Internet Reference Services Quarterly*, *27*(2), 1–9. doi:10.1080/10875301.2023.2181262

Chen, Y., Jensen, S., Albert, L. J., Gupta, S., & Lee, T. (2023). Artificial intelligence (AI) student assistants in the classroom: Designing chatbots to support student success. *Information Systems Frontiers*, *25*(1), 161–182. doi:10.100710796-022-10291-4

Cheng, X. Z. (n.d.). Exploring the metaverse in digital economy: An overview and research framework. *Journal of Electronic Business & Digital Economics*.

Chien-Chang Lin, A. Y. Q. H., & Stephen, J. H. (2023). A Review of AI-Driven Converstational Chatbots Implementation Methodologies and Challenges (1999-2022). *Sustainability*, *15*(5), 4012. Advance online publication. doi:10.3390u15054012

Choi, J. H., Hickman, K. E., Monahan, A. B., & Schwarcz, D. (2023). *ChatGPT Goes to Law School*. doi:10.2139srn.4335905

Company, M. A. (2023). *What is generative AI?* https://www.mckinsey.com/featured-insights/mckinsey-explainers/what-is-generative-ai

Dattathrani, S., & De', R. (2023). The Concept of Agency in the era of Artificial Intelligence: Dimensions and degrees. *Information Systems Frontiers*, *25*(1), 29–54. doi:10.100710796-022-10336-8

Dowling, M., & Lucey, B. (2023). ChatGPT for (Finance) research: The Bananarama Conjecture. *Finance Research Letters*, *53*, 103662. doi:10.1016/j.frl.2023.103662

Duan, Y., Ong, V. K., Xu, M., & Mathews, B. (2012). Supporting decision making process with "ideal" software agents–What do business executives want? *Expert Systems with Applications, 39*(5), 5534–5547. doi:10.1016/j.eswa.2011.11.065

Duong, D., & Solomon, B. D. (2023). *Analysis of large-language model versus human performance for genetics questions.* Cold Spring Harbor Laboratory. doi:10.1101/2023.01.27.23285115

Duong, D., & Solomon, B. D. (2023). Analysis of large-language model versus human performance for genetics questions. medRxiv. doi:10.1101/2023.01.27.23285115

Eloundou, T., Manning, S., Mishkin, P., & Rock, D. (2023). GPTs are GPTs: An Early Look at the Labor Market Impact Potential of Large Language Models. arXiv:2303.10130. Retrieved March 01, 2023, from https://ui.adsabs.harvard.edu/abs/2023arXiv230310130E

Else, H. (2023). Abstracts written by ChatGPT fool scientists. *Nature, 613*(7944), 423–423. doi:10.1038/d41586-023-00056-7 PMID:36635510

Felten, E., Raj, M., & Seamans, R. (2023). How will Language Modelers like ChatGPT Affect Occupations and Industries? arXiv:2303.01157. Retrieved March 01, 2023, from https://ui.adsabs.harvard.edu/abs/2023arXiv230301157F

Ghosal, S. (2023). ChatGPT on Characteristic Mode Analysis. TechRxiv. https://www.techrxiv.org/articles/preprint/ChatGPT_on_Characteristic_Mode_Analysis/21900342

Gilson, A., Safranek, C. W., Huang, T., Socrates, V., Chi, L., Taylor, R. A., & Chartash, D. (2023). How Does ChatGPT Perform on the United States Medical Licensing Examination? The Implications of Large Language Models for Medical Education and Knowledge Assessment. *JMIR Medical Education, 9*, e45312. doi:10.2196/45312 PMID:36753318

Greenwood, R., Suddaby, R., & Hinings, C. R. (2002). Theorizing change: The role of professional associations in the transformation of institutionalized fields. *Academy of Management Journal, 45*(1), 58–80. doi:10.2307/3069285

Guan, C., Ding, D., & Guo, J. (2022). *Web3.0: A Review And Research Agenda. 2022 RIVF International Conference on Computing and Communication Technologies*, Ho Chi Minh City, Vietnam.

Guan, C., Hung, Y.-C., & Liu, W. (2022). Cultural differences in hospitality service evaluations: Mining insights of user generated content. *Electronic Markets, 32*(3), 1061–1081. doi:10.100712525-022-00545-z

Haleem, A., Javaid, M., & Singh, R. P. (2022). An era of ChatGPT as a significant futuristic support tool: A study on features, abilities, and challenges. *BenchCouncil Transactions on Benchmarks, Standards and Evaluations, 2*(4), 100089.

Halloran, L. J. S., Mhanna, S., & Brunner, P. (2023). AI tools such as ChatGPT will disrupt hydrology, too. *Hydrological Processes, 37*(3), e14843. doi:10.1002/hyp.14843

Hartmann, J., Schwenzow, J., & Witte, M. (2023). *The political ideology of conversational AI: Converging evidence on ChatGPT's pro-environmental, left-libertarian orientation.* arXiv:2301.01768. Retrieved January 01, 2023, from https://ui.adsabs.harvard.edu/abs/2023arXiv230101768H

Haugeland, I., Fornell, K., Følstad, A., Taylor, C., & Bjørkli, C. A. (2022). Understanding the user experience of customer service chatbots: An experimental study of chatbot interaction design. *International Journal of Human-Computer Studies, 161*, 102788. doi:10.1016/j.ijhcs.2022.102788

Hoffman, A. J. (1999). Institutional evolution and change: Environmentalism and the US chemical industry. *Academy of Management Journal, 42*(4), 351–371. doi:10.2307/257008

Hu, G. (2023). Challenges for enforcing editorial policies on AI-generated papers. *Accountability in Research, 1-3*, 1–3. Advance online publication. doi:10.1080/08989621.2023.2184262 PMID:36840450

Hu, K. (2023). *ChatGPT sets record for fastest-growing user base* Reuters. https://www.reuters.com/technology/chatgpt-sets-record-fastest-growing-user-base-analyst-note-2023-02-01/

Jalil, S., Rafi, S. T., Moran, K., & Lam, W. (2023). *ChatGPT and Software Testing Education: Promises & Perils.* arXiv pre-print server.

Jeblick, K., Schachtner, B., Dexl, J., Mittermeier, A., Topalis, J., Weber, T., Wesp, P., Sabel, B., Ricke, J., & Ingrisch, M. (2022). *ChatGPT Makes Medicine Easy to Swallow: An Exploratory Case Study on Simplified Radiology Reports.* arXiv pre-print server.

Jeblick, K., Schachtner, B., Dexl, J., Mittermeier, A., Stüber, A. T., Topalis, J., Weber, T., Wesp, P., Sabel, B., Ricke, J., & Ingrisch, M. (2022). *ChatGPT Makes Medicine Easy to Swallow: An Exploratory Case Study on Simplified Radiology Reports.* arXiv:2212.14882. Retrieved December 01, 2022, from https://ui.adsabs.harvard.edu/abs/2022arXiv221214882J

Jena, L. K., & Goyal, S. (2022). Emotional intelligence and employee innovation: Sequential mediating effect of person-group fit and adaptive performance. *European Review of Applied Psychology, 72*(1), 100729. doi:10.1016/j.erap.2021.100729

Jenneboer, L., Herrando, C., & Constantinides, E. (2022). The Impact of Chatbots on Customer Loyalty: A Systematic Literature Review. *Journal of Theoretical and Applied Electronic Commerce Research, 17*(1), 212–229. doi:10.3390/jtaer17010011

Jurgen Rudolph, S. T. (2023). ChatGPT: Bullshit spewer or the end of traditional assessments in higher education? *Journal of Applied Learning & Teaching, 6*(1). Advance online publication. doi:10.37074/jalt.2023.6.1.9

Kasneci, E., Sessler, K., Küchemann, S., Bannert, M., Dementieva, D., Fischer, F., Gasser, U., Groh, G., Günnemann, S., Hüllermeier, E., Krusche, S., Kutyniok, G., Michaeli, T., Nerdel, C., Pfeffer, J., Poquet, O., Sailer, M., Schmidt, A., Seidel, T., ... Kasneci, G. (2023). ChatGPT for good? On opportunities and challenges of large language models for education. *Learning and Individual Differences, 103*, 102274. doi:10.1016/j.lindif.2023.102274

Khan, R. A., Jawaid, M., Khan, A. R., & Sajjad, M. (2023). ChatGPT - Reshaping medical education and clinical management. *Pakistan Journal of Medical Sciences, 39*(2). Advance online publication. doi:10.12669/pjms.39.2.7653 PMID:36950398

Kim, B., Kim, H., Lee, S.-W., Lee, G., Kwak, D., Park, S., Kim, S., Kim, S., Seo, D., Lee, H., Jeong, M., Lee, S., Kim, M., Suk, Kim, S., Park, T., Kim, J., Kang, S., . . . Sung, N. (2021). *What Changes Can Large-scale Language Models Bring? Intensive Study on HyperCLOVA: Billions-scale Korean Generative Pretrained Transformers.* arXiv pre-print server.

King, M. R. (2023). A Conversation on Artificial Intelligence, Chatbots, and Plagiarism in Higher Education. *Cellular and Molecular Bioengineering, 16*(1), 1–2. doi:10.100712195-022-00754-8 PMID:36660590

Kshetri, N., & Ajami, R. (2008). Institutional reforms in the Gulf Cooperation Council economies: A conceptual framework. *Journal of International Management, 14*(3), 300–318. doi:10.1016/j.intman.2008.01.005

Kung, T. H., Cheatham, M., Medenilla, A., Sillos, C., De Leon, L., Elepaño, C., Madriaga, M., Aggabao, R., Diaz-Candido, G., Maningo, J., & Tseng, V. (2023). Performance of ChatGPT on USMLE: Potential for AI-assisted medical education using large language models. *PLOS Digital Health, 2*(2), e0000198. doi:10.1371/journal.pdig.0000198 PMID:36812645

Kung, T. H., Cheatham, M., Medenilla, A., Sillos, C., De Leon, L., Elepaño, C., Madriaga, M., Aggabao, R., Diaz-Candido, G., Maningo, J., & Tseng, V. (2023). Performance of ChatGPT on USMLE: Potential for AI-assisted medical education using large language models. *PLOS Digit Health, 2*(2), e0000198. doi:10.1371/journal.pdig.0000198 PMID:36812645

Lanzi, P. L., & Loiacono, D. (2023). *ChatGPT and Other Large Language Models as Evolutionary Engines for Online Interactive Collaborative Game Design.* arXiv:2303.02155. doi:10.1145/3583131.3590351

Lund, B. D., & Wang, T. (2023). Chatting about ChatGPT: how may AI and GPT impact academia and libraries? *Library Hi Tech News.* doi:10.1108/LHTN-01-2023-0009

Luo, B., Lau, R. Y. K., Li, C., & Si, Y.-W. (2022). A critical review of state-of-the-art chatbot designs and applications. *WIREs Data Mining and Knowledge Discovery, 12*(1), 1434.

Macdonald, C., Adeloye, D., Sheikh, A., & Rudan, I. (2023). Can ChatGPT draft a research article? An example of population-level vaccine effectiveness analysis. *Journal of Global Health, 13,* 01003. doi:10.7189/jogh.13.01003 PMID:36798998

Maguire, S., Hardy, C., & Lawrence, T. B. (2004). Institutional entrepreneurship in emerging fields: HIV/AIDS treatment advocacy in Canada. *Academy of Management Journal, 47*(5), 657–679. doi:10.2307/20159610

Mariani, M. M., Hashemi, N., & Wirtz, J. (2023). Artificial intelligence empowered conversational agents: A systematic literature review and research agenda. *Journal of Business Research, 161,* 113838. doi:10.1016/j.jbusres.2023.113838

McKee, F., & Noever, D. (2023). *Chatbots in a Honeypot World.* arXiv:2301.03771. Retrieved January 01, 2023, from https://ui.adsabs.harvard.edu/abs/2023arXiv230103771M

Mhlanga, D. (2023). *Open AI in Education, the Responsible and Ethical Use of ChatGPT Towards Lifelong Learning.* Academic Press.

MimnoD.WallachH.TalleyE.LeendersM.McCallumA. (2011). Optimizing semantic coherence in topic models. *Proceedings of the 2011 Conference on Empirical Methods in Natural Language Processing.*

Mitrovic, S., Andreoletti, D., & Ayoub, O. (2023). *ChatGPT or Human? Detect and Explain. Explaining Decisions of Machine Learning Model for Detecting Short ChatGPT-generated Text.* arXiv pre-print server.

MollickE. R.MollickL. (2022). New Modes of Learning Enabled by AI Chatbots: Three Methods and Assignments. *Available at* SSRN. doi:10.2139/ssrn.4300783

Munn, L., Magee, L., & Arora, V. (2023). *Truth Machines: Synthesizing Veracity in AI Language Models.* arXiv:2301.12066. Retrieved January 01, 2023, from https://ui.adsabs.harvard.edu/abs/2023arXiv230112066M

Nastasi, A. J., Courtright, K. R., Halpern, S. D., & Weissman, G. E. (2023). Does ChatGPT Provide Appropriate and Equitable Medical Advice?: A Vignette-Based, Clinical Evaluation Across Care Contexts. medRxiv, 2023.2002.2025.23286451. doi:10.1101/2023.02.25.23286451

Nature. (2023). *Preparing your materials.* https://www.nature.com/nbt/submission-guidelines/preparing-your-submission

Nordheim, C. B., Følstad, A., & Bjørkli, C. A. (2019). An Initial Model of Trust in Chatbots for Customer Service—Findings from a Questionnaire Study. *Interacting with Computers*, *31*(3), 317–335. doi:10.1093/iwc/iwz022

Nov, O., Singh, N., & Mann, D. M. (2023). Putting ChatGPT's Medical Advice to the (Turing) Test. medRxiv, 2023.2001.2023.23284735. doi:10.1101/2023.01.23.23284735

O'Flaherty, J., & Phillips, C. (2015). The use of flipped classrooms in higher education: A scoping review. *The internet and higher education*, *25*, 85–95. doi:10.1016/j.iheduc.2015.02.002

Omar, R., Mangukiya, O., Kalnis, P., & Mansour, E. (2023). *ChatGPT versus Traditional Question Answering for Knowledge Graphs: Current Status and Future Directions Towards Knowledge Graph Chatbots.* arXiv pre-print server.

Ott, S., Hebenstreit, K., Liévin, V., Egeberg Hother, C., Moradi, M., Mayrhauser, M., Praas, R., Winther, O., & Samwald, M. (2023). *ThoughtSource: A central hub for large language model reasoning data.* arXiv:2301.11596. Retrieved January 01, 2023, from https://ui.adsabs.harvard.edu/abs/2023arXiv230111596O

Prieto, S. A., Mengiste, E. T., & García de Soto, B. (2023). Investigating the Use of ChatGPT for the Scheduling of Construction Projects. *Buildings, 13*(4), 857. https://www.mdpi.com/2075-5309/13/4/857

Qadir, J. (2022). *Engineering Education in the Era of ChatGPT: Promise and Pitfalls of Generative AI for Education.* Academic Press.

Rai, A., Constantinides, P., & Sarker, S. (2019). Next generation digital platforms: toward human-AI hybrids. *Management Information Systems Quarterly*, *43*(1), iii–ix.

Rao, A., Kim, J., Kamineni, M., Pang, M., Lie, W., & Succi, M. D. (2023). Evaluating ChatGPT as an Adjunct for Radiologic Decision-Making. medRxiv. doi:10.1101/2023.02.02.23285399

Rao, A., Kim, J., Kamineni, M., Pang, M., Lie, W., & Succi, M. D. (2023). *Evaluating ChatGPT as an Adjunct for Radiologic Decision-Making.* Cold Spring Harbor Laboratory. doi:10.1101/2023.02.02.23285399

Rudolph, J., Tan, S., & Tan, S. (2023). *ChatGPT: Bullshit spewer or the end of traditional assessments in higher education?* doi:10.37074/jalt.2023.6.1.9

Sakib Shahriar, K. H. (2023). *Let's have a chat! A Conversation with ChatGPT.* Technology, Applications, and Limitations.

Sakirin, T., & Said, R. B. (2023). *User preferences for ChatGPT-powered conversational interfaces versus traditional.* Academic Press.

Salah, M., Alhalbusi, H., Ismail, M. M., & Abdelfattah, F. (2023). *Chatting with ChatGPT: Decoding the Mind of Chatbot Users and Unveiling the Intricate Connections between User Perception, Trust and Stereotype Perception on Self-Esteem and Psychological Well-being.* Research Square., doi:10.21203/rs.3.rs-2610655/v2

Sallam, M. (2023). ChatGPT Utility in Healthcare Education, Research, and Practice: Systematic Review on the Promising Perspectives and Valid Concerns. *Health Care*, *11*(6), 887. doi:10.3390/healthcare11060887 PMID:36981544

Sallam, M., Salim, N. A., Al-Tammemi, A. B., Barakat, M., Fayyad, D., Hallit, S., Harapan, H., Hallit, R., & Mahafzah, A. (2023). ChatGPT Output Regarding Compulsory Vaccination and COVID-19 Vaccine Conspiracy: A Descriptive Study at the Outset of a Paradigm Shift in Online Search for Information. *Cureus*, *15*(2), e35029. doi:10.7759/cureus.35029 PMID:36819954

Sanmarchi, F., Bucci, A., & Golinelli, D. (2023). A step-by-step Researcher's Guide to the use of an AI-based transformer in epidemiology: an exploratory analysis of ChatGPT using the STROBE checklist for observational studies. medRxiv. doi:10.1101/2023.02.06.23285514

Sezgin, E., Sirrianni, J., & Linwood, S. L. (2022). Operationalizing and Implementing Pretrained, Large Artificial Intelligence Linguistic Models in the US Health Care System: Outlook of Generative Pretrained Transformer 3 (GPT-3) as a Service Model. *JMIR Medical Informatics*, *10*(2), 32875. doi:10.2196/32875 PMID:35142635

Shahriar, S., & Hayawi, K. (2023). *Let's have a chat! A Conversation with ChatGPT: Technology, Applications, and Limitations.* arXiv:2302.13817. Retrieved February 01, 2023, from https://ui.adsabs.harvard.edu/abs/2023arXiv230213817S

Shaji George, A. S. H. G., & Martin. (2023). A Review of ChatGPT AI's Impact on Several Business Sectors. *Partners Universal International Innovation Journal*, *01*(01), 15. doi:10.5281/zenodo.7644359

Singh, O. P. (2023). Artificial intelligence in the era of ChatGPT - Opportunities and challenges in mental health care. *Indian Journal of Psychiatry*, *65*(3), 2. doi:10.4103/indianjpsychiatry.indianjpsychiatry_112_23 PMID:37204980

Strang, D., & Meyer, J. (1993). Institutional conditions for diffusion. *Theory and Society*, *v*, 22.

Susnjak, T. (2022). *ChatGPT: The End of Online Exam Integrity?* arXiv pre-print server.

Thorp, H. H. (2023). ChatGPT is fun, but not an author. *Science, 379*(6630), 313–313. doi:10.1126cience. adg7879 PMID:36701446

Tirunillai, S., & Tellis, G. J. (2014). Mining marketing meaning from online chatter: Strategic brand analysis of big data using latent dirichlet allocation. *JMR, Journal of Marketing Research, 51*(4), 463–479. doi:10.1509/jmr.12.0106

Tlili, A., Shehata, B., Adarkwah, M. A., Bozkurt, A., Hickey, D. T., Huang, R., & Agyemang, B. (2023). What if the devil is my guardian angel: ChatGPT as a case study of using chatbots in education. *Smart Learning Environments, 10*(1), 15. Advance online publication. doi:10.118640561-023-00237-x

Tu, R., Ma, C., & Zhang, C. (2023). *Causal-Discovery Performance of ChatGPT in the context of Neuropathic Pain Diagnosis.* arXiv:2301.13819. Retrieved January 01, 2023, from https://ui.adsabs.harvard.edu/abs/2023arXiv230113819T

Vargo, S. L., Maglio, P. P., & Akaka, M. A. (2008). On value and value co-creation: A service systems and service logic perspective. *European Management Journal, 26*(3), 145–152. doi:10.1016/j.emj.2008.04.003

Wang, J., Hu, X., Hou, W., Chen, H., Zheng, R., Wang, Y., Yang, L., Huang, H., Ye, W., Geng, X., Jiao, B., Zhang, Y., & Xie, X. (2023). *On the Robustness of ChatGPT: An Adversarial and Out-of-distribution Perspective.* arXiv:2302.12095. Retrieved February 01, 2023, from https://ui.adsabs.harvard.edu/abs/2023arXiv230212095W

Wang, X., Bendle, N. T., Mai, F., & Cotte, J. (2015). The journal of consumer research at 40: A historical analysis. *The Journal of Consumer Research, 42*(1), 5–18. doi:10.1093/jcr/ucv009

Weissglass, D. E. (2022). Contextual bias, the democratization of healthcare, and medical artificial intelligence in low-and middle-income countries. *Bioethics, 36*(2), 201–209. doi:10.1111/bioe.12927 PMID:34460977

Weizenbaum, J. (1976). *Computer power and human reason: From judgment to calculation.* W. H. Freeman & Co.

Wirtz, J., Kunz, W. H., Hartley, N., & Tarbit, J. (2022). Corporate digital responsibility in service firms and their ecosystems. *Journal of Service Research.*

Yeo, Y. H., Samaan, J. S., Ng, W. H., Ting, P.-S., Trivedi, H., Vipani, A., Ayoub, W., Yang, J. D., Liran, O., Spiegel, B., & Kuo, A. (2023). Assessing the performance of ChatGPT in answering questions regarding cirrhosis and hepatocellular carcinoma. *Clinical and Molecular Hepatology, 29*(3), 721–732. Advance online publication. doi:10.3350/cmh.2023.0089 PMID:36946005

Yoshua Bengio, R. D., & Vincent. (2000). *A Neural Probabilistic Language Model* (Vol. 13). MIT Press. https://proceedings.neurips.cc/paper/2000/hash/728f206c2a01bf572b5940d7d9a8fa4c-Abstract.html

Zhavoronkov, A. (2022). Rapamycin in the context of Pascal's Wager: Generative pre-trained transformer perspective. *Oncoscience, 9*, 82–84. doi:10.18632/oncoscience.571 PMID:36589923

Zhou, Li, Yu, Liu, Wang, Zhang, Ji, Yan, He, Peng, Li, Wu, Liu, Xie, Xiong, Pei, Yu, & Sun. (2023). *A Comprehensive Survey on Pretrained Foundation Models: A History from BERT to ChatGPT.* Academic Press.

Chapter 8

Privacy and Security by Design:
A Case Study on Innovative Techniques for Secure Healthcare Data Research

Ana Ferreira
CINTESIS@RISE, FMUP-MEDCIDS, Porto, Portugal

Tiago Morais
Department of Information Technology, Unidade Local de Saúde de Matosinhos, Portugal

José Castanheira
Department of Information Technology, Unidade Local de Saúde de Matosinhos, Portugal

Tiago Taveira-Gomes
Department of Community Medicine, Faculdade de Medicina da Universidade do Porto, Portugal & Faculty of Health Sciences, Fernando Pessoa University, Portugal & MTG Research and Development Lab, Portugal

ABSTRACT

Privacy is a fundamental human right, and the need for information security to guarantee patients' privacy is essential. In today's world, where technology and connected devices are increasingly prevalent, cyber-attacks on critical infrastructures have grown significantly. The implementation of proactive privacy and security procedures and techniques is essential to protect data privacy, prevent information leakage, and mitigate cyber risks. This chapter focuses on innovative techniques for privacy by design and by default in the practice of accessing secondary health data for research. It presents a case study of a secure computation process and technology, which includes an architectural approach to provisioning a zero-trust research environment. By adopting a zero-trust research environment, healthcare institutions can mitigate the risks of cyber-attacks and data breaches while increasing data security for the benefit of patients. Ultimately, this chapter emphasizes the importance of implementing proactive privacy and security measures to protect sensitive data in healthcare.

DOI: 10.4018/978-1-6684-8422-7.ch008

1. INTRODUCTION

Legislation aims to enforce and support humans' fundamental right for privacy (UN, 1948), but legislation alone is not enough to build private, secure and resilient systems that can support and optimize users' activities as well as promote trust in their outcomes. All this is especially important in the healthcare domain where the impact is measured in adequate disease management and well-being. All these concepts are interconnected as shown in Figure 1.

As legislation and even user interactions can enforce and influence the way privacy is perceived and defined, we still need security solutions that can guarantee privacy in practice. Without proper security measures, adapted to the real needs of a specific healthcare ecosystem, it is not possible to provide privacy of data processing and, therefore, not possible to foster trust to promote continued, better and safer health services, as well as outcomes.

Figure 1. What influences privacy and promotes trust
Source: Ferreira et al. (2021)

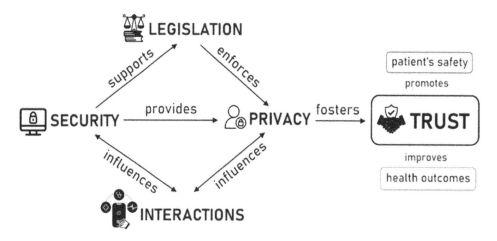

Legislation such as GDPR in The European Union (EU) (European Union, 2016) can give an indication, though generic, of the need for security solutions to integrate, above all, security by design and by default. What this means is that even before design, within ideation itself, security needs to be integrated as a main part of the solution. If the basic security and privacy principles are provided in the final products, these will be and provide, by default, secure interactions with their end-users and within their organizations.

In theory, this is what needs to work. According to the Network and Information Security (NIS) Directive (NIS, 2016), the EU-wide legislation that aims to increase security levels for critical infrastructures in the EU (recently updated to NIS2 (NIS2, 2022)), healthcare is one of those critical infrastructures that is vital for economy and society, and which relies heavily on Information and Communication Technologies (ICT). This means that healthcare services need to be both protected and available 24/7, as well as trustable, secure and resilient.

In practice, this is far from reality. Currently, healthcare is one of the most unprepared, vulnerable and attacked domains. Only in the last few years, attacks have exponentially increased, and in the height of COVID-19, there was an increase of 220% of phishing attacks (Warburton, 2020). Phishing attacks commonly precede ransomware attacks, one of the most dangerous and impactful attacks in healthcare (Eddie & Perlroth, 2020; Marks, 2021). Ransomware can render entire healthcare services or even institutions unavailable and hinder adequate patients' treatment.

Portugal is no exception. In 2021, there was an increase in 81% of incidents reporting by Portuguese SMEs, above the European average (51%) (CNCS, 2022). Besides this, healthcare is an under invested domain, with lack of human and infrastructural resources as well as talent and expertise, not to mention a great lack of awareness for the need of cybersecurity. In fact, no one thought that in such a short time, a medical record would be one of the most valuable on the black market in comparison with any other kind of records, even credit card records. A medical record can worth, on average, five times more than any other type of record (Trustwave, 2019).

For all these reasons, the healthcare domain needs to attract more investment as well as more interest by all stakeholders. Sometimes, it can be just a matter of really understanding the needs of a specific ecosystem, to decide amongst available capabilities and solutions, the ones that can be adapted to better protect that ecosystem. Indeed, personalized and automated cybersecurity solutions to take human errors as much as possible out of the loop, can increase their potential for success (Cranor, 2008).

The aim of this chapter is to describe a case study, implemented in a Portuguese healthcare setting, of a secure computation process and technology for secondary healthcare data research, which includes an architectural approach to provisioning a zero-trust research environment. This architecture securely stores and processes raw healthcare data extracted from electronic health records or other sources on-premises using machine-written software, ensuring replicability and reproducibility, with no need for human intervention.

Next section introduces, in more detail, some of the needed concepts in terms of cybersecurity and healthcare secondary data research, Section 3 illustrates the use of Zero Trust applied to secondary health research and Section 4 presents the architecture of the proposed solution and the description of the use-case in a real healthcare setting. Sections 5 and 6 discuss results and experiences of the presented solution and conclude this chapter, respectively.

2. BACKGROUND

2.1 From Trust to Zero-Trust

One of the seven grand challenges regarding Human Computer Interaction (HCI) is: Ethics, Privacy and Security (Antona et al., 2019). This means that, still today, it is very difficult to integrate these concepts into usable and successful technology. When these solutions are available they will be closer to foster trust (Figure 1) and improve HCI, bringing technology to a point that humans can trust and adhere to for longer periods of time.

In fact, societies in general and people in particular have thrived, not because they are experts in all domains, and with all devices they have created, but because they found trust to support their decision-making in complex situations (Siegrist et al., 2005). This can happen both online and offline as technologies can have a social presence to which people respond to (Hoff & Bashir, 2015). Within online environments it may be more difficult to gain trust and maintain it (Smiljana & Laura, 2019) because trust, as well as mistrust, depend on a multidimensional set of factors and conditions (Gao et al., 2019).

However, at a general level, trust is established via repeated interactions, during which individuals become confident in the outcome of similar interactions (Smiljana & Laura, 2019; Ng et al., 2020). Studies have shown that trust plays an important role in diverse online domains like e-commerce (Pappas, 2018), healthcare (Sillence et al., 2019), information security (Pienta et al., 2020) and social networks (Kumar et al., 2018). However, trust is dynamic (Hoff & Bashir, 2015) and very challenging, as it is slow to build and quick to collapse (Selin, 2006).

Trust can be a very important factor of technology success and continued use, when the human is necessary to intervene, but is very complex to model and adapt to all contexts. Moreover, as in any other domain, there is the need to ascertain that the less human intervention or input needed within a process, the less potential there will be for failing. So, in order to complement technology that should be trusted by their users as much as possible, there is the need for technology that totally discards trust but always verifies and ascertains the security of any kind of access request: the so-called zero-trust technology.

Zero Trust (ZT), as the name indicates, is a security model built around the idea that nothing inside or outside an organization can be trusted. In a ZT paradigm an enterprise must assume no implicit trust is granted to assets or user accounts based solely on their physical or network location, or on asset ownership; but continually analyze and evaluate the risks involved and enact protections to mitigate those risks (Rose et al., 2020).

Given the interconnected nature of the future with IoMT (Internet of Medical Things), augmented reality, robotics and remote workers, the current perimeter-based security model that most healthcare organizations use, will no longer be effective. All these changes create an expanding attack surface and this is particularly dangerous for healthcare organizations, which are relying on outdated trust models and small IT security teams to protect their infrastructure. To complicate things even further, medical equipment and other connected devices have little, if any, cybersecurity capabilities.

However, healthcare organizations cannot vet every outside app, device, and network encountered by their employees. A ZT model can help healthcare organizations provision access in a more effective manner by focusing on data, workloads and identity, keeping technology secure without exhausting resources in an effort to keep pace with exponentially increasing threats (BlackBerry, 2020).

A zero trust architecture (ZTA) is not a single architecture but a set of ZT guiding principles for workflow, system design and operations. Those ZT principles are designed to prevent data breaches and limit internal lateral movement. Changing to ZTA cannot simply be accomplished with a replacement of technology. An organization needs to evaluate risks and seek to incrementally implement zero trust principles, process changes, and technology solutions that protect their data assets by use case, as the one described in this chapter (Rose et al., 2020).

2.2 GDPR Compliance

As illustrated in Figure 1, security solutions should support legislation and ZT technology and models are an example of that. Besides providing for "Security of processing", as specified in Art. 32 of GDPR, to implement appropriate technical and organizational measures to ensure a level of security appropriate to the risk, a ZTA can also provide compliance for the:

- "Principles relating to processing of personal data", Art. 5:

      ◦   Alínea b) "Purpose limitation": ZTA allows the separation of data analysis as data are selected for a specific research project or goal, and so not further processed in a manner that is incompatible with those purposes;

      ◦   Alínea c) "Data minimisation": the use-case presented in this chapter allows only the required data for analysis/research to be extracted from original sources and accessed in a protected/authorized manner within a ZTA. This way, only the necessary and relevant data, at one specific time, are processed, and no need to deal with data that are not required for the ambit of a specific analysis;

      ◦   Alínea f) "Integrity and confidentiality": ZTA allows data to be processed in a manner that ensures appropriate security of the personal and health data, including protection against unauthorized or unlawful processing and against accidental loss, destruction or damage, using appropriate technical or organizational measures;

- "Processing of special categories of personal data", Art. 9: healthcare data are categorized as special category data in GDPR, where the processing is still necessary for: Alínea h) medical diagnosis and the provision of healthcare (and in other well-defined contexts) under GDPR, but their privacy and security measures need to be taken care in a more controlled manner. In fact, paragraph 3 of this article specifies that healthcare data can be processed for the purposes referred in h) when those data are processed by or under the responsibility of a professional subject to the obligation of professional secrecy under Union or Member State law. For healthcare professionals, this means they are subject to secrecy regarding patients' confidentiality, under the hippocratic oath and deontological code. However, this was defined pre-technology age. Nowadays, professionals not only decide in teams, but they perform medical diagnosis and treatments together with the technology. Technology extends the healthcare teams, so these "new" teams need to guarantee they will act with the same care and secrecy of the professionals alone, and help them maintain that throughout their daily activities. A ZTA provides that security extension to the relation professionals-technology in better identifying, separating and securing healthcare data;

- "Data protection by design and by default" in Art. 25: this article summarizes all that should be required from ideation, to development and implementation of private and secure technology. It requires that all that was pointed out in the previous points/articles (e.g., data minimization, legitimate purpose, adequate security measures, etc) will be integrated in an effective manner within the product and with the necessary safeguards into all data processing.

Finally, if ZTA can provide a protected silo to process data, and these data are by default already anonymized, and processed within a limited timeframe, GDPR requirements may not even apply.

2.3 Secondary Health Data for Research

Secondary data for research refers to the data that are re-used for other research purposes than the ones those data were collected for in the first place. It can be data as is, or aggregated from different sources. The advantages of re-using data are manifold: avoid delays from new studies' approval and data collection, triangulate data from multiple sources to answer existing or draw new hypotheses, or find relations that were not thought of before to solve existing problems. This can greatly improve quality, efficiency and efficacy of both clinical and medical research (Richter et al., 2021).

Legislation is not so clear for this type of research data. GDPR fails to provide a clear legal basis for the processing of personal data for secondary research purposes (Richter et al., 2021; Peloquin et al., 2020) and so it is very difficult for a researcher to know what are the required privacy and security measures in order to ideate and implement a study that requires processing of secondary healthcare data. This can hinder research and advances in many areas such as: genetics, genomics, biobanks, and so on.

ZTA can provide, in a standardized way, secure access and processing of data by separating them from their original sources and eliminating all traces from that processing after the timeframe is over. Research teams associated with a project can independently and confidently perform their healthcare data analysis, as a private and secure framework is automatically provided for them. Production and research environments are well separated and the solution proposed in this work allows a diversity of processes and interactions with healthcare data, for various purposes. It is never enough o stress that, being considered essential services, healthcare and healthcare data have a high degree of sensitivity as well as privacy/security needs.

3. HEALTHCARE AND ZTA

3.1 Common Data Model, Standardization, and ZTA

The Observation Health and Data Science and Informatics (OHDSI) community, among others, have played significant contributions in laying the ground for ZTA (OHDSI, 2021; Reinecke et al., 2021). At its heart, the OHDSI community develops and maintains a standardized Observational Medical Outcomes Partnership (OMOP) Common Data Model (CDM). The OMOP-CDM sets a functional specification of a tabular database schema that can be used to represent healthcare data in a standardized format that enables execution of standardized data analysis on top of the CDM. The standardization is both structural (tables and column names) and also semantic (concepts represented on the data are declared using standardized vocabularies) (Hripcsak et al., 2021).

The purpose of having a common data model is to increase replicability of analysis across multiple databases that may be able to collaborate and share evidence without sharing patient data. This enables evidence generation at scale. But a standardized CDM has other relevant advantages for the purpose of this work, namely, the ability to decouple analysis specification from source data representation. In essence, the CDM specification can serve as a contract between two parties: 1) for researchers looking to generate evidence, the contract specifies how data is represented structurally and semantically (what vocabularies are used), and thus enables the researchers to translate their research question into a standard set of CDM operations; 2) for a clinical data manager looking to ensure that data can be analyzed, the CDM serves as a basis for the development of extract-transform-load operations that take care of transforming the source data as it may exist in the underlying electronic health records and related software, and representing it according to the elements defined in the CDM. The OHDSI community maintains additional tools that report summary statistics of data and analyze its quality in such a way that evidence generation can be reliably derived from source data, without having ever the need to directly look at data.

Such approaches of standardization as set by the OMOP-CDM can serve as the basis to putting in place a broader ZTA architecture for evidence generation.

3.2 ZTA and Secondary Health Data Evidence

Healthcare institutions face an increased demand in generating evidence that may support all levels of decision-making, from a clinical, department and institution levels, up to government and regulators. Contemporary evidence is crucial for the decision process to be well-grounded and agile. Such type of approach has been successfully implemented throughout the world regarding infection prevention and control, which we will use as a use-case to illustrate the broader picture of evidence generation in healthcare (Cookson, 2005; Petrosino et al., 2001).

Infection control commissions, also known as infection prevention and control (IPC) committees, are multidisciplinary teams responsible for preventing and controlling healthcare-associated infections (HAIs) within healthcare facilities. These commissions play a crucial role in ensuring patient's safety, reducing morbidity and mortality, and maintaining a high standard of care in healthcare settings (Scheckler et al.,1998). The operation of these commissions typically involve activities ranging from establishing guidelines and protocols up to surveillance, auditing and reporting. IPCs monitor the incidence of HAIs within the healthcare facility, conduct investigations to identify the source of outbreaks, and implement appropriate interventions to control the spread of infections. Data collection and analysis play an essential role in this process, allowing the commission to track trends and measure the effectiveness of interventions (Reed & Kemmerly, 2009). These data are used to generate relevant evidence that may inform future review of guidelines and protocols such that the risk of HAIs is kept as minimal as possible across time (Sehulster & Chinn, 2019).

This exact cycle of continuous improvement based on evidence can be extended to any clinical or other healthcare related activities carried by healthcare institutions (Stelson et al., 2017). However, in order to carry out such activities at scale, means must be provided so that the source data, which is the pillar of support for this process, may be analyzed by parties internal and external to healthcare institutions in a timely fashion and without compromising patient data privacy and safety. The ability to collaborate with external institutions is paramount to the success of evidence generation. As usual, the complexities revolving around creating knowledge from observation data require very diverse multidisciplinary teams and leveraging of different skill sets (Henrique et al., 2021).

Such an ability is also critical for institutions to adhere to the 'FAIR Guiding Principles for scientific data management and stewardship' that are meant to improve the Findability, Accessibility, Interoperability, and Reuse of digital assets (Stanciu, 2023). The principles emphasize machine-actionability (i.e., the capacity of computational systems to find, access, interoperate, and reuse data with none or minimal human intervention) because humans increasingly rely on computational support to deal with data as a result of the increase in volume, complexity, and data creation speed (Sinaci et al., 2020).

Ultimately, a ZTA provides a promising approach, as it provides healthcare institutions with means to enable evidence generation at scale, following FAIR and, without having to trust in the internal or external parties involved.

The use-case presented in Section 4 can well illustrate this in a real setting and be generalized for similar needs and situations within other healthcare institutions.

4. PROPOSED ZTA SOLUTION

4.1 Case-Study

Unidade Local de Saúde de Matosinhos (ULSM), like every healthcare institution, has the need to generate evidence from its healthcare data to derive continuous improvement of the care that is being given to the population. In particular, ULSM is responsible for all levels of public healthcare for the region of Matosinhos, a town situated in the north west of Portugal, beside the second biggest city in Portugal, Porto. For such purposes ULSM has the need to process the vast amount of historical healthcare data that it generates in order to provide for that evidence. Moreover, questions to gather such evidence often require scientific formulation in order to be adequately defined, and yield conservative insights that adequately account for potential bias from observation data. Thus the entry point for conducting evidence generation in this case are the physician-researchers at ULSM.

These physician-researcher contact day-to-day with patients and are aware of medical progress in the field, as well as current unmet needs and sub optimized workflows that may require attention. Such professionals can then formulate observational research questions, as well as scientific protocols and statistical analysis plans that may provide the answer or the range of answers for each given question. In principle, such a study can be executed upon any given dataset.

A significant number of relevant research questions are dependent on the local context (such as the assessment of a missed opportunity of care in a patient pathway, or estimating cost attributable to an activity), and thus are not necessarily applicable to other settings. But a big number of questions are independent of local context (such as safety and effectiveness of a treatment, or prevalence of a disease). This means that multiple questions may hold different degrees of relevance to be applied in different contexts.

Regardless of that relevance, once a question is adequately formulated into a protocol and a statistical analysis plan, the next step is to analyze the data. For such purpose ULSM has implemented an automatic Extract, Transform and Load (ETL) pipeline that converts its source data into the OMOP-CDM format (Figure 2). The converted data is stored locally at ULSM in a non-production database in order not to compromise regular healthcare provisioning operation. This has been developed in the context of the EHDEN - European Healthcare Data and Evidence Network project (https://www.ehden.eu/).

Figure 2. Architecture of the ETL pipeline

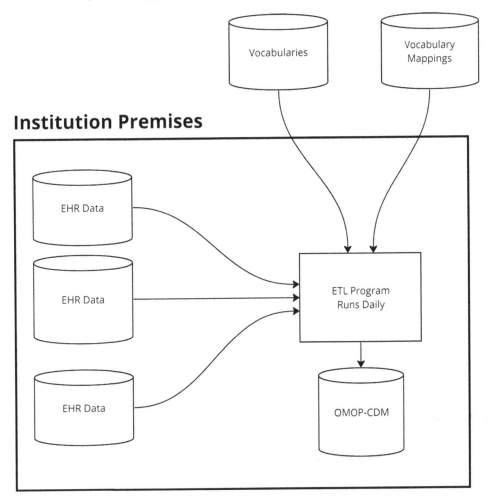

This ETL runs once every month to ensure that data is updated. Now it is important to ensure that researchers can get results for their research questions without having the need to access data at any point. This is because, on one hand, proper handling of healthcare data requires a degree of technical expertise that is not commonly found in healthcare professionals, and on the other, teams may include researchers external to the institution. Sharing healthcare data for research, assuming the need for sharing, may hold excess risk for the institution as even if data is pseudo anonymized, the risk of reverse identification is non-negligible and tracing data after it leaves the institution is not guaranteed.

As such, ULSM has a ZTA base that ensures that such clinical questions can be formulated, translated into software packages that are compliant with the OMOP CDM, and then automatically executed in sandboxed internal environments, ensuring that the totality of data transforms occurs on-premises and with total traceability and control of the institution. The aggregated results and coefficients that give answers to the formulated questions are shared with the researchers. This protocol has been used for generating evidence for local and international studies in collaboration with many different institutions (Figure 3) (Clemente-Teixeira et al., 2022).

Figure 3. Use-case workflow diagram

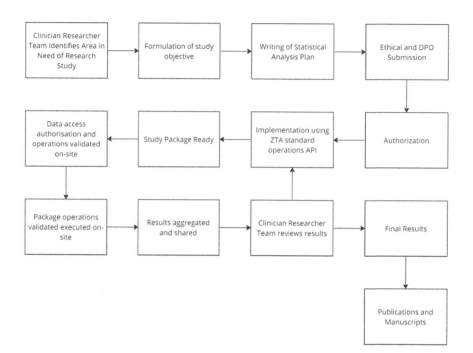

4.2 ZTA Requirements and Architecture

The ULSM ZTA integrates the following requirements:

• *Researchers are bound to define research questions considering a limited set of standardized computation operations using a standard data operations library.*

This allows for more control in terms of the allowed performed operations and their reproducibility and comparison in further studies.

• *There are policy documents put into place for data access that govern the scope of raw data that can be accessed by the researcher and by the project. This access is defined both at the column and at the row level in the source data.*

This allows for a fine-grained access control, which provides for more secure and private accesses as well as their constant auditing.

• *Project documentation for ethical and Data Protection Officer (DPO) assessment and authorization are generated from the study analytical package directly.*

This allows for a speedy and more standardized process regarding DPO and Ethical assessments.

- *After authorization, packages can be run automatically if the code signature matches the signature of the one that was authorized.*

This ensures that unauthorized minor changes and tweaks in the study protocol can be detected, therefore promoting for protocol integrity, as well as providing performance optimization, if there are no changes to the already authorized packages.

- *There is no need for human interaction at any point in the processing from source data to evidence.*

This allows for speedy processing as well as the protection of data and protocol integrity.

- *All data operations are logged and stored together with every intermediate and final datasets.*

This allows for close auditing of the executed protocol for further verification and optimization, if needed. Logging the operations using blockchain technology ensures the audit trail cannot be tampered with without detection.

- *All data operations happen in sandboxed environments that are disconnected from the network ensuring that no data communication can happen except for the one controlled locally by ULSM.*

This allows for the creation of a bidirectional controlled environment, as it will not leak into the production setting, nor will the ZTA ecosystem and associated results, be corrupted by any other data or processes that could be trying to communicate with it from other sites of the organization. Study packages can be executed safely and validated from previous signatures, and outputs can be shared to the desired endpoint.

- *In case of processed data yielding datasets of small individuals, prior to running statistical analysis or modeling datasets are injected with noise.*

This allows for privacy protection of minority groups that could easily lead to re-identification. The same applies to the next item.

- *Aggregate results can be returned to the researchers safely provided that for sensitive data attributes (such as rare diseases):*

  ◦ Small cell counts are clamped according to relevant limits (example if a report returns a summary report for 2 patients only, all counts are shown as "< 50")

AND

- Point estimates are replaced with categories (example if a summary reports for 2 patients only, with a mean age of 65 and a SD of 1, results are shown as [63 - 67]).

Figure 4 illustrates the two main settings of the USLM ZTA solution, how they are separated and how they connect. On the left, the ZTA solution on institutions premises and where all the processing is performed; on the right, the platform so that the physician-researcher can interact with the solution to define and execute the research questions.

Figure 4. Architecture of the presented ZTA solution

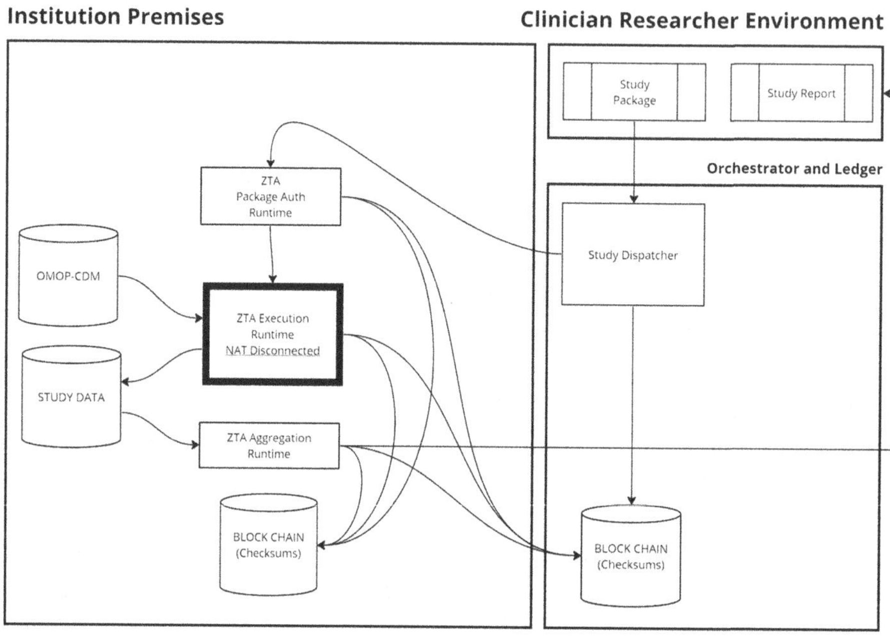

5. DISCUSSION

In order to generate evidence from healthcare data, it is not enough to collect data and simply perform what we think are the best analysis methods. To generate trusted and reproducible evidence there is the need to do it in a protected environment, with a standardized and automated protocol, and in a pool of data that is completely separate from production databases that are used daily to provide healthcare services. Moreover, all data needs to remain private and secure at all times and all processing needs to be compliant with current legislation.

Healthcare has the added requirement of comprising not only personal and identifiable data, but also data that is sensitive and confidential, which needs to be kept private ("special category data" as per GDPR). In addition, the healthcare environment generates a great amount of data daily, of various types and contexts, and in various formats and sizes. All these data are bound to be associated with a great number of research projects with the goal to study and improve health outcomes.

The described solution fulfills all these requirements. ZTA together with the OMOP Common Data Model create a secondary health data analysis architecture that allows for the separation of research data from all other data, avoiding also human intervention and associated errors while executing the pre-defined protocol and research questions on those data.

Although there is the need for some technological expertise to implement the solution, this use-case shows that it is not a matter of available solutions or technology but the need for the organizations themselves to understand and support these kinds of practices, policies and procedures. Once they acknowledge the advantages of such solutions, and can relate to similar contexts as the ones presented in this work, the practice of evidence generation will become more efficient and effective, and produce better results in shorter periods of time.

A general ZTA solution can be applied in similar scenarios however, there is always the need to adapt to the specific procedures, needs and resources available of the designated context. This is also a plus since one size fits all, specially with security solutions is frequently a bad option. As already mentioned, healthcare is one of the most vulnerable and attacked domains nowadays. The main attack vector is the human via phishing or similar social engineering attacks. These frequently end in ransomware attacks that may render services and organizations unavailable. With the separation of the evidence generation architecture from the production environment, access to those data will not be compromised and it may even constitute a temporary backup in the case of research projects.

6. CONCLUSION

Being a critical infrastructure, healthcare needs to find innovative, simple yet secure and tested solutions to process and analyze the vast amounts of daily collected data. Only this way will useful and trusted evidence be generated. The aim is always the same: to improve and optimize healthcare services on all fronts. Although privacy and security are the main motivators to protect data and thereby humans associated to those data, trust is, in the end, the link that keeps together any type of relation, being it between humans or between humans and the technology.

This work shows how trust can be increased by the Zero Trust paradigm. This may seem contradictory but by using an architecture that can provide all the necessary requirements for a private and secure, as well as safe data analysis, by taking out of the loop the probability of human and communication errors, this solution is, in fact, raising trust. And trust, as we all know, is the main drive to keep healthy and lasting relationships.

REFERENCES

Antona, M. (2019). Seven HCI Grand Challenges. *International Journal of Human-Computer Interaction*, *35*(14), 1229–1269. doi:10.1080/10447318.2019.1619259

BlackBerry. (2020). *Zero Trust, the Future of Healthcare Keep Technology Secure Without Exhausting Resources*. White paper. BlackBerry. https://cybersecuritycollaboration.com/wp-content/uploads/2020/10/BlackBerry_Zero-Trust-the-Future-of-Healthcare_White-Paper-1.pdf

Clemente-Teixeira, M., Magalhães, T., Barrocas, J., Dinis-Oliveira, R. J., & Taveira-Gomes, T. (2022). Health Outcomes in Women Victims of Intimate Partner Violence: A 20-Year Real-World Study. *International Journal of Environmental Research and Public Health*, *19*(24), 17035. doi:10.3390/ijerph192417035 PMID:36554916

CNCS - Centro Nacional de Cibersegurança. (2022). *Cybersecurity in Portugal. Relatório Sociedade 2022.* Centro Nacional de Cibersegurança. https://www.cncs.gov.pt/docs/rel-sociedade2022-observ-cncs15m.pdf

Cookson, R. (2005). Evidence-based policy making in health care: What it is and what it isn't. *Journal of Health Services Research & Policy, 10*(2), 118–121. doi:10.1258/1355819053559083 PMID:15831195

Cranor, L. (2008). A framework for reasoning about the human in the loop. *Proceedings of the 1st Conference on Usability, Psychology, and Security (UPSEC'08)*, 1-15.

Eddie, M., & Perlroth, N. (2020). Cyber Attack Suspected in German Woman's Death. *New York Times.* https://www.nytimes.com/2020/09/18/world/europe/cyber-attack-germany-ransomeware-death.html

Ferreira, A., Muchagata, J., Vieira-Marques, P., Abrantes, D., & Teles, S. (2021). Perceptions of Security and Privacy in mHealth. *23rd HCI International Conference Proceedings.* 10.1007/978-3-030-77392-2_19

Gao, Y., Li, X., Li, J., Gao, Y., & Yu, P. S. (2019). Info-Trust: A Multi-Criteria and Adaptive Trustworthiness Calculation Mechanism for Information Sources. *IEEE Access : Practical Innovations, Open Solutions, 7*, 13999–14012. doi:10.1109/ACCESS.2019.2893657

Henrique, D., Godinho Filho, M., Marodin, G., Jabbour, A., & Jabbour, C. (2021). A framework to assess sustaining continuous improvement in lean healthcare. *International Journal of Production Research, 59*(10), 2885–2904. doi:10.1080/00207543.2020.1743892

Hoff, K. A., & Bashir, M. (2015). Trust in automation: Integrating empirical evidence on factors that influence trust. *Human Factors, 57*(3), 407–434. doi:10.1177/0018720814547570 PMID:25875432

Hripcsak, G., Schuemie, M. J., Madigan, D., Ryan, P. B., & Suchard, M. A. (2021). Drawing Reproducible Conclusions from Observational Clinical Data with OHDSI. *Yearbook of Medical Informatics, 30*(1), 283–289. doi:10.1055-0041-1726481 PMID:33882595

Kumar, S., Kumar, P., & Bhasker, B. (2018). Interplay between trust, information privacy concerns and behavioural intention of users on online social networks. *Behaviour & Information Technology, 37*(6), 622–633. doi:10.1080/0144929X.2018.1470671

Marks, J. (2021). Ransomware attack might have caused another death. *The Washington Post.* https://www.washingtonpost.com/politics/2021/10/01/ransomware-attack-might-have-caused-another-death/

Ng, M., Coopamootoo, K., Toreini, E., Aitken, M., Elliot, K., & van Moorsel, A. (2020). Simulating the Effects of Social Presence on Trust, Privacy Concerns & Usage Intentions in Automated Bots for Finance. *IEEE European Symposium on Security and Privacy Workshops (EuroS&PW)*, 190-199. 10.1109/EuroSPW51379.2020.00034

NIS2. (2022). *Measures for a high common level of cybersecurity across the Union. Amending Regulation (EU) No 910/2014 and Directive (EU) 2018/1972, and repealing Directive (EU) 2016/1148. Directive (EU) 2022/2555.* European Parliament.

NIS. (2016). *Measures for a high common level of security of network and information systems across the Union. Directive (EU) 2016/1148.* European Parliament.

Official Journal of the European Union. (2016). General Data Protection Regulation (EU) 2016/679. *European Parliament and of the Council, L*, 119.

OHDSI. (2021). Observational Health Data Sciences and Informatics. In *The Book of OHDSI*. Independently Published. https://ohdsi.github.io/TheBookOfOhdsi/

Pappas, I. O. (2018). User experience in personalized online shopping: A fuzzy-set analysis. *European Journal of Marketing, 52*(7/8), 1679–1703. doi:10.1108/EJM-10-2017-0707

Peloquin, D., DiMaio, M., Bierer, B., & Barnes, M. (2020). Disruptive and avoidable: GDPR challenges to secondary research uses of data. *European Journal of Human Genetics, 28*(6), 697–705. doi:10.103841431-020-0596-x PMID:32123329

Petrosino, A., Boruch, R. F., Soydan, H., Duggan, L., & Sanchez-Meca, J. (2001). Meeting the Challenges of Evidence-Based Policy: The Campbell Collaboration. *The Annals of the American Academy of Political and Social Science, 578*(1), 14–34. doi:10.1177/000271620157800102

Reed, D., & Kemmerly, S. A. (2009). Infection control and prevention: A review of hospital-acquired infections and the economic implications. *The Ochsner Journal, 9*(1), 27–31. PMID:21603406

Reinecke, I., Zoch, M., Reich, C., Sedlmayr, M., & Bathelt, F. (2021). The Usage of OHDSI OMOP - A Scoping Review. *Studies in Health Technology and Informatics, 283*, 95–103. doi:10.3233/SHTI210546 PMID:34545824

Richter, G., Borzikowsky, C., Hoyer, B. F., Laudes, M., & Krawczak, M. (2021). Secondary research use of personal medical data: Patient attitudes towards data donation. *BMC Medical Ethics, 22*(1), 164. doi:10.118612910-021-00728-x PMID:34911502

Rose, S., Borchert, O., Mitchell, S., & Connelly, S. (2020). *Zero Trust Architecture*. NIST Special Publication 800-207. NIST - National Institute of Standards and Technology.

Scheckler, W. E., Brimhall, D., Buck, A. S., Farr, B. M., Friedman, C., Garibaldi, R. A., Gross, P. A., Harris, J. A., Hierholzer, W. J. Jr, Martone, W. J., McDonald, L. L., & Solomon, S. L. (1998). Requirements for infrastructure and essential activities of infection control and epidemiology in hospitals: A consensus panel report. Society for Healthcare Epidemiology of America. *American Journal of Infection Control, 26*(1), 47–60. doi:10.1016/S0196-6553(98)70061-6 PMID:9503113

Sehulster, L., & Chinn, RY. (2019). *Guidelines for environmental infection control in health-care facilities. Recommendations of CDC and the Healthcare Infection Control Practices Advisory Committee (HICPAC)*. MMWR Recomm Rep, 6;52(RR-10):1-42.

Selin, C. (2006). Trust and the illusive force of scenarios. *Futures, 38*(1), 1–14. doi:10.1016/j.futures.2005.04.001

Siegrist, M., Gutscher, H., & Earle, T. (2005). Perception of risk: The influence of general trust, and general confidence. *Journal of Risk Research, 8*(2), 145–156. doi:10.1080/1366987032000105315

Sillence, E., Blythe, J. M., Briggs, P., & Moss, M. (2019). A Revised Model of Trust in Internet-Based Health Information and Advice: Cross-Sectional Questionnaire Study. *Journal of Medical Internet Research, 21*(11), e11125. doi:10.2196/11125 PMID:31710297

Sinaci, A. A., Núñez-Benjumea, F. J., Gencturk, M., Jauer, M. L., Deserno, T., Chronaki, C., Cangioli, G., Cavero-Barca, C., Rodríguez-Pérez, J. M., Pérez-Pérez, M. M., Laleci Erturkmen, G. B., Hernández-Pérez, T., Méndez-Rodríguez, E., & Parra-Calderón, C. L. (2020). From Raw Data to FAIR Data: The FAIRification Workflow for Health Research. *Methods of Information In Medicine, 59*(S 01), e21–e32. . doi:10.1055/s-0040-1713684

Smiljana, A., & Laura, G. (2019). The internet: A brief history based on trust. *Sociologija, 61*(4), 464–477. doi:10.2298/SOC1904464A

Stanciu, A. (2023). Data Management Plan for Healthcare: Following FAIR Principles and Addressing Cybersecurity Aspects. A Systematic Review using InstructGPT Cold Spring Harbor Laboratory Press.

Stelson, P., Hille, J., Eseonu, C., & Doolen, T. (2017). What drives continuous improvement project success in healthcare? *International Journal of Health Care Quality Assurance, 30*(1), 43–57. doi:10.1108/IJHCQA-03-2016-0035 PMID:28105876

Trustwave. (2019). Global Security Report. *Trustwave.* https://www.trustwave.com/en-us/resources/library/documents/2019-trustwave-global-security-report/

UN - United Nations. (1948). *Fundamental Human Right, Article 12 - Privacy.* Universal Declaration of Human Rights.

Warburton, D. (2020). Phishing Attacks Soar 220% During COVID-19 Peak as Cybercriminal Opportunism Intensifies. *F5 Labs.* https://www.f5.com/company/news/features/phishing-attacks-soar-220--during-covid-19-peak-as-cybercriminal

Chapter 9
Advancements in Quantum Machine Learning for Intrusion Detection:
A Comprehensive Overview

Esteban Payares
Universidad Tecnologica de Bolivar, Colombia

Juan Carlos Martinez-Santos
https://orcid.org/0000-0003-2755-0718
Universidad Tecnologica de Bolivar, Colombia

ABSTRACT

This chapter provides a comprehensive overview of the recent developments in quantum machine learning for intrusion detection systems. The authors review the state of the art based on the published work "Quantum Machine Learning for Intrusion Detection of Distributed Denial of Service Attacks: A Comparative View" and its relevant citations. The chapter discusses three quantum models, including quantum support vector machines, hybrid quantum-classical neural networks, and a two-circuit ensemble model, which run parallel on two quantum processing units. The authors compare the performance of these models in terms of accuracy and computational resource consumption. Their work demonstrates the effectiveness of quantum models in supporting current and future cybersecurity systems, achieving close to 100% accuracy, with 96% being the worst-case scenario. The chapter concludes with future research directions for this promising field.

DOI: 10.4018/978-1-6684-8422-7.ch009

INTRODUCTION

Quantum computing is a field of computing that promises remarkable results in solving complex problems like factoring and unordered search problems (Havenstein et al., 2019). Over the years, the progress made in quantum technologies has led to the beginning of a quantum revolution, opening up opportunities for numerous other applications. Among the exciting possibilities is the potential of quantum computers to enhance machine learning (Killoran et al., 2019). In addition, this technology has the potential to transform the way computers address previously intractable problems (Havl´ıˇcek et al., 2019).

Machine learning has become a powerful tool for discovering data patterns due to the increasing computing power and algorithmic advances. However, quantum systems can produce outlier patterns that are difficult for classical methods to detect efficiently. This fact leads to the assumption that quantum computers may outperform classical computers in machine learning tasks (Biamonte et al., 2017). Therefore, quantum machine learning (QML) can improve applications of conventional machine learning (ML).

In the era of noisy intermediate-scale quantum (NISQ) computing, these technologies explore the potential of developing advanced quantum systems. With modern machine learning, we can access generative modeling techniques wellsuited for the emerging landscape of NISQ hardware (Torlai and Melko, 2020). For example, quantum technologies can develop robust security systems against computer threats. However, the emergence of quantum technologies also poses a significant cybersecurity threat that requires us to rethink how we encrypt our data (noa,). Two decades ago, we learned that practically all public-key cryptography would be compromised by quantum computers (Mosca, 2018). Therefore, studying the behavior of various quantum security systems is critical to prepare for this problem as the industry slowly transitions to using quantum technologies. Quantum computing holds immense promise in numerous areas, including medical research, artificial intelligence, weather forecasting, and more.

ADVANCEMENTS IN QUANTUM MACHINE LEARNING
FOR INTRUSION DETECTION SYSTEMS

Cybersecurity has become a significant concern with the increasing use of technology in our daily lives. Intrusion detection systems (IDS) are a crucial component in ensuring the security of computer networks by detecting and alerting the presence of any unauthorized access or malicious activity. However, the sheer volume and complexity of data that IDSs process make it challenging to detect new and sophisticated attacks. It is where quantum machine learning (QML) comes into play. QML has the potential to revolutionize the field of cybersecurity by offering a new approach to the processing and analysis of data that is faster and more efficient than classical computing. In this section, the authors will explore the recent advancements in QML for IDS and their potential to enhance the security of computer networks.

The paper "Quantum-Assisted Activation for Supervised Learning in Healthcare-Based Intrusion Detection Systems" proposes a novel method for IDS using quantum-assisted activation for supervised learning. The proposed method uses a neural network with a new activation function based on quantum mechanics that successfully capture patterns in the dataset while having less architectural memory footprint than classical solutions. The authors of this work claim that their method improves the performance of IDS and can achieve an accuracy rate as high as 99.9% (Laxminarayana et al., 2022).

Also, the work titled "Security Intrusion Detection Using Quantum Machine Learning Techniques" proposes a novel method for intrusion detection using quantum machine learning techniques. The authors claim that their method improves the performance of IDS by utilizing their dataset that implements the grouping of network packets into input streams that are suitable for quantum machine learning. Furthermore, they have developed a software solution that encodes network traffic streams ready for quantum computing. Experimental results show the QML-based intrusion detection's ability to process extensive data inputs with high accuracy (98%), providing a twice faster speed compared to the conventional machine learning algorithms utilized for the same task (Kalinin and Krundyshev, 2022).

On the other hand, The paper titled "A Quantum-Based Approach for Offensive Security Against Cyber Attacks in Electrical Infrastructure" proposes a unique, robust offensive security technique known as the "Alligator and Octopus" model for safeguarding the physical infrastructures of smart grids. The authors claim that their model safeguards present states and prevents future similar attacks. They explore state-space quantum attack and counter-attack mechanisms using Feynman concepts of quantum dynamics and attack and defend, threat and offend (ADTO) diagrams. They focus on the frequency stability and cyber-security of the LFC system. Using a QML technique, the authors of this work present a procedure for correct vulnerability prediction, exploitation, and execution strategy with an approximated likelihood of attack and its mode (D. et al., 2023).

Another work titled "Quantum Optimization for IoT Security Detection" presents an efficient and high-performance intrusion detection system based on Quantum Annealing for IoT security. The authors claim that their system can preserve systems confidentiality, integrity, and availability. In addition, they explore quantum computing and its ability to perform computational processes using classical optimization algorithms. The results show an optimization of computational time and an improvement in detection accuracy (Barletta et al., 2023).

Subsequently, in another work entitled "Automated Vulnerability Detection in Source Code Using Quantum Natural Language Processing", the authors present an efficient and scalable vulnerability detection method based on a deep neural network model Long Short-Term Memory (LSTM), and quantum machine learning model– Long Short-Term Memory (QLSTM), that can learn features extracted from the source codes1. The authors claim that their method can detect vulnerabilities in source code with high accuracy. Furthermore, they compared the results derived from the classical LSTM and quantum LSTM using classic feature representation and semantic and syntactic representation. We found that the QLSTM with semantic and syntactic features detects significantly accurate vulnerability and runs faster than its classical counterpart (Akter et al., 2023).

Another work entitled "Cyber-Physical System for Industrial Automation Using Quantum Deep Learning" presents a cyber-physical system for industrial automation using deep quantum learning. The authors claim that their system can make it easier for employees to get secure information and work better with people in other departments. To propose Cyber-Physical System for Industrial Automation Using Quantum Deep Learning, the authors proposed Cyber-Physical System for Industrial Automation that uses Quantum Learning to find attacking patterns (Rajawat et al., 2022).

Quantum Machine Learning for Distributed Denial of Service Attacks Detection

The authors will now focus on the implementation proposed for Distributed Denial of Service Attacks Detection using different QML models and their comparisons presented in work entitled "Quantum Machine Learning for Intrusion Detection of Distributed Denial of Service Attacks: A Comparative Overview". The authors employed three different approaches to building a classification model using their selected dataset to develop their implementation. The first approach involved using the QSVM model provided by QiskitAqua, a package designed for building algorithms and applications by Qiskit (IBM) (Abraham et al., 2019). The authors utilized the PennyLane framework for the other two models, a specialized QML framework developed by Xanadu Quantum Technologies Inc. (Bergholm et al., 2020). The methodology involved several general steps described below and summarized in Figure 1.

Figure 1. Overview of the methodology process. (A) Search and selection of the dataset. (B) Data pre-processing to improve model performance. (C) Construction and training of the models. (D) Generation of results, analysis, and conclusions.

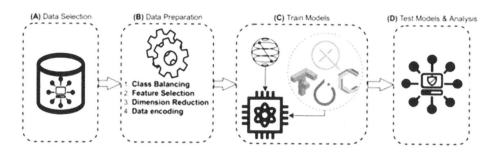

To ensure accurate results, the authors conducted three essential steps in data preparation: class balancing, feature selection and dimension reduction, and data encoding. To address the imbalance in the data, which represents network traffic and event logs per machine, the authors employed undersampling and oversampling algorithms, typically of the random type. Feature selection was a crucial step in the methodology as the initial dataset had 80 features, and some could interfere with the models' performance. The authors' feature selection process consisted of five approaches: removing features with a high percentage of missing values or a single unique value and eliminating collinear variables with a correlation coefficient above a specified threshold. To improve the algorithms' performance, the authors applied two types of normalization, scaling the data from $-\pi$ to π for the ensemble model and using a -1 to 1 scaling for the other models. Additionally, the authors implemented principal component analysis (PCA) to address the high dimensionality of their data and extract critical information from the table, reducing the data to only two features, as shown in Figure 2.

Data encoding is a crucial step in quantum machine learning, where classical data is represented as quantum states in a high-dimensional Hilbert space using a quantum feature map(Lloyd et al., 2020). The goal is to encode a classical

Figure 2. Training data used

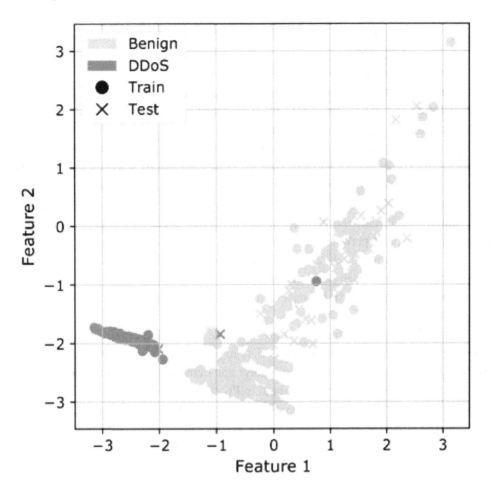

datapoint x into a quantum state $|\psi_x\rangle$ by mapping it into a set of gate parameters in a quantum circuit. In this study, the authors employed the embedding angle method, which encodes a set of N features into the rotation angles of n qubits, where $N \leq n$, using the Rx Gate, one of the Rotation Operators. Specifically, the Rx gate performs a single-qubit rotation around the x-axis of the Bloch Sphere by an angle θ (radians), as shown in Equation 1.

$$R_x\left(\theta\right) = \begin{bmatrix} \cos\left(\dfrac{\theta}{2}\right) & -i\sin\left(\dfrac{\theta}{2}\right) \\ -i\sin\left(\dfrac{\theta}{2}\right) & \cos\left(\dfrac{\theta}{2}\right) \end{bmatrix} \tag{1}$$

Models

In this section, the authors will briefly describe the models used in this implementation, which are practical adaptations of algorithms, concepts, and tools required to achieve results through quantum architectures, aiming for maximum reproducibility.

Quantum Support Vector Machine: For binary classification problems, Support Vector Machines (SVM) are a well-known type of supervised machine learning algorithm. This method maps the data into a higher dimensional input space and constructs an optimal separating hyperplane by solving a quadratic programming problem. Least Squares SVM (LS-SVM) is a version of SVM that approximates the hyperplane finding procedure of SVM by solving a linear equation (Suykens and Vandewalle, 1999).

The quantum version of SVM performs the LS-SVM algorithm using quantum computers (Rebentrost et al., 2014; J. et al., 2020). It calculates the kernel matrix using the quantum algorithm for the inner product on quantum random access memory, solves the linear equation using a quantum algorithm for solving linear equations, and performs the classification of query data using the trained qubits with a quantum algorithm (Rebentrost et al., 2014). However, since data is not typically a coherent superposition, we implemented the approach presented in (Havlíček et al., 2019). This classifier processes data classically and uses the quantum state space as a feature space through the QSVM algorithm of the Qiskit framework.

Ensemble Model: The authors presented an ensemble model that utilizes the quantum property of superposition to generate a set of quantum classifiers in parallel, similar to classical ensemble methods. The authors used four-qubit devices from the PennyLane default qubit and the PennyLane-Cirq plugin simulator to implement the circuits in two Quantum Processing Units (QPU). To encode the data, they employed the angle embedding process. The authors enacted the circuits for each system with a specific set of trainable parameters. The output of the circuits is a Pauli Z operator for measurement on two qubits, and the result is passed into a softmax function to obtain two two-dimensional probability vectors for the two classes. As a result, the ensemble model predicts the class with the highest average likelihood over all QPUs.

$$\sigma_z = \begin{bmatrix} 1 & 0 \\ 0 & -1 \end{bmatrix} \tag{2}$$

Hybrid Quantum-Classical Neural Network: The authors present a hybrid quantum-classical neural network model, which combines quantum and classical processors to overcome the limitations of noisy intermediate-scale quantum (NISQ) processors. This approach is appropriate for quantum simulation, optimization, and machine learning applications. The model comprises two dense classical layers and one quantum layer. Unlike the previous models, this model utilizes two qubits representing the bias neurons for the features extracted from the post-processed data. Following the circuit-centric classifier design, the quantum layer uses angle embedding and includes single-qubit rotations and entanglers. Like the ensemble model, two Pauli Z operators with a matrix defined in Equation 2 are created for measurements. The model's architecture includes a Rectified Linear Unit (ReLU) function in the first layer, a quantum variational circuit of two qubits in the second layer, and a Softmax function in the last layer.

The findings of this research provide valuable insights into the performance of quantum models for cybersecurity applications and demonstrate the potential of utilizing quantum machine learning techniques to address these challenges, depending on the specific use case. The author's results are presented in Table 1, which summarizes the performance metrics of each model.

Table 1. Summary of results.

Model	Accuracy Recall Precision F-Score Missclass CPU Time Memory Usage
ENSEMBLE 0.96836 0.96832 0.97024 0.96832 0.0316	32.1 s 546.69 MiB
QSVM 0.99661 0.99660 0.99661 0.99661 0.0034	122.4×10³ s 5.73 GiB
H-QNN 0.99887 0.99887 0.99887 0.99887 0.0011	5.265×10³ s 520.05 MiB

Table 1 presents the accuracy, recall, precision, F-score, misclassification rate, CPU time, and memory usage of each of the three models evaluated in this study: ENSEMBLE, QSVM, and H-QNN. The evaluation metrics provided in Table 1 offer insights into the performance of each model. Accuracy indicates the proportion of accurate predictions made on the test data. Precision measures the ratio of the true positive to all examples of a specific class. At the same time, recall indicates the proportion of examples belonging to a class among all examples belonging to the same class. The F-score, a composite of both recall and precision, provides an overall view of the model's performance. Finally, the Missclass metric represents the percentage of incorrect predictions made. As observed, the models exhibit varied behavior when subjected to the same test data, necessitating tuning to enhance their respective performance.

The results highlight the superior performance of the H-QNN model, achieving an accuracy of 0.99887 and outperforming the other models in all evaluated metrics except for memory usage. However, the QSVM model required significantly more CPU time and memory than the other models. The potential of overfitting for each model needs to be considered by the authors. Nevertheless, despite being parametrically robust, the models have shown considerable performance with the test data (Payares and Martinez-Santos, 2021).

FUTURE EXPECTATIONS

In recent times, groundbreaking research has unveiled a remarkable frontier in the realm of addressing cybersecurity challenges - the promising intersection of quantum machine learning (QML) techniques. The significance of these findings cannot be understated, as they shine a bright light on the potential of QML models like ENSEMBLE, QSVM, and the captivating H-QNN to revolutionize the landscape of cybersecurity. However, it's paramount to delve into the nuances and complexities that underlie this exciting emergence.

An intriguing highlight that emerges from the recent studies is the exceptional performance exhibited by the H-QNN model. This particular exemplar demonstrates, in unequivocal terms, the tremendous promise that QML holds within its grasp for reshaping the way we approach and tackle cybersecurity issues. One must recognize the monumental value of QML's ability to provide a holistic view of a model's performance, a feature that emerges as a cornerstone in the fight against the multifaceted challenges of cybersecurity. Nevertheless, the path forward is not without its hurdles, with the lurking specter of overfitting casting a necessary shadow that the authors must confront and navigate.

Peering into the horizon of possibilities, it's discernible that the trajectory of QML's evolution holds profound implications for the entire cybersecurity landscape. By artfully harnessing the distinctive capabilities that quantum computing bestows, QML techniques unlock a Pandora's box of security solutions that were once unfathomable within the confines of classical computing. The tantalizing prospect of dissecting colossal datasets in real-time, unveiling latent threats that could otherwise stealthily elude our notice, represents a quantum leap in the efficacy of cybersecurity measures.

Zooming in further, it becomes evident that QML techniques could aptly resolve some of the most formidable cybersecurity challenges that organizations grapple with in the contemporary milieu. Think about the prowess to effortlessly unmask and thwart the machinations of intricate cyber-attacks, effectively shielding communication networks from the incessant barrage of threats and fortifying the bulwarks that safeguard critical infrastructure from potentially catastrophic breaches.

As we stand at this juncture, where the crossroads of quantum innovation and cybersecurity merge in a harmonious symphony, it's undeniable that the tides of change are set to surge. The prospect of QML's integration into the cybersecurity arsenal is not merely a tantalizing possibility but rather an inevitability that has the potential to redefine the very fabric of digital security. And as we forge ahead, embracing this technological convergence with cautious optimism, it's imperative to tread the path with unwavering scrutiny, acknowledging both the remarkable potential and the underlying complexities that lie within the embrace of quantum machine learning for the realm of cybersecurity.

CONCLUSIONS AND FUTURE WORK

Summarizing the journey traversed in this chapter, we arrive at a comprehensive panorama of the strides taken in the domain of quantum machine learning for the pivotal task of intrusion detection. While the realm of quantum technologies still stretches out before us, it's discernible from this endeavor that the seeds of potential have been sown, indicating a fertile ground for quantum methodologies to flourish within the realm of artificial intelligence. This chapter acts as a beacon, showcasing how quantum machine learning techniques have surged forward, unveiling their prowess in the intricate dance of identifying and combatting cybersecurity threats, with a particular spotlight on the insidious DDoS attacks. What emerges strikingly is the unparalleled accuracy achieved, transcending the performance of their classical counterparts - a testament to the power latent within three distinct quantum models, each carving its own path with resounding success in its unique realm of applicability.

Yet, as we bask in the glow of these achievements, it's imperative to cast our gaze forward into the uncharted territories that beckon with promise. The road ahead presents the opportunity to dive into the depths of complexity, exploring the potential of more intricate data sets. Conceptualizing traffic representations that would find their resonance within the paradigm of a quantum internet introduces an electrifying avenue for exploration. The expanse of possibility extends further, inviting us to grapple with larger datasets, a move that holds the potential to bolster the reliability of the results, enhancing their robustness and real-world applicability.

In the grand tapestry of research, this chapter unfurls as a singular thread that contributes to the ever-growing fabric of knowledge surrounding the synergy of quantum machine learning and the intricate tapestry of cybersecurity. Not only does it offer insights and solutions, but it also lays bare the trajectory for future advancements. This endeavor embodies the spirit of progress, a glimpse into the unfolding chapters of this evolving narrative, where the marriage of quantum ingenuity and cybersecurity resilience is poised to script even more riveting tales of innovation. Thus, this research reverberates beyond its current pages, resonating as a testament to the boundless capacity that awaits in the intersection of quantum realms and the challenges of safeguarding our digital frontiers.

REFERENCES

A., Azaustre, C., AzizNgoueya, Banerjee, A., Bansal, A., Barkoutsos, P., Barnawal, A., Barron, G., Barron, G. S., Bello, L., Ben-Haim, Y., Bevenius, D., Bhobe, A., Bishop, L. S., Blank, C., Bolos, S., & Bosch, S. (2019). *Qiskit: An opensource framework for quantum computing*. Academic Press.

Akter, M. S., Shahriar, H., & Bhuiya, Z. A. (2023). Automated vulnerability detection in source code using quantum natural language processing. In *Communications in Computer and Information Science* (pp. 83–102). Springer Nature Singapore.

Barletta, V. S., Caivano, D., Vincentiis, M. D., Magr'ı, A., & Piccinno, A. (2023). Quantum optimization for IoT security detection. In *Lecture Notes in Networks and Systems* (pp. 187–196). Springer International Publishing.

Bergholm, V., Izaac, J., Schuld, M., Gogolin, C., Alam, M. S., Ahmed, S., Arrazola, J. M., Blank, C., Delgado, A., Jahangiri, S., McKiernan, K., Meyer, J. J., Niu, Z., Sza'va, A., & Killoran, N. (2020). PennyLane: Automatic differentiation of hybrid quantum-classical computations. arXiv: 1811.04968.

Biamonte, J., Wittek, P., Pancotti, N., Rebentrost, P., Wiebe, N., & Lloyd, S. (2017). Quantum machine learning. *Nature*, *549*(7671), 195–202. doi:10.1038/nature23474 PMID:28905917

D., L., Nagpal, N., Chandrasekaran, S., & D., J. H. (2023). A quantum-based approach for offensive security against cyber attacks in electrical infrastructure. *Applied Soft Computing*, *136*, 110071.

Havenstein, C., Thomas, D., and Chandrasekaran, S. (2019). Comparisons of Performance between Quantum and Classical Machine Learning. *SMU Data Science Review*, *1*(4).

Havlíček, V., Córcoles, A. D., Temme, K., Harrow, A. W., Kandala, A., Chow, J. M., & Gambetta, J. M. (2019). Supervised learning with quantum-enhanced feature spaces. *Nature*, *567*(7747), 209–212. doi:10.103841586-019-0980-2 PMID:30867609

J., A., Adedoyin, A., Ambrosiano, J., Anisimov, P., Ba¨rtschi, A., Casper, W., Chennupati, G., Coffrin, C., Djidjev, H., Gunter, D., Karra, S., Lemons, N., Lin, S., Malyzhenkov, A., Mascarenas, D., Mniszewski, S., Nadiga, B., O'Malley, D., Oyen, D., Pakin, S., Prasad, L., Roberts, R., Romero, P., Santhi, N., Sinitsyn, N., Swart, P. J., Wendelberger, J. G., Yoon, B., Zamora, R., Zhu, W., Eidenbenz, S., Coles, P. J., Vuffray, M., & Lokhov, A. Y. (2020). Quantum Algorithm Implementations for Beginners. arXiv: 1804.03719.

Kalinin, M., & Krundyshev, V. (2022). Security intrusion detection using quantum machine learning techniques. *Journal of Computer Virology and Hacking Techniques*, *19*(1), 125–136. doi:10.100711416-022-00435-0

Killoran, N., Bromley, T. R., Arrazola, J. M., Schuld, M., Quesada, N., & Lloyd, S. (2019). Continuous-variable quantum neural networks. *Physical Review Research*, *1*(3), 033063. doi:10.1103/PhysRevResearch.1.033063

Laxminarayana, N., Mishra, N., Tiwari, P., Garg, S., Behera, B. K., & Farouk, A. (2022). *Quantum-assisted activation for supervised learning in healthcare-based intrusion detection systems*. IEEE Transactions on Artificial Intelligence. doi:10.1109/TAI.2022.3187676

Lloyd, S., Schuld, M., Ijaz, A., Izaac, J., & Killoran, N. (2020). Quantum embeddings for machine learning. arXiv: 2001.03622.

Mosca, M. (2018). Cybersecurity in an era with quantum computers: Will we be ready? *IEEE Security and Privacy*, *16*(5), 38–41. doi:10.1109/MSP.2018.3761723

Payares, E., & Martinez-Santos, J. C. (2021). Quantum machine learning for intrusion detection of distributed denial of service attacks: a comparative overview. In P. R. Hemmer & A. L. Migdall (Eds.), *Quantum Computing, Communication, and Simulation*. SPIE. doi:10.1117/12.2593297

Rajawat, A. S., Goyal, S., Bedi, P., Constantin, N. B., Raboaca, M. S., & Verma, C. (2022). Cyber-physical system for industrial automation using quantum deep learning. In *2022 11th International Conference on System Modeling; Advancement in Research Trends (SMART)*. IEEE. 10.1109/SMART55829.2022.10047730

Rebentrost, P., Mohseni, M., & Lloyd, S. (2014). Quantum Support Vector Machine for Big Data Classification. *Physical Review Letters*, *113*(13), 130503. doi:10.1103/PhysRevLett.113.130503 PMID:25302877

Suykens, J., & Vandewalle, J. (1999). Article. *Neural Processing Letters*, *9*(3), 293–300. doi:10.1023/A:1018628609742

Torlai, G., & Melko, R. G. (2020). Machine-Learning Quantum States in the NISQ Era. *Annual Review of Condensed Matter Physics*, *11*(1), 325–344. doi:10.1146/annurev-conmatphys-031119-050651

Chapter 10
Organizational Transformation Projects:
The Role of Global Cyber Security and Crimes (RoGCSC)

Antoine Toni Trad
https://orcid.org/0000-0002-4199-6970
IBISTM, France

ABSTRACT

The implementation of organizational transformation projects (simply project) in the contexts of complex and dynamic businesses (or other application domains), need an optimal transformation framework and a holistic RoGCSC. The RoGCSC uses measurable cybersecurity and governance security risk (secRisk) critical factors, which are mitigated and tuned, to ensure project's successful evolution and predict/block cyber (or classical) crimes/misdeeds. The actual exponential rise of cybercrimes has become a major concern for countries, enterprises, and citizens; and that obliges projects to integrate polymathic-holistic security strategies. Actual cyberspace's resilience, control, and security concepts are siloed, insufficient, chaotic, and concentrate only on platforms' infrastructural aspects. Actual concepts focus on isolated hackers, where financial predators are the ones behind major cybercrimes. Global cybercrimes are closely related to global events and phenomena, like financial greediness, insecurity, conflicts, terrorism, pandemics, and societal crisis.

INTRODUCTION

Today many security Architectures (secArch) exist and unfortunately, they often inefficient. A *Project* supports the transformation of traditional businesses into secured Cyberbusinesses, by automating its security processes, which can face human resistances. The implementation of secOUs takes into account mainly intangible non-financial objectives, where security as the highest priority. A *Project* has various Enterprise's (simply *ENT*) Viewpoints, like "O" for organizational, "S" for Security... In this chapter

DOI: 10.4018/978-1-6684-8422-7.ch010

the focus is on Viewpoint "S" or *ENT*(S). *ENT*(S) is a sequence (or a set) of secRPs applied to secOUPs (*secRPOUP*), which goal is to disassemble *ENT(S)'*: Legacy OUs' archaic structure(s), Security concept, Organizational processes, Information system's administration, Resources/Artefacts, Applications, Working models, and Components; into dynamic reusable secCBBs which can be (re)used in standardized or In-House-Implemented (IHI) Organizational secBBs (secOBB). A secOU is a set of secOBBs and different secOUs can share common secOBBs and secCBBs. Legacy OUs' transformation need an IHI secured Methodology, Domain, and Technology Common Artefacts Standard (secMDTCAS) that maps to refactored secBBs, secCBBs and secOBBs. In the process of refactoring Micro-Artifacts (secMA) the secRP can face difficulties, because *ENT(S)'* heterogenous human profiles/cultures, system parts, secOU's Resistances (OUR), managers/stakeholders exaggerated financial ambitions, and *Project's* limited time/budgets. The author uses an adapted version of his Applied Holistic Mathematical Model (AHMM) for *RoGCSC* (AHMM4RoGCSC) (Trad, & Kalpić, 2020a) to support *secRPOUP's* capacity in the initial phase to generate a pool of secBBs. The secBBs are based on the secBBs that are generated by the secure Automated Refine Processes (secARP) based secUP. *Project*s are very complex to secure and they depend on the initial *Project's* phase, which is secARP/secUP. secCBBs are combined to offer reusable secOBBs, which are used to (re)build and resecure secOUs. The secARP/secUP based *secRPOUP* face difficulties because of various heterogenous security concepts and the AHMM4RoGCSC can check the integrity of the *RoGCSC*. Unfortunately, *Projects* are intended to deliver immediate tangible financial profits, and that is the reason for their high failure-rate, which is more than 70%; and if they succeed, they are unsecure. An IHI *RoGCSC* avoids *financial-only locked-in* strategies, products, and ensures success. It is important to define the levels of granularity and a mapping concept for the secMDTCAS, which enables the reuse of existing (or newly) refactored/refined secMAs/secBBs/secCBBs/secOBBs. As shown in Figure 1, the *RoGCSC* follows the secARP/secUP phase and if that step fails then a new *RoGCSC* has to be implemented. Otherwise, the *Project* can move to the next step and consider that an achievement was done. The *RoGCSC* chooses an initial secOU's module to be refactored by the secARP/secUP, to prove that its feasibility and tries to convince that *ENT(S)* can move to secOBB and the secure Process/collaboration Models (secOPM) based secure Dynamic Organizational Models (secDOM) refactoring phase, which is this chapter's scope.

Figure 1. Project's secured phases

Various *ENT* domains have critical security requests and the hyper evolution of various domains (security/technology), needs different security concepts, methodologies, and technologies, and that creates fatal general and security problems because of the gaps between the mentioned hyper-evolutions and *Projects'* progress, which take long-time to terminate. That implies the need for a transcendent secMDTCAS, which ensures *Project's* evolution independence from types of evolutions. The secMDTCAS based *RoGCSC* is an important success factor because secRPs unify Mas/secCBBs/secOBBs management in order to support the reorganization of secOUs; and to deliver *ENT(S)*. secCBB/secOBB refactoring is a risky *Project's* phase, because of secRP's complexity and the *RoGCSC* supports *Project* Managers (or simply *Managers*) and team, in refactoring/extracting and reusing secCBBs. secRP is not only disassembling (and reassembling) of secCBBs/secOBBs, but it is a structural and coherent reorganization of secOUs based *ENT*. A secCBB reuses secured models/diagrams/documents, secMAs/secBBs, and Architectural secBBs (ABB). The secured Transformation Development Methodology (secTDM) coordinates secRPs to deliver secCBBs/secOBBs, which are used in next *Project's* phases, as shown in Figure 1.

Figure 2. The project's security construct

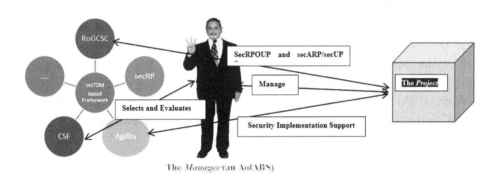

In many *Projects,* secARP/secUPs-secRPs operations are underestimated and that causes *Project's* failure(s). Therefore, secRP's success is mandatory for *Project's* next phases. secRP's activities and its transformed/generated IHI secCBBs/secOBBs, are independent of a specific brand/methodology, tool, or locked-in strategy. The AHMM4RoGCSC (Trad, & Kalpić, 2020a) supports the *RoGCSC* which uses secARP/secUP to refactor/extract secCBBs/secOBBs and takes into account secRP's complexity and applied a Polymathic- holistic approach. Such an approach needs an Enterprise Architecture (EA) based *RoGCSC* that can be used for any APplication Domain (APD). secRP's objective is to reengineer and secure common System and/or Domain Components (secSDC)... The *RoGCSC* is done in consequent steps and uses the Polymathic-AHMM4RoGCSC secRP, to surpass complexities (Trad, 2022a, 2022b, 2023a, 2023b). The AHMM4RoGCSC supports *secRPOUP* of legacy OUs, by using secMDTCAS and secTDM to integrate standard methodologies, like The Open Group's (TOG) Architecture Framework's (TOGAF) Architecture Development Method (ADM) (The Open Group, 2011a) and the Sherwood Applied Business Security Architecture (SABSA) (SABSA, 2020). The secured Information and Communications Systems' (secICS) related *Projects* use iterative/cyclic transformation phases, which includes secRPs. secRPs are used to refactor secSDCs that include secured: 1) Organizational refinement technics; 2) Development Secured and Operations (DevSecOps); 3) Automated tests/qualifications; 4) Extracting secCBBs/secOBBs; and 5) secCBBs/secOBBs/secDOMs modelling activities. The *RoGCSC* supports secRPs, which faces complexities due to: 1) The implementation of secured complex, chaotic, and heterogenous secCBB/secOBB/secSDCs; 2) secICS' hyper-evolution; 3) Incapacity to establish an secMDTCAS; 4) Resistance for Change (R4C) (or OUR), which should be checked with the Readiness to Transform (R2C); and 5) Maintenance difficulties (Koenig, Rustan, & Leino, 2016). The *RoGCSC* uses a Proof of Concept (PoC) and a related Applied Case Studies (ACS); where one ACS describes a leading *European Bank's* (simply *zBank*) secARPs/secUPs and secRPs and another one related to an insurance *Project ArchiSurance* (Jonkers, Band & Quartel, 2012). The *zBank Project* was mainly used to support a secRP of its legacy framework, ICS, and organizational structure, which was based on secTDM/ADM, ArchiMate, Mainframe and Java environments. The ADM based secTDM, managed underlying design/refinement, DevSecOps, secArch, and governance activities. As shown in Figure 2, a *Project* needs a qualified *Manager* (or Architect of Adaptive Business Information System-AofABIS), secArch/secRP specialists, and a skillful team. But for *zBank,* the team was the weakness which generated R4C/OUR, due to the lack of secTDM/ADM skills and secArch was ignored and that proves the need for *RoGCSC*. The secTDM managed refactored secCBBs/secOBBs/secSDCs and their storage in the *ENT(S)'/Enterprise Continuum* (Trad, 2022a, 2022b). Three refactoring/technics were applied: 1) Common secCBBs/secOBBs; 2) Mixed secCBBs which include ABBs and Solution secBBs (SBB), and create secSDCs' libraries (The Open Group, 2011a); 3) Imported secCBBs/secOBBs to be used by secDOMs; 4) Reorganize OUs; and 5) Support *ENTs*. As shown in Figure 2, *RoGCSC*' interaction includes: 1) Decision Making System (DMS) for *RoGCSC* (DMS4RoGCSC); 2) Knowledge Management System (KMS) for *RoGCSC* (KMS4RoGCSC); 3) Critical Success Factors (CSF) (and areas Critical Success Areas-CSA) Management System (CSFMS); and 4) An IHI *RoGCSC*. To prove *RoGCSC*' feasibility a PoC was implemented as well as a Research and Development Process (RDP) for *RoGCSC* (RDP4RoGCSC) concepts.

THE RDP FOR RoGCSC

The Polymathic Model's Basic Elements

The *RoGCSC* assesses strategic and critical *Project's* secRisks to guaranty secRP operations' coherency, by using the AHMM4RoGCSC and its basic elements:

- *m* mapping operator
- *i* instance of
- *R* U of Requirements
- *C* U of Constraints
- *H* HDT/Heuristics function
- *V* Valuate function, U of *H*
- *St* U of States
- *T* U of Sts
- *Sl* U of Solutions
- *F* Function
- *A* U of Actions/*Fs*
- *P* U of Problem
- *GID or GUID, is a **unique identifier** for all AHMM4RoGCSC objects*

- *FTR is a **feature**, of an ENT(S), Enterprise, Project, secICS...*
- *ART is an **artefact**, ...,*
- *CNT or **C's element** is a **constraint**, of an ENT(S), Enterprise, Project, secICS...*
- *RUL is a **rule**, of an ENT(S), Enterprise, Project, secICS...*
- *REL is a **relationship or association**, ...*
  - *Which can be three DIM [TYPE][GID][CSA/APD]*
- *PRB or **P's element** is a **problem**, of an Enterprise, Project, secICS...*
- *REQ or **R's element** is a **requirement**, of an Enterprise, Project, secICS...*
- *CLS is a **structure**, class, method-part,...*
- *OBJ is a **CLS instance**, object, exec code,...*
- *SRV is a **service***
- *DIA is a **Diagram**, UML, TOGAF, OOM, SA/SD,...*
- *APP is an **application***
- *RFA is an **Refinement Actions***
- *secARP is an **Automated Refinement Process***
- *UPS is an **Unbundling Process***
- *UPP is an **Unbundling Phase***
- *OUS is an **Organizational Unbundling Sub-Project***
- *secBB is a **Building Block***
- *ABB is an **Architecture Building Block***
- *SBB is a **Solution Building Block***
- *CMP is an secICS **structure**, like application, server...*
- *WGT is a **Weighting***
- *HDT is a **heuristics based ...***
- *SOL or **S's element** is a **solution***
- *AIM is a **AI models**, interaction, secBPM, UML/Collaboration,*
- *GAP is a **Project's gap analysis***
- *TSK is a **Project task***
- *CLD is a **Cloud or Distributed System***
- *EST is an **Enterprise System***

Figure 3. The AHMM4RoGCSC's nomenclature

<u>**ICS basics:**</u>

ART	= *m* SRV	(I1)
ǀART	= *m* DTB	(I2)
ART	= mcArtefact	(I3)
SRV	= $\underline{U}$ mcArtefact	(I4)
CLS	= $\underline{U}$ FUN *or* SRV + $\underline{U}$ VAR + $\underline{U}$ REL	(I5)
OBJ	= *i* CLS	(I6)
DIA	= $\underline{U}$ CLS + $\underline{U}$ REL	(I7)
DIA	= $\underline{U}$ OBJ + $\underline{U}$ REL	(I8)
SCR	= *i* DIA	(I9)
BB	= $\underline{U}$ DIA	(I9)
ABB	= $\underline{U}$ DIA	(I9)
SBB	= *i* SCR	(I9)
APP	= $\underline{U}$ SCR	(I10)
CMP	= $\underline{U}$ APP *or* IEL *or* DST	(I11)
ICS	= $\underline{U}$ CMP	(I12)
CLD	= $\underline{U}$ ICS	(I13)
EST	= $\underline{U}$ CLD	(I14)

<u>**Requirements:**</u>

mcREQ	= *m* KPI	(R1)
mcMapping mcArtefact/mcREQ	= mcArtefact + *m* mcREQ	(R2)
FTR	= mcREQ	(R3)
PRB	= *m* PRB	(R4)
REQ	= *m* CSF = $\underline{U}$ mcREQ	(R5)
REQ	= $\underline{U}$ FTR + $\underline{U}$ RUL + $\underline{U}$ CNT + $\underline{U}$ DIA + $\underline{U}$ REL	(R6)

AHMM4RoGCSC's basic elements are used to present secRP artefacts:

- *a* for atomic, for the atomization of an element
- *MVC* = $\underline{U}$ DIA + $\underline{U}$ REL (A1)
- *MVC* = $\underline{U}$ MVC + $\underline{U}$ REL (A2)
- *aBB* = $\underline{U}$ SRV + $\underline{U}$ REL (A3)
- *sBB* = $\underline{U}$ *i* SRV + *i* $\underline{U}$ REL (A4)

In this chapter the Viewpoint "S" is the central section of the applied Polymathic-holistic approach.

A Polymathic-Holistic Approach

Figure 4. Project's polymathic-holistic approach

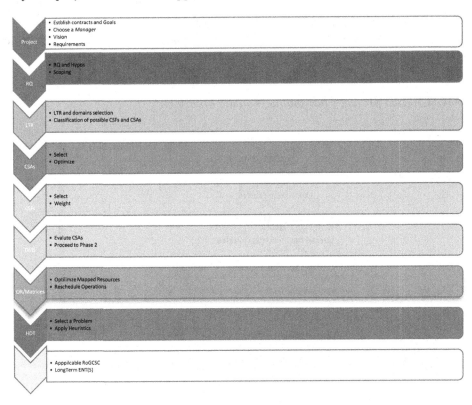

secARP/secUP and secRP has created a paradigmatic change in *Projects*, where archaic OUP's components use heterogenous structures, technologies, and methodologies; and their transformation in the form of secCBBs/secOBBs is supported by a Polymathic-holistic *RoGCSC*. As shown in Figure 4 the Viewpoint "S" focuses on refactoring secOUs to deliver *ENT*(S); which is related to the Viewpoint "O". Viewpoint's "S" elements are:

- $secMA = \sum aBB + \sum sBB + \sum aMVC$ (S1)
- $secBB = \sum secARP/secUP + \sum secMA + \sum secOPM$ (S2)
- $secCBB = \sum secBB + \sum secABB + \sum secSBB$ (S3)
- $secOBB = \sum secCBB$ (S4)
- $secSDC = \sum secOBB$ (S5)
- $secOU = \sum secSDC$ (S6)
- $secRP = \sum secARP/secUP$ (S7)
- $secDOM = \sum secRP$ (S8)
- $secRPOUP - \sum secDOM$ (S9)
- $secOU = \sum secRPOUP$ (S10)
- $ENT(S) = \sum OU(S)$ or $secOU$ (S11)

Transformed/refactored secMAs/secDOMs/secSDCs/secCBBs/secOBBs (objects, resources) are classified in repositories and they are identified by a GID. The RDP4RoGCSC supports the *RoGCSC* to refine secOU's components for the *ENT(s)*. secRP's main activity is to extract APD secDOMs and relate them to secCBBs/secOBBs/secSDCs. The RDP4RoGCSC supports the implementation of the ACSs/PoC. Figure 4 shows the Polymathic-holistic *RoGCSC* based *Project* for *zBank*. RDP4RoGCSC's first step was to establish the Research Question (RQ) and achieve a Literature Review Process (LRP) for *RoGCSC* (LRP4RoGCSC).

Figure 5. RoGCSC-based project's polymathic-holistic approach

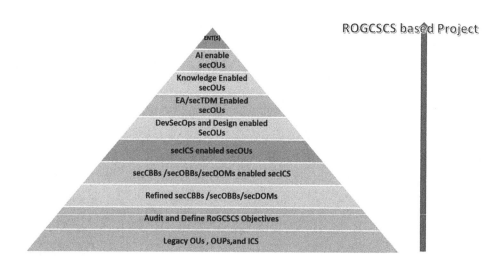

The RQ and LTR4RoGCSC

The RQ is: "Can *RoGCSC* support the implementation of secRP for secOUs and *ENT(S)*?". Where this chapter's auxiliary RQ is: "How can secDOMs/secCBBs/secOBBs support secSDCs?". Where the RDP4RoGCSC uses EA/secTDM, AHMM4RoGCSC, CSFMS, and DMS4RoGCSCS. LRP4RoGCSC's analysis showed that there isn't any similar approach to the Transformation Research Architecture Development framework (*TRADf*), *secTDM*, secARP/secUP/secRP, and AHMM4RoGCSC/RQ. And there are a small number of relevant scholar resources on basic UP technics. Concerning TOGAF, which is a usable and limited framework, and tackles minor *Project's* topics, like EA. Therefore, the AHMM4RoGCSC based RDP4RoGCSC (and related works), are pioneering, innovative and complete RQ's gap. The gap and high failure-rates were confirmed by the LRP4RoGCSC (Bishop, 2009; Capgemini, 2011). There is also a lack of a Polymathic-holistic approach, because such activities are done manually or by using commercial products. The LRP4RoGCSC used the following resources: 1) Articles and resources related to secRP/secOPM/secICS/*ENT(S)* reengineering; 2) The author's works related to security; 3) *RoGCSC's* feasibility and capacities; 4) Initial sets of CSAs/CSFs; and 5) The Empirical Engineering Research Model (EERM). All the author's works are based on *TRADf*, AHMM, secTDM, and RDP; which are today mature and can be applied in various APDs. The RDP4RoGCSC proved the existence of a gap and the necessity to deliver *RoGCSC* recommendations. The gap is due that there nothing similar to the

RoGCSC; but there are basic refinement approaches that concern exclusively code-sources, and which are manual processes. As shown in Figure 4, the next step is to select and classify the sets of CSFs and CSAs in the CSFMS.

CSAs, CSFs Management System

A CSA is a category (or set) of CSFs where in turn a CSF is a set of Key Performance Indicators (KPI), where a KPI maps (or corresponds) to a single *Project* or *RoGCSC*. For a *RoGCSC* requirement or problem, an initial set of CSAs, CSFs and KPIs are selected, to be used by the Heuristics Decision Tree (HDT) based DMS4RoGCSC. The requirements are mapped to sets of secCBBs/ABBs/SBBs/secDOMs/ secMAs. CSFs are used for the mapping between the requirements, secRP modules/secCBBs/secSDCs, OUs/OUPs, and DMS4RoGCSC/KMS4RoGCSC (Peterson, 2011). CSFs reflect areas that must meet the main strategic *Project* and *RoGCSC*'s goals/constraints. Measurement's technics, which are provided by *TRADf*, to evaluate performance for each CSA, where CSFs can one of the following: 1) *RoGCSC*'s status; 2) Mapping levels; 3) *Project's* gap analysis; and 2) DMS4RoGCSC/KMS4RoGCSC requests calls in real time, as shown in Figure 6. KPIs can be integrated in secSDCs, so HDT's based evaluation processes can automatically estimate the values of CSAs, and CSFs (Dick, 2001; Quinlan, 2015). As shown in Figure 5, CSFs' and- secRisks estimations have the following characteristics (Ylimäki, 2006): 1) Understanding secRP and DevSecOps activities; 2) CSFs based secTDM implementations' fallouts; 3) Mitigation strategy of secRisks are their mapping to CSFs; 4) CSFs are linked to KPIs which are secSDC variables; and 5) CSAs/CSFs/KPIs are tuned by the *Project team*. Sets of CSFs/CSAs are weighted by the DMS4RoGCSC/KMS4RoGCSC to offer sets of solutions for a *RoGCSC* problem.

Figure 6. The secRP and CSAs/CSFs integration with RDP4RoGCSC
Source: Trad and Kalpić (2020a)

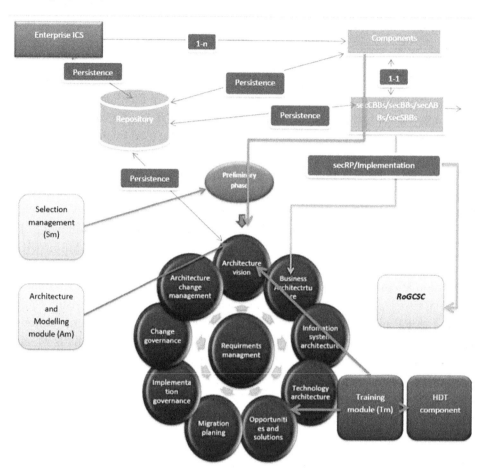

RDP4RoGCSCS' phases:

- Phase 1 (represented in decision Tables), forms the empirical part, which checks the following CSAs: 1) The RDP4RoGCSC, which is synthesized in Table 1; 2) The secICS/secPCP is synthesized in Table 2; 3) secArch is synthesized in Table 3; 4) The Polymathic approach synthesized in Table 4; 5) The *RoGCSC* based *Project*, which is synthesized in Table 5; and 6) This chapter's RDP4RoGCSC outcome, which is synthesised in Table 6. *TRADf* based *RoGCSC* delivers a set of (managerial and technical) recommendations and solutions, and a strategy for a *Project and ENT(S)*.

- Phase 2 checks problem solving capabilities and integration with *TRADf*.

RoGCSC's Integration With TRADf

As shown in Figure 6, *TRADf,* secTDM, and the *RoGCSC* support the transformation of legacy OUs/secOUPs/*ENT* into agile secSDCs/secCBBs/secOBBs/secMAs, which are designed, assembled, and implemented using secMDTCAS, independently of the types of: 1) secICS/technologies; 2) APDs; 3) secOUs' structures; 4) SecDevOps; and 5) Methodologies. The secMDTCAS ensures that *ENT(S)'s Projects* are not locked-in by global actors or the hyper-evolution of methodologies/technologies (Greefhorst, 2009).

Figure 7. TRADf's implementation interface

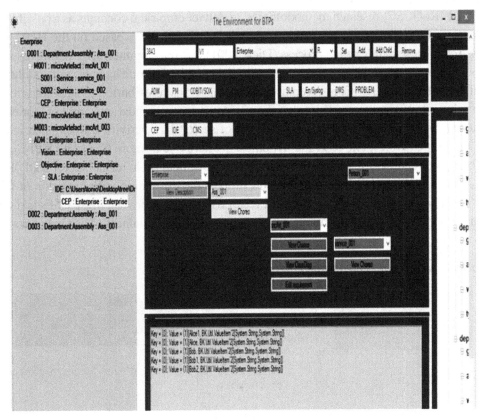

The *RoGCSC* is a complex concept and strategy, that is due to the unviable, heterogenous, and archaic OUP's and ICS' components, that makes the secRP very hard to extract secMAs/secCBBs/secOBBs and secSDCs. *RoGCSC*'s Polymathic-holistic approach supports complex secOU/secOUP's integration activities (Daellenbach, & McNickle, 2005). secRPs for APDs automate and refactor OUs. The *RoGCSC* is a part of *TRADf's: Software engineering or the Implementation module* (Im), and *Architecture module* (Am); where it is recommended to build a similar IHI framework and secTDM, which can be based on the ADM, as shown in Figure 7. The secTDM based *RoGCSC* supports DevSecOps, to extract secSDCs/secCBBs/ABBs/SBBs, which circulate through its phases. These elements contain their sets of CSFs and KPIs. The RDP4RoGCSC reuses the author's works/*TRADf*, and RDP4RoGCSC to solve the RQ. So, it is an iterative research process and all related topics are only referenced, because otherwise it would be tedious to understand this work. The RDP4RoGCSC is a non-conventional concept, in the field of *Project's* topics. The *RoGCSC* is Polymathic and is founded on a genuine RDP that is influenced by the EERM that in turn is based on *TRADf*/HDT, DMS4RoGCSC/KMS4RoGCSC, secTDM/ADM and secICS concepts (The Open Group, 2011a).

EERM's Usage

The EERM based RDP4RoGCSC is optimal for *Projects* and uses *TRADf* (where it applies a multi-level mixed research by using the HDT) that can be considered as different from conventional research models (Easterbrook, Singer, Storey, & Damian, 2008; Dick, 2001: Quinlan, 2015), and it includes: 1) Heuristics-Basic reasoning; 2) Quantitative Analysis for *RoGCSC* (QNT4RoGCSC); 3) Qualitative Analysis for *RoGCSC* (QLT4RoGCSC) research methodologies, to deliver empirical concepts as a possible approach for complex tuned mixed methods research; and 4) A learning process based on the HDT, which was inspired by Action Research learning process (Dick, 2001). *TRADf* can interface existing research methods, and the difference is just in the scope and depth of the method. Empirical research validity checks if the RDP, like the RDP4RoGCSC, is acceptable as an important contribution to existing scientific (and engineering) knowledge and to convince that the presented recommendations and PoC (or engineering experiment), are valid and reusable for various types of *secRPOUP* activities. In engineering, a PoC is a software prototype of a testable RQ (and hypothesis) where one or more CSFs and KPIs (or independent variables, in theoretical research) are processed to evaluate their influence on RDP4RoGCSC's dependent variables. As shown in Figure 8, PoCs support the evaluation with precision of CSFs/KPIs and if they are related, whether the cause–effect relationship exists between these CSFs and CSAs. The secTDM and *RoGCSC* are transformation centric and use existing standards (The Open Group, 2011a).

Figure 8. TRADf's RDP implementation environment

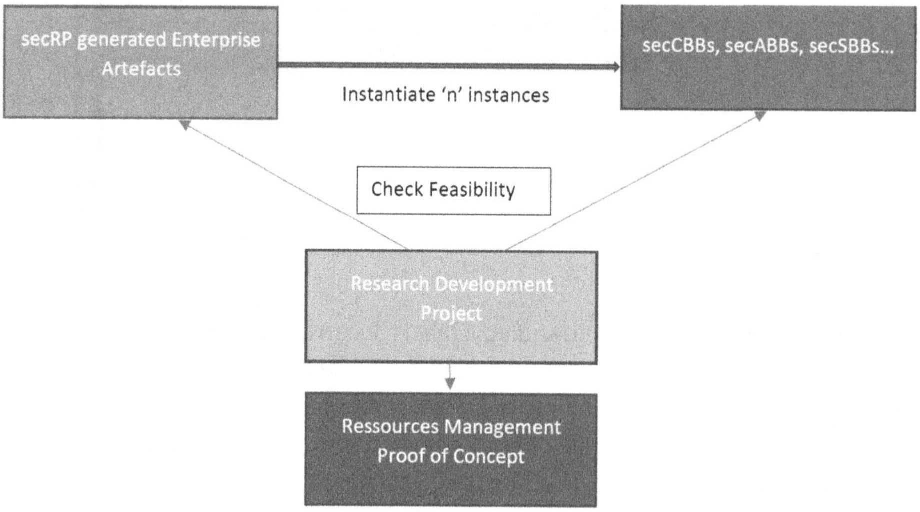

RoGCSC's author's related works are: 1) Enterprise Transformation Projects-Cloud Transformation Concept – Holistic Security Integration (CTC-HSI) (Trad, 2023c); 2) The Business Transformation Framework and the-Application of a Holistic Strategic Security Concept (Trad, & Kalpić, 2019a); 3) The Business Transformation Framework and Enterprise Architecture Framework for Managers in Business Innovation: The Role of Cyber and Information Technology Security (Trad, & Kalpić, 2019b); 4) Business Architecture and Transformation Projects: Enterprise Holistic Security Risk Management

(ESRM) (Trad, & Kalpić, 2019b); 5) *ENT* Transformation Projects: Security Management Concept (SMC) (Trad, & Kalpić, 2021c); 6) Advancing Cybersecurity for Business Transformation and Enterprise Architecture Projects: Deep Learning Integration for Projects (DLI4P) (Trad, & Kalpić, 2021b); 7) Using Applied Mathematical Models for Business Transformation (Trad, & Kalpić, 2020a); 8) Applied Holistic Mathematical Models for Dynamic Systems (AHMM4DS) (Trad, 2021a); 9) Business Transformation Projects-The Role of a Transcendent Software Engineering Concept (RoTSEC) (Trad, 2022a); 10) Business Transformation Projects-The Role of Requirements Engineering (RoRE) (Trad, 2022b); 11) Business Transformation Projects based on a Holistic Enterprise Architecture Pattern (HEAP)-The Basic Construction (Trad, & Kalpić, 2022c); 12) Integrating Holistic Enterprise Architecture Pattern-A Proof of Concept (Trad, & Kalpić, 2022d); 13) A Transformation Framework Proposal for Managers in Business Innovation and Business Transformation Projects-Intelligent atomic building block architecture (Trad, 2015a); 14) A Transformation Framework Proposal for Managers in Business Innovation and Business Transformation Projects-An Information System's Atomic Architecture Vision (Trad, 2015b); and 15) Organizational and Digital Transformation Projects-A Mathematical Model for Building Blocks based Organizational Unbundling Process (Trad, 2023b). But the *Project* should not underestimate *RoGCSC*' complexity, which is mainly due to a long and complex process; which needs R2C based transformation readiness checks.

The RoGCSC and Transformation Readiness Checks

The *RoGCSC* supports and secures all *Project* tasks, including the tools usage, processes, and secICS' management. An important CSF is to use *RoGCSC* to synchronize various secICS and secured Cloud Platforms (secCP). *secRPOUP*s are very complex and they are the cause of *Projects'* failures; which are mainly due to secARP/Ups and the following secRPs, which generate various types of problems, like (O'Riordan, 2021; Standish, 2011): 1) secRPs cannot be successfully finalized; 2) *Projects* have > 70% failure rates; 2) *Managers* use accountability justifications to select people to be accused, and to justify the failure's *only* financial aspects; where the main reason is *RoGCSC*'s complexities; 3) secOPM/secICS fields evolve fast and business schools graduate *Managers* are submerged by such complexities; 4) In an Oxford study, 90% of *Projects* were stopped because of budgets overruns, especially ICS budgets which have a 200% overruns rate; 5) Failure-rates are also due to the excessive demands of stakeholders to make excessive gains; 6) *Project* initiatives for change is a critical subject for *ENTs*; where various research show that the failure-rates of such initiatives are around 70-80%, while other *ENTs* are struggling for their survival; 9) The Chaos Reports, produced by the Standish Group over the last fifteen years; they assert that: ... *only about 29% of transformations come in on time and budget... So why continuing such Projects? Projects* need UPs and they need skills, IHI tools, and secTDM/ADM capabilities. Successful cases are due to *Enterprise's Capacity to Execute (EC2E)*, which is the ability of an *ENT* to perform all *RoGCSC* tasks and to make optimal *Project* decisions. The *RoGCSC* needs the following types of skills (The Open Group, 2011a): 1) secTDM/EA for RoGCSCs and to support *Business Transformation Readiness Assessment* capacities; 2) To support secRPs' executions; 3) To establish *EC2E* capacities; 4) DMS4RoGCSC based learning concept, to build secRP experiences; 4) To integrate secMDTCAS; and 5) Design and implement of secOPM System (secOPMS) and secDOM. The readiness for *RoGCSC* depends on secARP/secUP refined pool of secBBs.

secARP/secUP Refined secBBs

The *RoGCSC* depends on the critical secBBs based secUP, where secUPs are used for secOUPs. A secBB is a set of atomic BBs (aBB) (Greefhorst, 2009). *Projects* apply aBBs driven implementation which is based on a Pseudo-Bottomup-Approach (PBA), where aBBs are built on secured services' architecture frameworks (Trad, 2023b).

Figure 9. The model-view-control pattern
Source: Palermo et al. (2012)

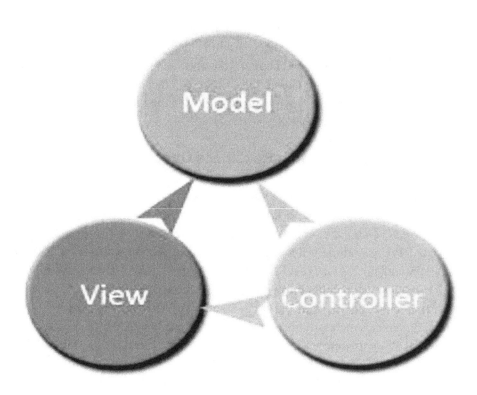

The ARP/UP supports secured services which are coordinated by the secMVC pattern as shown in Figure 9. secTDM manages ARPs/UPs in which ABBs are templates for instantiating SBBs. secTDM manages secBBs which provide conceptual and logical views of secured SRVs (secSRV) across various APDs. EA like TOGAF has generic BBs that correspond to ABBs, where a secBB uses standard security concepts (The Open Group, 1999).

RDP4RoGCSC's CSFs

Based on the AHMM4RoGCSC, LRP4RoGCSC and DMS4RoGCSC, this CSA's CSFs/KPI were weighted and the results are shown in Table 1. And the total result is 9.25, which is high and that is due to RDP4RoGCSC's maturity and that the secRP delivers secCBBs can be successful (Trad, 2023b). As RDP4RoGCSC's CSA presents positive results, the next CSA to be analyzed, is the role of ICS, OUP and secCP.

Table 1. This CSA has the average of 9.25.

Critical Success Factors	KPI		Weightings
CSF_RDP4RoGCSC_Polymathic_Approach	Proven	▼	From 1 to 10 **10 Selected**
CSF_RDP4RoGCSC_CSA_CSF_KPI_Integration	Proven	▼	From 1 to 10 **10 Selected**
CSF_RDP4RoGCSC_secRP_Integration	Complex	▼	From 1 to 10 **08 Selected**
CSF_RDP4RoGCSC_FERM	Feasible	▼	From 1 to 10 **09 Selected**
CSF_RDP4RoGCSC_Transformatio_Readiness	Feasible	▼	From 1 to 10 **09 Selected**
CSF_RDP4RoGCSC_Needed_Skills_Profiles	Feasible	▼	From 1 to 10 **09 Selected**
CSF_RDP4RoGCSC_IHI_TRADf	Possible	▼	From 1 to 10 **09 Selected**
CSF_RDP4RoGCSC_LTR4RoGCSC	Proven	▼	From 1 to 10 **10 Selected**

valuation

ICS, OUP, AND DISTRIBUTED/secCP SECURITY

Basic ICS Security

Cybersecurity is *ENT's* state that can be prone to dangers, where the *Project* delivers a secICS that provides maximum security (Oxford Dictionaries, 2017a). This section presents the CSFs that influence the secICS and OUP's Cybersecurity requirements. Cybersecurity depends on requirements related to: 1) Cybertechnologies; 2) (Inter)National contexts; and 4) *ENT*. Cybersecurity requirements are the most fundamental for *ENT*'s survival and they enclose various subdomains. A secArch should fit *ENT*'s secTDM that in turn is based on best practices. *RoGCSC* is a mixture of EA/technical solutions, APD/ business engineering, and security concepts, like DevSecOps. *RoGCSC* governance defines the interaction between various secICS components and their Cybertechnologies artefacts: Data, Technology, Networks, Web/ Internet of Things (IoT), and Applications.

DevSecOps' Integration

Applications development and operations are coordinated by DevSecOps which manages developers, operations and security specialists. The *Project* uses agile SecDevOps procedures to identify patterns for managing requirements. DevSecOps is a set of engineering practices that support secured collaboration between various *Project* teams. An *ENT* needs a fast implementation concept that includes software releases, like DevSecOps'; respecting secRisks, quality and benefits. DevSecOps can be controlled using the Secured Control and Logging Concept (SCLS).

The SCLS

Cyberbusiness platforms (or OUPs) are not APD agnostic and offer improved: 1) Performance; 2) Reliability; and 3) Cybersecurity/Tracing. OUPs are controlled/monitored in real-time by the SCLS to support the *RoGCSC*. SCLS' are optimal for monitoring and support presentation, sorting, and tuning. SCLSs can be designed to analyse, collect and store *RoGCSC* data from various secICS components. The SCLS can be integrated in secCBBs/secOBBs to ssynchronize dislocated activities. SCLS enables logging and logged-data is essential for maintaining, measuring, and optimizing performance and security. It is complex to leverage logged-data from heterogenous sources and these insights are used improve *ENT(S)*. SCLS log-media includes: Event-logs, Security-logs, Transaction-logs, Message-logs, and Audit-logs. To ensure cohesive aggregation process, the SCLS ingests, processes, and correlates logged-data. And takes in account legal constraints

Legal Constraints and Cybersecurity

RoGCSC supports *ENT's* legal integration to achieve legal support; CSFs assert/monitor legal artefacts and manages differences in Cyberbusiness/OUP's local and international laws. Cyberbusinesses must have the capacity to proactively recognize illegal/erroneous Cybertransactions. The European Union (EU) legislation governs/asserts Cyberbusiness laws and implements enforced APD-engineering national practices. Cybertransactions outcomes have to be continually legally asserted, traced, and their periodic summaries are reported to *Managers* (Fu & Mittnight, 2015). The legal regulation of Cybertransaction's security needs qualified time-stamps and certification. Cybertransaction is influenced by the Uniform Law Commissioners who promulgated the Uniform Electronic Transactions Act in 1999. It is the first adaptable effort to prepare a Cyberlaw for Cyberbusiness. Many countries have adopted Cyberbusiness regulations. The Uniform Electronic Transactions Act represents the first effort in providing some standardized rules to govern Cybertransactions. The integration of Mas/secCBBs/secOBBs has to be conform with legal predispositions, which supports data-protection-laws, contract-laws, procurement-laws, fraud-laws and many other laws. Facts show that international-law on Cybersecurity is inefficient and advanced states are hesitant to integrate international-law that is based on non-governmental norms. States insist on their traditional legal systems that marginalize inter-state governance of Cyberspace and secCPs.

secCP

secTDM and *RoGCSC* support the *ENT(S)* by using a scalable secCP's infrastructure and services layers. secCPs support the alignment of secBBs secSRVs, and security strategies, like the *RoGCSC* which recommends the use of a secured Private CP (SecPCP). An *ENT* can build its own SecPCP, uses secCPs, and avoids locked-in situations. The *RoGCSC* uses secPCPs' domains like Services, Processes, AI, Capacities, Infrastructure, Distributed computing, and secured Business Process Models (secBPM). The *RoGCSC* integrates various types of security challenges to support *ENT's* robustness, longevity, and sustainability. The *RoGCSC* supports the sharing of secured resources to ensure *Project's* coherence and uses secPCP models, which reduces costs and stays unlocked. A secPCP includes a set of distributed secSRVs and the management of secICS' components, which are IHI (Wikipedia, 2022a). *ENTs* have built their secPCP to become secure, agile and, supports public Infrastructure as a Service (IaaS) based secSRVs (Bala, Gill, Smith, Wright, & Ji, 2021). Basic secPCP activities are managing: 1) Passwords; 2)

Firewalls; 3) DevSecOps; 4) Antivirus/Viruses/Worms; 5) Emails; 6) Wireless Fidelity; 7) Malware; 8) Business rules for *ENT's* assets; 9) Policies; 10) Codified data/information assets' ownership/custody; 11) secRisk analysis, and 5) Data classification policies. The *RoGCSC* manages the flow of secICS/OUPS/ secPCP applications' fallout/abnormal flows, failure-modes, and the possibilities in which applications can be interrupted (or attacked). All *ENTs* have secPCP concerns and secArch's should be implemented with secTDM's support; that ensures that all *RoGCSC's* decisions are traceable and that secRisks are mitigated. secPCP's concerns are (Trad, 2021b; 2023c):

- Authentication: The substantiation of GIDs.
- Authorization: Enforcement of permitted capabilities for a person/GID has been established.
- Confirming: The secPCP/OUPS/secICS respects *RoGCSC* policies.
- Assurance: secTDM checks security attributes with accordance to *RoGCSC* policies.
- Availability: *ENT's* ability to function without secSRVs' interruption.
- Assets: The protection of information/assets from misdeeds.
- Administration: Managing *RoGCSC* policies and persons.
- secRisks: Managing *RoGCSC's* secRisks.
- Violations: Block attacks.

Violation Types and Protection Against Attacks

ENTs' activities are orthogonal to *RoGCSC*/Cybersecurity's requirements, where it defines the responsibilities for their resources. Cybertransactions outcomes must be asserted, traced, and summaries can be archived (Fu, & Mittnight, 2015). Common motivations for violations-attacks are: State Organized Financial Predators' (SOFP) greediness, Lack of ethics, Immoral education, Geopolitical interests/sabotage, and other. SOFPs drive to major violations-attacks, like, gigantic Cyberfinancial crimes, which are related to fraud/money-laundering that damage many countries, and this case it is related to major global financial institutions, like the Union des Banques Suisse (UBS) (Stupples, Sazonov, & Woolley, 2019), in which 32 trillion US dollars are *hidden*.. Under the cover of bank secrecy… SOFP is behind major Cyberattacks like (Trad, 2022a): 1) Denial-of-Service (DoS) and Distributed DoS (DDoS); 2) Man-in-the-Middle; 3) Phishing and spear-phishing; 4) Drive-by attack; 5) Passwords theft; 6) Structured Language Query (SQL) injections; 7) Cross-Site-Scripting (XSS); 8) Use of trojan Cyberfinance institutions; and 9) Eavesdropping attack. SOFP backed attacks need *RoGCSC*. Attacks are due to global IoT and SOFPs' bank secrecy concepts; the *RoGCSC* blocks by forbidding SOFPs' interaction and Cyberhackers. A Cyberhacker is a criminal who illegally accesses a secICS, and transfers assets in SOFP banks, like the UBS. *ENT(S)* counters threats like: 1) Cybercrime that includes Cyberattacker(s), which attack *ENTs* for financial goals; 2) Cyberattack, involves SOFP and/or politically motivated information theft; and 3) Cyberterrorism, undermines the secICS and causes damage. The secICS supports *ENT's* security and reduces secRisks related to attacks by, spreading information/knowledge to *ENT's* OUs, Verify personnel for *Social Engineering Attacks*, SOFP interactions, and other scams. An attack uses illegal access rights, and that can be hindered by: 1) Systemic password change/management; 2) Using screen-lock and face-recognition; 3) Blocking email-attachments from anonymous email-address(es); 4) Anti-virus software, 5) Not sharing personal-info; 6) Reporting security-loops; 7) Avoiding paper-documents; 8) Non-secured digital data; 9) Securing information handling; and 10) Providing of information over phone. secICSs need governance and legal-constraints to handle violations, for that goal CSFs are selected/asserted to monitor Cyberactivities. The Identity and Access Management (IAM) secSRV allows secICSs to specify which rights are attributed to users and its elements are: Identities and groups, Resources, Permissions, Roles, and Policies; used to manage:

- Identities and groups grant access permissions to users.
- Resources can be accessed by authorized users.
- Permissions are rights to perform actions on a secICS resource.
- Roles are sets of permissions and administrators grant roles to Identities, and not permissions.
- Policies enable the association of sets of roles and permissions with secICS resources.
- Data security provides multiple mechanisms for securing data in addition to IAM policies.
- Security principles enforce security design principles, like the Separation of Duties.
- General Data Protection Regulation (GDPR) is used to standardize privacy protections across the EU, by granting controls to individuals over their private information.

secICS and secPCP CSFs

Table 2. This CSA has the average of (rounded) 8.20

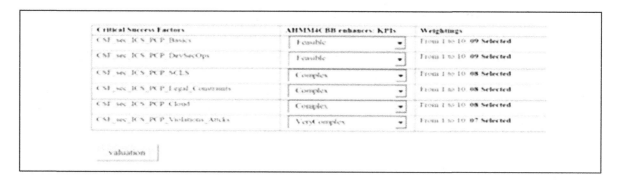

Based on the AHMM4RoGCSC, LRP4RoGCSC and DMS4RoGCSC, this CSA's CSFs/KPI were weighted and the results are shown in Table 2; which has the average of 8.20, which is low, is due to the fact that basic security integration is complex. As the RDP4RoGCSC's CSA presented low results, the next CSA to be analyzed the role and evolution of secArch.

SECURITY ARCHITECTURE

The Role of Secured Digital Transformation

As shown in Figure 1, the *RoGCSC* to secure *Project's* initial phases, and its goal is to create secOUPs based on secCBBs/secOBBs/secDOMs/secSRVs for a sustainable *ENT(S)*. secOUPs and secICS support secured Digital Transformations (secDT), which improves *ENT's Time-to-Market* and adapts to *RoGCSC* requirements.

Figure 10. An APD viewpoint on the rejection of DTs
Source: Eira (2022)

RoGCSC based secDTs are strategic for *ENTs* and that needs high-adoption rate of secICS/digital technologies. But *Project* based digitization are complex and more than 70% fail, even if in general *Managers* are the ones to be accused; the main reason is *RoGCSC's* integration misfits. As shown in Figure 10, *Managers* consider that APD strategy, team-members' concerns/R4C, secDTs, and customer experience, are the causes for failures, which from APD's perspective are not the real reasons (Eira, 2022). *RoGCSC* breaks down *ENT's* (mainly secOUP and secICS) silos, to enable secDT which use to digitized APD models and defines secDT's scope (Bizzdesign, 2022).

The Scope of RoGCSC-Based secDTs

RoGCSC depends on governance requirements and relies on: Infrastructure, secICS, APD-engineering, Frameworks, and Cybersecurity. secDT is managed by secTDM to face challenges to digitally transform secSRVs, and resources. The secTDM synchronizes *ENT(S), RoGCSC,* secOUP, and secICS, where secDT profoundly changes the way the *ENT* acts (Möhring, Keller, Schmidt, Sandkuhl, & Zimmermann, 2023).

Figure 11. secMDTCAS' implementation

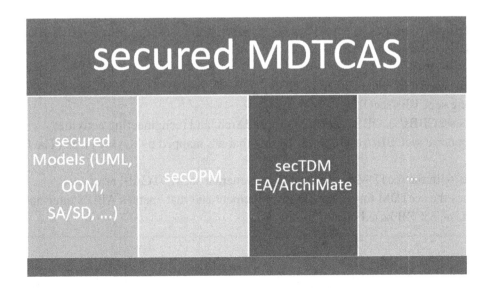

secDTs are difficult to scope because they depend on the APD, secOPMS, and secMDTCAS' integration. A secDT supports a *Project,* future APD's functions and (re)organization activities, which enhance *ENT's* functional performances. An agile secCBBs/secOBBs/ABBs/SBBs based APD models' development needs a secDT to adopt a Polymathic-holistic approach (Chaione, 2022). A *Project* must define a secMDTCAS, which is a mix of existing methodologies. secMDTCAS includes Object Oriented (OO) Methodology (OOM) and legacy methodologies, like the Structure Analysis and Structured Design (SA/SD). *RoGCSC* Adopts various types of diagrams like the Decision-Making-Notation (DMN) which is similar to *TRADf's* Tables' evaluations. The secMDTCAS interfaces standard methodologies which are based on OOM and which have OO features, which are inherited from three OOMs, namely Rumbaugh, Booch, and Jacobson methodologies. The methodologies are the fundaments of the most known modelling/secICS standard, the Unified Modelling Language (UML) (Liu, 2022). EA modelling languages like ArchiMate, have many artefacts, diagram types, views, and in this chapter only the UC View (UCV), Business Process Interaction View (BIV), and Business Process View (BPV) are used, to show how secMDTCAS can include common secOPMS, EA/ArchiMate artefacts and diagrams. Combining secOPMS with secTDM/EA in *Projects* are supported by secCBBs/secOBBs, which in turn support secOPMS in the *Business Architecture* phase aspect of ADM/secTDM (Rosing, Hove, Subbarao, & Preston, 2012). A well synchronized secTDM supports secOPMS, APD choreography, EA-models, to enable the *RoGCSC*. That needs a Polymathic-approach to enable structured *Project*. Automated and non-automated secOPMs have a key role in developing APD competencies, and where *Business Architecture* and secICS architecture are vital. The key to linking these two architectural domains are secured BPs (secBP), secOPMs, and secBPMs which are subsets of process architecture(s). Analyzing APDs security requirements in a siloed manner can generate problems and a Polymathic-holistic approach captures interdependencies, and the *RoGCSC* links secCBBs and secOBBs with secOPMSs (Rosing, Hove, Subbarao, & Preston, 2012). To align secBPs, secOPMs, and secBPMs/ secOPMSs (simply *Model*) with: secCBBs/ secOBBs/SBBs, and secOUs, there is a need to use secTDM/ADM's life-cycle. The *RoGCSC* establishes: Common secMAs for the secMDTCAS, secured Business Process Architecture (secBPA), *Models'* tools and management, DevSecOps, Test scenarios, Best practices, and secOUs' control (Luyckx, 2015).

The Role of secMDTCAS and Avant-Garde Domains

secMDTCAS supports the *RoGCSC* to refine legacy *Models* and uses secCBB/secOBBs-based secOPMS to deliver ABBs and instantiated SBBs. Where the *RoGCSC:*

- Offers the secRP to reuse refined secCBBs and actual refining concepts *reinvent the wheel* when extracting secCBBs/secOBBs.
- Delivers secCBBs/secOBBs/secDOMs for secArch, and reengineering activities
- Mixes generic secCBBs/secOBBs/secDOMs that are mapped by the secTDM (The Open Group, 2011a).
- Interacts with the secTDM to automate/auto-generate secMDTCAS' artefacts.
- Interfaces the secTDM for legacy-OUPs refinement and that enables APD's inter-operability.
- Supports a secCBB based vision.

Preparing secCBBs-Based Vision

The secTDM needs a secCBBs/secOBBs based vision to establish a secured *Architecture Vision (sec-CAV)*, as shown in Figure 12, to support: *RoGCSC*, ABBs, and secCBB's reusability principles. An adaptive secOUP/secICS is based on various secRP generated atomic resources like aBBs, sBBs, secSRVs, secured Model View Control (secMVC) which are coordinated by the secTDM phases. A secCBB is a set of secBBs, and secCAV delivers their mapping-patterns (Greefhorst, 2009). *Projects* apply secCBBs driven implementation which needs specific implementation skills and a secCBB/secOBB based PBA. The secTDM depends on *RoGCSC's* requirements, and secArch which supports the related secSRVs, interfaces, and standards that satisfy APD's requirements (The Open Group, 2011c). The secMDTCAS includes common and coherent sets of IHI secCBBs, used to compose secDOMs. The *RoGCSC* drives the use of secRPs to refine secCBBs/secOBBs, which can also emerge from *the best architecture & modeling practices*. secRPs apply *secured architecture & modeling extraction techniques*. IHI secRP models used secARP/secUPs to generate basic secBBs. Then secRPs include secCBBs/secOBBs, *Models*, and secBBs/secMAs in the secMDTCAS. As there are many standards and types of artefacts, the Object Management Group's (OMG) DMN will be presented; and it is used for secArch modeling decisions. DMN's models are shared between EA based secOUPs/secPCPs and the secMDTCAS interfaces DMN's *Models* (RedHat, 2022).

Figure 12. ADM-based secTDM's vision phase

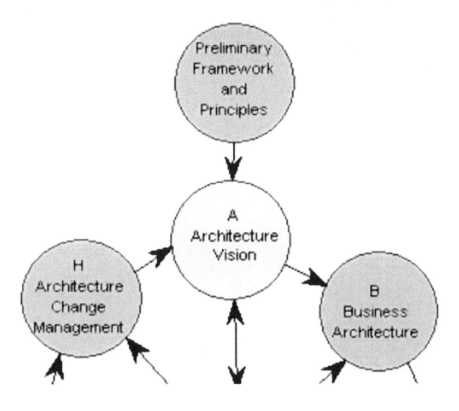

EA-Based secOUPs/secPCP

EA based OUPs/secPCPs support (Trad, 2023c):

- Protection by (Trad, & Kalpić, 2022c): 1) Localizing gaps in the infrastructures; 2) Review of security solutions; 3) Blocking cumulative-attacks; 4) Defining a security strategy; 5) Building a robust/ defensive secICS; 6) Integrating security in Cybertransactions; 6) Blocking SOFPs; and 8) Applying qualification procedures. secTDM's usage avoids: 1) Siloes and poor performances; 2) Lack of scalability; 3) To fail and to become un-maintainable; 4) Unsynchronized; 5) Interfacing market risk frameworks like the Committee of Sponsoring Organizations of the Treadway Commission (COSO), which is shown in Figure 13.
- Conversion: Of legacy siloed architectures to secArch and a secOUP/secPCP, which enables the automation of MAs, throughout secTDM's phases.
- Hosting: Of secPCP models by using secTDM's *On Premises Hosting Model*, where the *ENT* is responsible for IHI secPCP (Charles, 2021). *The IaaS Hosting Model* represents hosting in both *On Premise* and in the *Cloud/secPCP*, where *ENT* manages its EA-based secOUP/secPCP; and secRPs refine secOUP/secPCP's applications' cartography.
- Unifying: secPCP security aspects by aligning with standards like the National Institute of Standards and Technology (NIST), which has a list of best practices that can influence the *RoGCSC*. The NIST has created the necessary steps for an *ENT* to self-assess its secPCP security preparedness and to apply adequate security measures. These principles are built on the NIST's five pillars of Cybersecurity framework: Identify, Protect, Detect, Respond, and Recover. Another framework is the Cloud Security Posture Management (CSPM) which is designed to address common secTDM's integration (IBM, 2022a).

Figure 13. Integration of SABSA with TOGAF
Source: Kasarkod (2011)

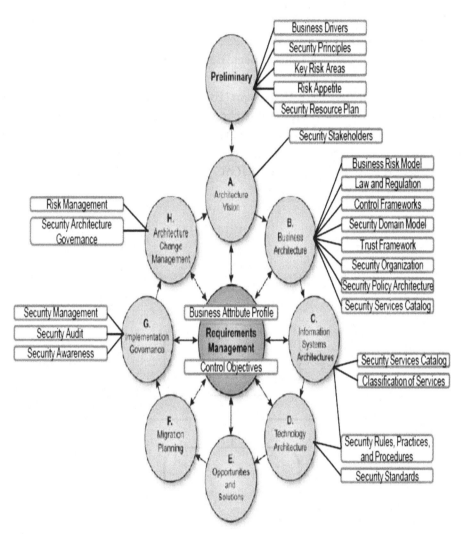

ENT's secTDM Integration

Classification domains (or CSAs) is used in secArch to reduce *RoGCSC*'s complexity in the design process which includes the following phases (Vulić, Prodanović, & Tot, 2019): 1) Phase I-Preparation for defining security-requirements; 2) Phase II-Security vulnerability analysis; 3) Phase III-Threats' modelling; 4) Phase IV-Determination of security requirements; 5) Phase V-sRisks assessment; 6) Phase VI-Categorization/prioritization; and 7) Phase VII-Documentation. The role of EA based secTDM is like in all civil engineering fields, is central and it is directly inspired from civil engineering. Urbanistic architecture for large cities, like Hausman's restructuring of Paris main aim was holistic security... So secArch is of crucial importance ! And standards can be considered as major security dangers, because if such knowledge is known and public, then it is easy to penetrate *ENT's* ICS. secTDM's basics are (Techopedia, 2022, Threat Intelligence, 2023)):

- Unifies security of all security artefacts, mitigates secRisks and applies security controls.
- Establishes design principles that are clear, has in-depth security control specifications, and includes connections between secCBBs/secOBBs.
- The key attributes are: Relationships/dependencies, Benefits, Form associates secICS with EA/secTDM, Drivers (like secRisk management, Benchmarking, Good practices, Financials, Legal and regulatory…).
- Key phases are: *Architecture Risk Assessment* (Evaluates influences of vital *ENT* assets), *Security Architecture and Design* (The design and secArch services), *Implementation* of secSRVs and processes, and *Operations and Monitoring* of secICS processes.
- An undeniable *ENT* needs requires robust security measures against Cyberthreats/Cyberbreach.
- Contains sets of *Models*, methods, and *RoGCSC* principles that align *ENT(S)* objectives.
- Offers a set of *RoGCSC* services.

RoGCSC Services

Figure 14. OSI architecture and service
Source: Threat Intelligence (2023)

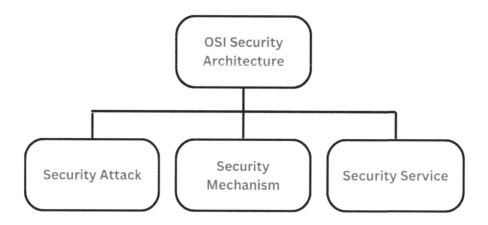

RoGCSC's basics services are (Threat Intelligence, 2023):

- A secSRV is processing improves the security of the data/code-modules by protecting the execution flow; it includes authentication, access-control, resources confidentiality/integrity, nonrepudiation, and availability.
- Sensitive data protection from Cyberthreats (DoS, Data-theft, SOFP, Malware-viruses-worms, and Trojans).
- Supports confidentiality, integrity, and availability, which are *RoGCSC* key principles. Confidentiality ensures that authorized users have access to sensitive secSRV. Integrity ensures that secSRV cannot modify without authorization.
- Supports secArch to secure data/resources as they move on the secICS, as shown in Figure 14.
- Authentication, verifies users authorized to access the secICS.

- Access control manages access to the secICS.
- Data confidentiality and integrity, maintains privacy of data/information.
- Non-repudiation blocks users from denying that they sent or received a specific message.
- Supports interfacing secArch frameworks like: TOGAF, SABSA, Open Security Architecture (OSA)...
- TOGAF focuses on secArch but does not offer specific *RoGCSC* solutions.
- SABSA is policy-driven that (superficially) supports secArch in asking: what, why, when, and who issues.... SABSA's goal is to ensure that after secArch of secSRVs, they are deployed and used in the secICS.
- The OSA supports technical/functional security controls and offers an overview of crucial security parts like principles, issues, and concepts that promote secArch decisions. But, OSA is used after secArch's finalization.
- secOUPs/secPCPs data are protected from unauthorized access, Cyberattacks, and other potential Cyberthreats. secOUPs/secPCPs service models are classified into three categories: Software as a Service, Platform as a Service, and IaaS; where each has its unique security requirements that and secArchs.
- Provides IAM services, encryption, firewall rules, and VPN services.
- Enterprise Information Security Architecture (EISA) is the framework for managing security measures for *ENT's* data; and provides a systematic mitigating secRisks and secArch. Where *ENTs* have difficulties in balancing security and APD needs, but EISA's goal is to provide a method to achieve this balance.
- Robustness to protect vital data/information and it reduces Cyberthreats.
- Proactive measurements of Cyberthreats/breaches by: Halting production processes, Product recalls, Integrate security at each production level...
- Mitigation measures, although Cyberbreachs' legislation consequences differ around the globe, it is known that *ENTs* try to prevent secRisks and reduce Cybervulnerabilities. Regulations help damage and with the introduction of GDPR, regulations are becoming stricter. But the hyper-evolution of technologies and the legislations are trying to follow. Therefore, as a business, having a robust secArch and using *RoGCSC's* processes to integrate security controls.

As shown in Figure 15, *ENT(S)* needs a Polymathic-holistic approach for secArch because it combines many security fields, and Cybersecurity is the central issue. So, it needs the secTDM, which interfaces frameworks like ADM, SAFe, COBIT, CISA... Unfortunately today, we are just tackling isolated fields like Software security, Network Security...

Figure 15. ENT's polymathic approach

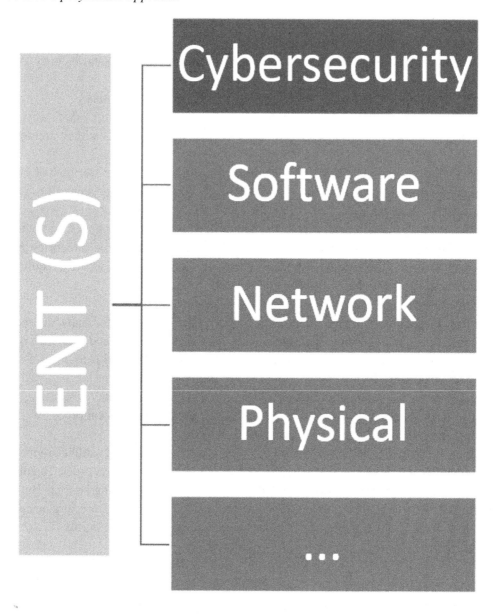

secArch's CSFs

Based on the AHMM4RoGCSC, LRP4RoGCSC and DMS4RoGCSC, for this CSA's CSFs/KPI were weight and the results are shown in Table 3. This CSA's result of 8.40, which is low, and that is due to the fact that the secArch is difficult to implement; and the next CSA is *ENT's* security.

Table 3. CSA's average is 8.20

Critical Success Factors	KPIs		Weightings
CSF_secArch_secArch	Complex	▼	From 1 to 10. 08 Selected
CSF_secArch_secMDTCAS	Feasible	▼	From 1 to 10. 09 Selected
CSF_secArch_Vision	Feasible	▼	From 1 to 10. 09 Selected
CSF_secArch_EA_secTDM_secOUPs secPCP	Complex	▼	From 1 to 10. 08 Selected
CSF_secArch_Services	Complex	▼	From 1 to 10. 08 Selected

valuation

ENT'S SECURITY

Basics Concepts

ENT's basic concepts includes (Raza, 2020):

- Strategies, techniques, and processes for securing secICS' data/information and assets against unauthorized access and secRisks.
- Technology, employees, and processes involved in maintaining the secICS' digital assets.
- Cybersecurity measures for all *ENT's* levels: 1) secICS/secPCP's scalable resources and activities, but voluminous data is complex to secure; 2) IoT's influx of connected devices are critical for *ENTs* and Cyberattackers damage IoT devices; 3) Huge data volume results in challenges that needs to secure user-information respecting ethical bounds of the secICS; and 4) Privacy awareness and regulations are integrated to block Cyberattacks.
- Best practices, which involve security measures across all *ENT's* parts; it ranges from secPCP to IoT endpoints. Cyberthreats can come from within the *ENT* (like human-errors) or from external Cyberattackers. Best practices for *ENTs'* improving its security capabilities are: 1) Protecting data flows and identifying data-assets that must be encrypted; 2) Establishing strong IAM controls by using the principle of least-privilege which allows users with limited access to the secICS; 3) Implement a disaster-recovery and secRisk mitigation plan, with a plan that includes responsibilities and workflows for disaster-recovery protocols. The plan must be adapted to counter Cyberthreats; 4) Educating employees for Cybersecurity to implement defense against Cyberthreats; 5) Managing endpoint security with monitoring; 6) Involving *Mangers* in *RoGCSC* implementation, in which Cyberthreats should not be ignored and to establish interfaces with secRisk management.

Interfaces and secRisk Management

RoGCSC interfaces various risk frameworks like the COSO, which is shown in Figure 16; and it is *a process, effected by an entity's board of directors, management and other personnel, applied in strategy setting and across the enterprise, designed to identify potential events that may affect the entity, and manage risks to be within its risk appetite, to provide reasonable assurance regarding the achievement of entity objectives*… COSO defines basic components, a common language and a roadmap for secRisk management. secRisks' management objectives are: 1) Strategic; 2) Operations; 3) Reporting; and 4) Compliance. And related CSFs are: 1) Organizational; 2) *RoGCSC's* interfacing; 3) secRisks' assessment; 4) Determining secRisks' possibilities; 5) Identifying secRisk responses; 6) Communication of secRisk results; and 7) Monitoring (Curtis, & Carey, 2012). *ENT* must establish a Digital Forensics and Incident Response (DFIR) Concept (DFIRC).

Figure 16. The COSO framework
Source: Curtis and Carey (2012)

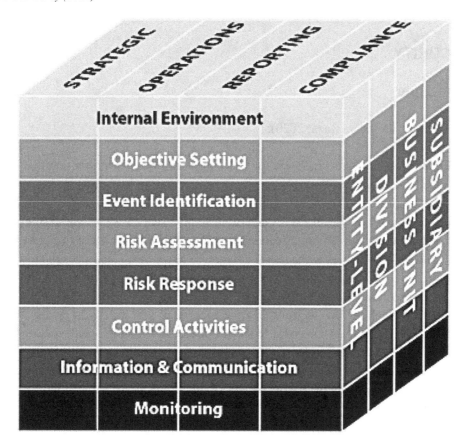

The DFIRC

A DFIRC is important for *RoGCSC* and is supported by ICS standards which can be integrated in secP-CPs, IoT-devices and other. A DFIRC includes: 1) secICS forensics that focuses on examining digital-components, to determine Cyberattack actions; and analyses digital-properties like networks, memory, digital-artifacts and other; 2) Capabilities and activities for: Data-acquisition, System transparency, Investigation-capabilities, Reporting, and other; 3) Six common steps: Preparing policies, Identifying attack-types, Containing damages, Remediating for best solutions, Incident-recovery, and Reporting and communication; 4) Digital and physical forensics levels support, where digital forensics concerns law enforcement and secICS properties. The *RoGCSC* includes a multi-platform systems' protection and secPCPs; and the capacity to mitigate secRisks (Watts, 2020). Such Cyberthreats result from SOFP motivations. The *RoGCSC* supports: Analyses of global financial, societal, and geopolitical security, Identifies recurrent patterns of organized SOFP misdeeds and related crimes, Offers measurable CSFs and CSAs which characterize the evaluation of secRisks. Such SOFPs are in general ranked as the most ethical organizations because such ranking organizations are chosen by SOFP-related circles. The *RoGCSC* supports proactive detection of SOFP irregularities, locked-in traps, and major Cybersecurity breaches and Cybercrimes, which can be fatal for *ENTs*. SOFP Cybercrimes are related to known financial centers, who enjoy a privileged position in transparency and ethical rankings (Transparency, 2020; Swissinfo, 2021). The reason for this global contradiction is that they have overwhelming legal, political, and financial advisory support, which blocks any attempt to divulge such Cybercrimes (Trad, 2023c).

ENT's Reorganization

secOPMS explains various types of inconsistencies and uses the AHMM4RoGCSC based DMS4RoGCSC to take the decisions to deliver optimal actions on how to reorganize secOUs. Using the right sequence of *RoGCSC* actions, can determine the *Projects* success. Such actions are based on *organizational routines* or *known actions*, knowing that there are various types of reorganizational *Models* (Kuwashima, 2014): 1) The Rational Actor Model (RAM), in which decisions (or sets of actions) of a large *ENT,* are under central control and RAM is an secOPM actor; 2) secOPM examines *ENT* actions and these actions are considered as an output of the secICS; the secOPM depends on the critical Management's Political Model (MPM); and 3) The MPM focuses on the group of important decision-makers and it considers actions as bargaining activities. The ARM, secOPM, and MPM support (re)organizational modelling (org secDOM) of an *ENT. ENT's* (re)organization represents an organization/structure, department, cost-center, division, sales-unit or any other secOU. As shown in Figure 17, typical *ENTs* incorporates: Business group, Company, Legal department, Sales Organization, Purchasing OU, Plant and warehouse (IBM, 2021). secCBB/secOBBs supports secDOMs' building or (re)assembling. secDOM based secOUs are a form of *ENT's* robotization which may provoke R2C.

R4C and Related Topics

Projects in general and *RoGCSC* specifically can face OUR and/or R2C, that is why *Managers* must implement a R4C in the *Project's* vision. R4C can be evaluated in all secTDM's phases. All the presented CSAs can be verified in the PoC's implementation.

Figure 17. Typical organization model
Source: IBM (2021)

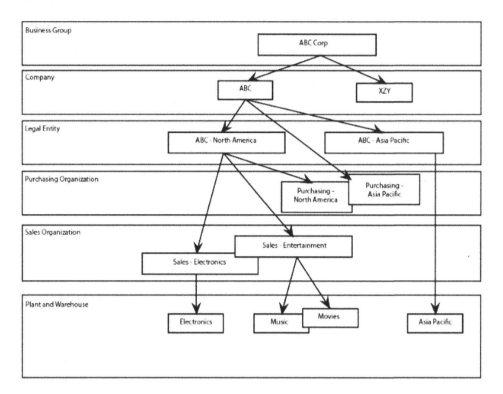

ENT Security's CSFs

Based on the AHMM4RoGCSC, LRP4RoGCSC and DMS4RoGCSC, for this CSA's CSFs/KPI were weighted and the results are shown in Table 4, with CSA's result of 8.60, which is low, and that is due to the fact that *ENT's* security is difficult to implement; and the next step is to implement the Polymathic approach.

Table 4. CSA's average is 8.60

Critical Success Factors	HMM enhances: KPIs	Weightings
CSF_ENT_sec_Basics	Feasible	From 1 to 10 09 Selected
CSF_ENT_sec_secRisk_Management	Possible	From 1 to 10 09 Selected
CSF_ENT_sec_DHRC	Complex	From 1 to 10 08 Selected
CSF_ENT_sec_Reorganization	Complex	From 1 to 10 08 Selected
CSF_ENT_sec_R4C	Feasible	From 1 to 10 09 Selected

valuation

A POLYMATHIC APPROACH

Evolution and secRisk of secRP-Based Project

The *RoGCSC* uses various mathematical domains to deliver a unique AHMM (Trad, & Kalpić, 2020a). As shown in Figure 18, a *Project* must select the optimal *RoGCSC*'s secRisk mitigation concepts, which is based on the following types of secRisks: 1) secRisk avoidance and prediction; 2) secRisk reduction; 3) Offers AHMM4RoGCSC actions to reduce secRisks; 4) Actions to transfer secRisks to third parties; and 5) secRisk acceptance. secRisk estimations includes (Pratap, & Predovich, 2020): AHMM4 RoGCSC based analysis, Remediation, Compliance, Coherent/Synchronization, User experiences, Reporting, Basic-advanced integration, and Real-time control-based assessments. secRisk mitigation artefacts are linked to the Polymathic AHMM4RoGCSC basic elements. AHMM4RoGCSC's nomenclature is presented in a basic form to be understandable by the readers. The AHMM4RoGCSC based *RoGCSC* and its main artefacts and characteristics are:

- secRP actions = supports secARP/secUP operations, DevSecOps activities, for finalizing *RoGCSC*.
- *Project* parts = $\sum$ *secRPOUP*(S) (for the secOUP, secICS, secSDCs, and its infrastructure/networks).
- *RoGCSC* = transformation of *Project's* parts + the defined goals of *Project* operations.
- *ENT(S,i)* = includes *Project's* parts + $\sum$ *RoGCSC*.
- *ENT(S)* = $\sum$ *ENT(S,i)*.

ENT(S)-RoGCSC-Based Model

As shown in Figure 18, the symbol $\sum$ indicates summation of all the relevant named set *RoGCSC* related members, while the indices and the set cardinality have been omitted. The summation should be understood in a generic sense, more like a set. The AHMM4RoGCSC uses services model to support the *RoGCSC* and is represented in a simplified form. The *RoGCSC* interfaces are based on the secTDM and uses services to enable the Polymathic transformation model. The AHMM4RoGCSC based secTDM is the combination of secTDM and AHMM4RoGCSC looks as follows:

The Polymathic Transformation Model

The AHMM4RoGCSC based secTDM model:
    AHMM_secTDM = AHMM4RoGCSC(secTDM) (G4).
    The *RoGCSC* transformation model is the combination of an AHMM4RoGCSCbsecTDM and *IterationGap* that can be modelled using the following formula:
    Project = AHMM_secTDM (*IterationGap*) (G5).
    The *Project's* model is based on the extraction of choreographies or *Models*.

Figure 18. The AHMM4RoGCSC main formulas

The Generic AHMM's Formulation

TDM	*is a **Transformation Development Method**, which can be ADM based...*	
AHMM	$= \bigcup \text{TDMs} + \bigcup \text{DMMs}$	(G1)

AHMM's Application and Instantiation for a Domain

Domain	$= \bigcup \text{APD}$	(G2)
AHMM4(*Domain*)	$= \bigcup \text{TDMs} + \text{DMMs}(Domain)$	(G3)

Extraction of secCBBs/secOBBs-Based Models

The *RoGCSC* depends on the results of secRPs' operations, which extract *Models* (or secBPM/choreography). The extracted *Models* are based on the HDT that uses secCBBs/secOBBs to support secDOMs. The AHMM4RoGCSC is composed of large number of interconnected nodes, to solve *RoGCSC* types of problems. *RoGCSC* secMAs are connected to each other, like nodes of the HDT and there is a WGT (a real number) and CSFs.

The Strategy and Evolution and a Decision Model

RoGCSC is supported by a predictive the KMS4RoGCSC based DMS4RoGCSC that depends on the selected CSFs, like the types of secRPs activities, types of *Project* risks, R2C, financial situation, types of secBPMs, skills, ... A *Project* should be adapted to a *RoGCSC* that can offer complex designs and eventual problems, which can be the source of risks and failures... *RoGCSC'* problems can be measured and weighted, where secRisks are not easy to measure. This explains the difficulty of estimating secRisks related to consequential sets of secRPs operations. The DMS4RoGCSC and selected weightings are used to deliver a set of possible *RoGCSC* actions. Weightings' DMS4RoGCSC concept supports the *RoGCSC* to deliver solutions and recommendations. The DMS4RoGCSC uses the HDT to solve *RoGCSC* types of problem(s). The *RoGCSC* adopts a holistic-systemic approach, which makes the *Project* robust and the secCBBs/secMAs management subsystem the basis of a successful *Project*. *RoGCSC's* secCBBs/secOBBs/SBBs are managed by the secTDM. The secMDTCAS provides support for refined secCBBs and the *RoGCSC* synchronizes *Project's* plans with the secTDM. The secTDM supports interactions between strategies, global processes, secSRVs, and secICS. The DMS4RoGCSC controls secRisks to implement secCBBs/secOBBs pools to support the implementation of secDOMs. *RoGCSC* contains the following concepts: 1) Agile DevSecOps for *RoGCSC*, secOBB, and secSDCs extractions; 2) secMDTCAS sets of artefacts; 3) secTDM's interfacing capabilities; 4) Mapping secMDTCAS artefacts; 5) secCBB's/secOBB's granularity; and 6) Requirements mapping to secCBBs. *RoGCSC'* capabilities to integrate emerging avant-garde domains, like *Models*, AI, EA, Refine techniques, and Scalable secOUPs/secICS (Sargent, 2021).

The Model's CSFs

Based on the AHMM4RoGCSC, LRP4RoGCSC and DMS4RoGCSC, for this CSA's CSFs/KPI were weight and the results are shown in Table 5, with the average of 8.40, which is low, and that is due to the complex Polymathic secRP approach is based on the AHMM.

Table 5. CSA's average is 8.40

Critical Success Factors	KPIs		Weightings
CSF_Polymathic_Approach_secRP_secRisk	Complex	▼	From 1 to 10. **08 Selected**
CSF_Polymathic_Approach_Model	Feasible	▼	From 1 to 10. **09 Selected**
CSF_Polymathic_Approach_Transformation	Feasible	▼	From 1 to 10. **09 Selected**
CSF_Polymathic_Approach_secCBBs	Complex	▼	From 1 to 10. **08 Selected**
CSF_Polymathic_Approach_DMS	Complex	▼	From 1 to 10. **08 Selected**

valuation

THE PoC's IMPLEMENTATION

RoGCSC's Basic Preparations

As shown in Figure 19, the first step is to prepare the PoC's environment by setting-up the Vision, sec-MDTCAS/secTDM, and extracted secCBBs/secOBBs from the secARP/secUP/secBBs (Trad, 2023b). Where in this chapter the focus is on Viewpoint "S" and this PoC uses the results of previous *TRADf's* PoCs.

Figure 19. PoC's basic preparation

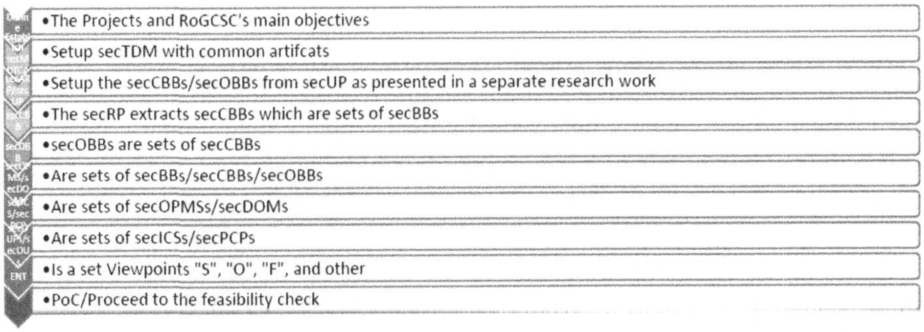

	• The Projects and RoGCSC's main objectives
	• Setup secTDM with common artifcats
	• Setup the secCBBs/secOBBs from secUP as presented in a separate research work
	• The secRP extracts secCBBs which are sets of secBBs
	• secOBBs are sets of secCBBs
	• Are sets of secBBs/secCBBs/secOBBs
	• Are sets of secOPMSs/secDOMs
	• Are sets of secICSs/secPCPs
	• Is a set Viewpoints "S", "O", "F", and other
	• PoC/Proceed to the feasibility check

RoGCSC's Feasibility Check

the extraction of secBBs as shown in Figure 19 (Trad, 2023b). secBBs are assembled to build secCBBs. And another PoC's part was used from a previous PoC, in which a secBB and Cybertransaction was experimented as shown in Figure 20, it also proved that the granularity level/approach can be used to refine the "1:1" mapping (Yalezo, Thinyane, 2013).

Figure 20. PoC's secCBBs/secOBBs'-based cybertransaction design

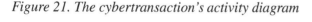

This PoC uses the author's previous PoC's secARP/secUP, which presents a logical view of a series of secCBBs/secOBB based Cybertransactions is presented in Figure 21, and their consumption of sec-SRVs, in the form of an activity diagram in which all the events are exchanged between various nodes, require encryption which is defined in the secTDM.

Figure 21. The cybertransaction's activity diagram

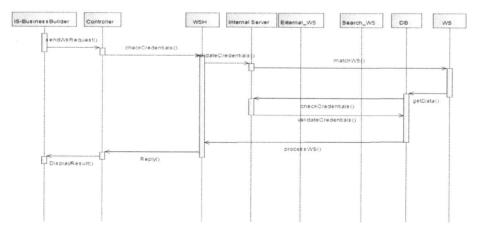

The Cybertransaction uses a set of secCBBs/secOBBs which are assembled in an secOPMS as presented in Figure 22. The secTDM uses ADM's phases B and D to implement the needed secOBB based Cybertransactions.

Figure 22. Cybertransaction's elements

secOUP-APD Environment	Provide APD secCBBs/secOBBs
Controller	Passes a secSRV request
Find secOBBs/secSRVs	Execute
Data Source	Return information

RoGCSC' Design and Implementation

An important PoC constraint, is the use of existing standards in a reduced form, by using artefacts that correspond to secMDTCAS, which makes it transcendent for secCBBs/secOBBs, and diagrams. These artefacts include secCBBs/secOBBs to be used to integrate secSDCs in OUPs/OUs/*ENT*. To select sets of CSAs' CSFs and test whether RQ's CSFs affect *RoGCSC*'s integration. The PoC uses the HDT based mixed qualitative and quantitative method, for CSFs' analysis as illustrated in Figure 23. The PoC in the beginning uses Phase 1 that is mainly based on the HDT tables, which use WGTs. Phase 1 is used to weight CSAs and CSFs for the usage of *RoGCSC* by using the DMS4RoGCSC/KMS4RoGCSC (Quang Phu, & Thi Yen Thao, 2017).

PoC's Phase 1

LRP4RoGCSC's outcome proves the existence of an important gap and it's (Phase 1's) outcome supports RQ's credibility, that is concluded by the LRP4RoGCSC and *TRADf*'s archive/knowledge-base, (that has an important set of references, previous author's works, documents, and links). After selecting CSA/CSFs, they were linked to HDT scenarios. The PoC uses CSFs' binding to specific RDP4RoGCSC resources, where the *RoGCSC* was prototyped using *TRADf*. The HDT represents the relationships between the RDP4RoGCSC's RQ/requirements, secCBBs/secOBBs/secMAs, and selected CSAs/CSFs. PoC's interfaces were achieved using Microsoft Visual Studio .NET environment and *TRADf*. The *RoGCSC* uses calls to resulting secCBBs/secOBBs, to execute HDT actions related to secRP requests and Cybertransactions. CSFs were selected and evaluated (using WGTs, HDT, and DMS4RoGCSC) and the results are illustrated in Table 6, which shows that the *RoGCSC* is a central phase and not an independent one. HDT's main constraint is that CSAs having an average result below 7.5, will be ignored. This fact, leaves *RoGCSC*'s CSAs (marked in green) effective for RDP4RoGCSC's conclusion(s). Phase 1, shows that the secRP part of the *Project* is very complex because of *RoGCSC*' extraction/refinement operations. The PoC can proceed to Phase 2.

Figure 23. RDP4RoGCSC's similar flow
Source: Phu & Thao (2017)

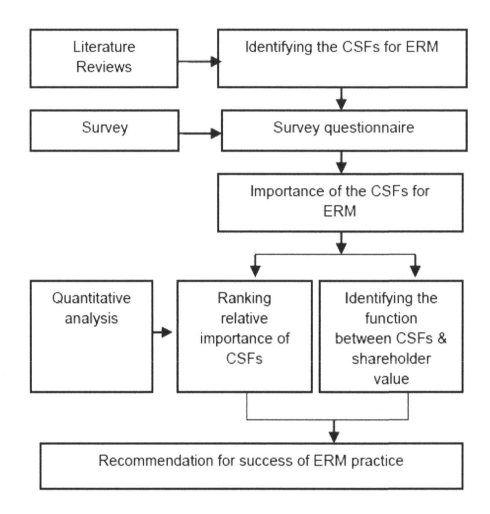

Table 6. The RoGCSC PoC's phase 1 outcome is (rounded) 8.50

CSA Category of CSFs/KPIs	Transformation Capability	Average Result	Table
The RDP4RoGCSC's Integration	Usable-Mature	From 1 to 10 9.25	1
secICS/secPCP's integration	Transformable-Possible-Complex	From 1 to 10 8.20	2
secArch's integration	Transformable-Possible-Complex	From 1 to 10 8.20	3
ENT's security integration	Transformable-Possible-Complex	From 1 to 10 8.60	4
The Polymathic Approach	Transformable-Possible-Complex	From 1 to 10 8.40	5

Evaluate First Phase

PoC's Phase 2

secMDTCAS/secTDM's Setup and CSFs' Selection

Phase's 2 setup includes: 1) Sub-phase A or the Architecture Vision phase's goals, establishes a secRP approach and goals; 2) Sub-phase B or the Business Architecture phase establishes *RoGCSC*'s target secTDM/EA and related secRPs' activities; 3) Sub-phase C shows and uses the Application Communication Diagram to describe secRPs activities; 4) Sub-phase D or the Target Technology Architecture shows the needed *RoGCSC*'s optimal infrastructure landscape; and 5) Sub-phases E and F, or the Implementation and Migration Planning, presents the transition secCAV based architecture, which proposes intermediate situation(s) and evaluates *RoGCSC*'s statuses. secCBBs/secOBBs and HDT based DMS4RoGCSC has mappings to *ENT(S)'s* resources and the *RoGCSC* defines relationships between secCBBs/secOBBs/ secMDTCAS' artefacts, and Requirements/PRBs.

PRBs Processing Control in a Concrete HDT Node

The DMS4RoGCSC solves *RoGCSC*'s PRBs, where CSFs link to specific secRP PRB type and has a set of actions that are processed in a concrete HDT node. For this goal, the action *CSF_RoGCSC_Extraction_Procedure* was called and delivered SOL(s). Solving PRBs involves the selection of actions and possible SOLs for multiple *Project* activities. The HDT is on mixed quantitative/qualitative and has a dual-objective that uses the following steps:

- In Phase 1, *TRADf's* interface implements HDT scripts to process the selected CSAs. And then relates PoC's resources to *CSF_RoGCSC_Extraction_Procedure.*
- The DMS4RoGCSC is configured to weight and tuned to support the HDT.
- Link the selected node to HDT to deliver the root node.
- The HDT starts with the *CSF_RoGCSC_Extraction_Procedure* and proposes SOL(s) in the form of secRP actions/improvements.

SOL Nodes

HDT scripts support AHMM4RoGCSC's instance that are processed in the background to deliver *RoGCSC* secRisk value(s). The hAHMM4RoGCSC based DMS4RoGCSC delivers *recommendations*; which are a set of secRPs actions and reorganized secOUs.

SOLUTION AND RECOMMENDATIONS

The set of *RoGCSC*'s technical and managerial recommendations ere:

- This chapter presents the possibility to implement an IHI *RoGCSC* which avoids locked-in strategies.
- secRP like the secARP/secUP, is a *Project's* critical phase.
- secCBBs/secOBBs stability and coherence are crucial for its evolution.

- secCBBs can be (re)used in an IHI secOBBs; where a secOU is a set of secOBBs and different secOUs can share secOBBs, and hence secCBBs.A *Project* needs a secTDM/secMDTCAS to support secRPs activities.
- secOBBs are used in secOPMs based DOM, which are OUPs' basis.
- *RoGCSC* interface *ENT(S)'s* secTDM and delivers the pool of secCBBs based DIAs.
- The secRP unbundles legacy-secOPMS to support secOU's/secOUPs and *ENT(S)*.
- Each *ENT(S)* constructs its own IHI *RoGCSC*.
- secTDM's and DevSecOps' integration enables the automation of secRPs' activities.
- Avoid consulting firms and to build internal secRP mechanisms.
- *RoGCSC* is very complex.

FUTURE RESEARCH DIRECTIONS

Based on the conclusions *TRADf's* future research will focus on the process model the secOPM based Dynamic Organizational Models (secDOM) to support *ENTs*, and how it can support transformation projects.

CONCLUSION

Legacy-OUs unbundling is a complex task and can be supported by using secCBBs/secOBBs and CAVs based strategies (IBM, 2014). secCAV uses a Polymathic-holistic approach and the PoC proved its application's complexities (Greefhorst, 2009). The *RoGCSC* support secCBB/secOBB based CAVs concept to facilitate secOUPs/secOUs reorganization. PBA is optimal for the *RoGCSC* which supports secured unbundling activities; and the LRP4RoGCSC presented a knowledge gap, that is due to the fact that are no similar research approaches and that there is a lack of a Polymathic-holistic approach. There are limited-manual unsecured refinement technics for legacy-OUs, but the *RoGCSC* presents the possibility to implement an IHI concept (Koenig, Rustan, & Leino, 2016). The RDP4RoGCSC is a part of a series of publications on *Projects*, secRP, secTDM/EA, Polymathic models... The *RoGCSC* uses the HDT and CSFs/CSAs to support *RoGCSC* activities. The *RoGCSC* focuses on evaluating the complex secRP and synchronizes a structured relationship between: secRP, secRisks, secTDM/ADM, constraints, and HDT based SOLs. *RoGCSC's* most important recommendation, is that the *Manager* must be skilled to manage *RoGCSC* activities. The PoC's Table 6 result of (rounded) 8.50 that used CSFs' binding to a RDP4RoGCSC resources, the DMS4RoGCSC/KMS4RoGCSC, RQ, and secCBBs, shows that the *RoGCSC* is very complex due to the risky secARP/secUP and secRP operations. The *RoGCSC* should be an IHI process, methodology and framework. In this chapter, the author proposes the following set of managerial recommendations:

- An *ENT* must build a holistic secArch to support Cybersecurity, to integrate underlying technology and to support Cybertransactions.
- Cybertechnologies replace traditional exchanges in order to improve productivity and enforce Cybersecurity.
- Applications' development and operations are coordinated by the SecDevOps.
- Cybertransaction is influenced by local and international Cyberlaw.
- The secRP supports the *RoGCSC* to reorganize OUs.
- The *RoGCSC* fits *ENT(S)'s* secTDM/EA framework.
- secTDM's integration with *RoGCSC* enables the automation of secRP activities.
- *ENT(S)* sustainability is orthogonal to its secRP capacities.
- To avoid locked-in scenario an *ENT* must an IHI *RoGCSC*.
- The *RoGCSC* can face OUR/R4C, which should be predicted by using R2C.
- All author's works are based on *TRADf*, AHMM, secTDM, and RDP; which are today mature and can be applied in various APDs.

REFERENCES

Bala, R., Gill, B., Smith, D., Wright, D., & Ji, K. (2021). *Magic Quadrant for Cloud Infrastructure and Platform Services*. Gartner Inc. https://www.gartner.com/doc/reprints?id=1-271SYZF2&ct=210802&st=sb

Bishop, M. (2009). *Standish Group CHAOS Report: Worst Project Failure Rate in a Decade*. Standish Group.

Bizzdesign. (2022). *Digital Transformation*. Bizzdesign. https://bizzdesign.com/blog-category/digital-transformation/

Capgemini. (2011). *Business transformation: From crisis response to radical changes that will create tomorrow's business*. A Capgemini Consulting Survey. Capgemini.

Chaione. (2022). *Digital Transformation-The 4 Types of Digital Transformation*. Chaione.com.

Charles. (2017). *Hosting and Cloud Software Delivery modelled in Archimate*. Agile Enterprise Architecture. https://agileea.com/2017/04/hosting-and-cloud-software-delivery-modelled-in-archimate/

Curtis, P., & Carey, M. (2012). *Committee of Sponsoring Organizations of the Treadway Commission-Risk Assessment in Practice*. Deloitte & Touche LLP.

Daellenbach, H., McNickle, D., & Dye, Sh. (2012). *Management Science. Decision-making through systems thinking* (2nd ed.). Plagrave Macmillian.

Dick, B. (2001). *Action research: action and research*. Southern Cross. University Press.

Easterbrook, S., Singer, J., Storey, M., & Damian, D. (2008). *Guide to Advanced Empirical Software Engineering-Selecting Empirical Methods for Software Engineering Research* (F. Shull, Ed.). Springer.

Eira, A. (2022). *72 Vital Digital Transformation Statistics: 2023 Spending, Adoption, Analysis & Data.* FinancesOnline. https://financesonline.com/digital-transformation-statistics/

Fu, Z., & Mittnight, E. (2015). *Critical Success Factors for Continually Monitoring, Evaluating and Assessing Management of Enterprise IT.* ISACA. https://www.isaca.org/COBIT/focus/Pages/critical-success-factors-for-continually-monitoring-evaluating-and-assessing-management-of-enterprise-it.aspx

Greefhorst, D. (2009). *Using the Open Group's Architecture Framework as a pragmatic approach to architecture. NIRIA. Jaarbeurs, Utrecht. KIVI NIRIA, afd.* Informatica.

IBM. (2021). *About organization modeling.* IBM. https://www.ibm.com/docs/en/order-management?topic=SSGTJF/productconcepts/c_OrganizationModeling.htm

IBM. (2022a). *An overview of cloud security.* IBM. https://www.ibm.com/topics/cloud-security

Jonkers, H., Band, I., & Quartel, D. (2012a). *ArchiSurance Case Study.* The Open Group.

Kasarkod, J. (2011). *Integration of SABSA Security Architecture Approaches with TOGAF ADM.* InfoQ. https://www.infoq.com/news/2011/11/togaf-sabsa-integration/

Koenig, J., Rustan, K., & Leino, M. (2016). *Programming Language Features for Refinement.* Stanford University. doi:10.4204/EPTCS.209.7

Kuwashima, K. (2014). How to Use Models of Organizational Decision Making? *Annals of Business Administrative Science, 13*, 215–230. www.gbrc.jp doi:10.7880/abas.13.215

Liu, A. (2022). *Rumbaugh, Booch and Jacobson Methodologies.* Opengenus. https://iq.opengenus.org/rumbaugh-booch-and-jacobson-methodologies/

Luyckx, F. (2015). *Advanced cycle: Advanced Delivery Management (ADM) life-cycle.* ARIS.

Möhring, M., Keller, B., Schmidt, R., Sandkuhl, L., & Zimmermann, A. (2023). Digitalization and enterprise architecture management: a perspective on benefits and challenges. *SN Bus Econ.* doi:10.1007/s43546-023-00426-3

O'Riordan, B. (2021). INNOVATION-Why Transformations Fail And How They Can Succeed With People Power. *Forbes.* https://www.forbes.com/sites/unit4/2021/10/11/why-transformations-fail-and-how-they-can-succeed-with-people-power/#:~:text=It%20is%20a%20bold%20decision,all%20major%20transformation%20projects%20fail

Oxford Dictionaries. (2017a). *Security*. London: Oxford Dictionaries. Retrieved on September 3, 2017, from: https://en.oxforddictionaries.com/definition/security

Palermo, J., Bogard, J., Hexter, E., Hinze, M., & Skinner, M. (2012). ASP.NET Model View Control 4. In *Action*. Manning.

Peterson, S. (2011). *Why it Worked: Critical Success Factors of a Financial Reform Project in Africa*. Faculty Research Working Paper Series. Harvard Kennedy School.

Pratap & Predovich. (2020). *The 2020 Gartner Magic Quadrant for IT Risk Management*. Gartner.

Quang Phu, T., & Thi Yen Thao, H. (2017). Enterprise Risk Management Implementation: The Critical Success Factors For Vietnamese Construction Companies. *Journal of Multidisciplinary Engineering Science Studies, 3*(2). http://www.jmess.org/wp-content/uploads/2017/02/JMESSP13420283.pdf

Quinlan, C. (2015). Business Research Methods. Dublin City University.

Raza, M. (2020). *Introduction to Enterprise Security*. BMC. https://www.bmc.com/blogs/enterprise-security/

RedHat. (2022). *Decision Model and Notation (DMN)*. RedHat. https://access.redhat.com/documentation/en-us/red_hat_process_automation_manager/7.1/html/designing_a_decision_service_using_dmn_models/dmn-elements-example-con

Rosing, M., Hove, M., Subbarao, R., & Preston, T. (2012). *Combining secBPM and EA in complex ERP projects (a Business Architecture discipline)*. Academic Press.

SABSA. (2020). *Sherwood Applied Business Security Architecture*. SABSA. https://sabsa.org/

Standish. (2011). *The Chaos Reports*. http://www.standish.com

Swissinfo. (2021). *Switzerland diplomatically rejects Biden's 'fiscal paradise' label*. Swissinfo. https://www.swissinfo.ch/eng/business/diplomacy_switzerland-diplomatically-rejects-biden-s—fiscal-paradise—label-/46578996

Techopedia. (2022). *Security Architecture*. https://www.techopedia.com/definition/72/security-architecture

The Open Group. (1999). *Building Blocks*. Introduction to Building Blocks. The Open Group.

The Open Group. (2011a). *Introduction to the Architecture Development Method (ADM)*. The Open Group.

The Open Group. (2011c). *Foundation Architecture: Technical Reference Model*. The Open Group. http://www.opengroup.org/public/arch/p3/trm/trm_dtail.htm

Threat Intelligence. (2023). *Security Architecture: What it is, Benefits and Frameworks*. https://www. threatintelligence.com/blog/security-architecture

Trad, A. (2022a). *Business Transformation Projects-The Role of a Transcendent Software Engineering Concept (RoTSEC)*. IGI Global.

Trad, A. (2022b). *Business Transformation Projects-The Role of Requirements Engineering (RoRE)*. IGI Global.

Trad, A. (2023a). *Organizational and Digital Transformation Projects-A Mathematical Model for Composite and Organizational Building Blocks*. IGI Global.

Trad, A. (2023b). *Organizational and Digital Transformation Projects-A Mathematical Model for Building Blocks based Organizational Unbundling Process*. IGI Global.

Trad, A. (2023c). *Enterprise Transformation Projects-Cloud Transformation Concept – Holistic Security Integration (CTC-HSI)*. WSEAS Transactions on Computers. doi:10.37394/23205.2022.21.41

Trad, A., & Kalpić, D. (2019a). The Business Transformation Framework and the-Application of a Holistic Strategic Security Concept. *Journal: E-leaders, Check Rep.*

Trad, A., & Kalpić, D. (2019b). *The Business Transformation Framework and Enterprise Architecture Framework for Managers in Business Innovation: The Role of Cyber and Information Technology Security. In Global Cyber Security Labor Shortage and International Business Risk*. IGI Global.

Trad, A., & Kalpić, D. (2020a). *Using Applied Mathematical Models for Business Transformation*. IGI Global. doi:10.4018/978-1-7998-1009-4

Trad, A., & Kalpić, D. (2021a). ENT Transformation Projects: Security Management Concept (SMC). *Proceedings of 12th SCF International Conference on Contemporary Issues in Social Sciences*, 326.

Trad, A., & Kalpić, D. (2021b). *Advancing Cybersecurity for Business Transformation and Enterprise Architecture Projects: Deep Learning Integration for Projects (DLI4P). In Handbook of Research on Advancing Cybersecurity for Digital Transformation*. IGI Global.

Trad, A., & Kalpić, D. (2022c). *Business Architecture and Transformation Projects: Enterprise Holistic Security Risk Management (ESRM). In Technological Development and Impact on Economic and Environmental Sustainability*. IGI Global.

Transparency. (2020). *Corruption perceptions index*. Transparency International. https://www.transparency.org/en/cpi/2020/index/nzl

Vulić, I., Prodanović, & Tot, R. (2019). An Example of a Methodology for Developing the Security of a Distributed Business System. Advances in Economics, Business and Management Research. In *5th IPMA SENET Project Management Conference (SENET 2019)*. Atlantis Press. 10.2991enet-19.2019.34

Watts, S. (2020). *Digital Forensics and Incident Response (DFIR): An Introduction.* BMC. https://www. bmc.com/blogs/dfir-digital-forensics-incident-response/

Wikipedia. (2022a). Cloud computing. In *Wikipedia.* https://en.wikipedia.org/wiki/Cloud_computing

Yalezo, S., & Thinyane, M. (2013). *Architecting and Constructing an Service Oriented Architecture Bridge for an Model View Control Platform.* IEEE Computer Society Washington.

Ylimäki, T. (2008). *Potential Critical Success Factors for Enterprise Architecture.* University of Jyväskylä, Information Technology Research Institute.

Chapter 11
Investigating the Dark Side of Gaming Chat Applications

Miloslava Plachkinova
Kennesaw State University, USA

ABSTRACT

The current study investigates the dark side of using gaming chat applications for illegal activities like selling credentials, stolen credit cards, private data, sexual exploitation, and organizing groups on white supremacy. With the shutdown of many Darknet websites and illegal marketplaces, criminals are now switching to chat platforms that allow them to resume their operations easily and quickly. In addition, such communities can be utilized for recruitment and for providing instructions on how to commit crimes to individuals anywhere in the world. The study is grounded in social learning theory, as it explains how crime is learned through interactions on these applications. The goal of the current work is to explore further these platforms and to provide law enforcement with guidance and recommendations on how to integrate digital forensic tools more effectively and efficiently for investigating data generated on gaming chat platforms and preventing future crimes facilitated through these platforms.

INTRODUCTION

Text communication such as instant messaging (IM) and text chat has been recognized as a powerful tool for both recreational and workplace activities. Many studies have been done to evaluate the effectiveness of such tools in the workplace (Herbsleb et al., 2002; O'Neill & Martin, 2003), collaborative learning environments (Mühlpfordt & Wessner, 2005), and even in healthcare (Wang et al., 2016). However, little research has been done to explore the use of gaming chat applications such as Discord, Mumble, and Team Speak for communication by cybercriminals. This is a relatively new topic of interest and while some examples of such utilization exist in practice, the problem is yet to be examined from a scientific perspective. With the growing number of cyberattacks in society such as distributed denial of service (DDoS), ransomware, phishing, Internet of Things (IoT) exploits, Crime as a Service (CaaS) and data breaches (McGuire, 2018), it is imperative to pay more attention to the means used by criminals for communication and information sharing. Being able to perform a digital forensic analysis of the content

DOI: 10.4018/978-1-6684-8422-7.ch011

exchanged by users in these applications can assist government agencies in protecting assets of national security. The current study offers a unique interdisciplinary perspective combining cybersecurity with a criminological theory–social learning theory–to explain the motivation of cybercriminals who use gaming chat applications for recruiting and communication (Korkmaz et al., 2014). Cybercriminals use gaming chat applications to recruit and train others to join their organizations and spread the word about performing criminal activities, thus exploring this intersection in more detail is crucial for further understanding how to identify and prevent future threats emerging from the chat applications. The current work bridges the gap between theory and practice and offers a relevant and innovative approach to investigate cybercriminal communications more comprehensively.

This study aims to answer the following research question:

Can social learning theory explain why cybercriminals use gaming chat applications?

Social learning theory is used to explain the utilization of gaming chat applications by cybercriminals because those chats offer an excellent opportunity to share their knowledge on illegal activities with others on the Internet. The global platform provides them access to individuals across the world who can be easily persuaded to commit crimes, whether cyber or physical. While video games have been extensively studied as recruiting channels for criminal organizations and promoting violence among youth (DeLisi et al., 2013; Ferguson, 2011; Herr & Allen, 2015), little research has been done to examine how chat applications associated with them facilitate the interactions between such organizations and their targets. It has already been established that video games affect social outcomes (Greitemeyer & Mügge, 2014). Thus, the current study extends this idea and applies social learning theory in the context of video game chat applications to establish whether these applications can be further utilized for recruiting and sharing knowledge on criminal activities online.

BACKGROUND

Social Learning Theory

Social learning theory is one of the best-known theories used in criminology to explain why individuals commit crime. It posits that people learn and engage in behavior by observing and imitating others. Social learning is a cognitive process and explains how deviant behavior and especially aggression can be modeled and learned by individuals. Akers (1973) was the first to integrate the principles of social learning into criminology. Burgess and Akers (1966) believed that criminal behavior is learned in social and non-social environments through direct reinforcement, vicarious reinforcement, explicit instruction, and observation. Gaming chat applications can be used for providing explicit instructions and reinforcement practices, either directly or indirectly. Gambetta (2011) further explained the process of how criminals communicate – they would typically ask a potential partner or recruit to give them evidence of having committed crimes. Such evidence can be easily transmitted as audio, video, or images through chat applications. These tools provide opportunities to give individuals explicit instructions on how to commit crimes and they can also be used to reinforce criminal behavior.

In the 1940s, Edwin Sutherland developed the concept of differential association, which argued that crime is learned through interactions with intimate peers where individuals acquire definitions that support or refute the violation of law (Sutherland et al., 2015). More specifically, the theory states that the process by which a person comes to engage in criminal behavior involves the following notions (Sutherland, 1947):

1. Criminal behavior is learned.
2. Criminal behavior is learned in interaction with other persons in a process of communication.
3. The principal part of the learning of criminal behavior occurs within intimate personal groups.
4. When criminal behavior is learned, the learning includes (a) techniques of committing the crime, which are sometimes very complicated, sometimes very simple, and (b) the specific direction of motives, drives, rationalization, and attitudes.
5. The specific direction of motives and drives is learned from definitions of the legal codes as favorable or unfavorable.
6. A person becomes delinquent because of an excess of definitions favorable to violation of law over definitions unfavorable to violation of law.
7. Differential associations may vary in frequency, duration, priority, and intensity.
8. The process of learning criminal behavior by association with criminal and anticriminal patterns involves all of the mechanisms that are involved in any other learning.
9. Although criminal behavior is an expression of general needs and values, it is not explained by those general needs and values, because noncriminal behavior is an expression of the same needs and values.

These principles follow in logical order as criminal behavior is learned in the process of symbiotic interaction with others, mainly in primary or intimate groups. Such groups are the foundation of gaming chat applications and serve the purpose of building and maintaining communities of individuals with similar interests. Social learning theory suggests that people learn criminal behavior through observation, imitation, and reinforcement (Akers, 1973; Akers et al., 2017). Social structure refers to the various patterns of social relationships, institutions, and norms that shape individuals' behavior and opportunities in society.

In the context of social learning theory, social structure can influence criminal behavior in several ways. First, individuals may observe and imitate criminal behaviors that are prevalent in their social environment. For example, if an individual grows up in a neighborhood where drug use is common and accepted, they may be more likely to engage in drug use themselves. Second, social structure can influence the rewards and punishments associated with criminal behavior. For example, in some neighborhoods, engaging in criminal behavior may be viewed as a way to gain status and respect, while in others, it may result in social isolation and disapproval.

Social structure can also influence the types of opportunities that are available to individuals. For instance, individuals who grow up in neighborhoods with limited access to education and employment opportunities may be more likely to engage in criminal behavior as a means of economic survival. Similarly, individuals who are socially marginalized or excluded may be more likely to engage in criminal behavior as a way of asserting their power and status.

While the nine principles of social learning were initially developed to explain street crime, they can also be applied to cybercrime, because the communication and personal group still exist, they are just taking place in cyberspace now (Morris & Blackburn, 2009; Morris & Higgins, 2010). Social learning theory is relevant to the current study because it can explain how individuals can be approached on gaming chat applications with instructions on how to commit crime and be recruited through intimate personal groups in a virtual environment. In addition, the Internet provides an opportunity for global communication and the downside is that these channels also allow criminals from all over the world to reach out to anyone using the applications. While these consequences are unintended, researchers and practitioners are still struggling to find ways to prevent criminals from utilizing these communication channels or at least retrieve digital forensic data.

Social learning theory is highly relevant to cybercrime, as it helps us understand how individuals learn to engage in cybercriminal behavior. Cybercrime refers to any criminal activity that involves the use of technology, such as hacking, identity theft, and cyberbullying (Deora & Chudasama, 2021). According to social learning theory, individuals learn to engage in criminal behavior through observation, imitation, and reinforcement. In the context of cybercrime, individuals may learn to engage in criminal behavior by observing and imitating the behavior of others, such as online forums or hacker communities. These groups may provide individuals with the necessary skills and knowledge to engage in cybercriminal activity, as well as a sense of validation and support (Benjamin et al., 2016). Reinforcement also plays a role in cybercrime, as individuals may receive rewards or positive feedback for engaging in criminal behavior. For example, hackers who successfully infiltrate a company's network may receive recognition and praise from their peers, which can reinforce their behavior and encourage them to continue engaging in cybercriminal activity (Coleman, 2005).

Social learning theory can also help us design more successful approaches and strategies how to prevent cybercrime. By understanding the social factors that contribute to cybercriminal behavior, policy makers can develop interventions that target these factors and reduce the likelihood of criminal behavior (Costello et al., 2017; Miró-Llinares et al., 2020). For example, interventions that focus on building positive social connections, providing alternative opportunities for learning and skill-building, and promoting ethical behavior can help prevent individuals from engaging in cybercrime.

Social learning theory is highly relevant to cybercrime, as it helps us understand how individuals learn to engage in criminal behavior and how it can be prevented. By applying social learning theory to the study and prevention of cybercrime, society can develop more effective interventions and policies that promote online safety and security (Shillair et al., 2015). To demonstrate the relevance of social learning in the context of cybercrime, the study explores how this theory has been already applied and evaluated.

Social learning theory is one of the most commonly tested theories to account for cybercrime, particularly software and movie piracy (Higgins, 2006; Higgins et al., 2006, 2007; Higgins & Makin, 2004a, 2004b; Higgins & Wilson, 2006). According to these prior studies, using a computer requires some learning and developing skills. And while such equipment has become significantly more user friendly and more widespread over time, the educational component inherent in computer use and abuse has not changed (Holt, 2007). At the same time, Holt (2007) states that "individuals must often gain some insights from others on the methods and tactics necessary to successfully engage in cybercrimes, such as music piracy or computer hacking. Thus, social learning theory is an intrinsically important framework to understand cybercrime and deviance" (p. 33). However, the influence of the social learning process for cybercrime cannot occur unless an individual is able to participate in and connect with other deviants and gaming chat applications provide a convenient channel for communication and information exchange. With the growing use of technology, it is necessary to address the problem of examining digital forensic data from these applications so that government agencies can leverage best practices and standards for investigating the retrieved data.

Social learning theory is relevant to both cybercrime and digital forensics, as it helps us understand how individuals learn to engage in cybercriminal behavior and how this behavior can be investigated and prosecuted through digital forensics. By understanding the social factors that contribute to cybercriminal behavior, law enforcement officials and digital forensic experts can better investigate and prosecute cybercrime.

Digital forensics involves the use of specialized tools and techniques to collect, analyze, and preserve digital evidence related to a crime. In the context of cybercrime, digital forensics plays a crucial role in identifying and prosecuting cybercriminals. Digital forensic experts use a variety of techniques, such as data recovery, network analysis, and forensic analysis, to collect and analyze digital evidence related to a cybercrime (Brown, 2015; Holt et al., 2022).

Social learning theory can help inform the techniques used in digital forensics by providing insights into how individuals learn and engage in criminal behavior online. For example, digital forensic experts may use social network analysis techniques to identify online communities or groups that are engaged in cybercriminal behavior (Rawat et al., 2021). They may also use psychological profiling techniques to understand the motivations and behaviors of cybercriminals, based on insights from social learning theory (Rogers, 2011). Thus, the current study argues that the integration of social learning theory and digital forensics is necessary for law enforcement to develop more effective and efficient strategies to combat cybercrime occurring in online gaming chat applications. A significant part of that process is understanding how technology can be leveraged by criminals, so next the study explores communication technologies in the context of cybercrime.

Communication Technologies

Social learning theory is also relevant to the current study because online games are becoming more and more popular for cybercriminals to use for communication and recruitment (Korkmaz et al., 2014). For example, for terrorism-related activities and the War on Terror, different groups have learned and expanded on covert communications such as email, text messaging, and chat applications. Adapting to their surroundings and using chats in video games with their coded language can give law enforcement agents an opportunity to better understand the attackers' motivation and to prevent some of these crimes. More specifically, Choo and Smith (2008) discuss how information and communications technologies (ICT) can be used by organized crime groups to infringe legal and regulatory controls. According to the authors, terrorist groups have been known to obtain information on and acquire chemical, biological and radiological materials via the Internet. The use of global telecommunications technologies can also be used to mount attacks against key critical infrastructures such as power plants, nuclear facilities, dams, power grids, etc. Very often members of terrorist groups include engineers and computer scientists (US NSTC 2006, p. 7) and they have been known to use the Internet as a medium for propaganda (e.g. publishing doctrines such as "The Global Islamic Resistance Call" on the Internet), recruitment and training of potential terrorists, and transferring information. That way the lower-level members of the criminal organization will suffer the consequences (often including death), while those up in the hierarchy will take all the credit.

Choo and Smith (2008) go on further by providing an example of how the Internet has been used in terrorist planning activities such as the case that was brought before the district court of Connecticut in the United States. The sentencing memorandum alleged that:

From approximately 1997 through at least August 2004, British nationals Babar Ahmad, Syed Talha Ahsan, and others, through an organization based in London called Azzam Publications, are alleged to have conspired to provide material support and resources to persons engaged in acts of terrorism through the creation and use of various internet Web sites, e-mail communications, and other means. One of the means Ahmad and his co-conspirators are alleged to have used in this effort was the management of various Azzam Publications websites, principally www.azzam.com, which, along with associated administrative email accounts, were hosted for a period of time on the servers of a Web hosting company located in the state of Connecticut. (US DoJ, 2014)

The Internet has been used for numerous illegal activities and often times offenders use anonymous browsers like The Onion Router (Tor)[1], the Invisible Internet Project (I2P)[2], Whonix[3], Subgraph[4], and The Amnesic Incognito Live System (TAILS)[5] to access the Darknet and engage in illegal activities such as buying or selling drugs, weapons, and stolen data, as well as engaging in other criminal activities like hacking and cyberstalking. While these tools can be used for illegal activities, they also have legitimate uses for people who need to protect their privacy, such as journalists, activists, and whistleblowers (Mirea et al., 2019). Here are some examples of how these tools work:

- Tor is a free and open-source software that enables anonymous communication. When someone uses Tor, their internet traffic is encrypted and routed through a network of volunteer-run servers called nodes. This makes it difficult for anyone to trace the user's internet activity back to their IP address or location (Ahmad et al., 2018).
- I2P is another anonymous network that allows users to communicate and browse the internet anonymously. It uses a similar system to Tor but is designed to be more secure and decentralized. I2P also includes features like hidden services, which allow websites to be hosted anonymously (Hoang et al., 2018).
- Whonix is a free and open-source operating system that runs on the Tor network. It is designed to provide a more secure and anonymous browsing experience than using Tor alone. Whonix routes all internet traffic through the Tor network and includes features like firewall protection and encryption (Gold, 2013).
- Subgraph is a security-focused operating system that includes a suite of privacy and security tools. It uses a modified version of the Tor network to provide anonymity and includes features like encryption, firewall protection, and application sandboxing (Scott-Hayward et al., 2015).
- TAILS is a live operating system that runs from a USB drive or DVD. It is designed to provide maximum privacy and anonymity and includes features like Tor integration, encryption, and secure deletion of files (Hassan et al., 2017).

Offenders may use these tools to access websites on the Darknet, which are not accessible through regular web browsers like Chrome or Firefox. These websites typically have URLs that end in ".onion" or ".i2p". Darknet markets like Silk Road and AlphaBay, which were shut down by law enforcement (Baravalle & Lee, 2018), have facilitated the sale of illegal goods and services, including drugs, weapons, and stolen data. However, cybercriminal organizations have significant resources and many of them switched from the Darknet to online gaming and chat communities where they can easily set up their operations and not just continue their illegal activities but actively recruit new members (Nurse & de Cominges, 2019).

Cryptocurrencies

Cryptocurrencies such as Bitcoin, Litecoin, Ethereum, and Ripple are increasingly being used to finance cybercrime, as they provide a secure, anonymous, and decentralized way of conducting financial transactions. Cryptocurrencies are digital or virtual tokens that use cryptography to secure and verify transactions and to control the creation of new units. Transactions are recorded on a decentralized public ledger called the blockchain (Habib et al., 2022). Because such currencies are not centrally regulated and the transactions are anonymous, they are becoming more and more popular for financing crime and money laundering. That is the reason why countries such as China, Russia, Thailand, Vietnam, Taiwan, Colombia, Ecuador, Bolivia, Bangladesh, and Kyrgyzstan have either banned cryptocurrencies or are planning to do it (Girasa, 2022; Taskinsoy, 2021).

Cybercriminals use cryptocurrencies to finance their activities in a variety of ways. One way is by using cryptocurrencies to pay for tools and services that are necessary for cybercrime, such as malware, hacking tools, and anonymous hosting services (Salas Conde et al., 2022). Cryptocurrencies provide a way for cybercriminals to pay for these services anonymously, making it difficult for law enforcement officials to track the transactions.

Another way that cryptocurrencies are used to finance cybercrime is through ransomware attacks. Ransomware is a type of malware that encrypts a victim's files and demands payment in exchange for the decryption key (Thakur et al., 2022). Cryptocurrencies such as Bitcoin are commonly used to pay the ransom, as they provide a fast and secure way for the victim to make the payment while maintaining their anonymity (Leo et al., 2022). Cybercriminals use cryptocurrencies to receive the ransom payments, making it difficult for law enforcement officials to trace the money (Ali, 2022).

Finally, cryptocurrencies are used to launder money obtained through cybercrime (Wronka, 2022). Cybercriminals can convert their cryptocurrency earnings into traditional currencies, such as US dollars, by using cryptocurrency exchanges. These exchanges allow users to convert cryptocurrencies into other currencies or to withdraw cash. By using multiple exchanges and mixing services, cybercriminals can obfuscate the source and destination of the funds, making it difficult for law enforcement officials to trace the money (Suryadi & Budianto, 2022).

As cryptocurrencies provide cybercriminals with a secure and anonymous way of financing their activities, this adds more complexity for law enforcement officials to investigate and prosecute cybercrime. Since cryptocurrencies continue to grow in popularity, it is likely that their use in cybercrime will also increase in the future. Thus, it is worthwhile to investigate further how online communities leverage this technology to facilitate criminal activities.

Crime as a Service

Like physical crime, cybercrime continues to evolve and today it exists in a highly organized form. It is becoming a big business now and this emerging market niche is attracting suppliers and vendors who offer a variety of illegal services and products to their customers. Cybercrime has evolved so much that it now represents a highly organized hierarchy involving leaders, engineers, infantry, and hired money mules and a worrying new phrase has entered the lexicon of cybercrime – Crime as a Service (CaaS) (Manky, 2013). The term CaaS is a reference to many other services that you can get on the Internet. For example, there is Software as a Service (SaaS), Platform as a Service (PaaS), and Infrastructure as a Service (IaaS). And while those allow customers to host servers and applications on the cloud, CaaS allows them to rent botnets, purchase malware and exploits, hire hitmen, obtain access to child pornography, or buy drugs online with just a few clicks (Hyslip, 2020). This growing new industry is becoming more and more popular as a resource to individuals who want to commit crime or learn more about illegal activities. And while the Federal Bureau of Investigation (FBI) is constantly trying to shut down websites on the Darknet that provide a platform for cybercriminals, it is very challenging for them to keep up because the cybercriminals can easily copy the source code and shortly after one site is taken down, a new version of it comes up. Silkroad is one of those sites – it is an online marketplace similar to Amazon but for offering illegal products and services (Lacson & Jones, 2016). Online communities play a significant role in facilitating Crime as a Service. Here are some examples to demonstrate how criminals use online communities to offer their services:

- Darknet Markets: Darknet markets are online marketplaces that are accessible only through the Tor network. These markets allow criminals to sell their services anonymously, including malware, hacking tools, and stolen data.
- Online Forums: There are many online forums and message boards where criminals can advertise their services or look for customers. These forums are often hidden from public view and require registration to access.
- Instant Messaging: Criminals can also use instant messaging services like WhatsApp or Telegram to communicate with potential customers. They may use encrypted chat groups to keep their conversations private.
- Social Media: Criminals may use social media platforms like Facebook or Twitter to promote their services or connect with potential customers. They may use fake accounts or profiles to avoid detection.
- Collaboration Platforms: Collaboration platforms like Slack or Discord can also be used by criminals to work together on hacking projects or to offer their services to others.

In these online communities, criminals can offer their services to a large audience without fear of being caught. They can communicate with potential customers anonymously, and the online nature of the transactions makes it difficult for law enforcement to track them down. Additionally, the use of cryptocurrencies for payment makes it hard for authorities to follow the money trail. The anonymity and ease of access provided by online communities make them an attractive platform for criminal activities.

Video Games

As a result of the constant law enforcement efforts to shut down Darknet websites and forums, criminal syndicates who use currently use the Darknet are now switching to chat apps. According to Auchard and Cohen (2017), "recruitment invitations into these underground markets have spiked upward over mainstream mobile messaging apps such as Facebook's WhatsApp, Telegram and Microsoft's Skype. But it is Discord, a lesser-known, two-year-old messaging app popular with video gamers that is becoming the "go-to app" for mobile dark web discussions, where thousands of links into criminal forums were tallied up." This study demonstrates how innovative and resilient cybercriminals are in spite of any law enforcement efforts to stop them. Thus, it is crucial to proactively address the problem of investigating these new communication channels and explore methods to forensically investigate data generated through such chat applications.

With these new opportunities that modern technologies create, there is also a lot of concern about the lack of regulations, accountability, and monitoring on the Internet. Now that cybercriminals are starting to explore more and more gaming chat applications like Discord, Mumble, and Team Speak, it is critical for law enforcement agencies to understand how forensic data from such applications can be preserved and examined. Gathering intelligence from these applications can shed light on a variety of criminal activities and can even prevent potential terrorist attacks (Ronczkowski, 2017).

Video games have been extensively explored from the lens of psychology and criminology but not much work has been devoted to understanding the chat applications that the gamers use to communicate with each other. For example, Al-Rawi (2018) looked at video games that deal with terrorist-related issues, especially in connection with the War on Terror. The author goes further to explain that organizations like ISIS are making full use of different technologies beyond just social media. They extensively use Twitter, but extend to video games, hacking by its Cyber Caliphate Army, apps, and the Darknet.

The idea of using video games to appeal to individuals is not new. In general, the target group of such games is young people who are attracted to violent and first shooter games because of the emotional appeal for young male adolescents to play such types of games (Jansz & Tanis, 2007). While females also play video games, only a small percentage of them identifies as gamers. According to the Pew Research Center, while 48% of women in the United States report having played a video game, only 6% identify as gamers, compared to 15% of men who identify as gamers (Duggan, 2015). The small number of female gamers is one of the reasons why males are a preferred target for cybercriminals. In addition, according to Olson et al. (2008) young males "experience fantasies of power and fame, to explore and master what they perceive as exciting and realistic environments (but distinct from real life), to work through angry feelings or relieve stress, and as social tools" (p. 55). In a virtual world, one can have the illusion of feeling much more important and finding their purpose compared to real life. Another study (Plaisier & Konijn, 2013) showed that there is a positive correlation between adolescents' anger, frustration, and peer rejection, on the one hand, and preference for antisocial media content and cyberbullying, on the other hand. These studies clearly identify that video games can be an excellent tool for recruiting young males who are attracted to violence, have low self-esteem and who crave power and popularity among their peers. Such an environment makes it very easy for cybercriminals to reach out to young males and attract them for their causes. Thus, being able to monitor chat applications and retrieve information that may have been intentionally deleted or encrypted should be a priority for law enforcement agencies focused, not just in the US but in any country in the world.

Digital Forensics

The Scientific Working Group (SWG) defined digital forensics as 'the use of scientifically derived and proven methods towards the preservation, collection, validation, identification, analysis, interpretation, documentation and presentation of digital evidence derived from digital sources for the purpose of facilitation or furthering the reconstruction of events found to be criminal, or helping to anticipate unauthorized actions shown to be disruptive to planned operations' (Palmer, 2001). There are many challenges for conducting a digital forensic investigation, especially when it is concerned with instant messaging applications. This is partially due to the fact that smartphones, used predominantly to access such applications, are always active and are constantly updating data, which can cause faster loss of evidentiary data. In addition, smartphone vendors tend to release operating system (OS) updates very often, making it hard for forensic examiners to keep up with the examination methods and tools required to forensically examine each release (Al Mutawa et al., 2012). The variety of proprietary hardware of smartphones is another issue faced by forensic examiners (Al-Zarouni, 2006).

Criminals are aware of these challenges and are actively using them to their benefit. They know that doing crimes using online mobile applications is secure as it is very tough task for extracting the information from mobile phone from which crime was committed (Mahajan et al., 2013). The authors explain this with the fact smartphones have very limited memory. In fact, their flash memory gets washed fast and easily for faster performance. Another reason of using mobile applications for doing any crime is that their application logs will not get saved on Internet Service Provider (ISP) side (Mahajan et al., 2013). Criminals are also using chat applications because it is easy for them to exchange and share information before, during, and after committing the crime. These issues are becoming an increasing concern for law enforcement agencies who need to recover evidence from gaming chat applications and mobile devices that individuals use to access them.

One of the most significant hurdles to investigating and prosecuting cybercrimes is the fact that data can potentially reside in multiple legal jurisdictions, leading to investigators relying on local laws and regulations regarding the collection of evidence (Ruan et al., 2013; Simou et al., 2014). From a technical standpoint, the fact that a single file can be split into a number of data blocks that are then stored on different remote nodes adds another layer of complexity thereby making traditional digital forensic tools redundant (Almulla et al., 2013; Chen et al., 2015). These increasing challenges to investigate cybercrimes are becoming a growing concern for law enforcement agencies all over the world. According to a recent report from MacAfee (2018), cybercrime losses in 2017 reach 1% of the world's gross domestic product (GDP) or over $75 trillion in one year alone. These numbers indicate the magnitude of the problem and highlight the need to address it on a global level, as it is not just a US concern. The current study addresses this issue and proposes an approach to forensically investigate data generated from gaming chat applications, which are increasingly used for criminal activities.

Privacy Issues

While it is imperative to be able to retrieve data from gaming chat applications to investigate and prevent cybercrimes, privacy concerns related to exposing sensitive personal data have to also be taken into consideration. Existing regulations in the European Union, General Data Protection Regulation (GDPR), and the US, California Consumer Privacy Act (CCPA) of 2018, demonstrate the changes in society's perceptions of private data. On the opposite site of the spectrum are the US Patriot Act and 18 U.S. Code Chapter 119 – Wire and Electronic Communications Interception and Interception of Oral Communications.

It is very difficult to balance individual rights with public safety, particularly in the context of monitoring online communities for illegal activities. On one hand, privacy is a fundamental right that must be protected, and individuals have the right to communicate and share information without fear of surveillance or censorship. On the other hand, public safety is a crucial concern, and law enforcement agencies have a responsibility to prevent and investigate criminal activity.

One of the challenges of monitoring online communities for illegal activities is that it can be difficult to distinguish between lawful and unlawful conduct (Décary-Hétu & Aldridge, 2015). For example, many people use encryption and other privacy tools to protect their communications from being intercepted, but these same tools can also be used by criminals to communicate and coordinate illegal activities. Therefore, any efforts to monitor online communities must be carefully balanced against individual privacy rights and should be conducted in accordance with applicable laws and regulations. Another challenge is that many online communities are hosted outside the jurisdiction of law enforcement agencies, making it difficult to enforce laws and regulations (Ghappour, 2017). Additionally, criminals may use multiple layers of encryption and other security measures to hide their activities, making it even harder to detect and prevent criminal activity (Aldridge & Askew, 2017).

To address these challenges, law enforcement agencies may use a variety of strategies, including collaboration with technology companies, development of specialized tools and techniques for monitoring online activity, and partnerships with other law enforcement agencies around the world. These efforts must be conducted in a way that respects individual privacy rights and is consistent with applicable laws and regulations. Balancing individual privacy rights with public safety is a complex issue, particularly in the context of monitoring online communities for illegal activities. While efforts to prevent and investigate criminal activity are important, they must be conducted in a way that respects individual privacy rights and is consistent with applicable laws and regulations. To address this concern, the current study aims to support the work of law enforcement agencies and rely on their objective assessment of the specific circumstances they encounter and that they would not abuse the knowledge provided in this work. While this presents a limitation to the current study, the issue is much broader and more complex to be addressed comprehensively in this paper.

CASE STUDIES

Methodology

To answer the research question, the author reviewed data from various gaming chat applications such as Discord, Mumble, and Team Speak and summarized findings so that law enforcement agencies can develop more reliable and useful protocols for forensic analysis in the future. This is a very new topic, and little scholarly work has been done to address the problem. In addition, as some of these cases are still currently being investigated, it can become very challenging to access the information. To address this limitation, the scope of the current study is focused exclusively on publicly available information on the Internet to identify instances when cybercriminals have relied on gaming chat applications for recruiting and for engaging them in criminal activities. There is no database for these new cases but through an Internet search, the author has discovered some examples such as the FBI's investigation on Discord and white papers done by information security companies that are gathering intelligence on the use of application messaging for cybercriminal activities. The following case study presents some recent examples of how gaming chat applications can be utilized by cybercriminals.

Discord Investigations

According to Brewster (2019), Discord is a $2 billion gaming chat application with over 150 million users. However, its original purpose to bring together gamers has significantly changed due to the rapid increase and lack of sufficient monitoring. As a result, Discord has become a chaotic space, where innocent gamers' voices have increasingly intermingled with those of shady criminals, child groomers, hate-mongers and, most notoriously, white supremacists. In fact, the FBI executed a search warrant against a group called Hells Gate selling stolen user credentials on the application. Other crimes being investigated on that application include selling credit card information, products, and drugs. A more recent case includes Jack Teixeira, 21, a member of the Massachusetts Air National Guard, who was arrested by the FBI in 2023 in connection with the leaking of classified Pentagon documents in a Discord chatroom (Perez et al., 2023). One explanation that Discord had become increasingly popular among digital crooks is that in 2018 law enforcement took down popular Darknet drug and weapons markets AlphaBay and Hansa. It is possible that those ex-dark web users believe that Discord can provide an acceptable degree of anonymity. However, these law enforcement actions prove that this is not the case. In spite of that, Discord is appealing to criminals because it allows them to quickly set up shop and easily reach out to a large audience. Another case illustrated how the application was used by a 22-year-old William Lee Dela Cruz to contact an unnamed 12-year-old. The government claimed they had used Discord to discuss, amongst other topics, having sex and masturbating. In another case, six men and one woman were arrested in Florida for sexually exploiting two teenage girls that were first approached through the platform. And finally, Discord has gained reputation as a hub for white supremacists with more than 20 communities that were "either directly about Nazism or white supremacy or reveled in sharing anti-Semitic and racist memes and imagery" (Glaser, 2018). These examples illustrate the need to be more proactive with regards to preventing Discord and other gaming chat applications from being used for facilitating cybercrime. The proposed recommendations can assist law enforcement in investigating and prosecuting individuals using these platforms to commit crime and recruit others to join them.

Other FBI Investigations

The FBI has also conducted a number of other investigations of illegal activities facilitated by online communities and chat rooms. For example, the U.S. Department of Justice's Internet Crimes Against Children Task Force Program conducted more than 71,200 investigations in 2018 alone, arresting more than 9,100 individuals who were targeting one of the most vulnerable populations–children. The ability to chat regularly, build relationships, respond with credibility and legitimacy, improvise on the spot, understand the violation, and accept failure while enjoying the successes is critical to success as an online undercover. Understanding the skill set needed in this type of work can assist future undercovers as they strive to protect the nation's children (Fowler et al., 2020). In 2012, the FBI conducted a two-week operation called "Operation Pacifier" that resulted in the arrest of over 200 individuals for accessing and sharing child pornography on a website called "Playpen." The FBI used a controversial tactic of taking over the website and running it themselves to collect evidence (Becker & Fitzpatrick, 2018). Even further back, in 2005 "Operation Safe Chat" targeted individuals who were using online chat rooms to engage in sexually explicit conversations with minors, resulting in the arrest of 50 individuals across the United States (McCarty et al., 2011). Other types of FBI operations involving chat rooms include human trafficking. In 2019, the FBI partnered with local law enforcement agencies on "Operation Cross Country" to conduct a nationwide operation targeting underage human trafficking. As part of the operation, the FBI identified and arrested individuals who were using online chat rooms to arrange the sexual exploitation of minors (Schwarz & Grizzell, 2020; Trautman & Moeller, 2020). These are important efforts to combat various types of crimes facilitated by online chat rooms and applications, but it is equally important to be able to gather and preserve evidentiary materials that can be used in court. It is also important to note that these investigations often involve complex and sensitive issues, and the FBI must navigate a variety of legal and ethical considerations in carrying out their work.

Digital Forensic Investigations of Discord

Researchers have demonstrated reliable methods for analyzing digital forensic data generated through gaming chat applications such as Discord. For instance, Gupta et al. (2023) successfully recovered a variety of artifacts such as payment information, sent messages, account settings, conversations, uploaded attachments, and much more, all of which could be utilized in a forensic investigation. Motyliński et al. (2020) created a novel tool called DiscFor designed for the extraction, analysis, and presentation of Discord data in a forensically sound manner. DiscFor creates a safe copy of said data, presenting the current cache state and converting data files into a readable format. Another aspect of this problem has been investigated by linguists (Howes & Kemp, 2017)who examine how language in Discord is used to developed shared understanding and community bonds, which demonstrate the relevance of social learning theory in gaming chat applications.

As Discord is becoming a popular chat and voice communication app used by millions of people around the world, further work needs to be done to develop sound techniques for digital forensic investigations of Discord to identify evidence related to criminal activities such as cyberstalking, cyberbullying, online harassment, and the distribution of illegal or harmful content. Here are some of the techniques and tools used in digital forensic investigations of Discord:

- Data Extraction: Digital forensic investigators use specialized tools to extract data from Discord servers, including message logs, voice chat recordings, user data, and metadata. Discord provides an API that can be used to extract data from the platform programmatically, and investigators can also use forensic imaging tools to extract data from individual devices.
- Data Analysis: Investigators use data analysis tools to search through large volumes of Discord data to identify relevant information. These tools can be used to search for specific keywords, usernames, IP addresses, and other metadata.
- Timeline Analysis: Investigators can use timeline analysis techniques to reconstruct a chronological timeline of events related to a particular case. This can be useful in identifying patterns of behavior and in identifying potential suspects.
- Reverse Engineering: In some cases, digital forensic investigators may need to reverse engineer the Discord app or other software components to identify vulnerabilities or other security issues. This can be a complex process that requires specialized skills and expertise.
- Chain of Custody: It is important for digital forensic investigators to maintain a proper chain of custody to ensure that the evidence they collect is admissible in court. This involves documenting the handling of evidence, including the extraction, analysis, and storage of data.

These are just a few of the techniques and tools used in digital forensic investigations of Discord. It is important for investigators to stay up to date with the latest technology and trends in order to effectively investigate and prosecute criminal activities on digital platforms like Discord. The current study aims to shed more light on the growing problem of forensically analyzing various types of Discord artifacts for investigations and prosecution.

LIMITATIONS

The current project does not come without any limitations. First, the research topic is quite new, so it is difficult to find existing literature in the field. Prior work has focused mostly on the relationship between aggression and the use of video and online games as well as the appeal of these games to male adolescents (Al-Rawi, 2018; Jansz & Tanis, 2007; Olson et al., 2008). In addition, digital forensics is a growing field, but its utilization in gaming chat applications is still limited. Thus, it may be challenging to identify sources for the theoretical foundation of the work in that area. However, law enforcement can rely on prior studied focused on smart phone forensics, cloud forensics, and digital forensics in general until a reliable methodology for gaming chat applications is established. Furthermore, a lot of the evidence retrieval, examination, and preservation practices are similar and will be applicable to their work.

Second, other scholars have looked mostly at data from self-reported studies when exploring the emotions of children who play video games. Thus, it may be difficult to assess their propensity to engage in crimes based on information exchange via gaming chat applications. To address this concern, the scope of the current work goes beyond gaming communities and it involves chat rooms in general to create a broader approach and a more comprehensive overview of the problem.

And third, while it is possible to conduct a forensic analysis on data from gaming chat applications, it mostly involving simulated data. A significant limitation for most academic studies is to obtain real data from actual cybercriminal groups who use the chat applications. It might be very challenging to observe the interactions in their natural environment. In addition, the case study data presented in this paper is obtained from publicly available sources. Some of it may be sensitive or part of ongoing investigations. Thus, the researcher relied on the accuracy and trustworthiness of the sources that are providing the information. To address this limitation, reasonable precautions were taken to evaluate all secondary data sources and to carefully vet them before including them as part of the case study. In addition, this work is more focused on providing law enforcement agencies with a deeper context to how gaming chat applications can be utilized to facilitate crime, rather than preventing the actual crimes. The current study is exploratory in nature and its goal is on raising awareness of this growing trend and shedding more light on the problem of gaming chat applications as a communication channel for cybercriminal activity.

FUTURE WORK

Exploring the demographic profile of gaming chat users is outside the scope of this project, but others are encouraged to focus on that particular aspect as it can add valuable insights. Specific demographic data may be able to assist law enforcement agencies to develop policies for potential individuals who may be easier targets of cybercriminal recruiting. Such policies can include information on how to identify cybercriminal activity, what to do in such instances, and how to respond if you are being approached by somebody with malicious intentions in a video game chat application.

CONCLUSION

The current study investigates the dark side of using gaming chat applications such as Discord, Mumble, and Team Speak for illegal activities. With the shutdown of many Darknet websites, criminals are now switching to chat platforms that allow them to resume their operations easily and quickly. In addition, such communities can be utilized for recruitment and reaching out to individuals anywhere in the world. Social learning is the theoretical lens of this research, as it best explains how crime can be learned in online communities using gaming chat applications. By exploring further these platforms, the study sheds more light on this problem of growing importance and answers the question "Can social learning theory explain why cybercriminals use gaming chat applications?" in the affirmative. Further work needs to be done to develop, test, and evaluate specific forensic tools that can assist law enforcement in their ongoing efforts to combat cybercrime facilitated by various online communities and chat rooms.

The current study contributes to the body of knowledge and establishes a solid foundation for further work in this area. As cybercrime continues to be on the rise, many individuals and businesses need to better understand how they can safely use chat applications without putting themselves and their organizations at risk. The study offers valuable insights to both academics and professionals who want to develop policies and tools to prevent cybercrime and its impact on society.

REFERENCES

Ahmad, I., Saddique, M., Pirzada, U., Zohaib, M., Ali, A., & Khan, M. (2018). A New Look at the TOR Anonymous Communication System. *Journal of Digital Information Management*, *16*(5), 223.

Akers, R. L. (1973). *Deviant behavior: A social learning approach*. Academic Press.

Akers, R. L., Sellers, C. S., & Jennings, W. G. (2017). *Criminological theories: Introduction, evaluation & application* (7th ed.). Oxford University Press.

Al Mutawa, N., Baggili, I., & Marrington, A. (2012). Forensic analysis of social networking applications on mobile devices. *Digital Investigation*, *9*, S24–S33. doi:10.1016/j.diin.2012.05.007

Al-Rawi, A. (2018). Video games, terrorism, and ISIS's Jihad 3.0. *Terrorism and Political Violence*, *30*(4), 740–760. doi:10.1080/09546553.2016.1207633

Al-Zarouni, M. (2006). *Mobile Handset Forensic Evidence: a challenge for Law Enforcement*. Academic Press.

Aldridge, J., & Askew, R. (2017). Delivery dilemmas: How drug cryptomarket users identify and seek to reduce their risk of detection by law enforcement. *The International Journal on Drug Policy*, *41*, 101–109. doi:10.1016/j.drugpo.2016.10.010 PMID:28089207

Ali, N. (2022). Crimes Related to Cryptocurrency and Regulations to Combat Crypto Crimes. *Journal of Policy Research*, *8*(3), 289–302.

Almulla, S., Iraqi, Y., & Jones, A. (2013). Cloud forensics: A research perspective. *2013 9th International Conference on Innovations in Information Technology (IIT)*.

Auchard, E., & Cohen, T. (2017). *Criminals try message apps to evade dark web crackdown: report*. Retrieved March 12 from https://www.reuters.com/article/us-cyber-summit-apps-messaging/criminals-try-message-apps-to-evade-dark-web-crackdown-report-idUSKBN1CU2SS

Baravalle, A., & Lee, S. W. (2018). Dark web markets: Turning the lights on AlphaBay. *Web Information Systems Engineering–WISE 2018: 19th International Conference,* Dubai, United Arab Emirates, November 12-15, 2018, *Proceedings, Part II*, 19.

Becker, K., & Fitzpatrick, B. (2018). In search of shadows: investigating and prosecuting crime on the Dark Web. *Dep't of Just. J. Fed. L. & Prac., 66*, 41.

Benjamin, V., Zhang, B., Nunamaker, J. F. Jr, & Chen, H. (2016). Examining hacker participation length in cybercriminal internet-relay-chat communities. *Journal of Management Information Systems, 33*(2), 482–510. doi:10.1080/07421222.2016.1205918

Brewster, T. (2019). Discord: The $2 Billion Gamer's Paradise Coming To Terms With Data Thieves, Child Groomers And FBI Investigators. *Forbes.* https://www.forbes.com/sites/thomasbrewster/2019/01/29/discord-the-2-billion-gamers-paradise-coming-to-terms-with-data-thieves-child-groomers-and-fbi-investigators/?utm_source=TWITTER&utm_medium=social&utm_content=2108057929&utm_campaign=sprinklrForbesMainTwitter#442d2a903741

Brown, C. S. (2015). Investigating and prosecuting cyber crime: Forensic dependencies and barriers to justice. *International Journal of Cyber Criminology, 9*(1), 55.

Burgess, R. L., & Akers, R. L. (1966). A differential association-reinforcement theory of criminal behavior. *Soc. Probs., 14*(2), 128–147. doi:10.2307/798612

Chen, L., Xu, L., Yuan, X., & Shashidhar, N. (2015). Digital forensics in social networks and the cloud: Process, approaches, methods, tools, and challenges. *2015 International Conference on Computing, Networking and Communications (ICNC)*.

Choo, K.-K. R., & Smith, R. G. (2008). Criminal exploitation of online systems by organised crime groups. *Asian Journal of Criminology, 3*(1), 37–59.

Coleman, J. W. (2005). *The criminal elite: Understanding white-collar crime*. Macmillan.

Costello, M., Hawdon, J., & Ratliff, T. N. (2017). Confronting online extremism: The effect of self-help, collective efficacy, and guardianship on being a target for hate speech. *Social Science Computer Review, 35*(5), 587–605. doi:10.1177/0894439316666272

Décary-Hétu, D., & Aldridge, J. (2015). Sifting through the net: Monitoring of online offenders by researchers. *European Review of Organised Crime, 2*(2), 122–141.

DeLisi, M., Vaughn, M. G., Gentile, D. A., Anderson, C. A., & Shook, J. J. (2013). Violent video games, delinquency, and youth violence: New evidence. *Youth Violence and Juvenile Justice, 11*(2), 132–142. doi:10.1177/1541204012460874

Deora, R. S., & Chudasama, D. (2021). Brief study of cybercrime on an internet. *Journal of Communication Engineering & Systems, 11*(1), 1–6.

Duggan, M. (2015). *Gaming and gamers*. https://www.pewinternet.org/2015/12/15/gaming-and-gamers/

Ferguson, C. J. (2011). Video games and youth violence: A prospective analysis in adolescents. *Journal of Youth and Adolescence, 40*(4), 377–391. doi:10.100710964-010-9610-x PMID:21161351

Fowler, M. J., Lybert, K. A., Owens, J. N., & Waterfield, J. M. (2020). *Undercover Chatting with Child Sex Offenders.* Retrieved March 12 from https://leb.fbi.gov/articles/featured-articles/undercover-chatting-with-child-sex-offenders

Gambetta, D. (2011). *Codes of the underworld: How criminals communicate.* Princeton University Press.

Ghappour, A. (2017). Searching places unknown: Law enforcement jurisdiction on the dark web. *Stanford Law Review*, *69*, 1075.

Girasa, R. (2022). International regulation. In Regulation of Cryptocurrencies and Blockchain Technologies: National and International Perspectives (pp. 313-377). Springer.

Glaser, A. (2018). *White Supremacists Still Have a Safe Space Online.* Slate. Retrieved March 12 from https://slate.com/technology/2018/10/discord-safe-space-white-supremacists.html

Gold, S. (2013). Getting lost on the Internet: The problem with anonymity. *Network Security*, *2013*(6), 10–13. doi:10.1016/S1353-4858(13)70069-2

Greitemeyer, T., & Mügge, D. O. (2014). Video games do affect social outcomes: A meta-analytic review of the effects of violent and prosocial video game play. *Personality and Social Psychology Bulletin*, *40*(5), 578–589. doi:10.1177/0146167213520459 PMID:24458215

Gupta, K., Varol, C., & Zhou, B. (2023). Digital forensic analysis of discord on google chrome. *Forensic Science International: Digital Investigation*, *44*, 301479.

Habib, G., Sharma, S., Ibrahim, S., Ahmad, I., Qureshi, S., & Ishfaq, M. (2022). Blockchain Technology: Benefits, Challenges, Applications, and Integration of Blockchain Technology with Cloud Computing. *Future Internet*, *14*(11), 341. doi:10.3390/fi14110341

Hassan, N. A., Hijazi, R., Hassan, N. A., & Hijazi, R. (2017). Online Anonymity. *Digital Privacy and Security Using Windows: A Practical Guide*, 123-194.

Herbsleb, J. D., Atkins, D. L., Boyer, D. G., Handel, M., & Finholt, T. A. (2002). Introducing instant messaging and chat in the workplace. *Proceedings of the SIGCHI Conference on Human Factors in Computing Systems*.

Herr, C., & Allen, D. (2015). Video games as a training tool to prepare the next generation of cyber warriors. *Proceedings of the 2015 ACM SIGMIS Conference on Computers and People Research*.

Higgins, G. E. (2006). Gender differences in software piracy: The mediating roles of self-control theory and social learning theory. *Journal of Economic Crime Management*, *4*(1), 1–30.

Higgins, G. E., Fell, B. D., & Wilson, A. L. (2006). Digital piracy: Assessing the contributions of an integrated self-control theory and social learning theory using structural equation modeling. *Criminal Justice Studies*, *19*(1), 3–22. doi:10.1080/14786010600615934

Higgins, G. E., Fell, B. D., & Wilson, A. L. (2007). Low self-control and social learning in understanding students' intentions to pirate movies in the United States. *Social Science Computer Review*, *25*(3), 339–357. doi:10.1177/0894439307299934

Higgins, G. E., & Makin, D. A. (2004a). Does social learning theory condition the effects of low self-control on college students' software piracy. *Journal of Economic Crime Management, 2*(2), 1–22.

Higgins, G. E., & Makin, D. A. (2004b). Self-control, deviant peers, and software piracy. *Psychological Reports, 95*(3), 921–931. doi:10.2466/pr0.95.3.921-931 PMID:15666930

Higgins, G. E., & Wilson, A. L. (2006). Low self-control, moral beliefs, and social learning theory in university students' intentions to pirate software. *Security Journal, 19*(2), 75–92. doi:10.1057/palgrave.sj.8350002

Hoang, N. P., Kintis, P., Antonakakis, M., & Polychronakis, M. (2018). An empirical study of the I2P anonymity network and its censorship resistance. *Proceedings of the Internet Measurement Conference 2018.*

Holt, T. J. (2007). Subcultural evolution? Examining the influence of on-and off-line experiences on deviant subcultures. *Deviant Behavior, 28*(2), 171–198.

Holt, T. J., Bossler, A. M., & Seigfried-Spellar, K. C. (2022). *Cybercrime and digital forensics: An introduction.* Routledge. doi:10.4324/9780429343223

Howes, L. M., & Kemp, N. (2017). Discord in the communication of forensic science: Can the science of language help foster shared understanding? *Journal of Language and Social Psychology, 36*(1), 96–111. doi:10.1177/0261927X16663589

Hyslip, T. S. (2020). Cybercrime-as-a-service operations. The Palgrave Handbook of International Cybercrime and Cyberdeviance, 815-846.

Jansz, J., & Tanis, M. (2007). Appeal of playing online first person shooter games. *Cyberpsychology & Behavior, 10*(1), 133–136. doi:10.1089/cpb.2006.9981 PMID:17305460

Korkmaz, B., Tuzcu, M., & Sözer, S. (2014). *Use of Massively Multiplayer Online Games for Intelligence Gathering, Recruitment, and Training Purposes. 7th International Conference on Information Security and Cryptography*, Istanbul, Turkey.

Lacson, W., & Jones, B. (2016). The 21st Century DarkNet Market: Lessons from the Fall of Silk Road. *International Journal of Cyber Criminology, 10*(1).

Leo, P., Isik, Ö., & Muhly, F. (2022). The ransomware dilemma. *MIT Sloan Management Review, 63*(4), 13–15.

Lewis, J. (2018). Economic Impact of Cybercrime-No Slowing Down. McAfee & CSI (Center for Strategic and International Studies).

Mahajan, A., & Dahiya, M., & Sanghvi, H. (2013). Forensic Analysis of Instant Messenger Applications on Android Devices. *International Journal of Computers and Applications, 68*(8), 38–44. doi:10.5120/11602-6965

Manky, D. (2013). Cybercrime as a service: A very modern business. *Computer Fraud & Security, 2013*(6), 9–13. doi:10.1016/S1361-3723(13)70053-8

McCarty, C., Prawitz, A. D., Derscheid, L. E., & Montgomery, B. (2011). Perceived safety and teen risk taking in online chat sites. *Cyberpsychology, Behavior, and Social Networking, 14*(3), 169–174. doi:10.1089/cyber.2010.0050 PMID:20677982

McGuire, M. (2018). *Hyper-Connected Web of Profit Emerges, as Global Cybercriminal Revenues Hit $1.5 Trillion Annually*. Bromium Inc. Retrieved June 29 from https://www.bromium.com/press-release/hyper-connected-web-of-profit-emerges-as-global-cybercriminal-revenues-hit-1-5-trillion-annually/

Mirea, M., Wang, V., & Jung, J. (2019). The not so dark side of the darknet: A qualitative study. *Security Journal, 32*(2), 102–118. doi:10.105741284-018-0150-5

Miró-Llinares, F., Drew, J., & Townsley, M. (2020). Understanding target suitability in cyberspace: An international comparison of cyber victimization processes. *International Journal of Cyber Criminology, 14*(1), 139–155.

Morris, R. G., & Blackburn, A. G. (2009). Cracking the code: An empirical exploration of social learning theory and computer crime. *Journal of Crime and Justice, 32*(1), 1–34. doi:10.1080/0735648X.2009.9721260

Morris, R. G., & Higgins, G. E. (2010). Criminological theory in the digital age: The case of social learning theory and digital piracy. *Journal of Criminal Justice, 38*(4), 470–480. doi:10.1016/j.jcrimjus.2010.04.016

Motyliński, M., MacDermott, Á., Iqbal, F., Hussain, M., & Aleem, S. (2020). Digital forensic acquisition and analysis of discord applications. *2020 International Conference on Communications, Computing, Cybersecurity, and Informatics (CCCI)*.

Mühlpfordt, M., & Wessner, M. (2005). Explicit referencing in chat supports collaborative learning. *Proceedings of the 2005 Conference on Computer Support for Collaborative Learning: Learning 2005: The Next 10 years!*

Nurse, J. R., & de Cominges, M. B. (2019). The group element of cybercrime: Types, dynamics, and criminal operations. *The Oxford handbook of cyberpsychology*.

O'Neill, J., & Martin, D. (2003). Text chat in action. *Proceedings of the 2003 international ACM SIG-GROUP conference on Supporting group work*.

Olson, C. K., Kutner, L. A., & Warner, D. E. (2008). The role of violent video game content in adolescent development: Boys' perspectives. *Journal of Adolescent Research, 23*(1), 55–75.

Palmer, G. (2001). *A road map for digital forensic research*. First Digital Forensic Research Workshop, Utica, NY.

Perez, E., Herb, J., Bertrand, N., Cohen, Z., & Liptak, K. (2023). *FBI arrests 21-year-old Air Force guardsman in Pentagon leak case*. https://www.cnn.com/2023/04/13/politics/us-government-intel-leak/index.html

Plaisier, X. S., & Konijn, E. A. (2013). Rejected by peers—Attracted to antisocial media content: Rejection-based anger impairs moral judgment among adolescents. *Developmental Psychology, 49*(6), 1165–1173. doi:10.1037/a0029399 PMID:22799588

Rawat, R., Mahor, V., Chirgaiya, S., & Rathore, A. S. (2021). Applications of social network analysis to managing the investigation of suspicious activities in social media platforms. In *Advances in Cybersecurity Management* (pp. 315–335). Springer. doi:10.1007/978-3-030-71381-2_15

Rogers, M. K. (2011). The psyche of cybercriminals: A psycho-social perspective. *Cybercrimes: A multidisciplinary analysis*, 217-235.

Ronczkowski, M. R. (2017). *Terrorism and organized hate crime: Intelligence gathering, analysis and investigations*. CRC Press. doi:10.4324/9781315203133

Ruan, K., Carthy, J., Kechadi, T., & Baggili, I. (2013). Cloud forensics definitions and critical criteria for cloud forensic capability: An overview of survey results. *Digital Investigation*, *10*(1), 34–43. doi:10.1016/j.diin.2013.02.004

Salas Conde, J. J., Martín Ortiz, M., & Carneiro Díaz, V. M. (2022). Methodology for Identification and Classifying of Cybercrime on Tor Network through the Use of Cryptocurrencies Based on Web Textual Contents. *Computación y Sistemas*, *26*(1), 347–356. doi:10.13053/cys-26-1-4178

Schwarz, C., & Grizzell, T. (2020). Trafficking spectacle: Affect and state power in operation cross country X. *Frontiers*, *41*(2), 57–81. doi:10.1353/fro.2020.a765265

Scott-Hayward, S., Natarajan, S., & Sezer, S. (2015). A survey of security in software defined networks. *IEEE Communications Surveys and Tutorials*, *18*(1), 623–654. doi:10.1109/COMST.2015.2453114

Shillair, R., Cotten, S. R., Tsai, H.-Y. S., Alhabash, S., LaRose, R., & Rifon, N. J. (2015). Online safety begins with you and me: Convincing Internet users to protect themselves. *Computers in Human Behavior*, *48*, 199–207. doi:10.1016/j.chb.2015.01.046

Simou, S., Kalloniatis, C., Kavakli, E., & Gritzalis, S. (2014). Cloud forensics solutions: A review. *International Conference on Advanced Information Systems Engineering*.10.1007/978-3-319-07869-4_28

Suryadi, P., & Budianto, A. (2022). Money Laundering And Tax Evasion Resulting From Cyber Crimes Through Digital Currency (Crypto Currency). *Proceedings of the 2nd International Conference on Law, Social Science, Economics, and Education, ICLSSEE 2022*.10.1007/978-3-319-07869-4_28

Sutherland, E. H. (1947). *Principles of Criminology* (4th ed.). JP Lippinco. 10.1007/978-3-319-07869-4_28

Sutherland, E. H., Williams, F., & McShane, M. (2015). Differential association. *On Analyzing Crime*.

TaskinsoyJ. (2021). *This Time is Different: Bitcoin Has More Reasons to Reach the Price of $100,000*. doi:10.2139/ssrn.3914299

Thakur, S., Chaudhari, S., & Joshi, B. (2022). Ransomware: Threats, Identification and Prevention. *Cyber Security and Digital Forensics*, 361-387.

Trautman, L., & Moeller, M. (2020). The Role of the Border and Border Policies in Efforts to Combat Human Trafficking: A Case Study of the Cascadia Region of the US-Canada Border. The Palgrave International Handbook of Human Trafficking, 985-999.

United States vs Babar Ahmad (United States Department of Justice (US DoJ). (2014). https://www.investigativeproject.org/documents/case_docs/2422.pdf

Wang, T., Huang, Z., & Gan, C. (2016). On mining latent topics from healthcare chat logs. *Journal of Biomedical Informatics*, *61*, 247–259. doi:10.1016/j.jbi.2016.04.008 PMID:27132766

Wronka, C. (2022). "Cyber-laundering": The change of money laundering in the digital age. *Journal of Money Laundering Control*, *25*(2), 330–344. doi:10.1108/JMLC-04-2021-0035

ENDNOTES

[1] https://www.torproject.org/, accessed on March 12, 2023
[2] https://geti2p.net/, accessed on March 12, 2023
[3] https://www.whonix.org/, accessed on March 12, 2023
[4] https://subgraph.com/, accessed on March 12, 2023
[5] https://tails.boum.org/, accessed on March 12, 2023

Chapter 12
A Modelling Approach to Privacy and Safety Issues in Cyber–Physical Systems

Rodrigo Martinez-Bejar
University of Murcia, Spain

María S. García-González
https://orcid.org/0000-0002-1640-9623
University of Murcia, Spain

Lorenzo Scalera
https://orcid.org/0000-0002-0770-0275
University of Udine, Italy

Alessandro Gasparetto
University of Udine, Italy

ABSTRACT

Safety issues are relevant in the interaction of human and robotic systems, as these might be a risk for humans' physical integrity. Robotic systems in the armies are a good example of such risk, since these systems are highly dependent on the software integrity that governs their behaviour. But in civil society there are examples of such issues as well. Also, medical applications are usually designed to be very accurate/precise, for instance, in surgery. If that accuracy/precision is threatened due to a cyberattack— as some of those robots are connected to communication networks—the patient could even die. In this chapter, the authors describe a modelling approach that categorizes the most relevant cybersecurity threats to robots from different analytical viewpoints. To illustrate the usefulness of this model, the main characteristics of a model addressing the cybersecurity threats to manufacturing robotic systems is shown in this work. Such a model has been implemented into machine-understandable software by using standard knowledge representation methods.

DOI: 10.4018/978-1-6684-8422-7.ch012

1. INTRODUCTION

Smart systems are becoming popular in society and economy, from industry to welfare services. Thus, it is expected that the use of home systems and services increases dramatically in the years to come (Abbas, 2021a). Therefore, it seems adequate to address some facets tied to such services and systems, including cybersecurity.

Usually, robots are capable of detecting, analysing and storing contextual data (Calo, 2011). Hence, both security issues related to the robot and its users and security aspects related to the data handled by the robot can be highlighted. Such issues are often addressed in cyber-physical (CPS) security (Lera, 2016).

CPS crimes have several features that should be addressed for CPS systems safety. In this work, we describe a modelling approach to deal with privacy and safety issues in CPS systems. In this respect, robotics systems have been reported to raise more and more concerns related to privacy issues. This is not surprising if one considers that technological advances in the last decade have made it possible to have (social/assistant) robots close to us in daily life at affordable prices for medium class families in countries like Japan, USA and to some extent in Europe. This kind of robots can be analysed as a kind of vector to introduce risks in our (human) safety from the privacy viewpoint due to the personal information they capture and process from the humans whom they interact with.

In this work, we describe a modelling approach that categorizes the most relevant cybersecurity threats to robots from different analytical viewpoints (e.g., type of human interrelation with robots, industrial sector, etc.). To illustrate the usefulness of this model, the main characteristics of a model addressing the cybersecurity threats to manufacturing robotic systems is shown in this work. Such model has been implemented into a machine-understandable software by using standard knowledge representation methods.

This paper is organized as follows. Section 2 presents the state of the art in relation to CPS threats definition. Also, the specific problem addressed and the objectives planned in this work are pointed out. In section 3, a categorization schema for cybersecurity threats to robots is presented. Section 4 shows how to model the cybersecurity threats to manufacturing robotic systems by taking into account the schema defined in this work. Finally, in section 5 the discussion and conclusion are put forward.

2. STATE OF THE ART

Smart systems use has spread to everything from manufacturing, education and healthcare to military and defence systems. Spending on smart home systems and services is expected to be 300 million by 2023 (Abbas, 2021a). Having this in mind, the study and research in smart systems, in particular human interaction, becomes important and faces numerous challenges. There is a need to understand and gain knowledge of certain aspects, including programming, human behaviour, machine learning, artificial intelligence and cybersecurity.

Robots are often designed to have the ability to detect, process and record information from their contexts (Calo, 2011). Therefore, two categories of security issues can be stated in relation to robot security, namely, security issues related to the robot and its users and, on the other hand, security related to the (received, processed, sent) data by the robot. This is usually addressed in the field of CPS security (Lera, 2016).

In the event that domestic or commercial robots were hacked, these could provide a lot of private information about the users interacting with the robots. This information can range from general data (e.g., age, size, etc.), private photographs, routine user information, financial information, etc. (Apa, 2017). On the other hand, people are also concerned about the possible damage that robots can cause if they are hacked. Sometimes, robots can be connected to communication networks that allow for remote operations. Moreover, in case that these communications are hijacked, those robots could cause real damage, such as fires, collisions with cars, etc. (Rawnsley, 2011).

Security risk analysis is generally based on two factors: the probability of a successful attack against an asset and the consequence of such attack (Byres, 2004). The literature presents several studies on cybersecurity threats targeting industrial environments (Ten, 2010). But according to Lera (2016), there are risks associated with domestic service robots.

Industrial IoT (IIoT) applications include smart manufacturing, where products and machines interact to each other to drive manufacturing materials and machines by communicating with the IIoT systems. Nowadays, there are factories with network machines and raw products. In the next years, it is expected that these elements will be interconnected within a comprehensive system where all machines, devices and materials will be sensor devices that will communicate and connect to each other, that is, they will be become CPS. Industry 4.0 is dependent on the CPS-based IIoT by communicating with and controlling each other. Smart manufacturing enables to perform information analysis automatically to optimize products and data-based decision making. In addition, there has been a dramatic reduction of sensors costs in the last years. As a consequence of this cost reduction, the application of sensors in industries is rapidly rising. This, in its turn, is facilitating the insights revelation and extraction from raw data (Chanchal & Sen, 2020).

Amongst the various CPS-IIoT challenges, security vulnerabilities is gaining momentum recently. Thus, the continuous disfiguring of high-profile aims keeps this issue regularly in the back of human minds. Changing the disinfectant blend ratio at a water treatment plant to stop the nuclear power plant cooling system could potentially place a city in immediate danger (Chanchal & Sen, 2020). Some of the major security concerns for CPS-IIoT systems include the arrangement of security temporal dimensions, the handle of the infrastructure, the management of the implementation processes, and the infrastructure needed to change of offline to online way of operation (Maximilian & Markl, 2018).

This work will be based on the following information facets: confidentiality, integrity and availability. Other works (Cavelty, 2013) have included also issues such as privacy, authentication, authorisation, auditability and non-repudiation issues. In addition to this, it is also necessary to add security issues associated with physical damage caused by a cyberattack (Lera, 2016).

For the categorisation of cybersecurity threats, it has been pointed out that, on smart robotic manufacturing systems, it is necessary to analyse the motivation of cyber attackers, manufacturing cyber vulnerabilities and protection technologies of smart manufacturing systems (Abbas, 2021b). In both manufacturing and non-manufacturing systems, cyberattacks could take place. However, certain attacks have dramatic consequences in manufacturing systems. Some examples of such attacks are: stealing manufacturers' trade secrets and intellectual property; cyber espionage; sabotaging production systems and altering design and process (Verizon, 2018); (Ward, 2018); (Zetter, 2014); (Fruhlinger, 2017).

Cyber-protection solutions in manufacturing systems need to take into account certain unique aspects specific to manufacturing system information and network components. In this respect, security must be considered in the design phase (Tuptuk and Hailes, 2019). According to these authors, secure software development practices which core is the prevention of software vulnerabilities (e.g., security requirements specification, security properties implementation, testing, code review, patch management) have not been adequately addressed during the implementation of such systems. They have stated also that in manufacturing systems, for instance, the focus so far has been more on operational efficiency and performance and not on the evolution of security issues.

So, it can be said that CPS crimes present several characteristics that need to be addressed for the security of CPS systems. In this regard, it has been reported that robotic systems are increasingly raising concerns related to privacy issues. This is not surprising considering that technological advances in the last decade have made it possible to have (social/assistant) robots close to us in everyday life at affordable prices for middle-class families in countries such as Japan, the US and, to some extent, in Europe. Such robots can be seen as a kind of vector that introduces risks to our (human) security from a privacy point of view, due to the personal information they capture and process from the humans they interact with.

Also, safety issues are relevant in the interaction of human and robotic systems, as they can pose a risk to the physical integrity of humans. Robotic systems in the military are a good example of such a risk, as these systems rely heavily on the integrity of the software that governs their behaviour. But in civil society there are also examples of such problems. For example, manufacturing systems are connected to each other and/or to communication network systems, making them potential targets for hijacking. In addition, medical applications are often designed to be very precise, e.g. in surgery. If that accuracy/precision is threatened by a cyber-attack - as some of these robots are connected to communication networks - the patient could even die.

The goal of this work was to engineer an information model of robotic systems that addresses relevant privacy and security issues for those systems in such a way that (1) at least 4 different types of robotic information systems, in terms of application domains, are included; (2) the most important information privacy factors for society are taken into account; (3) physical and psychological safety factors for humans are considered.

Also, the goal was to develop knowledge representation models of robotic systems that are reusable and shareable between application domains, in accordance with the following requirements: (4) the above referred number of application domains are considered; and (5) the conceptual elements shared across different application domains among those analyzed are identified.

3. CATEGORIZATION SCHEMA FOR CYBERSECURITY THREATS TO ROBOTS

The algorithm followed to obtain a categorization schema for cybersecurity threats to robots in indicated next.

Step 1: Knowledge capture on robotic systems in relation to human privacy and security parameters. This process involves (1) to collect the main relevant features of 4 different categories of robotic systems; and (2) to evaluate privacy and human security parameters in the inputs and outputs of the systems.
Step 2: Obtain a knowledge model of robotic systems in relation to human privacy and security parameters, which involves (1) to model the conceptual elements that are shared across different application domains; and (2) to model conceptual elements that are potentially reusable across a repertory of application domains.

Ontologies was used as the method (and model) of knowledge representation (Gruber, 2007). These allowed for the identification of the basic ontological elements (i.e., concepts, attributes, and (ranges of) values) as well as the relevant ontological relationships between the concepts. The Protégé software tool was used to edit the ontological models.

3.1. Robotic Systems in Relation to Human Privacy and Security

The amount and way in which data is generated, how it is collected, where it is stored and how it is processed are all major issues in CPS security. Thus, the problem arising for example from data collection is that there must be a boundary with the data source privacy, so providing trust and preventing more data than is permitted (in time, form or nature) from being collected. Establishing the boundary is one of the biggest challenges to prevent data from being used inadequately. In this sense, according to the previous lines and the scenario proposed in this work, the main characteristics of several categories of robotic systems in relation to security issues will be described next.

Before proceeding to categorising the cybersecurity threats according to their semantics, a taxonomy of robotic systems was obtained by attending to their application domains, namely, industry, healthcare, logistics, home, agriculture and livestock, smart cities, commerce and hospitality, etc. In this taxonomy, 5 subcategories of robots are included. One group of such subcategories includes fixed-location robots and robots that move around in their environment. The former includes autonomous mobile robots (AMR), automated guided vehicles (AGV), mobile humanoids and hybrids (i.e., robot systems that result from a combination of diverse robot types, for example, AMR with a robotic arm). The other group is composed by those robots having a fixed nature, such as articulated robots or co-bots, which are designed to work alongside humans.

With the purpose of modelling the main privacy and security factors in robotic systems, the causes that lead to the breach of robotic systems and their context must be identified. Having this in mind, all physical, natural causes, human factors, hardware and software factors were considered in this research. Thus, for instance, the physical components that a robotic system possesses, in addition to the elements of its mechanical structure, transmissions, connectors, terminal elements as well as the sensors and peripherals connected or installed in these systems were all taken into account. Through the components that may be installed, it is possible to collect a series of data or inputs, which were also handled in the proposed categorization.

With all, the next categories of robot categories are proposed.

(C1) Domestic robot: This type of robot is autonomously responsible for household chores, a private place with maximum privacy and with data that must have maximum protection. The following inputs can be obtained through this robot: mapping of the home, images and sounds, WiFi, radio or Bluetooth signals, equipment connected to the network such as a router or voice assistants, etc. The outputs obtained after processing the information collected are, above all, the execution of a set of algorithms or programmes based on a defined schedule. Examples of these are: the decision to modify a route after capturing an immobile element in an image; the recording of images and videos; sounds, voice commands, conversations, averages and physical mappings; temperature records; interruptions; schedules; connections; equipment connected to a network; recording of human interactions; hit counters; button presses; emptying of waste bags...etc.

The main threats and related concepts that can be elucidated for this kind of robot in relation to those threats are indicated next.

Main threats:

- Infringement of the security and privacy of people in their environment.
- Access to private and sensitive information (i.e., images and sounds)
- Capture of consumer behaviour and habits

Main threats-related concepts:

- Organizational assets vulnerability.
- Physical environment, which includes the domain, the personal context, and the organisational nature.
- Processed information.

(C2) Cobot system: It is intended for industry. It has the advantage of being able to work closely with people. Typical tasks of cobot systems are: carrying out production work; taking care of the heaviest, most precise and dangerous parts -while human operators take care of the most human part. Regarding the inputs, they are able, for example, to introduce all stuff passing through their hands into a system. Such stuff includes: materials that they process; products that they manufacture, package, move, etc. They can also scan everything that surrounds them, whether it be human personnel that interacts with them, machinery that is used around them, equipment. They may account for the relationship of time with their tasks, for instance, products per minute that are obtained, material consumption (e.g., energy, consumables, etc.) per minute, human production times, etc. As for outputs, it can be stated that they are able to store all the information obtained as input as data, relate them to each other, process them, and even learn from them. Some of the most common outputs are: work statistics, hours, products, risks, stoppages, consumption, interactions, etc.

The main threats and related concepts that can be established for this kind of robot in relation to those threats are indicated next.

Main threats:

- Infringement of the security and privacy of people in their environment.
- Access to private and sensitive information, including pictures and sounds.
- Access to confidential information.
- Profit (i.e., private/commercial interests).
- Cyber-vandalism.

Main threats-related concepts:

- Organizational assets vulnerability, which can be grouped in:
  ○ Vulnerability of Sw elements.
  ○ Vulnerability of Hw elements.
  ○ Vulnerability of communication elements.
- Physical environment in terms of personal context and organisational nature.
- Processed information

Conversational bot (C3): It is computer program that automatically performs reiterative tasks via the Internet through a series of commands or previous autonomous functions to assign an established role.

Conversational bots possess interaction capacities by changing their state to respond to a stimulus. They do not have individual hardware but they do use the hardware of the machines and equipment where they are running. In other words, they use microphones, keyboard inputs, mouse or other peripherals, cameras, and complements that are similar to those present in a phone, laptop, tablet or machine with a customised configuration. Their inputs are all those elements that are captured by the input of their respective equipment. These elements can be of various types, like sound, video, photo, text, etc. And their outputs can be interactions via screen, sound or print, as well as files and data streaming.

The main threats and related concepts that can be defined for this kind of robot in relation to those threats are indicated next.

Main threats:

- Infringement of the security and privacy of people in their environment.
- Access to private and sensitive information, including images and sounds.
- Capture of consumer behaviour and habits.

Main threats-related concepts:

- Organizational assets vulnerability.
- Physical environment, which encompasses all scope, personal context, and organisational nature.
- Processed information.

Robotic warehouse (C4): The philosophy of this type of robot is to maximise storage capacity in an autonomous facility. It is extremely useful in the manufacturing industry, warehouses of logistics companies and of any type such as supply companies, even robotised car parks. Robotic warehouses can have an ample repertory of inputs coming from systems such as: cameras that collect images of the objects to be stored and their environment; movement sensors for security; temperature, CO_2 or oxygen levels sensors; scanning lasers for volumes and measurements, weighing scales, unit counters; biometric detection to identify users. There are also robotic warehouses equipped with keyboards or more sophisticated peripherals, such as virtual reality glasses. All of them, at any given time, can improve the efficiency of their task or contribute to the security of personal and material goods. For instance, thermostats, particle detectors, or motion detectors can trigger beneficial commands and in this way, they can foresee risks or disasters and avoid them. However, this kind of robots can also provoke disasters, because the data they handle can harm a person or a company.

The main threats and related concepts that can be defined for this kind of robot in relation to those threats are indicated next.

Main threats:

- Access to private and sensitive information, including images and sounds.
- Capturing behaviour and consumption habits.
- Causing harm.

Main threats-related concepts:

- Vulnerability of Sw elements.

- Physical environment.
- Processed information.

Autonomous vehicle or AGV (AMR mobile robotics): It moves on predetermined tracks or routes, and it is not free to move beyond what has been programmed physically or virtually. Autonomous vehicles often require minimal human intervention. They have a wide variety of technologies, such as cameras, speed controllers, signal readers, temperature and humidity, GPS location, WiFi, GSM or 5G connection. Also, they can include photometer to check external light, movement of their environment, microphone that identifies sounds, etc. Autonomous vehicles are often able to record, connect to a server, satellite or mobile phone and get inputs from all of them. Their outputs are the diversity of reactions that a vehicle's behaviour can have. Such behaviour imitates and aims to improve the way a human being drives. They detect reactions of the environment and foresee safe actions. Other outputs can be labelled as sensitive, as they record images and sounds of indoors or outdoors personal life, locations connected with mapping records where the vehicle is driven and stopped, fuel consumed, consumption habits (e.g., petrol stations, roads, and in the case of industrial vehicles, economic, logistical or production data of the company in question).

The main threats and related concepts that can be set up for this kind of robot in relation to those threats are indicated next.

Main threats:

- Access to private and sensitive information, including images and sounds.
- Access to confidential information.
- Capture of behaviour and consumption.
- Causing harm.

Main threats-related concepts:

- Organizational assets vulnerability.
- Vulnerability of Sw elements.
- Vulnerability of Hw elements.
- Physical environment.
- Processed information.

3.2. Knowledge Model of Robotic Systems in Relation to Human Privacy and Security Parameters

From the robot systems' main threats and related concepts in relation to those threats obtained in the previous section, a set of 4 general relevant concepts, together with their respective attributes and values can be modelled as described below, where for each concept/sub-concept, their relevant attributes are expressed into square brackets, and some representative values of such attributes, if it is the case, are written into brackets:

1. vulnerability [affected component ∈ {Sw, Hw, communication}; organisational effect ∈ {psychological, physical, economic/financial, competitive, operational}].

1.1. vulnerability of Sw elements [affected component = 'Sw', software effects of the robotic system ∈ {configuration modification, system attack, malware infection, hidden downloads, information hijacking, software damage, productivity deficit}].

1.2. vulnerability of Hw elements [affected component = 'Hw', robotic hardware effect ∈ {change RAM blocks; destroy disk; malicious code (USB), inject flash memory}].

1.3. vulnerability of communication elements [affected component = 'communication', organisational effect, risk ∈ {access, identity theft, theft, sabotage, unauthorised use, tampering}].

2. physical environment [domain ∈ {medical (healthcare), industry, home, logistics, retail and catering, smart cities}; personal context ∈ {adults, minors}; organisational nature ∈ {public, private}].

3. technical characteristics [manufacturer; physical configuration ∈ {articulated, integrated, exoskeleton}; weight; power].

4. processed information [direction ∈ {input information, output information}; location ∈ {external information, internal information}; degree of privacy ∈ {confidential, private, public}; object ∈ {human identity, information flow, human behaviour, human habit, human consumption, location, information protocol, process, instruction, statistics, secrecy, intellectual property}].

4. MODELLING THE CYBERSECURITY THREATS TO MANUFACTURING ROBOTIC SYSTEMS

By using the knowledge model described in previous section, the cybersecurity threats to manufacturing robotic systems can be ontologically expressed as shown below. To do that, the Protégé toolkit was used.

Figure 1 shows the main conceptual categories as defined in previous section and to which manufacturing robotic systems is linked.

Figure 2 below illustrates how the kind of vulnerability that a manufacturing robotic system may have depending on the affected robot component, namely, a Hw, Sw or communication component.

Figure 3 illustrates the modelling of some of the features of the processed information that a manufacturing robotic system may have, like the object of the processed information, the degree of privacy, the location, etc.

Figure 1.

Figure 2.

Figure 3.

5. DISCUSSION AND CONCLUSION

In this work, a model that categorizes the most relevant cybersecurity threats to robots from different analytical viewpoints has been formulated. This model is based on the state-of-the-art of current robotic systems as found in literature. It consists of four main (top-level) concepts that address such threats by taking into account key aspects related to robot systems security, such as the kind of human relation with robots, the industrial sector/application domain, the information handled, etc.

The model approach that has been used to obtain the knowledge model is ontologies due to their properties facilitating knowledge modularity, sharing and reuse. Furthermore, the model has been implemented into OWL ontological language by means of Protégé. This language is the de facto standard of ontologies, so making the system machine-understandable and exchangeable world-wide. To illustrate the usefulness of this model, the main (top level) characteristics of a model addressing the cybersecurity threats to manufacturing robotic systems has been described.

As further work, we envisage two main directions. First, the model will be tested against some real settings (i.e., manufacturing robotic systems) to check that the model contains all the relevant features of manufacturing robotic systems and their context. Second, we plan to implement some software application that interacts with the model, so that it can be evaluated in some real industrial/corporate high level process.

REFERENCES

Abbas, M. (2021a). *The Human Elements in Artificial Intelligence, Robotics, and Cybersecurity*. CRC Press.

Abbas, M. (2021b). Cybersecurity in Smart and Intelligent Manufacturing Systemas. In M. Abbas (Ed.), *The Human Elements in Artificial Intelligence, Roboticas, and Cybersecurity* (pp. 149–160). CRC Press.

Apa, L., & Cerrudo, C. (2017). Hacking Robots Before Skynet. IOActive Inc.

Byres, E., & Lowe, J. (2004). The myths and facts behind cyber security risks for industrial control systems. *Proceedings of the VDE Kongress*.

Calo, R. M. (2011). Robots and privacy. In P. Bekey, G. Abney, & K. Lin (Eds.), *Robot Ethics: The Ethical and Social Implications of Robotics*. MIT Press.

Cavelty, M. D. (2013). From cyber-bombs to political fallout: Threat representations with an impact in the cyber-security discourse. *International Studies Review*, *15*(1), 105–122. doi:10.1111/misr.12023

Chanchal Dey, S. K., & Sen, D. K. (2020): Industrial 4.0: Industrial internet of things (IIOT). *Indus. Autom. Technol.*, 269–310.

Fruhlinger, J. (2017). What is Stuxnet, who created it and how does it work? Thanks to Stuxnet, we now live in a world where code can destroy machinery and stop (or start) a war. *CSO*. https://www.csoonline.com/article/3218104/what-is-stuxnetwho-created-it-and-how-does-it-work.html

Gruber, T. (2007). Automatically integrating heterogeneous ontologies from structured web pages. *International Journal on Semantic Web and Information Systems*, *3*(1), 1–11. doi:10.4018/jswis.2007010101

Lera, F. J. R., Balsa, J., Casado, F., Fernández, C., Rico, F. M., & Matellán, V. (2016). Cybersecurity in Autonomous Systems: Evaluating the performance of hardening ROS. Academic Press.

Maximilian, L., & Markl, E. M. A. (2018). Cybersecurity management for (industrial) internet of things–challenges and opportunities. *Journal of Information Technology & Software Engineering, 8*(5), 1–9.

Rawnsley, A. (2011). Iran's Alleged Drone Hack: Tough, but Possible. *Wired.* https://www.wired.com/2011/12/iran-drone-hack-gps

Ten, C. W., Manimaran, G., & Liu, C. C. (2010). Cybersecurity for critical infrastructures: Attack and defense modeling. *IEEE Transactions on Systems, Man, and Cybernetics. Part A, Systems and Humans, 40*(4), 853–865. doi:10.1109/TSMCA.2010.2048028

Tuptuk, N., & Hailes, S. (2018). Security of smart manufacturing systems. *Journal of Manufacturing Systems, 47*, 93–106. doi:10.1016/j.jmsy.2018.04.007

Verizon. (2018). *Data Breach Investigations Report.* Verizon. https://enterprise.verizon.com/resources/reports/DBIR_2018_Report.pdf

Ward, M. (2018). Staying one step ahead of the cyber-spies. *BBC News.* https://www.bbc.com/news/business-43259900

Zetter, K. (2014). An unprecedented look at stuxnet, the world's first digital weapon. *Wired.* https://www.wired.com/2014/11/countdown-to-zero-day-stuxnet/

Chapter 13

Detailing a Case of Cyber Fraud Through Telephone in Brazil:
From the Choice of Elderly Victims, Spoofing Until Social Engineering Manipulation

Eduardo M. Morgado
São Paulo State University, Brazil

Carla Gonçalves Távora
São Paulo State University, Brazil

João Pedro Albino
ⓘ https://orcid.org/0000-0001-5965-1869
São Paulo State University, Brazil

Ivany Bucchianico
ⓘ https://orcid.org/0009-0005-0094-1294
Universidade de São Paulo, Brazil

Ana Cláudia Pires Ferreira de Lima
São Paulo State University, Brazil

ABSTRACT

The goal is to initiate a discussion over the measures to protect the victims, whom unfortunately, in Brazil, composes 30% of elderly people (older than 60 years old). The case report portrays the scam through spoofing, programs that change the caller's identification in a communication, together with Social Engineering, to trick the victim into carrying out operations in the bank's application, thus encouraging transfers to the scammer's account. The victim ended up following these guidelines and made appointments to send money to the scammer, however, he ended up suspecting the situation, decided to interrupt that communication and seek the bank branch for clarification, thus managing to cancel the appointments and reverse the transfer amounts. Actions need to be taken, urgently, because the predictions show a gigantic increase of this type of fraud.

DOI: 10.4018/978-1-6684-8422-7.ch013

INTRODUCTION

The number of frauds and digital frauds associated to smartphones is increasing very fast throughout the last years. According to Serasa Experian's Attempted Frauds Indicator, in 2022, the **Brazilian population has suffered an attempted fraud at every 8 seconds.** Solely on June 2022, 32.219 attempted frauds happened through all over the Brazilian territory.

According to the Brazilian Banks Federation (Febraban), since the beginning of the Covid-19 Pandemic, in 2019, there has been a 165% increase of the smartphone-based frauds. There are many types of frauds, like extortion, identity theft, violation of personal data, nonpayment or non-delivery.

This is not a Brazilian phenomenon, the same is happening in other countries, like the United Kingdom, where the population is allegedly more enlightened and polite, but where the increase has been of 25% over the last year (ONS.gov.uk, 2022).

Frauds are more predominant amongst smartphone users, given their use by most of all of the population. In Brazil, according to IBGE'S 2021 census, an average of 84,4% of Brazilians had a cellphone for personal use; 90% of them with internet access e 79% of these Brazilian used some sort of "digital bank services" (Forbes, 2022).

The authors will describe in details one of these frauds, under the victims point of view, the technical analysis of the fraud and Brazilian legislation. This fraud or scam involved a big state bank, that the same way as all other involved, will not have its name revealed, although its actions and behaviors will.

The goal is to initiate a discussion over the measures to protect the victims, whom unfortunately, in Brazil, composes 30% of elderly people (older than 60 years old).

VICTIM'S NARRATIVE

I am 64 years of age, I have been a client of the Bank over 15 years now, and I was a victim of a cellphone fraud, called "hacker scam". I have an IPhone 11. At a Friday, at the end of the morning, the cellphone rang and on its screen showed "Bank" – this is the name of the agency where I keep my account for years and is registered amongst my contact list for years.

In order to appear "Bank", only two numbers could have called: XXXX XXXX, a corporative cellphone number from my "Bank's" Agency, or YYYY YYYY of the same agency. These numbers were registered on my contact list for years. Unsuspecting and sure that I was talking to my Manager, I answered saying "Hi Manager!" and "she" (already a scammer) greeted me with joy, but started the conversation scaring me, by saying that "my account was possibly hacked".

She asked me if I had done a few transfers that day. I told her no, but the scammer "said yes", and informed me "they were made to another Bank". She told me to write down a protocol number and said she was "running the system" to verify the amount of the transfers. After a few seconds, the scammer asked me to write down the "transfers" of R$4.253,00; R$4.050,00; R$4.500,00 and R$4.598,00; adding up to R$17.401,00.

With a calm voice, the scammer told me again, "the transfers were made to 'another Bank', but I could be assured because "she was already in contact with the Manager from the Fraud Sector from "the other Bank", asking me to write down the name of this "Manager from the other Bank". When I asked how could these transfers be possible, since no one has my passwords and I do not keep them written on an agenda, the scammer responded, "it is just like this, they invade the account and obtain the passwords easily". And added "the account was already being blocked".

Frightened, yet still confident I was talking to "my Bank's Manager", I asked if they had accessed my father's account, to which I am the second holder. The scammer asked me for a few seconds to verify and came back saying "yes, they had transferred around R$21.000,00 from his account".

She than asked me if I had done some loans to which I answered no. The scammer guided me through the cellphone App to hire a loan, because this would be the only way she could verify if they (the alleged invaders) had contracted it. I told her I would not do that, since there was no meaning to hiring a loan to make this verification. Realizing she could not get me to hire a loan, the scammer quickly said "It would not be necessary, because they (the scammers) had solicited a loan, which was not approved and to ease myself".

Even terrified, in the meanwhile, I checked my father's bank statement, mine, and realized it did not show any withdraws or money transfers. I told that to the scammer, but she informed me the "scammers freeze the balance's screen for 48 hours so the victim cannot get a hold of her balance. Starting to think this was all very strange, I questioned: "if you had frozen the accounts, how could I get access to the app or the statement?". The scammer told me she had unlocked it for my access, but she was blocking it again.

The scammer than told me she would guide me through the proceedings to enable my transfers via cellphone app so I could "receive the restitutions the other Bank's Manager would do". Thinking about the restitutions, I made a series of proceedings on the app's screen, clicking on pay/receive, but at the same time asking myself if I was not sending money instead of preparing to receive. The scammer told me "everything was fine, she was keeping track of what I was doing, and making sure I really was enabling my app to receive". Scared and nervous, and being pressured with the orientation of doing everything in a hurry, but still relying I was speaking with "my Manager's Bank account" I did the proceedings.

As there are daily limits for transfers, she insisted I enabled another type of transfer so I could receive. What I was doing, in fact, were transfers and I did not realized it. As there were daily limits for transfers, in a short amount of time I could not do it any longer. Therefore, she guided me "to make the habilitations, which were in fact, transfers scheduling for Saturday and Sunday".

Scared, nervous and completely unsure about these inverted transactions (getting out and not getting in), even certain I had talked to "my Bank's Manager", I interrupted the calls and personally went to the Bank's Agency of my city. I was quickly attended and informed I had been a victim of a fraud. The managers cancelled the schedules and reversed the transfers that were possible. However, the transfers made and withdrawn at the Receiving Agency could not be recovered. The gangs maintain people around the agencies, to make withdraws as quickly as possible of the transfers made.

TECHNICAL ANALYSIS OF THE FRAUD

From the Digital Security's point of view, the victim was initially approached by a technique called **"spoofing"** and subsequently by a strategy called **"Social Engineering"**.

- **Spoofing** means "to deceive or falsify", it is the use of programs that alter the caller's identification in a communication. There are many types of "spoofing": in this case it was telephone's.

"Spoofing" is used as mass strategy, where a computer does millions of calls – in this case only a few react positively to that call – exactly those with the number registered on their contact list. When this happens, the scammers move on to the next phase.

- **Social Engineering,** is a complex people manipulation strategy, where a gang tricks a person, exploiting their emotional and expecting human errors to occur. Its application follows a methodology where a trained gang tricks and manipulates the victims, searching to obtain information or induce actions to harm themselves.

This strategy can be applied online like this case, through telephone. It is also a mass strategy – millions are approached.

In this case, it makes no sense to discuss if she collaborated or not with the scammers, as **Social Engineering** searches exactly that – **to get collaboration**. The only way of helping the victims is through information, warning or previous counseling about the frauds being applied at the moment It is the Banks's obligation to inform.

Previously, the authors need to highlight the fact that all this frauds are applied by a group of scammers (gangs) and a computer system that makes several calls to many people, incessantly; given it is a machine, redirecting or creating data banks for other actions of all of those who reacted to the first round of attacks. Besides **"spoofing",** there are many other technical variations of attacks, as **"fishing", "vishing", "smishing"** and **"pharming".**

Social Engineering is the usual strategy after the targets are detected. To better understand this strategy the authors will describe its methodology:

1. **Preparation**: when the gang reunites basic information about a target or a group of targets.
2. **Infiltration**: connection and establishment of a relationship with the victim. Starts by building trust.
3. **Destabilization**: supply of impact information to scare or make the victim to become nervous.
4. **Pressure or exploitation**: through hurry urgency or higher fear, the gang convinces the victim to act fast, doing things without thinking.
5. **Dispersion**: disappearance, disconnection after goals were attained.

Social Engineering is very effective. The victims usually surrender everything, apparently without being coerced or threatened. Unfortunately, there is a massive prejudice, which tends to consider the "user collaborated" instead of the "user was a victim". This prejudice is, obviously, bigger amongst those that had not been victimized yet or did not study the problem (IC3, 2023). At this point, important questions have surfaced:

· **How did the scammers knew the victim had an account at the Bank?**

They did not! They only knew the number "XXXX XXXX" was used to call clients in the past, but was not being used to this means anymore, although it still existed to receive phone calls.

The scammers did the "spoofing" of "XXXX XXXX" in thousands or millions of people. They are machines that turn on and do not get tired. Who react recognizing the call as being the Bank's is transferred to the Engineering group.

· Why did the victim had this number XXXX XXXX in her contact list with the Bank's name since the Bank affirms this is the Agencies' number, but is not used to external calls?

Nowadays, this number can no longer call outside the agency, but it could in the past. And it needs, in fact, to be on my contacts, because it is one of the numbers used to talk to the Bank.

In the past this number called me and the victim and the authors saved it years ago. the authors do not know when did this number stopped making external calls.

When analyzing the Bank's strategies and actions regarding this scam, there is a way to technically show they were negligent when managing this issue. They failed to inform people they were at high risk.

The **Bank is familiar with this fraud**, calling it "fake call center", long ago. In addition, the Bank has it described in details in one of its Web pages.

But in order to find this description on its Web pages I had to make searches via Google using as search mechanisms the words "spoofing", "phishing" and "Bank". The search I made was one of a data processing specialist - an average client could hardly do it.

- **The Bank also describes this swindle in a much elaborated brochure or folder.**

Paradoxically, this brochure is only available at the Agency's desks. Meaning, people who uses the Cellphone Bank's app will rarely go to the Agency and, therefore, will not see this brochure.

- **Why the elderly predominate amongst the victims?**

Brazil, according to the 2017s Census (IBGE), has 30.2 millions of people above 60 years old. And as the authors have already seen it, the elderly are 30% of the victims of digital scams, notably "spoofing", strategy used in the "fake call center" swindle (Fintech, 2023; Kaspersky, 2022).

The authors notice a larger participation of elderly people in the virtual universe, mainly for leisure and communication with their family. Consequently, there is an increase of their number as virtual crimes' victims. The elderly population is an extremely vulnerable social class to these crimes. Amongst the many causes for this situation, the authors can quote the reduction of cognitive and physiologic functions due to the age; the unknowing and ingenuity over the adequate use of technology and its associated risks.

Elderly people are mostly retired, with limited groups of social relationship. They have more difficulties to accessing technology that updates at every second. Therefore, they have a lesser chance of being alerted about these swindles. Criminals uses the **Social Engineering** strategy which affects the psychological of the elderly, affecting their process in making decisions through emotions and due to the overload of information, as well as the ingenuity when believing the reciprocity of favors, on offers and the false construction of relationships

A very particular case – WhatsApp is the Champion in frauds involvement (Noia, 2023)

Research made with 14 thousand interviews reveals most people who fell for the frauds were tricked by messages received through WhatsApp, being 65.1% of which has suffered from the following types of scams:

- They had their app account cloned (22.1%);
- Clicked at fraudulent links they received through text message (20.7%);
- Payed false tickets with an adulterated bar code (20.8%);
- 49.5% transferred money to the scammers.

Unfortunately, 76.4% of consumers who were victims of frauds could not get their Money back and only 24.7% of them registered a police report. Around 30.1% had gave their personal data and bank information, 20.4% had their social security number and their names used in unauthorized shopping on behalf of strangers and 49.5% made financial transfers to the scammers. The authors can also see WhatsApp has added security measures, but has not been too effective when the scammers also use **Social Engineering**.

The installation of a spyware is the most a scammer can do, by distance, without being in hold of the device. The technique is always the same, the user is incited to click on a link but, as the authors have seen it, the spyware's installation will only occur after several confirmation. The possibility of a scammer to "capture" or "clone" or "copy" someone else's smartphone is not real. This is an urban legend. The authors could say that is impossible today in IOS and very and very difficult in Android.

THE FRAUD ANALYSIS THROUGH THE LIGHT OF THE BRAZILIAN LEGISLATION

The Criminal Classification

The spoofing techniques and social engineering were perpetrated to induce to victims to committing an error, using a ruse to fool the victim and making her transfer money to the bank accounts indicated by the criminal, who obtained illicit advantage, in the detriment of the victim.

The mentioned behaviors on the case are classified in the article 171, §2°-A of the Brazilian Criminal Code, being the embezzlement crime, qualified because of the electronic use:

Article 171 – To obtain, for yourself or others, illicit advantage, in detriment of other people, inducing or maintaining someone in error, through artifice, ruse, or any other fraudulent mean:

Sentence – reclusion, starting from one to five years, and fine of five hundred thousand réis to ten counts of réis.

Maurício Tamer observes the embezzlement crime victim "only agreed with the situation given the unfamiliarity this was a fraud" and highlights "In this case, there is no decrease to the victim's vigilance, but an altering (falsification) of reality in order to convince the victim to deliver an illicit advantage (patrimonial) undue to the criminal" (Tamer, 2023).

The Law n° 14.155/2021 created a qualification to the embezzlement crime when used electronic means, in which case there is a penalty increase. Therefore, if the fraud is committed with the use of technology, through phone contacts, social media, e-mails, or any other similar fraudulent mean, as well as instant messages apps, the qualification of the embezzlement crime exists, once made through electronic fraud, regulated in article 171, §2°-A of the Criminal Code:

Electronic Fraud

§ 2°-A. The sentence is reclusion, from 4 (four) to 8 (eight) years and fine, if the fraud is committed using information given by the victim or by a third party induced into error through social media, phone contacts or fraudulent e-mails, or by any other fraudulent similar mean.

If the embezzlement crime is committed against an elderly person, there is another qualification, regulated in the §4° of the same article:

Embezzlement Against Elderly or Vulnerable

§ 4° The sentence increases by 1/3 (one third) to the double if the crime is committed against elderly or vulnerable, considering the relevance of the seriousness of the result.

The beginning of the criminal persecution depends on the victim's representation, that need to be made on the statute of limitations of six months, beginning from the crime's author identification. It is, therefore, a crime of public criminal action conditioned to representation, meaning, the victim has to manifest its willing to the Public Prosecutor so to sue the crime's author on the criminal scope. There is no need of the victim's representation when it is a child or teenager, a person with mental deficiency, older than 70 years old or incapable or if the crime is perpetrated against the Public Administration, direct or indirect, regulated in the article 171, §5° of the Criminal Code.

Civil Responsibility of the Financial Institution Regarding the Digital Bank Frauds

The victim of the digital fraud on the banking sector must immediately report the fraud suffered, so they can try to obstruct or reverse the fraudulent transfers and to the police, so they can respond appropriately. However, the verification of the digital crimes authorship requires time and wide technique specialization, to track the accounts to which the bank transfers were made, besides requirement to the Justice System to break the secrecy of the telematics and cybernetics data to try to identify the fraudulent agent. Even so, once investigated the authorship, the criminal's complaint on the criminal sphere do not guarantee the reparation of the moral and material damages made to the victim.

In order for the victim to have her reparation, with restitution of the amount transferred through fraud, she has to sue the one who caused the damage. Depending on the peculiarities of the case, if there was omission on the bank's behalf over the adoption of safety measures or breach of its legal obligations, it can be held accountable for damage reparations.

The responsibility by a third party's fact is well explained by Maria Helena Diniz:

On the responsibility over a third party someone will answer, indirectly, for the loss resulting of the illicit practice by someone else, because it is connected to her, through legal dispositive. There are two agents, therefore, the one who causes the damage and the responsible for the compensation (Diniz, 2009, p.529).

The article 186 of the Civil Code defines the practice of the illicit act: *"The person who, by action or voluntary omission, negligence or imprudence, violates right and causes damage to someone, even if exclusively moral, commits an illicit act"*, being the obligation to compensate regulated in article 927 of the Civil Code:

Article 927. The person who, by illicit act (articles 186 and 187) causes damage to another, is obliged to compensate him.

Single paragraph. The obligation to compensate the damage will occur, regardless of guilt, on the cases described by the law, or when the activity usually developed by the author of the damage implies, by its nature, risk to the rights of others.

The single paragraph of the article 927 talks about the objective responsibility, regarding the risks of the activity, regardless of fault. Analyzing the matter on the consumerist relations ambit, the provider's objective civic responsibility because of insufficient information about its fruition and risks is expressively recognized in the article 14 of the Consumer's Defense Code (Law n° 8.078/90):

Article 14. The service provider answers, regardless of fault, for the compensation of the damages caused to consumers because of flaws regarding to provision of services, as well as for insufficient or inadequate information about its fruition and risks.

The civic responsibility in the Brazilian law, generally, is subjective, meaning, depends on the agent's fault over the damage caused in order to be held accountable to repair it. However, "considering the consumer's vulnerability in the market and based on the activity's risk theory" (Varalli, 2022, p.79) business, the Consumer's Law stablishes the objective responsibility of the product supplier and the service provider, in other words, regardless of fault, to the damage reparation caused to the consumer, according to VARALLI.

It is clear the service provider will not be held accountable when proven the consumers or the third party exclusive guilt, according to article 14, §3°, II of the Consumer's Defense Code. Nonetheless, in this case the bank's guilt was evidenced, by not fulfilling its obligation to adopt measures to protect its clients data and to give important information to its clients in order to prevent against banking scams.

Among others, according to article 6th of the Consumer's Law, these are basic consumer's rights:

I – the protection of life, health and security against the risks provoked by practices over the supply of products and services considered dangerous or harmful;

II- the education and disclosure over the adequate consume of products and services, assuring the liberty of choice and equality on hiring;

III – the adequate and clear information about different products and services, with correct specification on quantity, characteristics, composition, quality, taxes and price, as well as the risks they present;

IV – the protection against false and abusive advertisement, coercive and disloyal commercial methods, as well as against abusive practices and clauses or imposed on the supply of products and services;

VI – the effective prevention and reparation of patrimonial and moral damages, individuals, collective and diffuse; (our highlight)

The Banks are the main beneficiated by the digitalization of client's relations and need to assume an active role in enlighten its potential victims. After all, it is undeniable that the adoption of "digital bank resources" by 75% of cellphone users reduce drastically its operational costs and substantially increase its profits.

To watch over consumers rights, it is up to the Financial Institution to amplify its awareness campaigns along with its clients so they will not be victims of swindles already knows by the institution. According to the case, the bank did not adopt any measure along with its clients, by either e-mail, mail or telephone.

The General Law of Data Protection (Law n° 13.709/18), in its article 46, imposes to the data treatments agents the adoption of every technological measures possible in order to protect the personal data of its holders, which was also not fulfilled by the bank:

Article 46. The treatment agents must adopt safety methods as well as technical, and administrative able to protect personal data from unauthorized accesses and accidental situations or illicit of destruction, loss, alteration, and communication or any other mean of inadequate or illicit treatment.

Technology already have programs of Machine Learning that allow the program of algorithms so the banks can detect non-standard bank operations considering its clients profiles, for instance the reoccurring value transfer, allowing a quick understanding of bank frauds and its interception. The failure to adopt measures of security inherent to the business characterizes guilt by omission of the entrepreneur, who must be civilly held accountable by the damages caused to his clients.

Therefore, the banks must make a risk management of its activities, adopting every measure capable to avoid the digital bank frauds. Besides the softwares and other security devices, the banks have the duty to make educational campaigns to alert its clients about the bank swindles perpetrated repeatedly.

Aware that thousands of scams are applied daily and knowing of the "fake call center" fraud, the financial institution of the case mentioned did not adopt the law-required caution to protect its clients' data and to make them aware of the dangers of Social Engineering, which could be easily done through educational campaigns disclosed through e-mail, message apps, mail or telephone.

Before the obligation's breach to adopt security measures against transactions outside of its clients profiles and against the non-authorized access of their personal data, regulated in article 46 of the General Law of Data Protection and because of the omission by not clarifying its costumers against the risks of the recurring scams, the bank must answer for this inertia, compensating his costumer for the moral and material damages suffered with the false central fraud, under the 479 Landmark of the Superior Court of Justice, that demonstrates the Enterprise Risk Theory, recognizing the risks of the economic activities need to be endured by the company:

479 Landmark

The financial institutions respond objectively for the damage caused by internal fortuitous regarding to frauds and crimes committed by a third party on the scope of bank operations.

The Damage Reparation

In order to try to recover the lost values, the digital victim's fraud of the bank sector can sue the bank in case it did not adopt the cautionary measures to avoid the scam, given the reasons exposed on the topic before. The bank, by its turn, can sue the criminal back, to seek compensation for the damages caused.

For causes of until twenty minimum wages the victim can sue the bank at the Special Civil Court of her city, narrating the facts and elaborating its request personally, without a lawyer's representation, through a physical petition or transmitter via internet, adding the supporting documents of the facts occurred.

Besides the initial petition, adding an opinion of a professional on information technology can assist to prove the digital evidences, helping the judge's opinion formation for the trial of the action. The Technical Opinion of forensics computing can present the technical elements to identify the crime committed through the electronic means, with the example of metadata of received e-mail, message apps and cellphone identification of the person who got the call, besides describing the fraud's method of application.

Forensics computing "consists in the use of scientific methods for preservation, gathering, validation, indentification, analysis, interpretation, documentation and presenting digital evidences" (Pinheiro, 2021, p.280).

The gathering of digital evidences and its insertion on the lawsuit's files must observe the forensics computing techniques for preservation of the integrity, authenticity and its chain of custody, being these the three factors to give utility to the digital (Thamy & Tamer, 2020).

If the damage caused by the fraud represents a bulky amount, recommends the ploughing of a Notarial Act, under the article 348 of the Civil Procedure Code[1], so the notary certify all digital evidences presented by the victim, what can also be done with the help of a computer sciences expert.

The notary has public faith, to whom is delegated the exercise of the notarial and register activities, under the article 3° of the Law n° 8.935/94. It is important to highlight the veracity presumption imposed to the public document, according to the article 405 of the Civil Procedure Code: *"The public document proves not only its formation, but also the facts the clerk, the chief of secretariat, the notary or the server declare happened on their absence."*

By considering the article 374, IV of the Procedure Civil Code stablishes the facts "in favor of which there is a legal presumption of existence and veracity" does not need proof, only if there is an impeachment of the Notarial Act, whose content has the presumption of veracity, there will be need to producing proofs in the opposite direction.

The maximum value for the actions in Special Civil Court is forty minimum wages, with the need of a lawyer only if the action's value is above twenty minimum wages, according to article 9th of Law n° 9.099/95.

The Federal Constitution assures, in article 5th, X, *"the right to intimacy, to private life, to honor and to a person's image, assured the right to compensation in case of material or moral damage in case of its violation"*. Therefore, a person with her rights violated can seek civil reparation on the Justice System (article 186 and 927 of the Civil Code) [2] from the offense's author and/or of the co-responsible to pay for compensation for moral and/or material damages.

Omission of the bank in risks management led to the victim's material and moral damages, embodied on psychological disruption and nervousness because of the exposition and leaking of her data as being the victim of digital bank fraud. Fraud that could have been easily avoided with educational campaigns and direct orientation of the bank to the clients about the inactivation of that telephone number from the bank, being used for the application of the frauds.

In that regard, the following decisions, in which there were the ruling against the financial institutions that neglected to adopt suficient measures to avoid the practice of digital bank scams:

Appeal. Declaratory action of debt unenforceability. Bank fraud. "Motoboy Fraud". Use of the card by scammers. Failure in the security of the services provided by the defendants regarding the protection of the plaintiff's data. Transactions not relatable to the account holder's profile. Need for a declaration of unenforceability of the disputed debt. Sentence reformed. Appeal granted (TJSP – Civic Appeal n.º 1009889-23.2019.8.26.0348. Rel. Des. Eduardo Siqueira. Trial in: 30/06/2020).

Declaratory. Credit card. Contested expenses. Improper use due to fraud. Transactions not relatable to the account holder's profile. Objective liability of the service provider, considered failure to provide the service. Reversal of the burden of proof. Imposition of fine for non-compliance. Admissibility. Appeal not granted (TJSP – Civic Appeal n.º 1012255-76.2019.8.26.0011. Re. Des. Matheus Fontes. Trial in: 30/06/2020).

Regarding this motion, the defendant's responsibility comes from the risk of his activity, which is why he objectively responds for fraud or use of false documents.

This is a demand in which the plaintiff alleges she was the victim of a fraud through which third parties - who knew of her status as a client of the defendant - obtained access to her computer, her password and bank account to carry out illicit operations.

In this hypothesis, the consumption relation between both parties is clear, the plaintiff is a consumer and the defendant the supplier, so that the matter discussed attracts the rules of the Consumer's Law which, in its article 6, item VIII, regulates the facilitation of the defense of consumer rights, "including the reversal of the burden of proof, in their favor, in civil proceedings, when at the discretion of the judge, the allegation is credible or when he is hypo sufficient, according to ordinary rules of experience".

It is up to the financial institution to adopt security measures to prevent account holders or card-holders from disposing of high amounts on the same day, even more so when they flee from the usual consumer's behavior.

In this case, one can concludes that the operations carried out involving the plaintiff's accounts, limited to small expenses, completely deviate from her profile. About this detail, no evidence was provided by the bank on any other way.

Certainly, the scammers would not have been successful in their endeavor if the defendant had taken the necessary means to follow up or monitor an atypical transaction involving too much expressive amounts.

Besides, not even after being called quickly by the plaintiff, was the bank ready to solve the reported problem, nor did it provide the blocking of the irregular transactions made.

The risk theory of the enterprise applies to the case, meaning, due to the activity carried out, the financial institution must objectively answer for damages suffered by consumers resulting from the provision of the service.

Thus, even if resulting from fraud, the bank must compensate the losses suffered by the applicant, since it is an internal fortuitous event, being a risk inherent to the activity itself.

(...)

Finally, it is worth mentioning STJ's 479 Landmark, according to which "The financial institutions respond objectively for the damage caused by internal fortuitous regarding to frauds and crimes committed by a third party on the scope of bank operations."

Thus, the restitution of amounts criminally subtracted from the plaintiff's bank account is strictly required.

As for moral damage, it appears from the documentation in the case file that as soon as the plaintiff became aware of the fraud, she informed the bank about what happened, but it was not promptly attended to, as well as drawing up an incident report on pages 43.

Subsequently, the defendant did not accept his justification and dismissed the administrative procedure, as can be seen on pages 40.

The situation faced by the plaintiff is of extreme discomfort, embarrassment and distress, mainly due to the large amounts involved in the fraud indicated in the complaint and the clear violation of her bank account, all of which can be repaired.

Once shown the defect, the damage and the causal link the service's provider responsibility elapses, regardless of fault.

Compensation for moral damages has a dual purpose.

On the one hand, it seeks to comfort the victim of an illicit act, consisting of an intimate injury, which cannot be evaluated by objective criteria, but it is possible to estimate by attributing a pecuniary reparation to the victim, thus repairing the damage caused on an equitable way.

On the other hand, in terms of the theory of disincentives, it is necessary to impose a fine to the offender, on a preventive basis, and not repressive, with the goal of preventing similar events from happening again or being effectively discouraged.

In this way, and so the reparation for moral damage represents a compensation and not a source of unjust enrichment, the amount to be indemnified for this purpose is set at R$7,000.00.

Remind yourself, thus, according to Precedent 326 of the C. STJ, "In the compensation's demand for moral damage, the condemnation in an amount inferior to the postulated in the initial one does not imply reciprocal loss".

The parties should pay attention to the detail that opposition of clarification's motions outside the legal hypotheses and/or with infringing effects will impose the fine provided for in article 1026, paragraph 2, of CPC/15.

That said and considering the rest of the case file, **I RULE in favor of the plaintiff,** under the terms of article 487, I, of the CPC, for the purpose of: 1- condemning the defendant to refund to the plaintiff the amount of R$44,500,00, plus monetary correction from the date of undue subtraction of the amounts and interest of 1% per month from the citation; 2- order the defendant to pay the plaintiff, as compensation for pain and suffering, the amount of R$ 7,000.00, plus monetary correction from this date and interest of 1% per month from the date of summons.

Finally, the defendant will bear the payment of court costs, procedural costs and attorney fees, which I set at 10% of the total amount of the conviction.[3]

CONCLUSION

The cases of cybernetic crimes are increasingly frequent, mainly regarding financial institution's clients. The frauds need to be broadcasted to the consumers defense organs, mostly to the Public Prosecutor in order to install procedures, culminating into Conduct Adjustment Term so the Financial Institutions adopt all of the possible means to avoid frauds in bank operations, to give an example, by improving the security system, in order to stop operations that is not compatible with the costumers profile and awareness campaigns against theses bank scams frequently uses involving the institution, which will contribute to the Sustainable Development Goals n° 16 of UN, to "Promote peaceful and inclusive societies for sustainable development, provide access to justice for all and build effective, accountable and inclusive institutions at all levels".

This cybernetic crime case was described in an innovative form, counting with three versions, the victim's, of an IT specialist and a Brazilian Jurist. It will serve as an alert to all possible new victims, but mostly orients technically and legally the competent authorities.

Actions need to be taken, urgently, because the predictions show a gigantic increase on this type of fraud.

REFERENCES

Alleasy. (2018). *What is Phishing, Smishing and Vishing? Know the differences*! All Easy.

Brasil. Decree-Law No. 2848, of December 7, 1940. (Criminal Code).

Brasil. Law No. 13,105, of March 16, 2015. (Code of Civil Procedure)

Court Of Justice Of São Paulo. Process 1009836-11.2021.8.26.0562, of the 1st Civil Court of the District of Santos, Judge Paulo Sergio Mangerona, judged on 10/14/2021. https://www.conjur.com.br/dl/dano-moral-bb.pdf.

Datavisor. (2021). Digital fraudtrends report 2021. *Datavisor*. https://www.datavisor.com/wp-content/uploads/2021/11/DataVisor-Digital-Fraud-Trends-Report-2021-2.pdf.

Diniz, M. H. (2009). Course of Brazilian civil law.: Vol. 7. *Civil Liability*. Saraiva.

Serasa Experian. (2022). Experian, S. *Brazilians suffered more than 375,000 fraud attempts in January, reveals Serasa Experian*. Serasa Experian. https://www.serasaexperian.com.br/sala-de-imprensa/analise-de-dados/brasileiros-sofreram-mais-de-375-mil-tentativas-de-fraude-em-janeiro-revela-serasa-experian/. Access on: Feb. 11, 2023.

Serasa Experian. (2022). *People between 36 and 50 years old are the main targets of scammers, points out research by Serasa Experian*. Serasa Experian. https://www.serasaexperian.com.br/sala-de-imprensa/analise-de-dados/pessoas-entre-36-e-50-anos-sao-os-principais-alvos-de-golpistas-aponta-pesquisa-da-serasa-experian/.

IC3. (2021). *Internet Crime Report*. IC3. https://www.ic3.gov/Media/PDF/AnnualReport/2021_IC3Report.pdf.

Kaspersky. (2022). *Kaspersky Security Bulletin*. Kapersky. https://go.kaspersky.com/rs/802-IJN-240/images/KSB_statistics_2022_en_final.pdf.

Manzzi, A. C. (2022). *Know the main scams on the Internet and learn how to protect your data*. NIC.br. https://www.nic.br/noticia/na-midia/conheca-os-principais-golpes-na-internet-e-saiba-como-proteger-os-seus-dados/.

Maybank. (2022). *Top 4 most viral online scams right now*. Maybank. https://www.maybank.com/en/blogs/2022/11/14-scam-tactics.page.

Nassif, T. (2022). *Digital scams put cybersecurity to the test; see how to protect yourself*. CNN Brasil. https://www.cnnbrasil.com.br/business/golpes-digitais-colocam-ciberseguranca-a-prova-veja-como-se-proteger/.

Noia, J. (2023). *WhatsApp is a champion of internet fraud, shows research. Learn how to protect yourself.* Globo. https://extra.globo.com/economia-e-financas/whatsapp-campeao-de-fraudes-na-internet-mostra-pesquisa-saiba-como-se-proteger-25415122.html.

ONS.gov.uk. (2023). *Office for National Statistics.* Gov. UK Office for National Statistics for England and Wales. https://www.ons.gov.uk/.

Pancini, L. (2022). 58% dos brasileiros sofreram crimes cibernéticos, aponta estudo da Norton. *Exame.* https://exame.com/tecnologia/58-dos-brasileiros-sofreram-crimes-ciberneticos-aponta-estudo-da-norton/.

Pinheiro, P. P. (2021). *Digital Law.* Saraiva Educação.

Ratier, R. (2022). *Bolsonarist groups have pix coup attacks, fake notes and "gatonet".* UOL. https://www.uol.com.br/ecoa/colunas/rodrigo-ratier/2022/06/13/grupos-bolsonaristas-no-whatsapp-tem-golpe-do-pix-nota-falsa-e-gatonet.htm. Access on: Feb. 13, 2023.

Siqueira, F. (2022). *Find out about the most common digital crimes committed in Brazil and know how to protect yourself.* R7. https://noticias.r7.com/tecnologia-e-ciencia/conheca-os-crimes-digitais-mais-comuns-praticados-no-brasil-e-saiba-se-proteger-22042022#/foto/1.

Tamer, M. (2023). *Ebook 3 of the Module "Legal Theory of Economic Criminal Law and Cyber Crimes".* Theme Embezzlement and Electronic Fraud - I, from the Postgraduate Course in Digital Law at EBRADI.

Thamy, R. (2020). *Tamer, Mauricio. Evidence in Digital Law: concept of digital evidence, procedures and digital evidence in kind.* Thomson Reuters Brasil.

Transunion. (2022). *Digital fraud attempts migrate to new segments globally.* Trans Union. https://newsroom.transunion.com.br/tentativas-de-fraude-digital-migram-para-novos-segmentos-globalmente/.

Varalli, R. M. (2022). *Consumer Law.* Rideel.

Wojahn, A. S., Michael, C. da P., da Veiga, D. J. S., Lenz, R., da Silva, S. G., Rossetto, T. P., & dos Santos, M. L. (2022). The social vulnerability of the elderly against scams in the digital scope. Research, Society and Development. doi:10.33448/rsd-v11i11.33652

ENDNOTES

[1] Article 384. The existence and mode of existence of a fact can be attested or documented, by requirement of the person interested in it, through minutes drawn up by a notary. Single Paragraph. Data represented by image or sound recorded in electronic files may be included on the notary files.

[2] Article 186. The person who, by action or voluntary omission, negligence or imprudence, violates right and causes damage to someone, even if exclusively moral, commits an illicit act. Article. 927. The person who, by illicit act (articles 186 and 187) causes damage to another, is obliged to compensate him. Single paragraph. The obligation to compensate the damage will occur, regardless of guilt, on the cases described by the law, or when the activity usually developed by the author of the damage implies, by its nature, risk to the rights of others.

3   Court of Justice of São Paulo. Process 1009836-11.2021.8.26.0562, of the 1st Civil Court of the District of Santos, Judge Paulo Sergio Mangerona, judged on 10/14/2021.

Chapter 14
Cybercrime and Cybersecurity Laws in Current and Future Contexts With Evolving Crimes Across National Boundaries

Banhita Sarkar

https://orcid.org/0000-0002-6094-3831

Amity University, Kolkata, India

Anirban Mitra

https://orcid.org/0000-0002-6639-4407

Amity University, Kolkata, India

Sujoy Chatterjee

Amity University, Kolkata, India

ABSTRACT

This chapter intends to discuss cybercrime and cybersecurity laws in their current and future contexts. The initial part of this chapter discusses terms and issues related to the cyber world. This portion has touched areas where the requirement of cyber laws is increasing with the advancement of time, technology, and types of cybercrimes. The later section of this chapter will look at existing and widely used cybersecurity laws from around the world. We have emphasized on Cyber Security Laws in India, the US, and the UK. The reason for focusing on these countries is that there are many multinational organizations that have offices spread across these regions. However, it should be noted that cybercrime is not limited by national or geographical boundaries and once committed, is dealt with under international law and in accordance with the trade agreements between the countries involved. The authors have included two famous trans boundary cyber cases that were brought to justice.

DOI: 10.4018/978-1-6684-8422-7.ch014

1. INTRODUCTION

Crime is an inevitable phenomenon that has existed since the birth of mankind in the world. With the growing age crime also has changed its forms, ways of occurrence, the jurisdiction of its operation, and so on and so forth. As and when society has taken relief that it has successfully created a protective shield against a form of offence, the criminals have come forth with a new one. With the advancement of technology, the introduction of computers has become an essential element of modern life. Today, humans depend on computers and allied technology for all our needs, starting from education to our livelihood, relaxation to business, socializing to banking, etc. The operation of criminals has also not been far from this technology. Cybercrime, or in simple words crimes committed with the aid of computers, has become the greatest strength for people with malafide intentions. Crimes can be committed in two ways using technology and computers. First, new kinds of offences are committed like Data Theft, identity theft, banking fraud, etc., which had no existence prior to the introduction of computers and databases, and secondly, the old offences are committed using the new technology (Ritu, 2017).

The Internet is considered as one of the greatest inventions of mankind which has made communication and diffusion of information from one part of the world to another very smooth and hassle-free. However, this has both positive and negative impacts on our lives. On the positive end, the instantaneous sharing of information has a great impact on education, business, entertainment, and social interactions (Ritu, 2017). The world survived the covid era more smoothly because of the internet services which kept us living some of our daily chores even after being immobile and stuck at our homes. On the negative end, however, the internet and its amenities have provided a wide possibility for criminals to commit crimes, with the much lesser worry of being caught by the administrators and wide jurisdiction can be covered as cyber-crimes at a much lesser cost of commission of crimes. In contrast with traditional economic criminals, cyber criminals find it much easier to commit such crimes as the same can be done only with a click of the mouse (Haung, 2011).

In the post covid era, it was seen that an abnormal rise has occurred in the number of cybercrimes, particularly those of economic crimes such as phishing, where fraudulently a person is made to reveal his personal information like passwords, credit card pin etc. and has been subjected to huge economic losses. Experts say the probable cause for such an abnormal increase is probably compulsory confinement during the lockdown, fear and anxiety for the future. As per data gathered by Google and analyzed by Atlas VPN, there has been an abnormal increase of 350% in data phishing during the Covid period (Edward, 2020). The same situation exists across the globe. Increasing uses of viruses, worms, trojans, spyware, malware etc. has made the population on the verge of fraud that can be committed at any time, and everyone is at equal risk of getting defrauded (Radoini, 2022)

Figure 1. Growth in cyber phishing
(Edward, 2020)

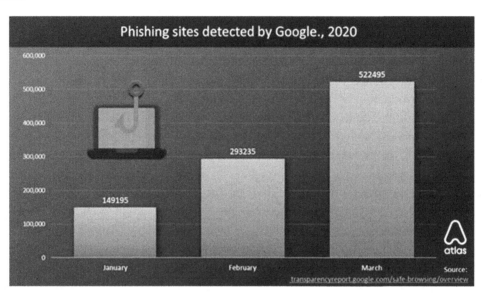

The above graph (Figure 1) depicts the humongous growth in cybercrimes during the Covid period of 2020, which is reported to be one of the most abnormal growth mankind has ever experienced.

2. DEFINING CYBER SPACE AND CYBER CRIME

To sufficiently understand the concept of cybercrimes and cyber law, it is prima facie essential to understand the concept of cyberspace. In the most common parlance, the word cyberspace means anything associated with Internet, computers, information technology, the internet, and associated matters (Rattan, 2017). It can be depicted as a village, electronically connected, where information can be shared instantly through electronic media. According to Webster's Dictionary, Cyberspace is the system of interconnected networks of computers that act as an endless environment facilitating access to data, information, interactive communication, and, in science fiction, a form of virtual reality (Malik, 2023).

The word cybercrime is frequently used in the present day to denote any crime which is committed using technology, computer, or data system. It is a combination of the two words Cyber & Crime. The word cyber means anything which is related to cyber space & crime is any wrongful act committed in contradiction of the criminal law of the land. Thus etymologically, the word cybercrime means any crime committed using cyber space, perpetuated using information technology. Hence characteristically there is hardly any difference between a crime of the traditional nature and cybercrime. However, there is no statutory definition of the term cybercrime in the Indian Statutes. Even after the amendment of the Indian Penal Code, 1860 by the Information Technology (Amendment) Act, 2008, there is no definition of cybercrimes in the Indian Penal Code, 1860. The Information Technology Act, 2000 which is the prime legislation on cyber law in India also does not contain the definition of Cybercrimes.

Cybercrime is considered as any unlawful activity carried out using a computing or communication device or any other internet-connected electronic device. Cybercrime can be committed by single individuals or small groups of persons having minimum technical expertise or even by highly organized international criminal organizations with relatively brilliant developers and specialists.

Most cybercrimes are committed by experts who are commonly known as hackers. Hackers are categorized into black hats, white hats, and grey hats. Black hats and in some cases, grey hats hackers are considered cybercriminals. Apart from the intention to make money, these hackers also work with an intention to damage the networks or to steal vital information. Cybercrime is a problem that is affecting both individuals and businesses. Cybercriminals uses networks, communication, or computing devices to deliver malware, viruses, pornographic content, harmful files and illegal data.

It is frequently observed that Cybercriminals are using a variety of profit-driven criminal activities to get money, including stealing, and selling identities, getting access to financial details, and using credit cards fraudulently for making financial transactions.

2.1 Common Type of Cyber Crimes

This section discusses some cybercrimes, that are common and frequently hard in our society.

Stolen credit card information:

The most frequent type of cybercrime involves the theft of a person's credit card information, which is then fraudulently used to obtain or pay for goods or services on the internet.

Intrusion into a Government website:

Modifying confidential government data is a different kind of criminality.

Theft of user accounts:

In one such case, between 2013 and 2016, Yahoo suffered a significant data breach that led to the theft of three billion user accounts. The attackers were successful in extracting passwords and other confidential data required to log into user accounts for various online services. Even today, the dark web still has access to most of this data.

Compromised IoT devices:

In 2016, hackers who took advantage of software flaws were able to infect more than one million linked IoT devices. The global DNS experienced failures because of this DDoS attack, which affected numerous well-known services including Twitter, PayPal, Netflix and few more. It is the greatest DDoS attack to date.

Loss of control and access to content:

Ransomware that encrypted user content was released during the WannaCry attack in 2017, which was purportedly carried out by North Korea. 300,000 machines were infected globally as this ransomware quickly spread. The cost of recovering the victims' data ran into the hundreds.

Phishing operations:

Phishing technique penetrates to enter corporate networks by sending users in an organization email that impersonate legitimate communications and persuade them to take actions like downloading attachments or clicking on links. Once on the systems, the viruses or malware propagate until they reach the networks of the organizations.

Other frequent examples of cybercrimes include soliciting, producing, distributing, or possessing child pornography, as well as the selling of illegal products like drugs, weapons, or counterfeit goods.

2.2 Classification of Cyber Crimes

Cybercrimes are broadly categorized into three different fields, Individual, Property, and Government.

Individual is the type of cybercrime where a single person uses the internet to spread harmful or illegal content. The harmful information may include information on human trafficking, pornography, online stalking and so on.

Property types of cybercrime involves getting hold of someone's bank account or credit card details. Using this information for accessing money, doing online transactions, or even using phishing to trick people with compromised personal information.

Government type, despite being rare are the cybercrimes are nevertheless regarded as serious offence and this includes hacking into government databases or official websites and playing with the data.

2.3 Various Types of Cybercrimes

Hacking or unauthorized access to a computer system: Criminal prosecution for hacking or unauthorized access to a computer system is a common legal solution. The punishment for this crime may include imprisonment, fines, or both.

Cyberbullying or online harassment: Civil lawsuits, restraining orders, or charges of stalking, harassment, or making threats may be used as legal remedies for cyberbullying or online harassment.

Identity theft: Legal solutions for identity theft may include civil lawsuits for damages or criminal charges for fraud or theft.

Phishing scams: Legal solutions for phishing scams can include civil lawsuits for damages or criminal charges for fraud or theft.

Distribution of malware or viruses: Legal solutions for the distribution of malware or viruses may include criminal charges for damage to computer systems, theft of data, or invasion of privacy.

Cyber espionage: Legal solutions for cyber espionage may include criminal charges for theft of trade secrets or espionage.

2.4 Various Forms of Cybercrime

There are many kinds of cybercrimes; the most frequently occurring crimes include social media fraud, clickjacking, email fraud, spyware, banking fraud, ransomware attacks, cyber espionage, and identity theft. We have briefly discussed some of such crimes in the following paragraphs.

Malware: Trojans, viruses, and worms are examples of the diverse types of cyberattacks that can be categorized as "malware." Malware is simply computer program aims to steal data or harm the computer components.

Viruses: A virus is a file attached with some clean files and it infect the other available files. Viruses have the property to spread uncontrollably and continue damaging the functionality and file systems of a computer. Commonly, viruses are injected through executable files downloaded from the Internet.

Trojan: This kind of malware poses as trustworthy software. Once penetrated, it operates covertly and allows more viruses to get into the system. Trojans are also responsible for breach of administrative privileges of a computer.

Worms: Worms use the network's interface to infect a large network of devices locally or remotely. Worms have a tendency to penetrate into a greater number of devices and subsequently infect them.

Phishing: Phishing has intentions to capture personal information stored in digital platforms. Users unknowingly shares their personal information through the link in phishing emails.

It was observed that many times consumers may not be able to classify between a legitimate and fraudulent request that intends to capture information, due to the complexity of phishing emails. Spam emails and phishing emails are sometimes combined; however, spam emails are much more harmful than straightforward advertisements.

Usually, five step process is followed to execute phishing. These steps include ***Preparation*** (where the phisher decide about the target and generate methods for obtaining emails), ***Setup*** (in this stage, the phisher creates and distribute the attack), ***Executing the attack*** (this step may include injecting the attack, anonymizing it so as it looks to be from an authentic source), ***Recoding data*** (tracks information that victims inserts through websites or pop-up windows, and is recorded by the phisher), ***Identity theft and fraud*** (the final step where the phisher uses the data gathered to conduct illegal transactions or commit other types of fraud).

Attack by DDoS: A denial-of-service (DoS) attack is carried out to disrupt or damage network service. Usually, the attackers flood the network with data traffic, causing the network to become overwhelmed and malfunction.

Man-in-the-middle Attack: By pretending to be the endpoints in the online information exchange, a man-in-the-middle attack can receive data from the end-user and the entity they are speaking with. To exemplify, this kind of attack, one can consider the situation while online money transaction, the intruder will place as an agent or will remain hidden and would communicate with the user as bank. During this process, this intruder would collect sensitive financial as well as personal information and going to use that information for unlawful activities.

Drive-by Download Attack: Through this technique, one no longer need to click to accept a download or apply a software update to get infected. Viewing or browsing a compromised webpage could result in the installation of harmful code on the device and the device including the data stored is no longer secure or stable. This technique often take advantage of exploiting vulnerable operating system, app, or browser of the victim's device.

Cybersecurity knowledge can be used to reduce cybercrime. Adopting strict legislation is another strategy for reducing crime. This chapter develops the possibility of legislation and legal issues related to cybercrimes.

3. CYBER LAWS ACROSS THE GLOBE

The growing limbs of technology has grasped the entire world within its ambit. Mankind can hardly imagine their life without the assistance of computers and allied technologies. Despite of the vices of its usage, we use it to meet all our needs, giving no heed to the huge losses which it can commit. Economic cybercrimes are the most dangerous as it affects not only individuals but also the business houses that makes use of technologies to expand their market not only within the country but in multiple countries. In the recent phase, it is seen that the world has become a global village, where all of us are connected through the fine lines of information, and hence trans-boundary communications in the field of business, education, social interaction has become very common. People with malice intent take advantage of the situation and commits crimes without regard to the country boundaries. It has thus become essential that cyber laws should be framed in a way where national boundary should not be a hindrance for registering the crimes and getting hold of the criminals.

Let us discuss here, what are the existing legislative and judicial response to cybercrimes in India, USA & UK.

3.1 Legislative and Judicial Response to Cybercrimes in United States of America (USA)

The United States of America was one of the first countries to have developed the legal defense against cybercrimes. At the very onset, it also became a victim to the cyber slaughtering, but very brilliantly it gave a befitting reply to the growing threat of cybercrimes with various statutes, legislations, policy framing and strategic legal management of the cyber users by making them fully aware (Brackman, 2010). The United States Department of Justice defines cybercrimes as any violations of criminal law that invokes knowledge of cyber technology for their occurrence, investigation, or prosecution (Computer Crime Law & Legal Definition, n.d.), (McEwen, 1995).

The US codes contain several legislations to combat cybercrimes. The primary legislation being Computer Fraud & Abuse Act, 1984 which mainly punishes unauthorized uses of computers and violation of the data contained therein (McEwen, 1995). This Act also restricts the uses of a computer in interstate commerce to "transmit a program or command which damages a computer system or network", or interrupts the use of a cyber system, "trafficking" in passwords to United States of America's Government computers; and the use of interstate commerce to transmit passwords with the intent to defraud (Elliott, 1999).The cyber criminals are punished in the same manner as other criminals by the federal courts following the USSG i.e. United States Sentencing Guidelines.

In the year 2004, the Fourth Plenary Session of the Organization of American States General Assembly passed the "Adoption of a Comprehensive Inter-American Strategy to Combat Threats to Cyber security: A multidimensional and Multidisciplinary Approach to Creating a Culture of Cyber security" to sought a profound cyber security strategy that ensures the protection of the network of information systems comprising of the Internet, government and industry (Thomas, 2007).

Along with the legislation, the Judiciary also plays a very effective role in combatting cybercrimes. Each of the federal states of the US are free to frame their own criminal laws for restricting the cybercrimes at state levels, but within the four corners of the federal law.

In *United States v. Morris*, the Circuit Court held that s. 1030 (a) (5)(A) of the Computer Fraud & Abuse Act, 1984 does not require the Government to particularly state that the defendant intentionally prevented authorized use and thereby caused damages (United States Vs Morris, 1991).

In another case of *Regan Gerard Gilmour v. Director of Public Prosecutions* (Regan Gerard Gilmour v. Director of Public Prosecutions, 1995), the Court held that a person commits an offence under section 76C of the Crimes Act, 1914 if he dearth the authority to insert the information into a computer, notwithstanding that he has general authority to insert other information into such computer (Regan Gerard Gilmour v. Director of Public Prosecutions, 1995). The Court further held that any entry made purposefully without lawful excuse and known to be false is made without lawful authority.

3.2 Legislative and Judicial Response to Cybercrimes in United Kingdom (UK)

The growing age of cybercrime did not spare the United Kingdom as well, and the strokes hit high at UK, when it started framing its legislative response to combat such online infractions. The development of cyber law in the UK occurred in two phases. In the initial stages, the regular criminal law was applied to online crimes as well. But the result was not very satisfactory. It paved the way for the second stage where dedicated law was passed to sufficiently deal with cybercrimes. The Computer Misuse Act, 1990 is the prime legislation for combating cybercrimes in the UK National Crime Agency, 2023).

The UK has been a breeding ground for online crimes and the graph went on increasing, which required a constant monitoring and upgradation of law. The Data Protection Act, 1998 was passed for the purpose of protecting data stored in the computer system. The United Kingdom Audit Commission Report portrayed an abnormal increase from a total of 77 incidents of computer crime in 1984 to a total of 510 such incidents in 1998 (Furnel, 2003).

Despite having huge legislations, the curve of cybercrimes in the United Kingdom is always high and the judiciary plays a very active role in combating the crimes. At times even the courts are at loss because jurisdictional question poses the court to step back, even in cases of grave cybercrimes. Vide report of The National Crime Agency (NCA) released on July 7, 2016, the need for stronger law enforcement and business partnership to fight cybercrime was enumerated. According to the NCA cybercrime consists of the largest chunk of total crime in the U.K. with "cyber enabled fraud" consisting of 36% of all crime reported and computer misuse accounting for 17% (National Crime Agency, 2023).

There has been a plethora of judgements where the English Courts have strictly applied the law to create a check on the growing cybercrimes. In a landmark judgement of R *vs Bow Street Magazine,* the accused made unauthorized access to the American Express Computer System with malafide intentions and modified its content. The accused was made liable for the same (R vs Bow Street Magazine, 1994).

3.3 Legislative and Judicial Response to Cybercrimes in INDIA

India being one of the largest countries of the world with huge population, the threat of the country to the growing arena of cybercrime is also equally huge. The Indian legislation and the judiciary have always worked hand on hand to combat all forms of threats and cybercrime is no exception. While the legislation has come up with a wide range of provisions for checking crimes, the judiciary has successfully implemented those law. The primary legislation in India dealing with cybercrimes is Information Technology Act, 2000.

When there has been a huge transformation from the paper-based commerce to E Commerce, the UN General Assembly adopted the United Nations Commission on International Trade Law (UNCITRAL) to successfully regulate commercial relations across the globe. The Indian legislation on Information Technology was formulated on the same spirit to give effect to the UN resolution. The Act further amends the Indian Penal Code, 1860, the Indian Evidence Act, 1872, the Bankers Books Evidence Act, 1891 and the Reserve Bank of India Act,1934.

Even after more than a decade of passing of the law, its practical implication has remained a distant dream since the law enforcing agencies fail to understand its technical terminology. Moreover, the law is more fitted for combating economic cyber frauds but not very efficient in dealing with other forms of cybercrimes like data theft, cyber pornography, cybersquatting, etc.

3.4 An Overview of Statistics on Cybercrime in India

This and the next subsection present a brief overview on the data available related to cybercrime that took place in a specific time frame. The following facts on cybercrime in India are taken from the National Crime Records Bureau's (NCRB) "Crime in India" report for 2019:

India recorded 44,546 cybercrime cases in total in 2019, a 63.5% rise from the previous year. [1] Cheating/fraud accounted for 50.4% of cybercrime cases, with sexual exploitation coming in at 7.5% and bringing bad reputation on the Internet at 4.8%. The most cases of reported cybercrime (18.5%) involved "Computer-related offences," which were followed by "cyber harassment" (16.3%) and "identity theft" (13.1%).

The state with the most reported instances of cybercrime in India was Maharashtra (9,081), followed by Uttar Pradesh (6,677) and Karnataka (4,770). It is worth noting that these statistics are based only on reported cases, and the actual number of cybercrimes may be higher since not all incidents are reported to the authorities. Additionally, the NCRB's report for 2020 has not been released yet, so the most recent statistics available are from 2019.

3.5 An Overview of Statistics on Cybercrime in Abroad

The COVID-19 pandemic's start was followed by a 20% spike in cybercrime events, according to a 2020 study from the European Union Agency for Cybersecurity (ENISA, 2020).

61% of adults in Europe experienced cybercrime in the previous 12 months, according to the 2021 Norton Cyber Safety Insights Report. Phishing, malware assaults, and ransomware attacks are the three types of cybercrime that are most frequently reported in Europe.

Cybercrime has a substantial financial impact on European enterprises; estimates place the annual cost at over €600 billion. According to the European Cybercrime Centre (EC3), small and medium-sized businesses are the most frequent targets of cybercrime in Europe, followed by major corporations. The United Kingdom, Germany, France, and Spain have the highest rates of cybercrime in Europe. Now it is a global issue, and many of the assaults on persons and businesses in Europe come from non-European nations.

4. APPLICATION OF CYBER LAWS INTEGRATED WITH IT OVER INTERNET BASED PLATFORM: COMBINING SOCIAL MEDIA ANALYTICS AND CROWDSOURCING FOR CYBERCRIME DETECTION

Through this section, the authors have discussed issues of cybercrimes based on crowdsourcing and social media activities. Crowdsourcing is a technique of gathering data or information from a crowd mainly through digital platforms like the Internet. Social media analytics works like crowdsourcing. The gathered information can be used for a number of applications like understanding customer behavior, crowd movement patterns, policy framing, advertisement, opinion imposing and even in politics. Since the platform consists of details of many users (crowd), the data becomes highly vulnerable (Raykar, 2011).

Depending on the individual laws and regulations in each nation, there are several legal solutions for various sorts of cybercrime. The legal solutions for cybercrime depend on the nature and severity of the crime, as well as the specific laws and regulations in each jurisdiction. It is important to consult with a legal professional to understand the specific legal solutions available in the corresponding situation.

As there is huge distinction between the number of reported cases and unreported cases in identifying several cybercrimes happening around the world. On the other hand, although the number of training data for analyzing the various typical patterns for cybercrime is not so easy. Hence, providing different legal solutions pertaining to the various types of cybercrime is highly needed. Moreover, there is a requirement to identify some new legal challenges based on some unobserved cybercrime cases. A potential solution to identify the various crime problems and providing in the fight against cybercrime is using social media analytics and crowdsourcing. The following are some ways that social media analytics/ crowdsourcing can aid in combating cybercrime, and it can be helpful for the organization to keep more secure. Here, there are a few important techniques (Awal, 2014).

Crowdsourcing and artificial intelligence (AI) can be used together to judge different cybercrimes reported on different social media platforms in a more efficient and effective way. Some ways that can be helpful for understanding the various cybercrime and many challenges are through following stages.

Cybercrime reporting and monitoring: Cybercrime reporting and monitoring can be aided by crowdsourcing. By creating online reporting platforms or apps, people can report incidents of cybercrime they have witnessed or experienced (Whitehill, 2009).

Data Collection: Crowdsourcing platforms can be used to collect reports of cybercrime from different social media platforms. These reports can be analyzed using natural language processing (NLP) algorithms to identify key information such as the type of crime, the identity of the victim and perpetrator, and the context in which the crime occurred.

Filtering and Classification: AI algorithms can be used to filter and classify the reported incidents based on predefined criteria such as the severity of the crime, the credibility of the report, and the impact it had on the victim. This can help prioritize which reports require immediate attention.

Evaluation: Based on predetermined criteria, the crowdsourcing platform can subsequently be utilized to assess the reported instances. The volunteers might be asked, for instance, to assess the veracity of the report, the seriousness of the incident, and the effect it had on the victim. This can make it easier to decide which reports need to be addressed right away. The volunteers can provide additional context, analyze the evidence, and provide their judgment on the credibility and severity of the reported incidents.

Ranking: The crowdsourcing platform can be used to rank the reported incidents according to their seriousness and urgency after they have been assessed. This can help law enforcement agencies and other relevant authorities to prioritize their responses and allocate their resources accordingly.

Feedback: AI algorithms can be used to provide feedback to the volunteers who participated in the evaluation process. This can help improve the accuracy and reliability of the evaluations over time and ensure that the platform is being used effectively.

Overall, combining crowdsourcing and artificial intelligence can provide a more efficient and effective way of judging different cybercrimes reported on social media platforms. By leveraging the power of AI to filter and classify the reported incidents, and the collective intelligence of a large group of volunteers to evaluate and rank them, we can improve our response to cybercrime and prevent further harm to victims.

4.1 Various Judgment Analysis Methods for Performing Aggregation From Various Crowd Opinions

To get decisions from many crowds, a variety of judgement analysis methods can be applied (Kouloumpis, 2021).

The often-employed algorithms include:

Majority Voting: This algorithm is straightforward, and it bases its choice on which option received the greatest support from the crowd. It is applied in circumstances where there are just two choices available.

Kemeny-Young Method: This method takes into account all feasible options' orderings and chooses the one that comes the closest to the voters' individual ranks.

Weighted voting: This method gives various voters varied weights based on their qualifications or reputation. The decision is subsequently made using the total weights assigned to each vote.

Borda Count: This method rates each choice according to the number of votes it receives, and the choice is chosen based on the combined score of all choices.

Condorcet's Method: This algorithm takes pairwise comparisons of all the alternatives into account and chooses the option that receives the most favourable pairwise comparisons.

Copeland's Method: This algorithm considers the number of times each option wins in pairwise comparisons with other options, and the decision is made based on the option with the highest number of wins.

These algorithms can be used in a variety of industries, including market research, sports, politics, and economics, among others. The algorithm selected will depend on the particular needs of the circumstance and the decision-makers' preferences.

4.2 Impact of Social Media Analytics for Accounting Cybercrimes

We can use a variety of methods and methodologies to determine the sentiment analysis of various social posts on various social crimes on social media (Awal 2014).

The stages that one can follow to list the social crimes, can be elaborated in the following paragraphs.

Choose the Best Social Media Platforms: Choose the social media channels that are most pertinent to the social crime you want to study. For instance, if anyone wants to concentrate on websites like Twitter, Facebook, and Instagram if we want to examine attitudes towards hate crimes.

Gather Social Media Posts: Get social media postings that are pertinent to the social crime you wish to examine using data scraping technologies. We can filter the posts you gather using hashtags and phrases associated with social crime.

Data Preprocessing: prepare the gathered data based on some techniques. We can also use natural language processing (NLP) techniques to remove stop words, punctuation, and other noise from the text.

Conduct Sentiment Analysis: Examine the posts' sentiment using tools for sentiment analysis like TextBlob, VADER, or IBM Watson. These tools can assist in determining if the posts are favorable, unfavorable, or neutral.

Thus, through social media analytics, relevant collected data can be used to derive valuable and behavioral insights about the happenings of cybercrimes, that might have not been promptly reported so far. Analysis on obtained data will provide information on various type of cybercrimes, change and pattern in occurrence of cybercrime and most importantly how best legal process can be used for decision-making towards prevention of crime as well as providing justice to the victims Hovy, 2013), (Kouloumpis, 2021).

5. TRANS BOUNDARY OR TRANSNATIONAL CYBERCRIMES

With the advancement of time and technology, leading to implementation of high-speed data connectivity and communication (including Internet), IT and its services are no longer confined to a single place rather is spread across the Globe. Cybercrimes are not exceptional and in multiple case cybercrimes are found as trans boundary crime or transnational crimes. Since the chapter is specifically focusing on cybercrimes, let's mention these terms as Trans boundary Cybercrime or Transnational Cybercrimes With the word Trans, these cybercrimes are across the multiple nations, beyond the international boundary (Buchan, 2016). Assuming an example related to cybercrime, where a hacker belongs to country 'X', has hacked a bank account of a person who seems to be citizen of Country 'Y', and the bank is in the country 'Z'. The broad scenarios of transnational cybercrimes include:

1.   Cybercrimes where more than one country is involved,
2.   Cybercrimes planned in one country but committed in another,
3.   Cybercrimes committed in one country by groups operating in many countries,
4.   Cybercrimes committed in one country that have effects on other countries.

Extradition treaties comes into effect while handling the operatives involved in trans boundary cybercrimes or transnational cybercrimes. Extradition treaties are formal process of understanding between two countries, where each country will legally cooperate the prosecution or punishment for cybercrimes committed in the requesting country's jurisdiction.

5.1 Two Early Successful Cases of Handling Trans Boundary Cybercrimes

Believed to be one of the first cybercrime cases, it was a case of bank robbery through Internet (FBI (USA) Case File, 2014). During July 1994, a group of enterprising cybercriminals located in multiple continents, led by a young computer programmer Levin staying in St. Petersburg, Russia, hacked into the electronic systems of a major U.S. bank and secretly started stealing money. In March 1995, he was lured to London, where he was arrested and later extradited back to the United States. He pled guilty in January 1998.

Operation Shrouded Horizon (FBI (USA) Case File, 2015) successfully carried out by FBI (the Federal Bureau of Investigation is the domestic intelligence and security service of the United States), during July 2015, is a one of the famous examples of effective way to combat cybercrime with law enforcement response transcending national borders. This operation was one of the largest-ever coordinated law enforcement efforts directed towards cyber criminals. FBI shut down a major resource for cyber criminals, law enforcement infiltrated a closed criminal forum to obtain the intelligence and evidence needed to identify and prosecute these cybercriminals. During the operation, FBI member tracked those cybercriminals responsible for developing, distributing, facilitating, and supporting complex cybercriminal schemes targeting victims and financial systems around the world. The complex scheme includes buying, selling, and trading malware, botnets, stolen personally identifiable information, credit card information, hacked server credentials, and other pieces of data and software that facilitated complex cybercrimes. Hundreds of cybercriminal members were arrested in 20 countries across the globe for bringing them under Justice.

6. CONCLUSION

This chapter has discussed terms, issues, and cases related to cybercrime, cybersecurity, and related laws with respect to the current and future contexts. The intention is to enlighten the reader on basic terminologies and functioning of online platforms to create basic awareness among users so as they can avoid themselves being the victim of cybercrimes. Cyber law of three countries (USA, UK and India) situated in three different continents has been discussed. This part opens further studies on comparative analysis of existing Laws on IT and Cybercrime used by three culturally heterogeneous countries. The reason for focusing on India, the US, and the UK, is that there are many multinational organizations, including software and financial firms, that have offices and development units spread across these regions. Trans boundary or Transnational Cybercrimes and extradition treats has been discussed keeping this context. We have briefly discussed using social networks and crowdsourcing to find out cybercrimes that might have remained unaccountable. Two of the famous early cybercrime cases that were brought to justice have been included. This chapter opens the scope of further study on transboundary cybercrimes, the use of extradition treaties for handling cybercriminals, and cases studies on transboundary cybercrimes.

REFERENCES

Awal, G., & Bharadwaj, K. K. (2014). Team formation in social networks based on collective intelligence – an evolutionary approach. *Applied Intelligence, 41*(2), 627–648. doi:10.100710489-014-0528-y

Brackman, D. (2010). *2009 Annual Report on Cyber Crime.* FBI.

Buchan, R. (2016). Cyberspace, Non-State Actors and the Obligation to Prevent Transboundary Harm. *Journal of Conflict and Security Law, 21*(3), 429–453. doi:10.1093/jcsl/krw011

Case Reference: Regan Gerard Gilmour v. Director of Public Prosecutions, Commonwealth No. 60488 (1995).

Chauhan, S. (2017). *Cyber crimes National and International Perspective.* HDL. http://hdl.handle. net/10603/188293

Cyber-crime during the COVID-19 Pandemic - f3magazine.unicri.it. (2021, December 23). F3 Magazine. f3magazine.unicri.it. https://f3magazine.unicri.it/?p=2085

Cyber Criminal Forum Taken Down. (2017, January 12). Federal Bureau of Investigation. https://www. fbi.gov/news/stories/cyber-criminal-forum-taken-down

Edward, G. (2020, March 26), Google Registers a 350% Increase in Phishing Websites Amid Quarantine. atlasvpn.com. https://atlasvpn.com/blog/google-registers-a-350-increase-in-phishing-websites-amid-quarantine)

Elliott, T. L. (1999). *International Responses to Cyber Crime, University of Petroleum and Energy Studies Review,* 39-40. Hoover. https://www.hoover.org/sites/default/files/uploads/documents/0817999825_35. pdf)

ENISA Threat Landscape 2020: Cyber Attacks Becoming More Sophisticated, Targeted, Widespread and Undetected. (n.d.). ENISA. https://www.enisa.europa.eu/news/enisa-news/enisa-threat-landscape-2020

FBI (USA) Case File. (2014). *Major cyber crime cases over the years: A Byte Out of History.* FBI. https://www.fbi.gov/news/stories/a-byte-out-of-history-10-million-hack)

Furnell, S. (2003). Cybercrime: Vandalizing the Information Society. In Springer eBooks (pp. 8–16). doi:10.1007/3-540-45068-8_2

Hovy, D., Berg-Kirkpatrick, T., Vaswani, A., & Hovy, E. (2013). Learning Whom to Trust with MACE. In *North American Chapter of the Association for Computational Linguistics* (pp. 1120–1130). https://www.aclweb.org/anthology/N13-1132.pdf

Huang, W., & Wang, S. K. (2011). THE EVOLUTIONAL VIEW OF THE TYPES OF IDENTITY THEFTS AND ONLINE FRAUDS IN THE ERA OF THE INTERNET. *Internet Journal of Criminology.* https://www.internetjournalofcriminology.com/Wang_Huang_The_Evolutional_View_of_the_Types_of_Identity_Thefts_and_Online_Frauds_in_the_Era_of_Internet_IJC_Oct_2011.pdf

Kouloumpis, E., Wilson, T., & Moore, J. D. (2011). Twitter Sentiment Analysis: The Good the Bad and the OMG! *Proceedings of the International AAAI Conference on Web and Social Media, 5*(1), 538–541. 10.1609/icwsm.v5i1.14185

Malik, D. K. (2023). Information Technology & Cyber Law. Allahabad Law Agency (SKU: 978-93-95759-22-9), India.

McEwen, J. T. (1995). *Dedicated computer crime units.* DIANE Publishing.

National Crime Agency (Government of UK). (n.d.). *Cyber Crime Assessment.* National Crime Agency. https://www.nationalcrimeagency.gov.uk/publications/709-cyber-crime-assessment-2016/file)

Rattan, D. J. (2017). *Cyber Laws & Information Technology.* Bharat Law House, India.

Raykar, V. C., & Yu, S. (2012). Eliminating spammers and ranking annotators for crowdsourced labeling tasks. *Journal of Machine Learning Research, 13*(1), 491–518. doi:10.5555/2188385.2188401

United States Vs Morris, (1991) 504 F 2d (1991). https://ncrb.gov.in/sites/default/files/CII%202019%20SNAPSHOTS%20STATES.pdf)

R. vs Bow Street Magazine, (1994) 4 All ER 1 (1994).

Thomas, J. M. (2007). The Computer Fraud and Abuse Act: A Powerful Weapon vs. Unfair Competitors and Disgruntled Employees. *Employment Law Magazine.* https://www.williamskastner.com/uploaded-Files/ThomasIDQ200703.pdf)

Whitehill, J., Wu, T., Bergsma, J., Movellan, J. R., & Ruvolo, P. (2009). Whose Vote Should Count More: Optimal Integration of Labels from Labelers of Unknown Expertise. *Neural Information Processing Systems, 22,* 2035–2043. https://papers.nips.cc/paper/3644-whose-vote-should-count-more-optimal-integration-of-labels-from-labelers-of-unknown-expertise.pdf

Compilation of References

A., Azaustre, C., AzizNgoueya, Banerjee, A., Bansal, A., Barkoutsos, P., Barnawal, A., Barron, G., Barron, G. S., Bello, L., Ben-Haim, Y., Bevenius, D., Bhobe, A., Bishop, L. S., Blank, C., Bolos, S., & Bosch, S. (2019). *Qiskit: An opensource framework for quantum computing*. Academic Press.

AACAP. (2018). *What is a Psychiatric Emergency?* American Academy of Child and Adolescent Psychiatry. Available at: https://www.aacap.org/AACAP/Families_ and_ Youth/Facts_ for_ Families/FFFGuide/What_is_a_Psychiatric_Emergency_126.aspx

Abad, C. (2005). The economy of phishing.

Abbas, M. (2021a). *The Human Elements in Artificial Intelligence, Robotics, and Cybersecurity*. CRC Press.

Abbas, M. (2021b). Cybersecurity in Smart and Intelligent Manufacturing Systemas. In M. Abbas (Ed.), *The Human Elements in Artificial Intelligence, Roboticas, and Cybersecurity* (pp. 149–160). CRC Press.

Abroshan, H., Devos, J., Poels, G., & Laermans, E. (2021). Phishing Happens Beyond Technology: The Effects of Human Behaviors and Demographics on Each Step of a *Phishing* Process. *IEEE Access : Practical Innovations, Open Solutions*, *9*, 44928–44949.

Adamson, G. (2023). Explaining technology we don't understand. *IEEE Transactions on Technology and Society*. doi:10.1109/TTS.2023.3240107

Adesso, G. (2023). Towards The Ultimate Brain: Exploring Scientific Discovery with ChatGPT AI. In: Authorea Preprints.

Agencies Need to Address Aging Legacy Systems. (n.d.). Retrieved from https://www.gao.gov/assets/gao-19-491.pdf

Ahmad, A., Waseem, M., Liang, P., Fehmideh, M., Shamima Aktar, M., & Mikkonen, T. (2023). *Towards Human-Bot Collaborative Software Architecting with ChatGPT*. arXiv:2302.14600. doi:10.1145/3593434.3593468

Ahmad, A., Maynard, S. B., Desouza, K. C., Kotsias, J., Whitty, M. T., & Baskerville, R. L. (2021). How can organizations develop situation awareness for incident response: A case study of management practice. *Computers & Security*, *101*, 102122. doi:10.1016/j.cose.2020.102122

Ahmad, I., Saddique, M., Pirzada, U., Zohaib, M., Ali, A., & Khan, M. (2018). A New Look at the TOR Anonymous Communication System. *Journal of Digital Information Management*, *16*(5), 223.

Ahn, C. (2023). Exploring ChatGPT for information of cardiopulmonary resuscitation. *Resuscitation*, *185*, 109729. doi:10.1016/j.resuscitation.2023.109729 PMID:36773836

Akers, R. L. (1973). *Deviant behavior: A social learning approach.* Academic Press.

Akers, R. L., Sellers, C. S., & Jennings, W. G. (2017). *Criminological theories: Introduction, evaluation & application* (7th ed.). Oxford University Press.

Akter, M. S., Shahriar, H., & Bhuiya, Z. A. (2023). Automated vulnerability detection in source code using quantum natural language processing. In *Communications in Computer and Information Science* (pp. 83–102). Springer Nature Singapore.

Al Mutawa, N., Baggili, I., & Marrington, A. (2012). Forensic analysis of social networking applications on mobile devices. *Digital Investigation, 9,* S24–S33. doi:10.1016/j.diin.2012.05.007

Alabdan, R. (2020). *Phishing* Attacks Survey: Types, Vectors, and Technical Approaches. *Future Internet, 12*(10), 1–39. doi:10.3390/fi12100168

Alami, H., Gagnon, M. P., Ahmed, M. A. A., Fortin, J. P., Alami, H., Gagnon, M. P., Ahmed, M. A. A., & Fortin, J. P. (2019). Digital health: Cybersecurity is a value creation lever, not only a source of expenditure. *Health Policy and Technology, 8*(4), 319–321. doi:10.1016/j.hlpt.2019.09.002

Alberts, C., & Dorofee, A. (2005). *Mission Assurance Analysis Protocol (MAAP): Assessing Risk in Complex Environments. CMU/SEI-2005-TN-032.* Carnegie Mellon University. doi:10.21236/ADA441906

Albladi, S. M., & Weir, G. R. S. (2018). User characteristics that influence judgment of social engineering attacks in social networks. *Human-centric Computing and Information Sciences, 8*(5), 1–24. doi:10.118613673-018-0128-7

Aldridge, J., & Askew, R. (2017). Delivery dilemmas: How drug cryptomarket users identify and seek to reduce their risk of detection by law enforcement. *The International Journal on Drug Policy, 41,* 101–109. doi:10.1016/j.drugpo.2016.10.010 PMID:28089207

Aleroud, A., & Zhou, L. (2017). Phishing environments, techniques, and countermeasures: A survey. *Computers & Security, 68,* 160–196.

Ali, N. (2022). Crimes Related to Cryptocurrency and Regulations to Combat Crypto Crimes. *Journal of Policy Research, 8*(3), 289–302.

Alleasy. (2018). *What is Phishing, Smishing and Vishing? Know the differences!* All Easy.

Almulla, S., Iraqi, Y., & Jones, A. (2013). Cloud forensics: A research perspective. *2013 9th International Conference on Innovations in Information Technology (IIT).*

Al-Rawi, A. (2018). Video games, terrorism, and ISIS's Jihad 3.0. *Terrorism and Political Violence, 30*(4), 740–760. doi:10.1080/09546553.2016.1207633

Al-Zarouni, M. (2006). *Mobile Handset Forensic Evidence: a challenge for Law Enforcement.* Academic Press.

Amin, M. M., Cambria, E., & Schuller, B. W. (2023). *Will Affective Computing Emerge from Foundation Models and General AI? A First Evaluation on ChatGPT.* arXiv:2303.03186. Retrieved March 01, 2023, from https://ui.adsabs.harvard.edu/abs/2023arXiv230303186A

Andrei Kucharavy, Maréchal, Wursch, Dolamic, Sabonnadiere, David, Mermoud, & Lenders. (2023). Fundamentals of Generative Large Language Modelsand Perspectives in Cyber-Defense. arXiv pre-print server.

Antona, M. (2019). Seven HCI Grand Challenges. *International Journal of Human-Computer Interaction, 35*(14), 1229–1269. doi:10.1080/10447318.2019.1619259

Apa, L., & Cerrudo, C. (2017). Hacking Robots Before Skynet. IOActive Inc.

Arachchilage, N. A. G., & Love, S. (2013). A game design framework for avoiding Phishing attacks. *Computers in Human Behavior, 29*(3), 706–714. doi:10.1016/j.chb.2012.12.018

Arora, N., & Kuriakose, D. (2019). Cybersecurity in healthcare: A review. *Journal of Healthcare Information Management, 33*(3), 139–146.

Auchard, E., & Cohen, T. (2017). *Criminals try message apps to evade dark web crackdown: report.* Retrieved March 12 from https://www.reuters.com/article/us-cyber-summit-apps-messaging/criminals-try-message-apps-to-evade-dark-web-crackdown-report-idUSKBN1CU2SS

Awal, G., & Bharadwaj, K. K. (2014). Team formation in social networks based on collective intelligence – an evolutionary approach. *Applied Intelligence, 41*(2), 627–648. doi:10.100710489-014-0528-y

Baidoo-Anu, D., & Ansah, L. O. (2023). *Education in the Era of Generative Artificial Intelligence (AI): Understanding the Potential Benefits of ChatGPT in Promoting Teaching and Learning.* Academic Press.

Bala, R., Gill, B., Smith, D., Wright, D., & Ji, K. (2021). *Magic Quadrant for Cloud Infrastructure and Platform Services.* Gartner Inc. https://www.gartner.com/doc/reprints?id=1-271SYZF2&ct=210802&st=sb

Baravalle, A., & Lee, S. W. (2018). Dark web markets: Turning the lights on AlphaBay. *Web Information Systems Engineering–WISE 2018: 19th International Conference,* Dubai, United Arab Emirates, November 12-15, 2018, *Proceedings, Part II,* 19.

Barletta, V. S., Caivano, D., Vincentiis, M. D., Magr'ı, A., & Piccinno, A. (2023). Quantum optimization for IoT security detection. In *Lecture Notes in Networks and Systems* (pp. 187–196). Springer International Publishing.

Barraclough, P. A., Fehringer, G., & Woodward, J. (2021). Intelligent cyber-Phishing detection for online. *Computers & Security, 104,* 1–17. doi:10.1016/j.cose.2020.102123

Becker, K., & Fitzpatrick, B. (2018). In search of shadows: investigating and prosecuting crime on the Dark Web. *Dep't of Just. J. Fed. L. & Prac., 66,* 41.

Belk, R. (2021). Ethical issues in service robotics and artificial intelligence. *Service Industries Journal, 41*(13-14), 860–876. doi:10.1080/02642069.2020.1727892

Benjamin, V., Zhang, B., Nunamaker, J. F. Jr, & Chen, H. (2016). Examining hacker participation length in cybercriminal internet-relay-chat communities. *Journal of Management Information Systems, 33*(2), 482–510. doi:10.1080/07421222.2016.1205918

Bergholm, V., Izaac, J., Schuld, M., Gogolin, C., Alam, M. S., Ahmed, S., Arrazola, J. M., Blank, C., Delgado, A., Jahangiri, S., McKiernan, K., Meyer, J. J., Niu, Z., Sza'va, A., & Killoran, N. (2020). PennyLane: Automatic differentiation of hybrid quantum-classical computations. arXiv: 1811.04968.

Biamonte, J., Wittek, P., Pancotti, N., Rebentrost, P., Wiebe, N., & Lloyd, S. (2017). Quantum machine learning. *Nature, 549*(7671), 195–202. doi:10.1038/nature23474 PMID:28905917

Birkinshaw, J., & Cohen, J. (2013). Make Time for Work that Matters. *Harvard Business Review.*

Bishop, M. (2009). *Standish Group CHAOS Report: Worst Project Failure Rate in a Decade.* Standish Group.

Bizzdesign. (2022). *Digital Transformation.* Bizzdesign. https://bizzdesign.com/blog-category/digital-transformation/

BlackBerry. (2020). *Zero Trust, the Future of Healthcare Keep Technology Secure Without Exhausting Resources.* White paper. BlackBerry. https://cybersecuritycollaboration.com/wp-content/uploads/2020/10/BlackBerry_Zero-Trust-the-Future-of-Healthcare_White-Paper-1.pdf

Blei, D. M. (2012). Probabilistic topic models. *Communications of the ACM, 55*(4), 77–84. doi:10.1145/2133806.2133826

Blei, D. M., Ng, A. Y., & Jordan, M. I. (2003). Latent Dirichlet Allocation. *Journal of Machine Learning Research, 3,* 993–1022.

Blomqvist, K. (1997). The many faces of trust. *Scandinavian Journal of Management, 13*(3), 271–286.

Brackman, D. (2010). *2009 Annual Report on Cyber Crime.* FBI.

Brasil. Decree-Law No. 2848, of December 7, 1940. (Criminal Code).

Brasil. Law No. 13,105, of March 16, 2015. (Code of Civil Procedure)

Breidbach, C. F., & Maglio, P. (2020). Accountable algorithms? The ethical implications of data-driven business models. *Journal of Service Management, 31*(2), 163–185. doi:10.1108/JOSM-03-2019-0073

Brewster, T. (2019). Discord: The $2 Billion Gamer's Paradise Coming To Terms With Data Thieves, Child Groomers And FBI Investigators. *Forbes.* https://www.forbes.com/sites/thomasbrewster/2019/01/29/discord-the-2-billion-gamers-paradise-coming-to-terms-with-data-thieves-child-groomers-and-fbi-investigators/?utm_source=TWITTER&utm_medium=social&utm_content=2108057929&utm_campaign=sprinklrForbesMainTwitter#442d2a903741

Brody, R. G., Mulig, E., & Kimball, V. (2007). PHISHING, PHARMING AND IDENTITY THEFT. Academy of Accounting & Financial Studies Journal, 11(3).

Brown, C. S. (2015). Investigating and prosecuting cyber crime: Forensic dependencies and barriers to justice. *International Journal of Cyber Criminology, 9*(1), 55.

Buchan, R. (2016). Cyberspace, Non-State Actors and the Obligation to Prevent Transboundary Harm. *Journal of Conflict and Security Law, 21*(3), 429–453. doi:10.1093/jcsl/krw011

Buckley, P., & Muggleton, S. (2019). A survey of healthcare cybersecurity incident response. *Journal of Healthcare Information Management, 33*(4), 168–173.

Budler, L. C., Gosak, L., & Stiglic, G. (2023). Review of artificial intelligence-based question-answering systems in healthcare. *WIREs Data Mining and Knowledge Discovery, 13*(2), e1487.

Burgess, R. L., & Akers, R. L. (1966). A differential association-reinforcement theory of criminal behavior. *Soc. Probs., 14*(2), 128–147. doi:10.2307/798612

Busey, T. A., Tunnicliff, J., Loftus, G. R., & Loftus, E. F. (2000). Accounts of the confidence-accuracy relation in recognition memory. *Psychonomic Bulletin & Review, 7*(1), 26–48. doi:10.3758/BF03210724

Butler, R. (2007). A framework of anti-phishing measures aimed at protecting the online consumer's identity. *The Electronic Library.*

Butler, R., & Butler, M. (2018). *Assessing the information quality of phishing-related content on financial institutions' websites.* Information & Computer Security.

Byres, E., & Lowe, J. (2004). The myths and facts behind cyber security risks for industrial control systems. *Proceedings of the VDE Kongress.*

Calo, R. M. (2011). Robots and privacy. In P. Bekey, G. Abney, & K. Lin (Eds.), *Robot Ethics: The Ethical and Social Implications of Robotics.* MIT Press.

Canfield, C. I., Fischhoff, B., & Davis, A. (2016). Quantifying Phishing Susceptibility for Detection and Behavior Decisions. *Human Factors, 58*(8), 1158–1172. doi:10.1177/0018720816665025

Capgemini. (2011). *Business transformation: From crisis response to radical changes that will create tomorrow's business.* A Capgemini Consulting Survey. Capgemini.

Case Reference: Regan Gerard Gilmour v. Director of Public Prosecutions, Commonwealth No. 60488 (1995).

Cavelty, M. D. (2013). From cyber-bombs to political fallout: Threat representations with an impact in the cybersecurity discourse. *International Studies Review, 15*(1), 105–122. doi:10.1111/misr.12023

Centro Nacional de Cibersegurança. (2022a). Relatório Cibersegurança em Portugal – Economia – maio de 2022. Avaliable at https://www.cncs.gov.pt/docs/relatorio-economia2022-obciber-cncs.pdf

Centro Nacional de Cibersegurança. (2022b). Relatório de Cibersegurança em Portugal: Riscos e Conflitos. Avaliable at https://www.cncs.gov.pt/docs/relatorio-riscosconflitos2022-obciber-cncs.pdf

Chaiken, S. (1987). The heuristic model of persuasion. *Hillsdale, NJ: Lawrence Erlbaum.* Symposium conducted at the meeting of the Social influence: the Ontario symposium. *5* (3-39).

Chaiken, S. (1980). Heuristic versus systematic information processing and the use of source versus message cues in persuasion. *Journal of Personality and Social Psychology, 39*(5), 752.

Chaione. (2022). *Digital Transformation-The 4 Types of Digital Transformation.* Chaione.com.

Chanchal Dey, S. K., & Sen, D. K. (2020): Industrial 4.0: Industrial internet of things (IIOT). *Indus. Autom. Technol.,* 269–310.

Charles. (2017). *Hosting and Cloud Software Delivery modelled in Archimate.* Agile Enterprise Architecture. https://agileea.com/2017/04/hosting-and-cloud-software-delivery-modelled-in-archimate/

Chatterjee, J., & Dethlefs, N. (2023). This new conversational AI model can be your friend, philosopher, and guide ... and even your worst enemy. *Patterns, 4*(1), 100676.

Chauhan, S. (2017). *Cyber crimes National and International Perspective.* HDL. http://hdl.handle.net/10603/188293

Cheng, X. Z. (n.d.). Exploring the metaverse in digital economy: An overview and research framework. *Journal of Electronic Business & Digital Economics.*

Cheng, Y., Deng, J., Li, J., DeLoach, S. A., Singhal, A., & Ou, X. (2014). Metrics of Security. In A. Kott, C. Wang, & R. Erbacher (Eds.), *Cyber Defense and Situational Awareness. Advances in Information Security* (Vol. 62). Springer.

Chen, L., Xu, L., Yuan, X., & Shashidhar, N. (2015). Digital forensics in social networks and the cloud: Process, approaches, methods, tools, and challenges. *2015 International Conference on Computing, Networking and Communications (ICNC)*.

Chen, R., Gaia, J., & Rao, H. R. (2020). An examination of the effect of recent Phishing encounters on *Phishing* susceptibility. *Decision Support Systems, 133*, 1–14. doi:10.1016/j.dss.2020.113287

Chen, S., & Chaiken, S. (1999). The heuristic-systematic model in its broader context. In S. Chaiken & Y. Trope (Eds.), *Dual-process Theories in Social and Cognitive Psychology* (pp. 73–96). Guilford.

Chen, W., & Wellman, B. (2004). The global digital divide–within and between countries. *ITandSociety, 1*(7), 39–45.

Chen, X. (2023). ChatGPT and Its Possible Impact on Library Reference Services. *Internet Reference Services Quarterly, 27*(2), 1–9. doi:10.1080/10875301.2023.2181262

Chen, Y., Jensen, S., Albert, L. J., Gupta, S., & Lee, T. (2023). Artificial intelligence (AI) student assistants in the classroom: Designing chatbots to support student success. *Information Systems Frontiers, 25*(1), 161–182. doi:10.100710796-022-10291-4

Chien-Chang Lin, A. Y. Q. H., & Stephen, J. H. (2023). A Review of AI-Driven Converstational Chatbots Implementation Methodologies and Challenges (1999-2022). *Sustainability, 15*(5), 4012. Advance online publication. doi:10.3390u15054012

Choi, J. H., Hickman, K. E., Monahan, A. B., & Schwarcz, D. (2023). *ChatGPT Goes to Law School.* doi:10.2139srn.4335905

Choo, K.-K. R., & Smith, R. G. (2008). Criminal exploitation of online systems by organised crime groups. *Asian Journal of Criminology, 3*(1), 37–59.

Clemente-Teixeira, M., Magalhães, T., Barrocas, J., Dinis-Oliveira, R. J., & Taveira-Gomes, T. (2022). Health Outcomes in Women Victims of Intimate Partner Violence: A 20-Year Real-World Study. *International Journal of Environmental Research and Public Health, 19*(24), 17035. doi:10.3390/ijerph192417035 PMID:36554916

CNCS - Centro Nacional de Cibersegurança. (2022). *Cybersecurity in Portugal. Relatório Sociedade 2022.* Centro Nacional de Cibersegurança. https://www.cncs.gov.pt/docs/rel-sociedade2022-observ-cncs15m.pdf

Cohen, L. E., & Felson, M. (1979). Social change and crime rate trends: A routine activity approach. *American Sociological Review*, ●●●, 588–608.

Coleman, J. W. (2005). *The criminal elite: Understanding white-collar crime.* Macmillan.

Company, M. A. (2023). *What is generative AI?* https://www.mckinsey.com/featured-insights/mckinsey-explainers/what-is-generative-ai

Cookson, R. (2005). Evidence-based policy making in health care: What it is and what it isn't. *Journal of Health Services Research & Policy, 10*(2), 118–121. doi:10.1258/1355819053559083 PMID:15831195

Cooper, T., & Fuchs, K. (2013). Technology risk assessment in healthcare facilities. *Biomedical Instrumentation & Technology*, *47*(3), 202–207. doi:10.2345/0899-8205-47.3.202 PMID:23692102

Costello, M., Hawdon, J., & Ratliff, T. N. (2017). Confronting online extremism: The effect of self-help, collective efficacy, and guardianship on being a target for hate speech. *Social Science Computer Review*, *35*(5), 587–605. doi:10.1177/0894439316666272

Court Of Justice Of São Paulo. Process 1009836-11.2021.8.26.0562, of the 1st Civil Court of the District of Santos, Judge Paulo Sergio Mangerona, judged on 10/14/2021. https://www.conjur.com.br/dl/dano-moral-bb.pdf.

Cranor, L. (2008). A framework for reasoning about the human in the loop. *Proceedings of the 1st Conference on Usability, Psychology, and Security (UPSEC'08)*, 1-15.

Curtis, P., & Carey, M. (2012). *Committee of Sponsoring Organizations of the Treadway Commission-Risk Assessment in Practice*. Deloitte & Touche LLP.

Cyber Criminal Forum Taken Down. (2017, January 12). Federal Bureau of Investigation. https://www.fbi.gov/news/stories/cyber-criminal-forum-taken-down

Cyber-crime during the COVID-19 Pandemic - f3magazine.unicri.it . (2021, December 23). F3 Magazine. f3magazine.unicri.it. https://f3magazine.unicri.it/?p=2085

D., L., Nagpal, N., Chandrasekaran, S., & D., J. H. (2023). A quantum-based approach for offensive security against cyber attacks in electrical infrastructure. *Applied Soft Computing*, *136*, 110071.

Daellenbach, H., McNickle, D., & Dye, Sh. (2012). *Management Science. Decision-making through systems thinking* (2nd ed.). Plagrave Macmillian.

Darwish, A., El Zarka, A., & Aloul, F. (2013). Towards understanding Phishing victims' profile. In *2012 International Conference on Computer Systems and Industrial Informatics* (pp. 1-5). IEEE.

Das, T. K., & Teng, B. S. (2004). The risk-based view of trust: A conceptual framework. *journal of Business and Psychology, 19*, 85-116.

Datavisor. (2021). Digital fraudtrends report 2021. *Datavisor*. https://www.datavisor.com/wp-content/uploads/2021/11/DataVisor-Digital-Fraud-Trends-Report-2021-2.pdf.

Dattathrani, S., & De', R. (2023). The Concept of Agency in the era of Artificial Intelligence: Dimensions and degrees. *Information Systems Frontiers*, *25*(1), 29–54. doi:10.100710796-022-10336-8

Décary-Hétu, D., & Aldridge, J. (2015). Sifting through the net: Monitoring of online offenders by researchers. *European Review of Organised Crime*, *2*(2), 122–141.

DeLisi, M., Vaughn, M. G., Gentile, D. A., Anderson, C. A., & Shook, J. J. (2013). Violent video games, delinquency, and youth violence: New evidence. *Youth Violence and Juvenile Justice*, *11*(2), 132–142. doi:10.1177/1541204012460874

Deora, R. S., & Chudasama, D. (2021). Brief study of cybercrime on an internet. *Journal of Communication Engineering & Systems*, *11*(1), 1–6.

Department of Health and Human Services. (2018). *Health Industry Cybersecurity Practices: Managing Threats and Protecting Patients*. Retrieved from https://www.phe.gov/Preparedness/planning/405d/Pages/hic-practices.aspx

Dhamija, R., & Tygar, J. D. (2005, July). The battle against phishing: Dynamic security skins. In *Proceedings of the 2005 symposium on Usable privacy and security* (pp. 77-88).

Dhamija, R., Tygar, J. D., & Hearst, M. (2006, April). Why Phishing works. In *Proceedings of the SIGCHI conference on Human Factors in computing systems* (pp. 581-590).

Dick, B. (2001). *Action research: action and research*. Southern Cross. University Press.

Diniz, M. H. (2009). Course of Brazilian civil law.: Vol. 7. *Civil Liability*. Saraiva.

Dowling, M., & Lucey, B. (2023). ChatGPT for (Finance) research: The Bananarama Conjecture. *Finance Research Letters*, *53*, 103662. doi:10.1016/j.frl.2023.103662

Downs, J. S., Holbrook, M. B., & Cranor, L. F. (2006). Decision strategies and susceptibility to Phishing. In *Proceedings of the second symposium on Usable privacy and security* (pp. 79-90).

Downs, J. S., Holbrook, M., & Cranor, L. F. (2007). Behavioral response to Phishing risk. In *Proceedings of the anti-Phishing working groups 2nd annual eCrime researchers summit* (pp. 37-44).

Duan, Y., Ong, V. K., Xu, M., & Mathews, B. (2012). Supporting decision making process with "ideal" software agents–What do business executives want? *Expert Systems with Applications*, *39*(5), 5534–5547. doi:10.1016/j.eswa.2011.11.065

Duggan, M. (2015). *Gaming and gamers*. https://www.pewinternet.org/2015/12/15/gaming-and-gamers/

Duong, D., & Solomon, B. D. (2023). *Analysis of large-language model versus human performance for genetics questions*. Cold Spring Harbor Laboratory. doi:10.1101/2023.01.27.23285115

Easterbrook, S., Singer, J., Storey, M., & Damian, D. (2008). *Guide to Advanced Empirical Software Engineering-Selecting Empirical Methods for Software Engineering Research* (F. Shull, Ed.). Springer.

Eddie, M., & Perlroth, N. (2020). Cyber Attack Suspected in German Woman's Death. *New York Times*. https://www.nytimes.com/2020/09/18/world/europe/cyber-attack-germany-ransomeware-death.html

Edward, G. (2020, March 26), Google Registers a 350% Increase in Phishing Websites Amid Quarantine. atlasvpn.com. https://atlasvpn.com/blog/google-registers-a-350-increase-in-phishing-websites-amid-quarantine)

Egelman, S., Cranor, L. F., & Hong, J. (2008, April). You've been warned: an empirical study of the effectiveness of web browser phishing warnings. *In Proceedings of the SIGCHI Conference on Human Factors in Computing Systems* (pp. 1065-1074).

Eira, A. (2022). *72 Vital Digital Transformation Statistics: 2023 Spending, Adoption, Analysis & Data*. FinancesOnline. https://financesonline.com/digital-transformation-statistics/

Elliott, T. L. (1999). *International Responses to Cyber Crime, University of Petroleum and Energy Studies Review*, 39-40. Hoover. https://www.hoover.org/sites/default/files/uploads/documents/0817999825_35.pdf)

Eloundou, T., Manning, S., Mishkin, P., & Rock, D. (2023). GPTs are GPTs: An Early Look at the Labor Market Impact Potential of Large Language Models. arXiv:2303.10130. Retrieved March 01, 2023, from https://ui.adsabs.harvard.edu/abs/2023arXiv230310130E

Else, H. (2023). Abstracts written by ChatGPT fool scientists. *Nature, 613*(7944), 423–423. doi:10.1038/d41586-023-00056-7 PMID:36635510

ENISA Threat Landscape 2020: Cyber Attacks Becoming More Sophisticated, Targeted, Widespread and Undetected. (n.d.). ENISA. https://www.enisa.europa.eu/news/enisa-news/enisa-threat-landscape-2020

European Commission (EC). (2020). *Digital Europe Programme 2021-2027 Fact Sheet.* https://ec.europa.eu/newsroom/dae/document.cfm?doc_id=67268

European Commission (EC). (2021). *The European Defence Fund Fact Sheet.* https://defence-industry-space.ec.europa.eu/system/files/2022-05/Factsheet%20-%20European%20Defence%20Fund.pdf

European Parliament (EP). (2013). *European Parliament resolution of 12 September 2013 on a Cybersecurity Strategy of the European Union: An Open, Safe and Secure Cyberspace (2013/2606(RSP)).* https://eur-lex.europa.eu/legal-content/EN/TXT/PDF/?uri=CELEX:52013IP0376&qid=1681210748084&from=EN

European Parliament, Council of the European Union (EPCEU). (2016). *Directive (EU) 2016/1148 of the European Parliament and of the Council of 6 July 2016 concerning measures for a high common level of security of network and information systems across the Union.* https://eur-lex.europa.eu/legal-content/EN/TXT/PDF/?uri=CELEX:32016L1148&from=EN

European Parliament, Council of the European Union (EPCEU). (2019). *Regulation (EU) 2019/881 of the European Parliament and of the Council of 17 April 2019 on ENISA (the European Union Agency for Cybersecurity) and on information and communications technology cybersecurity certification and repealing Regulation (EU) No 526/2013 (Cybersecurity Act).* https://eur-lex.europa.eu/legal-content/EN/TXT/PDF/?uri=CELEX:32019R0881&qid=1681208226017&from=EN

European Parliament, Council of the European Union (EPCEU). (2021). *Regulation (EU) 2021/887 of the European Parliament and of the Council of 20 May 2021 establishing the European Cybersecurity Industrial, Technology and Research Competence Centre and the Network of National Coordination Centres.* https://eur-lex.europa.eu/legal-content/EN/TXT/PDF/?uri=CELEX:32021R0887&qid=1681208461508&from=EN

European Parliament, Council of the European Union (EPCEU). (2022). *Directive (EU) 2022/2555 of the European Parliament and of the Council of 14 December 2022 on measures for a high common level of cybersecurity across the Union, amending Regulation (EU) No 910/2014 and Directive (EU) 2018/1972, and repealing Directive (EU) 2016/1148 (NIS 2 Directive).* https://eur-lex.europa.eu/legal-content/EN/TXT/PDF/?uri=CELEX:32022L2555&from=EN

European Union (EU). (2016). *Shared Vision, Common Action: A Stronger Europe, A Global Strategy for the European Union's Foreign And Security Policy.* https://www.eeas.europa.eu/sites/default/files/eugs_review_web_0.pdf

European Union (EU). (2018). *Towards a stronger EU on security and defence.* https://eeas.europa.eu/headquarters/headquarters-homepage/35285/eu-strengthens-cooperation-security-and-defence_en

European Union (EU). (2021). *Permanent Structured Cooperation (PESCO)'s projects – Overview.* https://www.consilium.europa.eu/media/53013/20211115-pesco-projects-with-description.pdf

European Union (EU). (2021a). *PESCO Projects Fact Sheet.* https://www.eeas.europa.eu/sites/default/files/pesco_projects_15nov_002.pdf

European Union (EU). (2023). *Permanent Structured Cooperation (PESCO) Official Site*. https://www.pesco.europa.eu/

European Union (EU). (2023). *The European Union Agency for Cybersecurity*. https://www.enisa.europa.eu/about-enisa

Faure, M., & Partain, R. (2019). Environmental crime. In Environmental Law and Economics: Theory and Practice (pp. 211-232). Cambridge University Press. doi:10.1017/9781108554916.011

FBI (USA) Case File. (2014). *Major cyber crime cases over the years: A Byte Out of History*. FBI. https://www.fbi.gov/news/stories/a-byte-out-of-history-10-million-hack)

Felten, E., Raj, M., & Seamans, R. (2023). How will Language Modelers like ChatGPT Affect Occupations and Industries? arXiv:2303.01157. Retrieved March 01, 2023, from https://ui.adsabs.harvard.edu/abs/2023arXiv230301157F

Ferguson, C. J. (2011). Video games and youth violence: A prospective analysis in adolescents. *Journal of Youth and Adolescence*, *40*(4), 377–391. doi:10.100710964-010-9610-x PMID:21161351

Ferreira, A., Muchagata, J., Vieira-Marques, P., Abrantes, D., & Teles, S. (2021). Perceptions of Security and Privacy in mHealth. *23rd HCI International Conference Proceedings*. 10.1007/978-3-030-77392-2_19

Flores, W. R., Holm, H., Nohlberg, M., & Ekstedt, M. (2015). Investigating personal determinants of Phishing and the effect of national culture. *Information & Computer Security*, *23*(2), 178–199.

Fotios, S., Uttley, J., Cheal, C., & Hara, N. (2015). Using eye-tracking to identify pedestrians' critical visual tasks, Part 1. Dual task approach. *Lighting Research & Technology*, *47*, 133–1.

Fowler, M. J., Lybert, K. A., Owens, J. N., & Waterfield, J. M. (2020). *Undercover Chatting with Child Sex Offenders*. Retrieved March 12 from https://leb.fbi.gov/articles/featured-articles/undercover-chatting-with-child-sex-offenders

Fruhlinger, J. (2017). What is Stuxnet, who created it and how does it work? Thanks to Stuxnet, we now live in a world where code can destroy machinery and stop (or start) a war. *CSO*. https://www.csoonline.com/article/3218104/what-is-stuxnetwho-created-it-and-how-does-it-work.html

Fu, Z., & Mittnight, E. (2015). *Critical Success Factors for Continually Monitoring, Evaluating and Assessing Management of Enterprise IT*. ISACA. https://www.isaca.org/COBIT/focus/Pages/critical-success-factors-for-continually-monitoring-evaluating-and-assessing-management-of-enterprise-it.aspx

Furnell, S. (2003). Cybercrime: Vandalizing the Information Society. In Springer eBooks (pp. 8–16). doi:10.1007/3-540-45068-8_2

Gaevskaja, E. J. (2016). On the issue of criminal law impact on environmental crime. *Bulletin of the Omsk Law Academy*, *3*(32), 40–45.

Gambetta, D. (2011). *Codes of the underworld: How criminals communicate*. Princeton University Press.

Gao, Y., Li, X., Li, J., Gao, Y., & Yu, P. S. (2019). Info-Trust: A Multi-Criteria and Adaptive Trustworthiness Calculation Mechanism for Information Sources. *IEEE Access : Practical Innovations, Open Solutions*, *7*, 13999–14012. doi:10.1109/ACCESS.2019.2893657

Gavett, B. E., Zhao, R., John, S. E., Bussell, C. A., Roberts, J. R., & Yue, C. (2017). Phishing suspiciousness in older and younger adults: The role of executive functioning. *PLoS One*, *12*(2), e0171620.

Ghappour, A. (2017). Searching places unknown: Law enforcement jurisdiction on the dark web. *Stanford Law Review*, *69*, 1075.

Ghazi-Tehrani, A. K., & Pontell, H. N. (2021). Phishing Evolves: Analyzing the Enduring Cybercrime. *Victims & Offenders*, *16*(3), 316–342. doi:10.1080/15564886.2020.1829224

Ghosal, S. (2023). ChatGPT on Characteristic Mode Analysis. TechRxiv. https://www.techrxiv.org/articles/preprint/ChatGPT_on_Characteristic_Mode_Analysis/21900342

Gilson, A., Safranek, C. W., Huang, T., Socrates, V., Chi, L., Taylor, R. A., & Chartash, D. (2023). How Does ChatGPT Perform on the United States Medical Licensing Examination? The Implications of Large Language Models for Medical Education and Knowledge Assessment. *JMIR Medical Education*, *9*, e45312. doi:10.2196/45312 PMID:36753318

Girasa, R. (2022). International regulation. In Regulation of Cryptocurrencies and Blockchain Technologies: National and International Perspectives (pp. 313-377). Springer.

Glaser, A. (2018). *White Supremacists Still Have a Safe Space Online*. Slate. Retrieved March 12 from https://slate.com/technology/2018/10/discord-safe-space-white-supremacists.html

Gold, S. (2013). Getting lost on the Internet: The problem with anonymity. *Network Security*, *2013*(6), 10–13. doi:10.1016/S1353-4858(13)70069-2

Gopavaram, S., Dev, J., Grobler, M., Kim, D., Das, S., & Camp, L. J. Cross-National Study on *Phishing* Resilience. *2021 Workshop on Usable Security and Privacy (USEC), 1-11.*

Graham, R., & Triplett, R. (2017). Capable guardians in the digital environment: The role of digital literacy in reducing phishing victimization. *Deviant Behavior*, *38*(12), 1371–1382.

Greefhorst, D. (2009). *Using the Open Group's Architecture Framework as a pragmatic approach to architecture. NIRIA. Jaarbeurs, Utrecht. KIVI NIRIA, afd.* Informatica.

Greenwood, R., Suddaby, R., & Hinings, C. R. (2002). Theorizing change: The role of professional associations in the transformation of institutionalized fields. *Academy of Management Journal*, *45*(1), 58–80. doi:10.2307/3069285

Greitemeyer, T., & Mügge, D. O. (2014). Video games do affect social outcomes: A meta-analytic review of the effects of violent and prosocial video game play. *Personality and Social Psychology Bulletin*, *40*(5), 578–589. doi:10.1177/0146167213520459 PMID:24458215

Grilli, M. D., McVeigh, K. S., Hakim, Z. M., Wank, A. A., Getz, S. J., Levin, B. E., ... Wilson, R. C. (2021). Is this phishing? Older age is associated with greater difficulty discriminating between safe and malicious emails. *The Journals of Gerontology: Series B*, *76*(9), 1711–1715.

Gruber, T. (2007). Automatically integrating heterogeneous ontologies from structured web pages. *International Journal on Semantic Web and Information Systems*, *3*(1), 1–11. doi:10.4018/jswis.2007010101

Guan, C., Ding, D., & Guo, J. (2022). *Web3.0: A Review And Research Agenda. 2022 RIVF International Conference on Computing and Communication Technologies*, Ho Chi Minh City, Vietnam.

Guan, C., Hung, Y.-C., & Liu, W. (2022). Cultural differences in hospitality service evaluations: Mining insights of user generated content. *Electronic Markets*, *32*(3), 1061–1081. doi:10.100712525-022-00545-z

Gupta, K., Varol, C., & Zhou, B. (2023). Digital forensic analysis of discord on google chrome. *Forensic Science International: Digital Investigation*, *44*, 301479.

Habib, G., Sharma, S., Ibrahim, S., Ahmad, I., Qureshi, S., & Ishfaq, M. (2022). Blockchain Technology: Benefits, Challenges, Applications, and Integration of Blockchain Technology with Cloud Computing. *Future Internet*, *14*(11), 341. doi:10.3390/fi14110341

Haleem, A., Javaid, M., & Singh, R. P. (2022). An era of ChatGPT as a significant futuristic support tool: A study on features, abilities, and challenges. *BenchCouncil Transactions on Benchmarks, Standards and Evaluations*, *2*(4), 100089.

Halloran, L. J. S., Mhanna, S., & Brunner, P. (2023). AI tools such as ChatGPT will disrupt hydrology, too. *Hydrological Processes*, *37*(3), e14843. doi:10.1002/hyp.14843

Hardee, J. B., West, R., & Mayhorn, C. B. (2006). To download or not to download: an examination of computer security decision making. *interactions, 13*(3), 32-37.

Harries, D., & Yellowlees, P. M. (2013). Cyberterrorism: Is the U.S. healthcare system safe? *Telemedicine Journal and e-Health*, *19*(1), 61–66. doi:10.1089/tmj.2012.0022 PMID:23113795

Harrison, B., Vishwanath, A., Ng, Y. J., & Rao, R. (2015). Examining the impact of presence on individual Phishing victimization. *IEEE 48th Hawaii International Conference on System Sciences*. 3483-3489. Doi: 10.1109/HICSS.2015.419

Hartmann, J., Schwenzow, J., & Witte, M. (2023). *The political ideology of conversational AI: Converging evidence on ChatGPT's pro-environmental, left-libertarian orientation*. arXiv:2301.01768. Retrieved January 01, 2023, from https://ui.adsabs.harvard.edu/abs/2023arXiv230101768H

Hassan, N. A., Hijazi, R., Hassan, N. A., & Hijazi, R. (2017). Online Anonymity. *Digital Privacy and Security Using Windows: A Practical Guide*, 123-194.

Hassandoust, F., Singh, H., & Williams, J. (2020). The Role of Contextualization in Individuals' Vulnerability to Phishing Attempts. *AJIS. Australasian Journal of Information Systems*, *24*, 1–32.

Haugeland, I., Fornell, K., Følstad, A., Taylor, C., & Bjørkli, C. A. (2022). Understanding the user experience of customer service chatbots: An experimental study of chatbot interaction design. *International Journal of Human-Computer Studies*, *161*, 102788. doi:10.1016/j.ijhcs.2022.102788

Havenstein, C., Thomas, D., and Chandrasekaran, S. (2019). Comparisons of Performance between Quantum and Classical Machine Learning. *SMU Data Science Review*, *1*(4).

Havlíček, V., Córcoles, A. D., Temme, K., Harrow, A. W., Kandala, A., Chow, J. M., & Gambetta, J. M. (2019). Supervised learning with quantum-enhanced feature spaces. *Nature*, *567*(7747), 209–212. doi:10.103841586-019-0980-2 PMID:30867609

Health Care Industry Cybersecurity Task Force Report on Improving Cybersecurity in the Health Care Industry. (2017). Department of Health and Human Service.

Healthcare Information and Management Systems Society (HIMSS). (2018). *2018 HIMSS Cybersecurity Survey.* Retrieved from https://www.himss.org/2018-himss-cybersecurity-survey

Henrique, D., Godinho Filho, M., Marodin, G., Jabbour, A., & Jabbour, C. (2021). A framework to assess sustaining continuous improvement in lean healthcare. *International Journal of Production Research, 59*(10), 2885–2904. doi:10.1080/00207543.2020.1743892

Herbsleb, J. D., Atkins, D. L., Boyer, D. G., Handel, M., & Finholt, T. A. (2002). Introducing instant messaging and chat in the workplace. *Proceedings of the SIGCHI Conference on Human Factors in Computing Systems.*

Herr, C., & Allen, D. (2015). Video games as a training tool to prepare the next generation of cyber warriors. *Proceedings of the 2015 ACM SIGMIS Conference on Computers and People Research.*

Higgins, G. E. (2006). Gender differences in software piracy: The mediating roles of self-control theory and social learning theory. *Journal of Economic Crime Management, 4*(1), 1–30.

Higgins, G. E., Fell, B. D., & Wilson, A. L. (2006). Digital piracy: Assessing the contributions of an integrated self-control theory and social learning theory using structural equation modeling. *Criminal Justice Studies, 19*(1), 3–22. doi:10.1080/14786010600615934

Higgins, G. E., Fell, B. D., & Wilson, A. L. (2007). Low self-control and social learning in understanding students' intentions to pirate movies in the United States. *Social Science Computer Review, 25*(3), 339–357. doi:10.1177/0894439307299934

Higgins, G. E., & Makin, D. A. (2004a). Does social learning theory condition the effects of low self-control on college students' software piracy. *Journal of Economic Crime Management, 2*(2), 1–22.

Higgins, G. E., & Makin, D. A. (2004b). Self-control, deviant peers, and software piracy. *Psychological Reports, 95*(3), 921–931. doi:10.2466/pr0.95.3.921-931 PMID:15666930

Higgins, G. E., & Wilson, A. L. (2006). Low self-control, moral beliefs, and social learning theory in university students' intentions to pirate software. *Security Journal, 19*(2), 75–92. doi:10.1057/palgrave.sj.8350002

HIPAA Journal. (n.d.). https://www.hipaajournal.com/tallahassee-memorial-healthcare-patient-data-stolen-in-cyberattack/

Hoang, N. P., Kintis, P., Antonakakis, M., & Polychronakis, M. (2018). An empirical study of the I2P anonymity network and its censorship resistance. *Proceedings of the Internet Measurement Conference 2018.*

Hoff, K. A., & Bashir, M. (2015). Trust in automation: Integrating empirical evidence on factors that influence trust. *Human Factors, 57*(3), 407–434. doi:10.1177/0018720814547570 PMID:25875432

Hoffman, A. J. (1999). Institutional evolution and change: Environmentalism and the US chemical industry. *Academy of Management Journal, 42*(4), 351–371. doi:10.2307/257008

Holt, T. J. (2007). Subcultural evolution? Examining the influence of on-and off-line experiences on deviant subcultures. *Deviant Behavior, 28*(2), 171–198.

Holt, T. J., Bossler, A. M., & Seigfried-Spellar, K. C. (2022). *Cybercrime and digital forensics: An introduction.* Routledge. doi:10.4324/9780429343223

Hong, J. (2012). The state of phishing attacks. *Communications of the ACM, 55*(1), 74–81. doi:10.1145/2063176.2063197

Hong, K. W., Kelley, C. M., Tembe, R., Murphy-Hill, E., & Mayhorn, C. B. (2013). Keeping up with the Joneses: Assessing Phishing susceptibility in an email task. *Proceedings of the Human Factors and Ergonomics Society Annual Meeting*, *57*(1), 1012–1016.

Hovy, D., Berg-Kirkpatrick, T., Vaswani, A., & Hovy, E. (2013). Learning Whom to Trust with MACE. In *North American Chapter of the Association for Computational Linguistics* (pp. 1120–1130). https://www.aclweb.org/anthology/N13-1132.pdf

Howes, L. M., & Kemp, N. (2017). Discord in the communication of forensic science: Can the science of language help foster shared understanding? *Journal of Language and Social Psychology*, *36*(1), 96–111. doi:10.1177/0261927X16663589

Hripcsak, G., Schuemie, M. J., Madigan, D., Ryan, P. B., & Suchard, M. A. (2021). Drawing Reproducible Conclusions from Observational Clinical Data with OHDSI. *Yearbook of Medical Informatics*, *30*(1), 283–289. doi:10.1055-0041-1726481 PMID:33882595

Hu, K. (2023). *ChatGPT sets record for fastest-growing user base* Reuters. https://www.reuters.com/technology/chatgpt-sets-record-fastest-growing-user-base-analyst-note-2023-02-01/

Huang, W., & Wang, S. K. (2011). THE EVOLUTIONAL VIEW OF THE TYPES OF IDENTITY THEFTS AND ONLINE FRAUDS IN THE ERA OF THE INTERNET. *Internet Journal of Criminology*. https://www.internet-journalofcriminology.com/Wang_Huang_The_Evolutional_View_of_the_Types_of_Identity_Thefts_and_Online_Frauds_in_the_Era_of_Internet_IJC_Oct_2011.pdf

Hu, G. (2023). Challenges for enforcing editorial policies on AI-generated papers. *Accountability in Research*, *1-3*, 1–3. Advance online publication. doi:10.1080/08989621.2023.2184262 PMID:36840450

Hyslip, T. S. (2020). Cybercrime-as-a-service operations. The Palgrave Handbook of International Cybercrime and Cyberdeviance, 815-846.

IBM. (2021). *About organization modeling*. IBM. https://www.ibm.com/docs/en/order-management?topic=SSGTJF/productconcepts/c_OrganizationModeling.htm

IBM. (2022a). *An overview of cloud security*. IBM. https://www.ibm.com/topics/cloud-security

IC3. (2021). *Internet Crime Report*. IC3. https://www.ic3.gov/Media/PDF/AnnualReport/2021_IC3Report.pdf.

International Committee of the Red Cross (ICRC). (2015). *International rules and standards for policing*. Available at: https://www.icrc.org/en/doc/assets/files/other/icrc-002-0809.pdf

International Committee of the Red Cross (ICRC). (2022). *The use of force in law enforcement operations*. ICRC.

International Telecommunications Union (ITU). (2008). ITU-T X.1205 - Overview of Cybersecurity. In *Series X: Data Networks, Open System Communications and Security - Telecommunication Security*. Telecommunication Standardization Sector of ITU (ITU-T).

International Telecommunications Union (ITU). (2011). *The ITU National Cybersecurity Strategy Guide*. Telecommunication Standardization Sector of ITU (ITU-T). https://www.itu.int/ITU-D/cyb/cybersecurity/docs/itu-national-cybersccurity-guidc.pdf

ISO/IEC 27001:2022 – Information Security Management Systems

J., A., Adedoyin, A., Ambrosiano, J., Anisimov, P., Ba¨rtschi, A., Casper, W., Chennupati, G., Coffrin, C., Djidjev, H., Gunter, D., Karra, S., Lemons, N., Lin, S., Malyzhenkov, A., Mascarenas, D., Mniszewski, S., Nadiga, B., O'Malley, D., Oyen, D., Pakin, S., Prasad, L., Roberts, R., Romero, P., Santhi, N., Sinitsyn, N., Swart, P. J., Wendelberger, J. G., Yoon, B., Zamora, R., Zhu, W., Eidenbenz, S., Coles, P. J., Vuffray, M., & Lokhov, A. Y. (2020). Quantum Algorithm Implementations for Beginners. arXiv: 1804.03719.

Jakobsson, M. (2007). The human factor in phishing. *Privacy & Security of Consumer Information*, 7(1), 1–19.

Jakobsson, M., & Menczer, F. (2007). Social Phishing. *Communications of the ACM*, ●●●, 1–10. doi:10.1145/12 90958.1290958.1290968

Jakobsson, M., & Myers, S. (Eds.). (2006). *Phishing and countermeasures: understanding the increasing problem of electronic identity theft*. John Wiley & Sons.

Jalali, M. S., & Kaiser, J. P. (2018). Cybersecurity in Hospitals: A Systematic, Organizational Perspective. *Journal of Medical Internet Research*, 20(5), e10059. doi:10.2196/10059 PMID:29807882

Jalil, S., Rafi, S. T., Moran, K., & Lam, W. (2023). *ChatGPT and Software Testing Education: Promises & Perils*. arXiv pre-print server.

Jannetti, M. C. (2014). Safeguarding patient information in electronic health records. *AORN Journal*, 100(3), C7–C8. doi:10.1016/S0001-2092(14)00873-4 PMID:24730081

Jansz, J., & Tanis, M. (2007). Appeal of playing online first person shooter games. *Cyberpsychology & Behavior*, 10(1), 133–136. doi:10.1089/cpb.2006.9981 PMID:17305460

Jeblick, K., Schachtner, B., Dexl, J., Mittermeier, A., Stüber, A. T., Topalis, J., Weber, T., Wesp, P., Sabel, B., Ricke, J., & Ingrisch, M. (2022). *ChatGPT Makes Medicine Easy to Swallow: An Exploratory Case Study on Simplified Radiology Reports*. arXiv:2212.14882. Retrieved December 01, 2022, from https://ui.adsabs.harvard.edu/abs/2022arXiv221214882J

Jeblick, K., Schachtner, B., Dexl, J., Mittermeier, A., Topalis, J., Weber, T., Wesp, P., Sabel, B., Ricke, J., & Ingrisch, M. (2022). *ChatGPT Makes Medicine Easy to Swallow: An Exploratory Case Study on Simplified Radiology Reports*. arXiv pre-print server.

Jena, L. K., & Goyal, S. (2022). Emotional intelligence and employee innovation: Sequential mediating effect of person-group fit and adaptive performance. *European Review of Applied Psychology*, 72(1), 100729. doi:10.1016/j.erap.2021.100729

Jenneboer, L., Herrando, C., & Constantinides, E. (2022). The Impact of Chatbots on Customer Loyalty: A Systematic Literature Review. *Journal of Theoretical and Applied Electronic Commerce Research*, 17(1), 212–229. doi:10.3390/jtaer17010011

Jennifer, M. P., Abigail, L. D., Lawrence, P., & Laura, M. P. (2010). Emergency Psychiatry. In Massachusetts General Hospital Handbook of General Hospital Psychiatry (6th ed.). Academic Press. doi:10.1176/appi.ajp.21060614

Joint Commission. (2018). *Improving the Safety of Health Information Technology*. Retrieved from https://www.jointcommission.org/-/media/tjc/documents/resources/patient-safety-topics/improving_safety_of_health_information_technology_5_22_18_final.pdf

Jonkers, H., Band, I., & Quartel, D. (2012a). *ArchiSurance Case Study*. The Open Group.

Jurgen Rudolph, S. T. (2023). ChatGPT: Bullshit spewer or the end of traditional assessments in higher education? *Journal of Applied Learning & Teaching*, *6*(1). Advance online publication. doi:10.37074/jalt.2023.6.1.9

Kalinin, M., & Krundyshev, V. (2022). Security intrusion detection using quantum machine learning techniques. *Journal of Computer Virology and Hacking Techniques*, *19*(1), 125–136. doi:10.100711416-022-00435-0

Kasarkod, J. (2011). *Integration of SABSA Security Architecture Approaches with TOGAF ADM*. InfoQ. https://www.infoq.com/news/2011/11/togaf-sabsa-integration/

Kasneci, E., Sessler, K., Küchemann, S., Bannert, M., Dementieva, D., Fischer, F., Gasser, U., Groh, G., Günnemann, S., Hüllermeier, E., Krusche, S., Kutyniok, G., Michaeli, T., Nerdel, C., Pfeffer, J., Poquet, O., Sailer, M., Schmidt, A., Seidel, T., ... Kasneci, G. (2023). ChatGPT for good? On opportunities and challenges of large language models for education. *Learning and Individual Differences*, *103*, 102274. doi:10.1016/j.lindif.2023.102274

Kaspersky. (2022). *Kaspersky Security Bulletin*. Kapersky. https://go.kaspersky.com/rs/802-IJN-240/images/KSB_statistics_2022_en_final.pdf.

Khan, R. A., Jawaid, M., Khan, A. R., & Sajjad, M. (2023). ChatGPT - Reshaping medical education and clinical management. *Pakistan Journal of Medical Sciences*, *39*(2). Advance online publication. doi:10.12669/pjms.39.2.7653 PMID:36950398

Khonji, M., Iraqi, Y., & Jones, A. (2013). Phishing Detection: A Literature Survey. *IEEE Communications Surveys and Tutorials*, *15*(4). Advance online publication. doi:10.1109/SURV.2013.032213.00009

Kigerl, A. (2021). Routine activity theory and malware, fraud, and spam at the national level. *Crime, Law, and Social Change*, *76*(2), 109–130.

Killoran, N., Bromley, T. R., Arrazola, J. M., Schuld, M., Quesada, N., & Lloyd, S. (2019). Continuous-variable quantum neural networks. *Physical Review Research*, *1*(3), 033063. doi:10.1103/PhysRevResearch.1.033063

Kim, B., Kim, H., Lee, S.-W., Lee, G., Kwak, D., Park, S., Kim, S., Kim, S., Seo, D., Lee, H., Jeong, M., Lee, S., Kim, M., Suk, Kim, S., Park, T., Kim, J., Kang, S., ... Sung, N. (2021). *What Changes Can Large-scale Language Models Bring? Intensive Study on HyperCLOVA: Billions-scale Korean Generative Pretrained Transformers*. arXiv pre-print server.

King, M. R. (2023). A Conversation on Artificial Intelligence, Chatbots, and Plagiarism in Higher Education. *Cellular and Molecular Bioengineering*, *16*(1), 1–2. doi:10.100712195-022-00754-8 PMID:36660590

Koenig, J., Rustan, K., & Leino, M. (2016). *Programming Language Features for Refinement*. Stanford University. doi:10.4204/EPTCS.209.7

Korkmaz, B., Tuzcu, M., & Sözer, S. (2014). *Use of Massively Multiplayer Online Games for Intelligence Gathering, Recruitment, and Training Purposes. 7th International Conference on Information Security and Cryptography*, Istanbul, Turkey.

Kouloumpis, E., Wilson, T., & Moore, J. D. (2011). Twitter Sentiment Analysis: The Good the Bad and the OMG! *Proceedings of the International AAAI Conference on Web and Social Media*, *5*(1), 538–541. 10.1609/icwsm.v5i1.14185

Kruse, C. S., Frederick, B., Jacobson, T., & Monticone, D. K. (2017). Cybersecurity in healthcare: A systematic review of modern threats and trends. *Technology and Health Care*, *25*(1), 1–10. doi:10.3233/THC-161263 PMID:27689562

Kshetri, N., & Ajami, R. (2008). Institutional reforms in the Gulf Cooperation Council economies: A conceptual framework. *Journal of International Management*, *14*(3), 300–318. doi:10.1016/j.intman.2008.01.005

Kumaraguru, P., Rhee, Y., Acquisti, A., Cranor, L. F., Hong, J., & Nunge, E. (2007, April). Protecting people from phishing: the design and evaluation of an embedded training email system. In *Proceedings of the SIGCHI conference on Human factors in computing systems* (pp. 905-914).

Kumaraguru, P., Sheng, S., Acquisti, A., Cranor, L. F., & Hong, J. (2009). Teaching Johnny Not to Fall for Phish. *ACM Transactions on Internet Technology*, *5*, 1–30.

Kumaraguru, P., Sheng, S., Acquisti, A., Cranor, L. F., & Hong, J. (2010). Teaching Johnny not to fall for phish. *ACM Transactions on Internet Technology*, *10*(2), 1–31.

Kumar, S., Kumar, P., & Bhasker, B. (2018). Interplay between trust, information privacy concerns and behavioural intention of users on online social networks. *Behaviour & Information Technology*, *37*(6), 622–633. doi:10.1080 /0144929X.2018.1470671

Kung, T. H., Cheatham, M., Medenilla, A., Sillos, C., De Leon, L., Elepaño, C., Madriaga, M., Aggabao, R., Diaz-Candido, G., Maningo, J., & Tseng, V. (2023). Performance of ChatGPT on USMLE: Potential for AI-assisted medical education using large language models. *PLOS Digital Health*, *2*(2), e0000198. doi:10.1371/journal.pdig.0000198 PMID:36812645

Kuwashima, K. (2014). How to Use Models of Organizational Decision Making? *Annals of Business Administrative Science, 13*, 215–230. www.gbrc.jp doi:10.7880/abas.13.215

Lacson, W., & Jones, B. (2016). The 21st Century DarkNet Market: Lessons from the Fall of Silk Road. *International Journal of Cyber Criminology*, *10*(1).

Lanzi, P. L., & Loiacono, D. (2023). *ChatGPT and Other Large Language Models as Evolutionary Engines for Online Interactive Collaborative Game Design*. arXiv:2303.02155. doi:10.1145/3583131.3590351

Lastdrager, E. E. (2014). Achieving a consensual definition of phishing based on a systematic review of the literature. *Crime Science*, *3*(1), 1–10.

Laxminarayana, N., Mishra, N., Tiwari, P., Garg, S., Behera, B. K., & Farouk, A. (2022). *Quantum-assisted activation for supervised learning in healthcare-based intrusion detection systems*. IEEE Transactions on Artificial Intelligence. doi:10.1109/TAI.2022.3187676

Le Bris, A., & El Asri, W. (2017). State of Cybersecurity & Cyber Threats in healthcare organizations: applied Cybersecurity strategy for managers. Cergy: ESSEC Bus Sch.

Leo, P., Isik, Ö., & Muhly, F. (2022). The ransomware dilemma. *MIT Sloan Management Review*, *63*(4), 13–15.

Lera, F. J. R., Balsa, J., Casado, F., Fernández, C., Rico, F. M., & Matellán, V. (2016). Cybersecurity in Autonomous Systems: Evaluating the performance of hardening ROS. Academic Press.

Leukfeldt, E. R. (2015). Comparing victims of phishing and malware attacks: Unraveling risk factors and possibilities for situational crime prevention. *arXiv preprint arXiv:1506.00769*.

Leukfeldt, E. R. (2014). Phishing for suitable targets in the Netherlands: Routine activity theory and phishing victimization. *Cyberpsychology, Behavior, and Social Networking, 17*(8), 551–555.

Leukfeldt, E. R., & Yar, M. (2016). Applying routine activity theory to cybercrime: A theoretical and empirical analysis. *Deviant Behavior, 37*(3), 263–280. doi:10.1080/01639625.2015.1012409

Lewis, J. (2018). Economic Impact of Cybercrime-No Slowing Down. McAfee & CSI (Center for Strategic and International Studies).

Lin, T., Capecci, D. E., Ellis, D. M., Rocha, H. A., Dommaraju, S., Oliveira, D. S., & Ebner, N. C. (2019). Susceptibility to spear-*Phishing* emails: Effects of internet user demographics and email content. [TOCHI]. *ACM Transactions on Computer-Human Interaction, 26*(5), 1–28. doi:10.1145/3336141

Liu, A. (2022). *Rumbaugh, Booch and Jacobson Methodologies*. Opengenus. https://iq.opengenus.org/rumbaugh-booch-and-jacobson-methodologies/

Liu, Musen, & Chou. (2015). Data breaches of protected health information in the United States. *J Am Med Assoc, 313*(14), 1471-1473. doi:10.1001/jama.2015.2252

Lloyd, S., Schuld, M., Ijaz, A., Izaac, J., & Killoran, N. (2020). Quantum embeddings for machine learning. arXiv: 2001.03622.

Lund, B. D., & Wang, T. (2023). Chatting about ChatGPT: how may AI and GPT impact academia and libraries? *Library Hi Tech News*. doi:10.1108/LHTN-01-2023-0009

Luo, B., Lau, R. Y. K., Li, C., & Si, Y.-W. (2022). A critical review of state-of-the-art chatbot designs and applications. *WIREs Data Mining and Knowledge Discovery, 12*(1), 1434.

Luyckx, F. (2015). *Advanced cycle: Advanced Delivery Management (ADM) life-cycle*. ARIS.

Lyons, J. B., Stokes, C. K., Eschleman, K. J., Alarcon, G. M., & Barelka, A. J. (2011). Trustworthiness and IT suspicion: An evaluation of the nomological network. *Human Factors, 53*(3), 219–229. doi:10.1177/0018720811406726

Macdonald, C., Adeloye, D., Sheikh, A., & Rudan, I. (2023). Can ChatGPT draft a research article? An example of population-level vaccine effectiveness analysis. *Journal of Global Health, 13*, 01003. doi:10.7189/jogh.13.01003 PMID:36798998

Maguire, S., Hardy, C., & Lawrence, T. B. (2004). Institutional entrepreneurship in emerging fields: HIV/AIDS treatment advocacy in Canada. *Academy of Management Journal, 47*(5), 657–679. doi:10.2307/20159610

Mahajan, A., & Dahiya, M., & Sanghvi, H. (2013). Forensic Analysis of Instant Messenger Applications on Android Devices. *International Journal of Computers and Applications, 68*(8), 38–44. doi:10.5120/11602-6965

Malik, D. K. (2023). Information Technology & Cyber Law. Allahabad Law Agency (SKU: 978-93-95759-22-9), India.

Manky, D. (2013). Cybercrime as a service: A very modern business. *Computer Fraud & Security, 2013*(6), 9–13. doi:10.1016/S1361-3723(13)70053-8

Manzzi, A. C. (2022). *Know the main scams on the Internet and learn how to protect your data*. NIC.br. https://www.nic.br/noticia/na-midia/conheca-os-principais-golpes-na-internet-e-saiba-como-proteger-os-seus-dados/.

Mariani, M. M., Hashemi, N., & Wirtz, J. (2023). Artificial intelligence empowered conversational agents: A systematic literature review and research agenda. *Journal of Business Research, 161*, 113838. doi:10.1016/j.jbusres.2023.113838

Marks, J. (2021). Ransomware attack might have caused another death. *The Washington Post*. https://www.washingtonpost.com/politics/2021/10/01/ransomware-attack-might-have-caused-another-death/

Maximilian, L., & Markl, E. M. A. (2018). Cybersecurity management for (industrial) internet of things–challenges and opportunities. *Journal of Information Technology & Software Engineering, 8*(5), 1–9.

Maybank. (2022). *Top 4 most viral online scams right now*. Maybank. https://www.maybank.com/en/blogs/2022/11/14-scam-tactics.page.

McCarty, C., Prawitz, A. D., Derscheid, L. E., & Montgomery, B. (2011). Perceived safety and teen risk taking in online chat sites. *Cyberpsychology, Behavior, and Social Networking, 14*(3), 169–174. doi:10.1089/cyber.2010.0050 PMID:20677982

McEwen, J. T. (1995). *Dedicated computer crime units*. DIANE Publishing.

McGuire, M. (2018). *Hyper-Connected Web of Profit Emerges, as Global Cybercriminal Revenues Hit $1.5 Trillion Annually*. Bromium Inc. Retrieved June 29 from https://www.bromium.com/press-release/hyper-connected-web-of-profit-emerges-as-global-cybercriminal-revenues-hit-1-5-trillion-annually/

McKee, F., & Noever, D. (2023). *Chatbots in a Honeypot World*. arXiv:2301.03771. Retrieved January 01, 2023, from https://ui.adsabs.harvard.edu/abs/2023arXiv230103771M

Medical Device Safety Action Plan. (2018). 2017 HIMSS Cybersecurity survey. Chicago: HIMSS.

Mhlanga, D. (2023). *Open AI in Education, the Responsible and Ethical Use of ChatGPT Towards Lifelong Learning*. Academic Press.

Michael, H. A., Peter, F., Joseph, Z., & Glenn, C. (2002). *Report and Recommendations Regarding Psychiatric Emergency and Crisis Services: A Review and Model Program Descriptions*. APA Task Force on Psychiatric Emergency Services.

Mimno D. Wallach H. Talley E. Leenders M. McCallum A. (2011). Optimizing semantic coherence in topic models. *Proceedings of the 2011 Conference on Empirical Methods in Natural Language Processing*.

Ministry of Health (MoH). (2018). *Clinical orientation manual: psychiatric emergencies; emergency medical services division, Bhutan*. Available at: https://www.moh.gov.bt/wp-content/uploads/moh-files/2017/10/Chapter-16-Psychiatric-Emerfgencies.pdf

Mirea, M., Wang, V., & Jung, J. (2019). The not so dark side of the darknet: A qualitative study. *Security Journal, 32*(2), 102–118. doi:10.105741284-018-0150-5

Miró-Llinares, F., Drew, J., & Townsley, M. (2020). Understanding target suitability in cyberspace: An international comparison of cyber victimization processes. *International Journal of Cyber Criminology, 14*(1), 139–155.

Mitrovic, S., Andreoletti, D., & Ayoub, O. (2023). *ChatGPT or Human? Detect and Explain. Explaining Decisions of Machine Learning Model for Detecting Short ChatGPT-generated Text.* arXiv pre-print server.

Miyamoto, D., Iimura, T., Blanc, G., Tazaki, H., & Kadobayashi, Y. (2014). EyeBit: Eye-Tracking Approach for Enforcing *Phishing* Prevention Habits. *Third International Workshop on Building Analysis Datasets and Gathering Experience Returns for Security* (BADGERS). Doi: 10.1109/BADGERS.2014.14

Möhring, M., Keller, B., Schmidt, R., Sandkuhl, L., & Zimmermann, A. (2023). Digitalization and enterprise architecture management: a perspective on benefits and challenges. *SN Bus Econ.* doi:10.1007/s43546-023-00426-3

MollickE. R.MollickL. (2022). New Modes of Learning Enabled by AI Chatbots: Three Methods and Assignments. *Available at* SSRN. doi:10.2139/ssrn.4300783

Moody, G. D., Galletta, D. F., & Dunn, K. (2017). Which phish get caught? An explanatory study of individuals' susceptibility to *Phishing. European Journal of Information Systems, 26*(6), 564–584. doi:10.105741303-017-0058-x

Morris, R. G., & Blackburn, A. G. (2009). Cracking the code: An empirical exploration of social learning theory and computer crime. *Journal of Crime and Justice, 32*(1), 1–34. doi:10.1080/0735648X.2009.9721260

Morris, R. G., & Higgins, G. E. (2010). Criminological theory in the digital age: The case of social learning theory and digital piracy. *Journal of Criminal Justice, 38*(4), 470–480. doi:10.1016/j.jcrimjus.2010.04.016

Mosca, M. (2018). Cybersecurity in an era with quantum computers: Will we be ready? *IEEE Security and Privacy, 16*(5), 38–41. doi:10.1109/MSP.2018.3761723

Motyliński, M., MacDermott, Á., Iqbal, F., Hussain, M., & Aleem, S. (2020). Digital forensic acquisition and analysis of discord applications. *2020 International Conference on Communications, Computing, Cybersecurity, and Informatics (CCCI).*

Mühlpfordt, M., & Wessner, M. (2005). Explicit referencing in chat supports collaborative learning. *Proceedings of the 2005 Conference on Computer Support for Collaborative Learning: Learning 2005: The Next 10 years!*

Munn, L., Magee, L., & Arora, V. (2023). *Truth Machines: Synthesizing Veracity in AI Language Models.* arXiv:2301.12066. Retrieved January 01, 2023, from https://ui.adsabs.harvard.edu/abs/2023arXiv230112066M

Nasser, G., Morrison, B. W., Bayl-Smith, P., Taib, R., Gayed, M., & Wiggins, M. W. (2020). The role of cue utilization and cognitive load in the recognition of phishing emails. *Frontiers in big data, 3*, 546860.

Nassif, T. (2022). *Digital scams put cybersecurity to the test; see how to protect yourself.* CNN Brasil. https://www.cnnbrasil.com.br/business/golpes-digitais-colocam-ciberseguranca-a-prova-veja-como-se-proteger/.

Nastasi, A. J., Courtright, K. R., Halpern, S. D., & Weissman, G. E. (2023). Does ChatGPT Provide Appropriate and Equitable Medical Advice?: A Vignette-Based, Clinical Evaluation Across Care Contexts. medRxiv, 2023.2002.2025.23286451. doi:10.1101/2023.02.25.23286451

National Crime Agency (Government of UK). (n.d.). *Cyber Crime Assessment.* National Crime Agency. https://www.nationalcrimeagency.gov.uk/publications/709-cyber-crime-assessment-2016/file)

National Institute of Standards and Technology. (2018). *Framework for Improving Critical Infrastructure Cybersecurity.* Retrieved from https://www.nist.gov/publications/framework-improving-critical-infrastructure-cybersecurity

Nature. (2023). *Preparing your materials.* https://www.nature.com/nbt/submission-guidelines/preparing-your-submission

Nehinbe, J. (2023). Classification Models for Preventing Juvenile Crimes Committed with Malware Apps. *Malware - Detection and Defense*, doi:10.5772/intechopen.107188

Neves, R. A. C. (2022). Vitimação por phishing: um estudo empírico.

Newhouse, W. (2017). *NICE Cybersecurity Workforce Framework: National Initiative for Cybersecurity Education, Special Publication (NIST SP 800-181).* National Institute of Standards and Technology. doi:10.6028/NIST.SP.800-181

Ng, M., Coopamootoo, K., Toreini, E., Aitken, M., Elliot, K., & van Moorsel, A. (2020). Simulating the Effects of Social Presence on Trust, Privacy Concerns & Usage Intentions in Automated Bots for Finance. *IEEE European Symposium on Security and Privacy Workshops (EuroS&PW)*, 190-199. 10.1109/EuroSPW51379.2020.00034

NIS. (2016). *Measures for a high common level of security of network and information systems across the Union. Directive (EU) 2016/1148.* European Parliament.

NIS2. (2022). *Measures for a high common level of cybersecurity across the Union. Amending Regulation (EU) No 910/2014 and Directive (EU) 2018/1972, and repealing Directive (EU) 2016/1148. Directive (EU) 2022/2555.* European Parliament.

Noia, J. (2023). *WhatsApp is a champion of internet fraud, shows research. Learn how to protect yourself.* Globo. https://extra.globo.com/economia-e-financas/whatsapp-campeao-de-fraudes-na-internet-mostra-pesquisa-saiba-como-se-proteger-25415122.html.

Nordheim, C. B., Følstad, A., & Bjørkli, C. A. (2019). An Initial Model of Trust in Chatbots for Customer Service—Findings from a Questionnaire Study. *Interacting with Computers, 31*(3), 317–335. doi:10.1093/iwc/iwz022

North Atlantic Treaty Organization (NATO). (2014). *NATO Summit Updates Cyber Defence Policy, from NATO Cyber Defence Policy at the NATO Summit in Wales on 4-5 September 2014.* https://ccdcoe.org/incyder-articles/nato-summit-updates-cyber-defence-policy/

North Atlantic Treaty Organization (NATO). (2014a). *Wales Summit Declaration, Paragraph 72, NATO Summit Updates Cyber Defence Policy, from NATO Cyber Defence Policy at the NATO Summit in Wales on 4-5 September 2014.* https://www.nato.int/cps/en/natohq/official_texts_112964.htm

North Atlantic Treaty Organization (NATO). (2016). *Point 3. of the Joint Declaration signed by the President of the European Council, the President of the European Commission, and the Secretary General of the North Atlantic Treaty Organization, Brussels, Belgium, Dec. 2016.* https://www.nato.int/cps/en/natohq/official_texts_138829.htm

North Atlantic Treaty Organization (NATO). (2016a). *Cybersecurity Reference Curriculum, 27 Sept. 2016, Norfolk, USA.* https://www.nato.int/nato_static_fl2014/assets/pdf/pdf_2016_10/1610-cybersecurity-curriculum.pdf

North Atlantic Treaty Organization (NATO). (2019). *NATO Cyber Defence Factsheet.* https://www.nato.int/nato_static_fl2014/assets/pdf/pdf_2019_02/20190208_1902-factsheet-cyber-defence-en.pdf

North Atlantic Treaty Organization (NATO). (2023). *Cyber defence.* https://www.nato.int/cps/en/natohq/topics_78170.htm

Nov, O., Singh, N., & Mann, D. M. (2023). Putting ChatGPT's Medical Advice to the (Turing) Test. medRxiv, 2023.2001.2023.23284735. doi:10.1101/2023.01.23.23284735

Nurse, J. R., & de Cominges, M. B. (2019). The group element of cybercrime: Types, dynamics, and criminal operations. *The Oxford handbook of cyberpsychology*.

O'Connor, A. M., Judges, R. A., Lee, K., & Evans, A. D. (2021). Can adults discriminate between fraudulent and legitimate e-mails? Examining the role of age and prior fraud experience. *Journal of Elder Abuse & Neglect*, •••, 1–25. doi:10.1080/08946566.2021.1934767

O'Flaherty, J., & Phillips, C. (2015). The use of flipped classrooms in higher education: A scoping review. *The internet and higher education*, *25*, 85–95. doi:10.1016/j.iheduc.2015.02.002

O'Neill, J., & Martin, D. (2003). Text chat in action. *Proceedings of the 2003 international ACM SIGGROUP conference on Supporting group work.*

O'Riordan, B. (2021). INNOVATION-Why Transformations Fail And How They Can Succeed With People Power. *Forbes.* https://www.forbes.com/sites/unit4/2021/10/11/why-transformations-fail-and-how-they-can-succeed-with-people-power/#:~:text=It%20is%20a%20bold%20decision,all%20major%20transformation%20projects%20fail

Official Journal of the European Union. (2016). General Data Protection Regulation (EU) 2016/679. *European Parliament and of the Council, L*, 119.

OHDSI. (2021). Observational Health Data Sciences and Informatics. In *The Book of OHDSI*. Independently Published. https://ohdsi.github.io/TheBookOfOhdsi/

Olson, C. K., Kutner, L. A., & Warner, D. E. (2008). The role of violent video game content in adolescent development: Boys' perspectives. *Journal of Adolescent Research*, *23*(1), 55–75.

Omar, R., Mangukiya, O., Kalnis, P., & Mansour, E. (2023). *ChatGPT versus Traditional Question Answering for Knowledge Graphs: Current Status and Future Directions Towards Knowledge Graph Chatbots*. arXiv pre-print server.

ONS.gov.uk. (2023). *Office for National Statistics*. Gov. UK Office for National Statistics for England and Wales. https://www.ons.gov.uk/.

Ott, S., Hebenstreit, K., Liévin, V., Egeberg Hother, C., Moradi, M., Mayrhauser, M., Praas, R., Winther, O., & Samwald, M. (2023). *ThoughtSource: A central hub for large language model reasoning data*. arXiv:2301.11596. Retrieved January 01, 2023, from https://ui.adsabs.harvard.edu/abs/2023arXiv230111596O

Oxford Dictionaries. (2017a). *Security*. London: Oxford Dictionaries. Retrieved on September 3, 2017, from: https://en.oxforddictionaries.com/definition/security

Palermo, J., Bogard, J., Hexter, E., Hinze, M., & Skinner, M. (2012). ASP.NET Model View Control 4. In *Action*. Manning.

Palmer, G. (2001). *A road map for digital forensic research*. First Digital Forensic Research Workshop, Utica, NY.

Pancini, L. (2022). 58% dos brasileiros sofreram crimes cibernéticos, aponta estudo da Norton. *Exame*. https://exame.com/tecnologia/58-dos-brasileiros-sofreram-crimes-ciberneticos-aponta-estudo-da-norton/.

Pappas, I. O. (2018). User experience in personalized online shopping: A fuzzy-set analysis. *European Journal of Marketing*, *52*(7/8), 1679–1703. doi:10.1108/EJM-10-2017-0707

Parmar, B. (2012). Protecting against spear-*Phishing*. *Computer Fraud & Security*, (1), 8–11. doi:10.1016/S1361-3723(12)70007-6

Parsons, K., Butavicius, M., Pattinson, M., Calic, D., Mccormac, A., & Jerram, C. (2016). Do users focus on the correct cues to differentiate between phishing and genuine emails? *arXiv preprint arXiv:1605.04717*.

Parsons, K., Butavicius, M., Delfabbro, P., & Lillie, M. (2019). Predicting susceptibility to social influence in Phishing emails. *International Journal of Human-Computer Studies*, *128*, 17–26.

Parsons, K., McCormac, A., Pattinson, M., Butavicius, M., & Jerram, C. (2013, July). Phishing for the truth: A scenario-based experiment of users' behavioural response to emails. In *IFIP international information security conference* (pp. 366–378). Springer.

Paus, T., Keshavan, M., & Giedd, J. (2008). Why do many psychiatric disorders emerge during adolescence? *Nature Reviews. Neuroscience*, *9*(12), 947–957. doi:10.1038/nrn2513 PMID:19002191

Payares, E., & Martinez-Santos, J. C. (2021). Quantum machine learning for intrusion detection of distributed denial of service attacks: a comparative overview. In P. R. Hemmer & A. L. Migdall (Eds.), *Quantum Computing, Communication, and Simulation*. SPIE. doi:10.1117/12.2593297

Peloquin, D., DiMaio, M., Bierer, B., & Barnes, M. (2020). Disruptive and avoidable: GDPR challenges to secondary research uses of data. *European Journal of Human Genetics*, *28*(6), 697–705. doi:10.103841431-020-0596-x PMID:32123329

Perez, E., Herb, J., Bertrand, N., Cohen, Z., & Liptak, K. (2023). *FBI arrests 21-year-old Air Force guardsman in Pentagon leak case*. https://www.cnn.com/2023/04/13/politics/us-government-intel-leak/index.html

Perrault, E. K. (2017). Using an Interative Online Quiz to Recalibre College Students' Attitudes and Behavioral Intentions About *Phishing*. *Journal of Education Computing*, *0*(0), 1–14. doi:10.1177/0735633117699232

Petersen, R., Santos, D., Wetzel, K., Smith, M., & Witte, G. (2020). *Workforce Framework for Cybersecurity (NICE Framework), Special Publication (NIST SP 800-181r1)*. National Institute of Standards and Technology. doi:10.6028/NIST.SP.800-181r1

Peterson, S. (2011). *Why it Worked: Critical Success Factors of a Financial Reform Project in Africa*. Faculty Research Working Paper Series. Harvard Kennedy School.

Petrosino, A., Boruch, R. F., Soydan, H., Duggan, L., & Sanchez-Meca, J. (2001). Meeting the Challenges of Evidence-Based Policy: The Campbell Collaboration. *The Annals of the American Academy of Political and Social Science*, *578*(1), 14–34. doi:10.1177/000271620157800102

Pinheiro, P. P. (2021). *Digital Law*. Saraiva Educação.

Plaisier, X. S., & Konijn, E. A. (2013). Rejected by peers—Attracted to antisocial media content: Rejection-based anger impairs moral judgment among adolescents. *Developmental Psychology*, *49*(6), 1165–1173. doi:10.1037/a0029399 PMID:22799588

Portuguese National Cybersecurity Centre (PNCSC). (2023). *Mission*. https://www.cncs.gov.pt/en/about-us/#missao

Portuguese Parliament (PP). (2018) *Establishes the legal framework for cyberspace security by transposing Directive (EU) 2016/1148 of the European Parliament and of the Council of 6 July 2016 on measures to ensure a high common level of network and information security across the Union, Law no. 46/2018, 13 August, Diário da República n.º 155/2018, Série I de 2018-08-13, p 4031–4037.* https://files.dre.pt/1s/2018/08/15500/0403104037.pdf

Pratap & Predovich. (2020). *The 2020 Gartner Magic Quadrant for IT Risk Management.* Gartner.

Presidency of the Council of Ministers (PCM). (2012). *Approves the organic of the National Security Office, Decree-Law n. 3/2012, of 16 January, Diário da República n. 11/2012, Série I de 2012-01-16, p. 174-177.* https://files.dre.pt/1s/2012/01/01100/0017400177.pdf

Presidency of the Council of Ministers (PCM). (2015). *Aproves the National Strategy for the CyberSpace Security, Resolution of the Council of Ministers no. 36/2015, 12 june, Diário da República n. 113/2015, Série I de 2015-06-12, p. 3738 – 3742.* https://files.dre.pt/1s/2015/06/11300/0373803742.pdf

Presidency of the Council of Ministers (PCM). (2017). *Creation of the group "Cyberspace Security Superior Council", Resolution of the Council of Ministers no. 115/2017, 24 August, Diário da República n. 163/2017, Série I de 2017-08-24, p. 5035 – 5037.* https://files.dre.pt/1s/2017/08/16300/0503505037.pdf

Presidency of the Council of Ministers (PCM). (2019). *Aproves the National Strategy for the CyberSpace Security 2019-2023, Resolution of the Council of Ministers no. 92/2019, 5 june, Diário da República, 1.ª série — N.º 108 — 5 de junho de 2019, p 2888-2895.* https://files.dre.pt/1s/2019/06/10800/0288802895.pdf

Presidency of the Council of Ministers (PCM). (2022). *Aproves the National Strategy for Cyberdefense, Resolution of the Council of Ministers no. 106/2022, 2 november, Diário da República n. 211/2022, Série I de 2022-11-02, p. 13–22.* https://files.dre.pt/1s/2022/11/21100/0001300022.pdf

Presidency of the Council of Ministers (PCM). (2022a). *Regulates the Legal Framework for Cyberspace Security and sets out the cybersecurity certification obligations under Regulation (EU) 2019/881 of the European Parliament of 17 April 2019, Decree-Law n. 65/2021, 30 june, Diário da República n.º 147/2021, Série I de 2021-07-30, p. 8 – 21.* https://files.dre.pt/1s/2021/07/14700/0000800021.pdf

Prieto, S. A., Mengiste, E. T., & García de Soto, B. (2023). Investigating the Use of ChatGPT for the Scheduling of Construction Projects. *Buildings, 13*(4), 857. https://www.mdpi.com/2075-5309/13/4/857

Qadir, J. (2022). *Engineering Education in the Era of ChatGPT: Promise and Pitfalls of Generative AI for Education.* Academic Press.

Quang Phu, T., & Thi Yen Thao, H. (2017). Enterprise Risk Management Implementation: The Critical Success Factors For Vietnamese Construction Companies. *Journal of Multidisciplinary Engineering Science Studies, 3*(2). http://www.jmess.org/wp-content/uploads/2017/02/JMESSP13420283.pdf

Quinlan, C. (2015). Business Research Methods. Dublin City University.

R. vs Bow Street Magazine, (1994) 4 All ER 1 (1994).

Rai, A., Constantinides, P., & Sarker, S. (2019). Next generation digital platforms: toward human-AI hybrids. *Management Information Systems Quarterly, 43*(1), iii–ix.

Rajawat, A. S., Goyal, S., Bedi, P., Constantin, N. B., Raboaca, M. S., & Verma, C. (2022). Cyber-physical system for industrial automation using quantum deep learning. In *2022 11th International Conference on System Modeling; Advancement in Research Trends (SMART)*. IEEE. 10.1109/SMART55829.2022.10047730

Rao, A., Kim, J., Kamineni, M., Pang, M., Lie, W., & Succi, M. D. (2023). Evaluating ChatGPT as an Adjunct for Radiologic Decision-Making. medRxiv. doi:10.1101/2023.02.02.23285399

Ratier, R. (2022). *Bolsonarist groups have pix coup attacks, fake notes and "gatonet"*. UOL. https://www.uol.com.br/ecoa/colunas/rodrigo-ratier/2022/06/13/grupos-bolsonaristas-no-whatsapp-tem-golpe-do-pix-nota-falsa-e-gatonet.htm. Access on: Feb. 13, 2023.

Rattan, D. J. (2017). *Cyber Laws & Information Technology*. Bharat Law House, India.

Rawat, R., Mahor, V., Chirgaiya, S., & Rathore, A. S. (2021). Applications of social network analysis to managing the investigation of suspicious activities in social media platforms. In *Advances in Cybersecurity Management* (pp. 315–335). Springer. doi:10.1007/978-3-030-71381-2_15

Rawnsley, A. (2011). Iran's Alleged Drone Hack: Tough, but Possible. *Wired.* https://www.wired.com/2011/12/iran-drone-hack-gps

Raykar, V. C., & Yu, S. (2012). Eliminating spammers and ranking annotators for crowdsourced labeling tasks. *Journal of Machine Learning Research*, *13*(1), 491–518. doi:10.5555/2188385.2188401

Raza, M. (2020). *Introduction to Enterprise Security*. BMC. https://www.bmc.com/blogs/enterprise-security/

Rebentrost, P., Mohseni, M., & Lloyd, S. (2014). Quantum Support Vector Machine for Big Data Classification. *Physical Review Letters*, *113*(13), 130503. doi:10.1103/PhysRevLett.113.130503 PMID:25302877

RedHat. (2022). *Decision Model and Notation (DMN)*. RedHat. https://access.redhat.com/documentation/en-us/red_hat_process_automation_manager/7.1/html/designing_a_decision_service_using_dmn_models/dmn-elements-example-con

Reed, D., & Kemmerly, S. A. (2009). Infection control and prevention: A review of hospital-acquired infections and the economic implications. *The Ochsner Journal*, *9*(1), 27–31. PMID:21603406

Reinecke, I., Zoch, M., Reich, C., Sedlmayr, M., & Bathelt, F. (2021). The Usage of OHDSI OMOP - A Scoping Review. *Studies in Health Technology and Informatics*, *283*, 95–103. doi:10.3233/SHTI210546 PMID:34545824

Richter, G., Borzikowsky, C., Hoyer, B. F., Laudes, M., & Krawczak, M. (2021). Secondary research use of personal medical data: Patient attitudes towards data donation. *BMC Medical Ethics*, *22*(1), 164. doi:10.118612910-021-00728-x PMID:34911502

Rogers, M. K. (2011). The psyche of cybercriminals: A psycho-social perspective. *Cybercrimes: A multidisciplinary analysis*, 217-235.

Ronczkowski, M. R. (2017). *Terrorism and organized hate crime: Intelligence gathering, analysis and investigations*. CRC Press. doi:10.4324/9781315203133

Rose, S., Borchert, O., Mitchell, S., & Connelly, S. (2020). *Zero Trust Architecture*. NIST Special Publication 800-207. NIST - National Institute of Standards and Technology.

Rosing, M., Hove, M., Subbarao, R., & Preston, T. (2012). *Combining secBPM and EA in complex ERP projects (a Business Architecture discipline)*. Academic Press.

Ruan, K., Carthy, J., Kechadi, T., & Baggili, I. (2013). Cloud forensics definitions and critical criteria for cloud forensic capability: An overview of survey results. *Digital Investigation, 10*(1), 34–43. doi:10.1016/j.diin.2013.02.004

SABSA. (2020). *Sherwood Applied Business Security Architecture*. SABSA. https://sabsa.org/

Sakib Shahriar, K. H. (2023). *Let's have a chat! A Conversation with ChatGPT*. Technology, Applications, and Limitations.

Sakirin, T., & Said, R. B. (2023). *User preferences for ChatGPT-powered conversational interfaces versus traditional*. Academic Press.

Salah, M., Alhalbusi, H., Ismail, M. M., & Abdelfattah, F. (2023). *Chatting with ChatGPT: Decoding the Mind of Chatbot Users and Unveiling the Intricate Connections between User Perception, Trust and Stereotype Perception on Self-Esteem and Psychological Well-being*. Research Square., doi:10.21203/rs.3.rs-2610655/v2

Salas Conde, J. J., Martín Ortiz, M., & Carneiro Díaz, V. M. (2022). Methodology for Identification and Classifying of Cybercrime on Tor Network through the Use of Cryptocurrencies Based on Web Textual Contents. *Computación y Sistemas, 26*(1), 347–356. doi:10.13053/cys-26-1-4178

Sallam, M. (2023). ChatGPT Utility in Healthcare Education, Research, and Practice: Systematic Review on the Promising Perspectives and Valid Concerns. *Health Care, 11*(6), 887. doi:10.3390/healthcare11060887 PMID:36981544

Sallam, M., Salim, N. A., Al-Tammemi, A. B., Barakat, M., Fayyad, D., Hallit, S., Harapan, H., Hallit, R., & Mahafzah, A. (2023). ChatGPT Output Regarding Compulsory Vaccination and COVID-19 Vaccine Conspiracy: A Descriptive Study at the Outset of a Paradigm Shift in Online Search for Information. *Cureus, 15*(2), e35029. doi:10.7759/cureus.35029 PMID:36819954

Salloum, S., Gaber, T., Vadera, S., & Shaalan, K. (2021). Phishing email detection using natural language processing techniques: A literature survey. *Procedia Computer Science, 189*, 19–28.

Sanmarchi, F., Bucci, A., & Golinelli, D. (2023). A step-by-step Researcher's Guide to the use of an AI-based transformer in epidemiology: an exploratory analysis of ChatGPT using the STROBE checklist for observational studies. medRxiv. doi:10.1101/2023.02.06.23285514

Sarno, D. M., Lewis, J. E., Bohil, C. J., Shoss, M. K., & Neider, M. B. (2017). Who are Phishers luring?: A Demographic Analysis of Those Susceptible to Fake Emails. *Proceedings of the Human Factors and Ergonomics Society Annual Meeting, 61*(1), 1735–1739. doi:10.1177/1541931213601915

Sarno, D. M., & Neider, M. B. (2021). So Many Phish, So Little Time: Exploring E-mail Task Factors and Phishing Susceptibility. *Human Factors, 00*(0), 1–25. doi:10.1177/0018720821999174

Scheckler, W. E., Brimhall, D., Buck, A. S., Farr, B. M., Friedman, C., Garibaldi, R. A., Gross, P. A., Harris, J. A., Hierholzer, W. J. Jr, Martone, W. J., McDonald, L. L., & Solomon, S. L. (1998). Requirements for infrastructure and essential activities of infection control and epidemiology in hospitals: A consensus panel report. Society for Healthcare Epidemiology of America. *American Journal of Infection Control, 26*(1), 47–60. doi:10.1016/S0196-6553(98)70061-6 PMID:9503113

Schwarz, C., & Grizzell, T. (2020). Trafficking spectacle: Affect and state power in operation cross country X. *Frontiers*, *41*(2), 57–81. doi:10.1353/fro.2020.a765265

Scott-Hayward, S., Natarajan, S., & Sezer, S. (2015). A survey of security in software defined networks. *IEEE Communications Surveys and Tutorials*, *18*(1), 623–654. doi:10.1109/COMST.2015.2453114

Sehulster, L., & Chinn, RY. (2019). *Guidelines for environmental infection control in health-care facilities. Recommendations of CDC and the Healthcare Infection Control Practices Advisory Committee (HICPAC)*. MMWR Recomm Rep, 6;52(RR-10):1-42.

Selin, C. (2006). Trust and the illusive force of scenarios. *Futures*, *38*(1), 1–14. doi:10.1016/j.futures.2005.04.001

Serasa Experian. (2022). Experian, S. *Brazilians suffered more than 375,000 fraud attempts in January, reveals Serasa Experian*. Serasa Experian. https://www.serasaexperian.com.br/sala-de-imprensa/analise-de-dados/brasileiros-sofreram-mais-de-375-mil-tentativas-de-fraude-em-janeiro-revela-serasa-experian/. Access on: Feb. 11, 2023.

Serasa Experian. (2022). *People between 36 and 50 years old are the main targets of scammers, points out research by Serasa Experian*. Serasa Experian. https://www.serasaexperian.com.br/sala-de-imprensa/analise-de-dados/pessoas-entre-36-e-50-anos-sao-os-principais-alvos-de-golpistas-aponta-pesquisa-da-serasa-experian/.

Sezgin, E., Sirrianni, J., & Linwood, S. L. (2022). Operationalizing and Implementing Pretrained, Large Artificial Intelligence Linguistic Models in the US Health Care System: Outlook of Generative Pretrained Transformer 3 (GPT-3) as a Service Model. *JMIR Medical Informatics*, *10*(2), 32875. doi:10.2196/32875 PMID:35142635

Shahriar, S., & Hayawi, K. (2023). *Let's have a chat! A Conversation with ChatGPT: Technology, Applications, and Limitations*. arXiv:2302.13817. Retrieved February 01, 2023, from https://ui.adsabs.harvard.edu/abs/2023arXiv230213817S

Shaji George, A. S. H. G., & Martin. (2023). A Review of ChatGPT AI's Impact on Several Business Sectors. *Partners Universal International Innovation Journal*, *01*(01), 15. doi:10.5281/zenodo.7644359

Sheng, S., Holbrook, M., Kumaraguru, P., Cranor, L., & Downs, J. (2010). Who Falls for Phish? A Demographic Analysis of Phishing Susceptibility and Effectiveness of Interventions, *Proceedings of the 28th International Conference on Human Factors in Computing Systems*, CHI 2010, Atlanta, Georgia, USA. doi: 10.1145/1753326.1753326.1753383

Shillair, R., Cotten, S. R., Tsai, H.-Y. S., Alhabash, S., LaRose, R., & Rifon, N. J. (2015). Online safety begins with you and me: Convincing Internet users to protect themselves. *Computers in Human Behavior*, *48*, 199–207. doi:10.1016/j.chb.2015.01.046

Siegrist, M., Gutscher, H., & Earle, T. (2005). Perception of risk: The influence of general trust, and general confidence. *Journal of Risk Research*, *8*(2), 145–156. doi:10.1080/1366987032000105315

Sillence, E., Blythe, J. M., Briggs, P., & Moss, M. (2019). A Revised Model of Trust in Internet-Based Health Information and Advice: Cross-Sectional Questionnaire Study. *Journal of Medical Internet Research*, *21*(11), e11125. doi:10.2196/11125 PMID:31710297

Simou, S., Kalloniatis, C., Kavakli, E., & Gritzalis, S. (2014). Cloud forensics solutions: A review. *International Conference on Advanced Information Systems Engineering*.10.1007/978-3-319-07869-4_28

Sinaci, A. A., Núñez-Benjumea, F. J., Gencturk, M., Jauer, M. L., Deserno, T., Chronaki, C., Cangioli, G., Cavero-Barca, C., Rodríguez-Pérez, J. M., Pérez-Pérez, M. M., Laleci Erturkmen, G. B., Hernández-Pérez, T., Méndez-Rodríguez, E., & Parra-Calderón, C. L. (2020). From Raw Data to FAIR Data: The FAIRification Workflow for Health Research. *Methods of Information In Medicine*, *59*(S 01), e21–e32. . doi:10.1055/s-0040-1713684

Singh, O. P. (2023). Artificial intelligence in the era of ChatGPT - Opportunities and challenges in mental health care. *Indian Journal of Psychiatry*, *65*(3), 2. doi:10.4103/indianjpsychiatry.indianjpsychiatry_112_23 PMID:37204980

Siqueira, F. (2022). *Find out about the most common digital crimes committed in Brazil and know how to protect yourself.* R7. https://noticias.r7.com/tecnologia-e-ciencia/conheca-os-crimes-digitais-mais-comuns-praticados-no-brasil-e-saiba-se-proteger-22042022#/foto/1.

Smiljana, A., & Laura, G. (2019). The internet: A brief history based on trust. *Sociologija*, *61*(4), 464–477. doi:10.2298/SOC1904464A

Spapens, T. (2017). Cross-border police cooperation in tackling environmental crime. Transnational Environmental Crime, 505-518. doi:10.4324/9781315084589-30

Stanciu, A. (2023). Data Management Plan for Healthcare: Following FAIR Principles and Addressing Cybersecurity Aspects. A Systematic Review using InstructGPT Cold Spring Harbor Laboratory Press.

Standish. (2011). *The Chaos Reports.* http://www.standish.com

Stelson, P., Hille, J., Eseonu, C., & Doolen, T. (2017). What drives continuous improvement project success in healthcare? *International Journal of Health Care Quality Assurance*, *30*(1), 43–57. doi:10.1108/IJHCQA-03-2016-0035 PMID:28105876

Strang, D., & Meyer, J. (1993). Institutional conditions for diffusion. *Theory and Society, v*, 22.

Sudarsanan, S., Chaudhury, S., Pawar, A. A., Salujha, S. K., & Srivastava, K. (2004). Psychiatric Emergencies. *Medical Journal, Armed Forces India*, *60*(1), 59–62. doi:10.1016/S0377-1237(04)80162-X PMID:27407580

Sun, J. C. Y., Yu, S. J., Lin, S. S., & Tseng, S. S. (2016). The mediating effect of anti-phishing self-efficacy between college students' internet self-efficacy and anti-phishing behavior and gender difference. *Computers in Human Behavior*, *59*, 249–257.

Susnjak, T. (2022). *ChatGPT: The End of Online Exam Integrity?* arXiv pre-print server.

Sutherland, E. H., Williams, F., & McShane, M. (2015). Differential association. *On Analyzing Crime.*

Suykens, J., & Vandewalle, J. (1999). Article. *Neural Processing Letters*, *9*(3), 293–300. doi:10.1023/A:1018628609742

Swissinfo. (2021). *Switzerland diplomatically rejects Biden's 'fiscal paradise' label.* Swissinfo. https://www.swissinfo.ch/eng/business/diplomacy_switzerland-diplomatically-rejects-biden-s—fiscal-paradise—label-/46578996

Tamer, M. (2023). *Ebook 3 of the Module "Legal Theory of Economic Criminal Law and Cyber Crimes".* Theme Embezzlement and Electronic Fraud - I, from the Postgraduate Course in Digital Law at EBRADI.

TaskinsoyJ. (2021). *This Time is Different: Bitcoin Has More Reasons to Reach the Price of $100,000.* doi:10.2139/ssrn.3914299

Techopedia. (2022). *Security Architecture.* https://www.techopedia.com/definition/72/security-architecture

Tembe, R., Hong, K. W., Murphy-Hill, E., Mayhorn, C. B., & Kelley, C. M. (2013, June). American and Indian conceptualizations of phishing. In *2013 Third Workshop on Socio-Technical Aspects in Security and Trust* (pp. 37-45). IEEE.

Ten, C. W., Manimaran, G., & Liu, C. C. (2010). Cybersecurity for critical infrastructures: Attack and defense modeling. *IEEE Transactions on Systems, Man, and Cybernetics. Part A, Systems and Humans*, 40(4), 853–865. doi:10.1109/TSMCA.2010.2048028

Thakur, S., Chaudhari, S., & Joshi, B. (2022). Ransomware: Threats, Identification and Prevention. *Cyber Security and Digital Forensics*, 361-387.

Thamy, R. (2020). *Tamer, Mauricio. Evidence in Digital Law: concept of digital evidence, procedures and digital evidence in kind*. Thomson Reuters Brasil.

The Open Group. (1999). *Building Blocks*. Introduction to Building Blocks. The Open Group.

The Open Group. (2011a). *Introduction to the Architecture Development Method (ADM)*. The Open Group.

The Open Group. (2011c). *Foundation Architecture: Technical Reference Model*. The Open Group. http://www.opengroup.org/public/arch/p3/trm/trm_dtail.htm

Thielmann, I., & Hilbig, B. E. (2015). Trust: An integrative review from a person–situation perspective. *Review of General Psychology*, 19(3), 249–277.

Thomas, J. M. (2007). The Computer Fraud and Abuse Act: A Powerful Weapon vs. Unfair Competitors and Disgruntled Employees. *Employment Law Magazine*. https://www.williamskastner.com/uploadedFiles/ThomasIDQ200703.pdf)

Thorp, H. H. (2023). ChatGPT is fun, but not an author. *Science*, 379(6630), 313–313. doi:10.1126cience.adg7879 PMID:36701446

Threat Intelligence. (2023). *Security Architecture: What it is, Benefits and Frameworks*. https://www.threatintelligence.com/blog/security-architecture

Tirunillai, S., & Tellis, G. J. (2014). Mining marketing meaning from online chatter: Strategic brand analysis of big data using latent dirichlet allocation. *JMR, Journal of Marketing Research*, 51(4), 463–479. doi:10.1509/jmr.12.0106

Tjostheim, I., & Waterworth, J. A. (2020). Predicting personal susceptibility to phishing. In *Information Technology and Systems* [Springer International Publishing.]. *Proceedings of ICITS*, 2020, 564–575.

Tlili, A., Shehata, B., Adarkwah, M. A., Bozkurt, A., Hickey, D. T., Huang, R., & Agyemang, B. (2023). What if the devil is my guardian angel: ChatGPT as a case study of using chatbots in education. *Smart Learning Environments*, 10(1), 15. Advance online publication. doi:10.118640561-023-00237-x

Torlai, G., & Melko, R. G. (2020). Machine-Learning Quantum States in the NISQ Era. *Annual Review of Condensed Matter Physics*, 11(1), 325–344. doi:10.1146/annurev-conmatphys-031119-050651

Trad, A., & Kalpić, D. (2019a). The Business Transformation Framework and the-Application of a Holistic Strategic Security Concept. *Journal: E-leaders, Check Rep.*

Trad, A., & Kalpić, D. (2021a). ENT Transformation Projects: Security Management Concept (SMC). *Proceedings of 12th SCF International Conference on Contemporary Issues in Social Sciences*, 326.

Trad, A. (2022a). *Business Transformation Projects-The Role of a Transcendent Software Engineering Concept (RoTSEC)*. IGI Global.

Trad, A. (2022b). *Business Transformation Projects-The Role of Requirements Engineering (RoRE)*. IGI Global.

Trad, A. (2023a). *Organizational and Digital Transformation Projects-A Mathematical Model for Composite and Organizational Building Blocks*. IGI Global.

Trad, A. (2023b). *Organizational and Digital Transformation Projects-A Mathematical Model for Building Blocks based Organizational Unbundling Process*. IGI Global.

Trad, A. (2023c). *Enterprise Transformation Projects-Cloud Transformation Concept – Holistic Security Integration (CTC-HSI)*. WSEAS Transactions on Computers. doi:10.37394/23205.2022.21.41

Trad, A., & Kalpić, D. (2019b). *The Business Transformation Framework and Enterprise Architecture Framework for Managers in Business Innovation: The Role of Cyber and Information Technology Security. In Global Cyber Security Labor Shortage and International Business Risk*. IGI Global.

Trad, A., & Kalpić, D. (2020a). *Using Applied Mathematical Models for Business Transformation*. IGI Global. doi:10.4018/978-1-7998-1009-4

Trad, A., & Kalpić, D. (2021b). *Advancing Cybersecurity for Business Transformation and Enterprise Architecture Projects: Deep Learning Integration for Projects (DLI4P). In Handbook of Research on Advancing Cybersecurity for Digital Transformation*. IGI Global.

Trad, A., & Kalpić, D. (2022c). *Business Architecture and Transformation Projects: Enterprise Holistic Security Risk Management (ESRM). In Technological Development and Impact on Economic and Environmental Sustainability*. IGI Global.

Transparency. (2020). *Corruption perceptions index*. Transparency International. https://www.transparency.org/en/cpi/2020/index/nzl

Transunion. (2022). *Digital fraud attempts migrate to new segments globally*. Trans Union. https://newsroom.transunion.com.br/tentativas-de-fraude-digital-migram-para-novos-segmentos-globalmente/.

Trautman, L., & Moeller, M. (2020). The Role of the Border and Border Policies in Efforts to Combat Human Trafficking: A Case Study of the Cascadia Region of the US-Canada Border. The Palgrave International Handbook of Human Trafficking, 985-999.

Trustwave. (2019). Global Security Report. *Trustwave*. https://www.trustwave.com/en-us/resources/library/documents/2019-trustwave-global-security-report/

Tu, R., Ma, C., & Zhang, C. (2023). *Causal-Discovery Performance of ChatGPT in the context of Neuropathic Pain Diagnosis*. arXiv:2301.13819. Retrieved January 01, 2023, from https://ui.adsabs.harvard.edu/abs/2023arXiv230113819T

Tuptuk, N., & Hailes, S. (2018). Security of smart manufacturing systems. *Journal of Manufacturing Systems, 47*, 93–106. doi:10.1016/j.jmsy.2018.04.007

UN - United Nations. (1948). *Fundamental Human Right, Article 12 - Privacy*. Universal Declaration of Human Rights.

United Kingdom (UK). (2009). *Cyber Security Strategy of the United Kingdom - Safety, Security and Resilience in Cyber Space, UK Office of Cyber Security and UK Cyber Security Operations Centre, Crown, Richmond, Surrey.* https://assets.publishing.service.gov.uk/government/uploads/system/uploads/attachment_data/file/228841/7642.pdf

United Kingdom (UK). (2011). *The UK Cyber Security Strategy, Cabinet Office, Crown, London.* https://assets.publishing.service.gov.uk/government/uploads/system/uploads/attachment_data/file/60961/uk-cyber-security-strategy-final.pdf

United Nations General Assembly (UN). (2010). *A/RES/64/211: Creation of a Global Culture of Cybersecurity and taking stock of national efforts to protect Critical Information Infrastructures. in Sixty Fourth Session of the United Nations (UN) General Assembly – Resolution adopted by the General Assembly, New York, United Nations.* https://digitallibrary.un.org/record/673712/files/A_RES_64_211-EN.pdf?ln=en

United States Air Force. (2023). *Air Force Doctrine Publication 3-12, Cyberspace Operations.* Available at https://www.doctrine.af.mil/Portals/61/documents/AFDP_3-12/3-12-AFDP-CYBERSPACE-OPS.pdf

United States Joint Chiefs of Staff (USJCS). (2018). *Joint Publication 3-12, Cyberspace Operations, June 8 2018.* https://nsarchive.gwu.edu/sites/default/files/documents/4560063/Joint-Chiefs-of-Staff-Joint-Publication-3-12.pdf

United States vs Babar Ahmad (United States Department of Justice (US DoJ). (2014). https://www.investigative-project.org/documents/case_docs/2422.pdf

United States Vs Morris, (1991) 504 F 2d (1991). https://ncrb.gov.in/sites/default/files/CII%202019%20SNAP-SHOTS%20STATES.pdf)

Varalli, R. M. (2022). *Consumer Law.* Rideel.

Vargo, S. L., Maglio, P. P., & Akaka, M. A. (2008). On value and value co-creation: A service systems and service logic perspective. *European Management Journal, 26*(3), 145–152. doi:10.1016/j.emj.2008.04.003

Verizon. (2018). *Data Breach Investigations Report.* Verizon. https://enterprise.verizon.com/resources/reports/DBIR_2018_Report.pdf

Verma, R., Shashidhar, N., & Hossain, N. (2012). Detecting phishing emails the natural language way. In *Computer Security–ESORICS 2012: 17th European Symposium on Research in Computer Security, Pisa, Italy, September 10-12, 2012.* [Springer Berlin Heidelberg.]. *Proceedings, 17,* 824–841.

Vishwanath, A., Harrison, B., & Ng, Y. J. (2018). Suspicion, Cognition, and Automaticity Model of Phishing Susceptibility. *Communication Research, 45*(8), 1146–1166. doi:10.1177/0093650215627483

Vishwanath, A., Herath, T., Chen, R., Wang, J., & Rao, H. R. (2011). Why do people get phished? Testing individual differences in Phishing vulnerability within an integrated, information processing model. *Decision Support Systems, 51,* 576–586. doi:10.1016/j.dss2011.03.002

von Solms, R., & van Niekerk, J. (2013, October). From information security to cyber security, Elsevier Science Direct. *Computers & Security, 38,* 97–102. doi:10.1016/j.cose.2013.04.004

Vulić, I., Prodanović, & Tot, R. (2019). An Example of a Methodology for Developing the Security of a Distributed Business System. Advances in Economics, Business and Management Research. In *5th IPMA SENET Project Management Conference (SENET 2019).* Atlantis Press. 10.2991enet-19.2019.34

Wang, J., Hu, X., Hou, W., Chen, H., Zheng, R., Wang, Y., Yang, L., Huang, H., Ye, W., Geng, X., Jiao, B., Zhang, Y., & Xie, X. (2023). *On the Robustness of ChatGPT: An Adversarial and Out-of-distribution Perspective.* arXiv:2302.12095. Retrieved February 01, 2023, from https://ui.adsabs.harvard.edu/abs/2023arXiv230212095W

Wang, J., Li, Y., & Rao, H. R. (2016). Overconfidence in Phishing email detection. *Journal of the Association for Information Systems*, *17*(11), 759–783.

Wang, J., Li, Y., & Rao, H. R. (2016). Overconfidence in Phishing e-mail detection. *Journal of the Association for Information Systems*, *17*(11), 759–783.

Wang, T., Huang, Z., & Gan, C. (2016). On mining latent topics from healthcare chat logs. *Journal of Biomedical Informatics*, *61*, 247–259. doi:10.1016/j.jbi.2016.04.008 PMID:27132766

Wang, X., Bendle, N. T., Mai, F., & Cotte, J. (2015). The journal of consumer research at 40: A historical analysis. *The Journal of Consumer Research*, *42*(1), 5–18. doi:10.1093/jcr/ucv009

Warburton, D. (2020). Phishing Attacks Soar 220% During COVID-19 Peak as Cybercriminal Opportunism Intensifies. *F5 Labs*. https://www.f5.com/company/news/features/phishing-attacks-soar-220--during-covid-19-peak-as-cybercriminal

Ward, M. (2018). Staying one step ahead of the cyber-spies. *BBC News*. https://www.bbc.com/news/business-43259900

Watts, S. (2020). *Digital Forensics and Incident Response (DFIR): An Introduction.* BMC. https://www.bmc.com/blogs/dfir-digital-forensics-incident-response/

Weissglass, D. E. (2022). Contextual bias, the democratization of healthcare, and medical artificial intelligence in low-and middle-income countries. *Bioethics*, *36*(2), 201–209. doi:10.1111/bioe.12927 PMID:34460977

Weizenbaum, J. (1976). *Computer power and human reason: From judgment to calculation.* W. H. Freeman & Co.

Welk, A. K., Hong, K. W., Zielinska, O. A., Tembe, R., Murphy-Hill, E., & Mayhorn, C. B. (2015). Will the "Phisher-Men" Reel You In?: Assessing individual differences in a Phishing detection task. [IJCBPL]. *International Journal of Cyber Behavior, Psychology and Learning*, *5*(4), 1–17. doi:10.4018/IJCBPL.2015100101

Wetzel, R. (2005). Tackling phishing. *Business Communications Review*, *35*(2), 46–49.

Whitehill, J., Wu, T., Bergsma, J., Movellan, J. R., & Ruvolo, P. (2009). Whose Vote Should Count More: Optimal Integration of Labels from Labelers of Unknown Expertise. *Neural Information Processing Systems, 22*, 2035–2043. https://papers.nips.cc/paper/3644-whose-vote-should-count-more-optimal-integration-of-labels-from-labelers-of-unknown-expertise.pdf

Whittaker, C., Ryner, B., & Nazif, M. (2010). Large-scale automatic classification of phishing pages. Conference: Proceedings of the Network and Distributed System Security Symposium, NDSS 2010, San Diego, California, USA.

Wikipedia. (2022a). Cloud computing. In *Wikipedia*. https://en.wikipedia.org/wiki/Cloud_computing

Williams, E. J., Beardmore, A., & Joinson, A. N. (2017). Individual differences in susceptibility to online influence: A theoretical review. *Computers in Human Behavior*, ●●●, 412–421. doi:10.1016/j.chb.2017.03.002

Williams, E. J., Hinds, J., & Joinson, A. N. (2018). Exploring susceptibility to phishing in the workplace. *International Journal of Human-Computer Studies*, *120*, 1–13.

Williams, E. J., & Polage, D. (2019). How persuasive is Phishing e-mail? The role of authentic design, influence and current events in e-mail judgement. *Behaviour & Information Technology, 38*(2), 184–197. doi:10.1080/014 4929X.2018.1519599

Wilson, M., deZafra, D., Pitcher, S., Tressler, J., & Ippolito, J. (1998). *Information Technology Security Training Requirements: A Role- and Performance-Based Model, Special Publication (NIST SP 800-16)*. National Institute of Standards and Technology. doi:10.6028/NIST.SP.800-16

Wilson, M., & Hash, J. (2003). *Building an Information Technology Security Awareness and Training Program, Special Publication (NIST SP 800-50)*. National Institute of Standards and Technology. https://tsapps.nist.gov/publication/get_pdf.cfm?pub_id=151287

Wirtz, J., Kunz, W. H., Hartley, N., & Tarbit, J. (2022). Corporate digital responsibility in service firms and their ecosystems. *Journal of Service Research*.

Wojahn, A. S., Michael, C. da P., da Veiga, D. J. S., Lenz, R., da Silva, S. G., Rossetto, T. P., & dos Santos, M. L. (2022). The social vulnerability of the elderly against scams in the digital scope. Research, Society and Development. doi:10.33448/rsd-v11i11.33652

Wright, R. T., & Marett, K. (2010). The Influence of Experiential and Dispositional Factors in *Phishing*: An Empirical Investigation of the Deceived. *Journal of Management Information Systems, 27*(1), 273–303. doi:10.2753/MIS0742-1222270111

Wronka, C. (2022). "Cyber-laundering": The change of money laundering in the digital age. *Journal of Money Laundering Control, 25*(2), 330–344. doi:10.1108/JMLC-04-2021-0035

Yalezo, S., & Thinyane, M. (2013). *Architecting and Constructing an Service Oriented Architecture Bridge for an Model View Control Platform*. IEEE Computer Society Washington.

Yar, M. (2005). The Novelty of 'Cybercrime' An Assessment in Light of Routine Activity Theory. *European Journal of Criminology, 2*(4), 407-427. doi: 101177/147737080556056

Yeo, Y. H., Samaan, J. S., Ng, W. H., Ting, P.-S., Trivedi, H., Vipani, A., Ayoub, W., Yang, J. D., Liran, O., Spiegel, B., & Kuo, A. (2023). Assessing the performance of ChatGPT in answering questions regarding cirrhosis and hepatocellular carcinoma. *Clinical and Molecular Hepatology, 29*(3), 721–732. Advance online publication. doi:10.3350/cmh.2023.0089 PMID:36946005

Yermek, A. B., Zhanna, A. K., Canzada, S., & Nurlan, Zh. A. (2020). Legislative Regulation of Criminal Liability for Environmental Crimes. *Journal of Environmental Accounting and Management, 8*(4), 323–334. doi:10.5890/JEAM.2020.12.002

Ylimäki, T. (2008). *Potential Critical Success Factors for Enterprise Architecture*. University of Jyväskylä, Information Technology Research Institute.

Yoshua Bengio, R. D., & Vincent. (2000). *A Neural Probabilistic Language Model* (Vol. 13). MIT Press. https://proceedings.neurips.cc/paper/2000/hash/728f206c2a01bf572b5940d7d9a8fa4c-Abstract.html

Yu, W. D., Nargundkar, S., & Tiruthani, N. (2008). A *Phishing* vulnerability analysis of web based systems. *2008 Symposium on Computers and Communications*, 326-331. IEEE.

Zetter, K. (2014). An unprecedented look at stuxnet, the world's first digital weapon. *Wired.* https://www.wired.com/2014/11/countdown-to-zero-day-stuxnet/

Zhavoronkov, A. (2022). Rapamycin in the context of Pascal's Wager: Generative pre-trained transformer perspective. *Oncoscience*, *9*, 82–84. doi:10.18632/oncoscience.571 PMID:36589923

Zhou, Li, Yu, Liu, Wang, Zhang, Ji, Yan, He, Peng, Li, Wu, Liu, Xie, Xiong, Pei, Yu, & Sun. (2023). *A Comprehensive Survey on Pretrained Foundation Models: A History from BERT to ChatGPT*. Academic Press.

Zielinska, O. A., Welk, A. K., Mayhorn, C. B., & Murphy-Hill, E. (2016). A temporal analysis of persuasion principles in Phishing e-mails. *Proceedings of the Human Factors and Ergonomics Society Annual Meeting*, *60*(1), 765–769.

About the Contributors

Nuno Mateus-Coelho is an Adjunct Professor of Cybersecurity at the Polytechnic Institute of Cavado and Ave; an Associate Professor at the Universidade Lusófona; Cyber Security Adviser at FORVIA; CEO of NRMC.PT; Judicial Expert of the Ministry of Justice; and CISO & DPO of several prominent national organizations. He holds a Bachelor's degree in Information Systems Engineering, a Master's degree in Computer Engineering (Cybersecurity) from the Higher Institute of Engineering of Porto, and a Ph.D. in Computer Science (Cybersecurity) from the University of Trás-os-Montes and Alto Douro. He is currently a post-doctoral researcher in Cybersecurity at the Universidade Lusófona. Nuno Mateus-Coelho serves as the Chief Editor of the scientific journal ARIS2-Journal, Director of LAPI2S - Laboratory of Privacy and Information Systems Security, General Chair of the iSCSi - International Conference on Industry Sciences and Computer Sciences Innovation, and he is also the author of numerous works, books, and scientific articles on Cybersecurity. He is a Senior Engineer and Specialist of the Order of Engineers and is accredited by the European Commission as an expert in information and Cybersecurity projects. Nuno Mateus-Coelho speaks at TED, IEEE, and Web Summit Lisbon on Technology and Cybersecurity. He is a cybersecurity and cyberterrorism expert commentator on CNN Portugal and TVI, with an opinion column. In 2021, he won the international Inncyber Innovation Award for "Best European Research" in Cybersecurity, which included a week of immersion at the University of California-Riverside. One of his most significant achievements was the Vent2Life project, which aimed to repair hospital ventilators during the COVID crisis, and this project successfully recovered two hundred pieces of equipment.

Maria Manuela Cruz-Cunha is a Full Professor in the School of Technology at the Polytechnic Institute of Cavado and Ave, Portugal. She holds a Dipl. Eng. (5 years) in the field of Systems and Informatics Engineering, an M.Sci. in the field of Computer Integrated Manufacturing, a Dr.Sci in of Production Systems Engineering and Habilitation in Informatics Engineering. She teaches subjects related with Information Systems, Information Technologies and Organizational Models to undergraduate and post-graduate studies. She has authored and edited 28 books and her work appears in 200 papers published in journals, book chapters and conference proceedings. She is founder and conference chair of the "CENTERIS – Conference on ENTERprise Information Systems", "ViNOrg – Conference on Virtual and Networked Organizations Emergent Technologies and Tools" and "SeGAH – Serious Games and Applications for Health". She is the editor-in-chief of the "International Journal of Web Portals" and serves as associate editor of some journals.

***

Jimmy Adebesin Benson is an Independent Mental health Practitioner with over 13 years experience working for NHS England. He has co-authored several books and journals in the areas of ICT and Mental health.

João Albino is Professor and Lecturer at the Graduate Program in Media and Technology at Universidade Estadual Paulista.

Ivany Bucchianico has a Bachelor in Nursing from the University of São Paulo at Ribeirão Preto.

Carla Cardoso has a Ph.D. in Biomedical Sciences from the Institute of Biomedical Sciences Abel Salazar of the University of Porto. Assistant Professor at the Faculty of Law of the University of Porto (FDUP), teaches in all three cycles of studies in Criminology. She is a founding and integrated member of the Center for Interdisciplinary Research-Crime, Justice, and Security (CJS) of the FDUP.

Isabel Chumbo is an adjunct professor at the Polytechnic University of Bragança. Her research interests are in the field of translation and intercultural studies. She has been involved in several European projects related to the improvement of teaching in higher education through digital technologies.

Ding Ding is Associate Professor and the Vice Dean of the School of Business at the Singapore University of Social Sciences (SUSS) where she has worked since 2008. She received her PhD in Economics from the Nanyang Technological University, and is a Chartered Financial Analyst (CFA). Prior to her current role, she was the head of B.Sc. in Finance programme at SUSS during 2012-2018, and taught various finance courses at the undergraduate, postgraduate, and executive training levels. Her research interests include Financial Technology and Innovation, Financial Markets, Development and International Economics.

Ana Ferreira, PhD, is a researcher and IT Specialist at the Service of Informatics at the Faculty of Medicine, University of Porto, Portugal (since 2004) and a member of the Health Informatics research group at CINTESIS (Center for Health Technology and Services Research). She got her MSc in Information Security at Royal Holloway, University of London (2002) and a PhD (2010) in Computer Science, a joint supervision between the University of Porto and the University of Kent, UK, working mainly on studying, improving and modelling access control for the healthcare domain. The PhD thesis was internationally awarded by Fraunhofer. Current research is devoted to access control for Electronic Patient Records, socio-technical security, usable security, human computer interaction and social engineering. She authored several scientific articles and book chapters (a list of relevant publications can be consulted at).

María García González is a Lecturer in the Information and Documentation Department at the University of Murcia (UMU). Phd in Information and Documentation. He is part of the TECNOMOD UM research group. Author of several publications on quality in content management systems in organizations; research methods for documenting uses experiences; data, information and knowledge management (DIC); semantic web; competitive Intelligence; Information management systems; research and standards initiatives relating to the use of metadata; issues related to information needs and access; Enterprice Content Management (ECM - BPM); e-Government and archivals – digital records.

317

Guan Chong is Associate Professor and Director in Centre for Continuing and Professional Education, Singapore University of Social Sciences (SUSS), Singapore. Chong completed her Ph.D in Marketing at Nanyang Business School, Nanyang Technological University, and her undergraduate studies in Marketing at Guanghua School of Management, Peking University, China. Her research interests lie in the area of data-driven digital marketing. Her publications appear in leading journals such as European Journal of Marketing, Journal of Interactive Marketing, Journal of Business Research and Telecommunications Policy. She is an editorial board member of Internet Research.

Inês Guedes has a Master and Ph.D. in Criminology from the Faculty of Law of the University of Porto (FDUP). Assistant Professor at the same University. She is a founding and integrated member of the Center for Interdisciplinary Research-Crime, Justice, and Security (CJS) of the FDUP and a collaborating member of the Center for Legal, Economic, and Environmental Studies (CEJEA).

Priyanka Gupta is a Senior Lecturer in Business Analytics Programmes in the School of Business at the Singapore University of Social Sciences. She holds a PhD in Quantitative Marketing from Nanyang Technological University, Singapore. Priyanka had worked in FMCG industry across Sales and Marketing which has given her a good exposure of field realities and managerial issues. Her training as an empirical researcher combined with her managerial experience puts her in good stead to connect the methodological rigor of her analysis to real-world solutions. Her research answers the intriguing question regarding how and to what extent does spatial interaction affects marketers' and retail managers' decisions. In addition to research, Priyanka has a passionate interest in teaching.

Yu-chen Hung is a senior lecturer in the Singapore University of Social Science. Her research interests include consumer psychology, innovation adoption, digital platform strategy, and experiential marketing. Her publications appear in various international journals, such as International Journal of Research in Marketing, European Journal of Marketing, Journal of Business Research, Transportation, and Journal of Marketing Management, Electronic Markets, Journal of Product and Brand Management, etc.

Jiang Zhiying is the Head of the Master of Digital Marketing Progamme. Her research interest is using quantitative modeling methods to generate consumer and market insights. Her publications appear in the Journal of Interactive Marketing, International Journal of Innovation Studies, etc.

Eugénia Maria Garcia Jorge Anes is a Professor at the School of Health of the Polytechnic Institute of Bragança Degree in Nursing Specialist in Community Nursing Master in Health Management and Economics Doctor in Psychology and Intervention Throughout the Life Cycle

Vandana Dixit Kaushik is working as Associate Professor in the Department of Computer Science and Engineering, Harcourt Butler Technical University, Kanpur, U.P., India (formerly Harcourt Butler Technological Institute, Kanpur, U.P., India). She has vast teaching and research experience. She teaches various subjects like Digital Image Processing, Database Management, Operating Systems, E-Commerce etc both at graduate and under graduate levels. She completed her Ph.D. in 2011 from Dr. APJ Abdul Kalam University, Lucknow, U.P., India and she is currently guiding four Ph.D. scholars in areas of current international needs. Her three PhD students have completed PhD under her guidance. She Worked in close collaboration with various other Academic institutes like HNB Garhwal University (Archaeology

Department), Guindy College of Engineering, IISC Bengaluru, Indian Institute of Technology, Kanpur and with industries like Intel. She was the member of Multicore Curriculum Development team at UG level under the convenorship of Prof. H.S. Jamadagni, Chairman, CEDT, IISc, Bengaluru. This entire curriculum development project was sponsored by Intel, Bengaluru. Has reviewed many International Journal and Conference papers of good impact. She is currently the member of Board of Studies of CS/ IT/ MCA of Dr. APJ Abdul Kalam University, Lucknow and H.B.T.U, Kanpur. She has presented papers and attended many international conferences in India and abroad and published many research papers in international conferences and journals of good impact. Research Areas • 3D Image Blurring and Deblurring • Medical Imaging • Data indexing • 3D Face Recognition • Biometrics •Image Processing

Ana Claudia Lima is a Student of the Graduate Program in Media and Technology (Doctorate) at Universidade Estadual Paulista

Juan Carlos Martínez Santos is an accomplished researcher and lecturer with over 19 years of experience in electronic and computer engineering. He received his bachelor's degree in electronic engineering and master's in electric power from the Universidad Industrial de Santander, Bucaramanga, Colombia, in 2001 and 2004, respectively. He then earned his Ph.D. in computer engineering from Northeastern University, Boston, MA, USA, in 2013. Dr. Martínez Santos received numerous accolades throughout his career for his research and teaching, including the Fulbright Scholar-Colciencias-DNP in 2007. He has been a Researcher and a Lecturer with the Universidad Tecnológica de Bolívar since 2004, where he has been a Professor since 2017. Between 2012 and 2020, he led a group of interdisciplinary work in Computer Science. Currently, Dr. Martínez Santos is a Teacher at the Faculty of Engineering, where he is responsible for teaching courses in computer architecture (computer engineering), microprocessors (electronics engineering), microcontrollers (mechatronics engineering), and advanced techniques of digital design (graduate course, M.Sc., and Ph.D.). He is also an active researcher in several areas, including Cloud computing, the Internet of Things, Architectural support for security enhancement, Information assurance, Embedded systems, Blockchain applications, and Quantum Computing. In 2018, he was under a Research License at Ormuco Inc. (Montreal, CA). Dr. Martínez Santos' expertise in his field has led to numerous publications in top-tier academic journals, and he has also presented his research at various international conferences.

Rodrigo Martínez-Béjar is a Professor of Computer Science in the Department of Information and Communication Engineering at the University of Murcia in Spain. He received his Master Degree in Computer Science from the University of Malaga in 1992 and his Ph.D. degree from the University of Murcia in Spain in 1997. Also, he holds a Master degree in Applied Sociology from the University of Murcia. He has held visiting positions at several European, Australian and Latin-American Universities, including the Australian Universities of Adelaide and New South Wales, and the French University of Southern Paris. He has served on several Editorial Boards and has co-authored abour 150 scientific publications, most of them in peer-reviewed journals and conferences and led more than 30 national or international competitive grants and research contracts with industry. In 2006, he became the Head of an institutional, inter-disciplinary University research group.

Anirban Mitra, (Ph.D. in Science & Technology - Computer Science) is working as an Associate Professor of Computer Science and Engineering in the School of Engineering and Technology at Amity University, Kolkata, India. He is a senior member of IEEE and ACM.

Eduardo Morgado is a Professor at the Computing Department, Fac de Ciências – UNESP – Bauru, since 1985. Degree in Engineering from Escola Politécnica/USP in 1980. Master in Business Administration from FEA/USP in 1991 – in the area of Quantitative Methods and Informatics, research on the Internet. Doctorate in Administration from FEA/USP in 1996 - in the area of Quantitative Methods and Informatics, research on IT Management in the Banking Sector. Postdoctoral in Technological Innovation by INSEAD/France in 2012. He is a professor in the Computer Science and Information Systems courses, where he teaches Advanced Topics in Information Technology III. Advanced Topics in Computing IV; Cloud computing; Machine Learning and Entrepreneurship. He is an accredited professor at the Graduate Program in Media and Technology at FAAC, where he teaches Cloud Computing and New Uses of the Cloud in Education I and II. Currently researching Data Security, Artificial Intelligence, Machine Learning and Alexa Development

Joshua Ojo Nehinbe obtained Ph.D. in Computer Science from the University of Essex, UK in 2011 and M.Sc. in Computer Science (with research) from the University of Agriculture, Abeokuta in Nigeria in 2004. He has worked in the banking sector as a Software engineer; Globus support specialist, Head of IT and auditor of Information Systems. He also had cognate experience in IT consultancy with local and international firms. Joshua Nehinbe teaches Undergraduates and Post graduates students in the areas of Cyber security and forensics, database design and management, software engineering, Leading E-Strategy and data mining. He has published over 40 reputable journal papers, conference papers and co-authored book chapters with foreign experts in the areas of best industrial practices, security and forensics in Cyber Physical Systems. He is a professional member of the Institute of Electrical and Electronics Engineers (IEEE), British Computer Society (BCS), British Academy of Forensic Sciences (BAFS) and Nigeria Computer Society (NCS).

Miloslava Plachkinova is an Assistant Professor of Information Security and Assurance at Kennesaw State University. Her research focuses on information security, cybercrime, and policy implications. Dr. Plachkinova's work has been published in journals such as Journal of the Association for Information Systems, Information Systems Frontiers, Journal of Computer Information Systems, Communications of the Association of Information Systems, and Journal of Information Systems Education. She is a Certified Information Systems Security Professional (CISSP), Certified Cloud Security Professional (CCSP), Certified Information Security Manager (CISM), Certified Information Systems Auditor (CISA), Certified Data Privacy Solutions Engineer (CDPSE), Certified in Risk and Information Systems Control (CRISC), and a Project Management Professional (PMP®).

Liliana Ribeiro has a Degree in Criminology from the Faculty of Law of the University of Porto (FDUP). Currently, Master's student in the same Faculty. Develops research in the areas of security and cybercrime.

Banhita Sarkar has submitted her PhD Thesis and is waiting for final defense. Apart from being an active researcher, she is presently heading the Law School of Amity University Kolkata.

Lorenzo Scalera achieved the Master Degree in Mechanical Engineering (cum laude) at University of Trieste in 2015, and the PhD Degree in Industrial and Information Engineering at University of Udine in 2019. In 2018 he was a visiting PhD student at the Stevens Institute of Technology in Hoboken (NJ, USA). In 2019 he was a Post Doc Research Fellow at Free University of Bozen-Bolzano. Since 2020 he is Assistant Professor of Mechanics Applied to Machines at the Polytechnic Department of Engineering and Architecture of the University of Udine. His research interests include dynamic modeling of robotic systems, trajectory planning, collaborative robotics, and mobile robotics.

Vineeta Singh is working as assistant professor (Research and Development Wing) in Computer Engineering and Applications Department in GLA University, Mathura. Her area of research is image processing, biometrics and Data Mining. She has presented and published more than 13 research papers in international reputed conference proceedings publishers such as Springer, Taylor and Francis, Apple Academic Press, Elsevier SSRN etc. and published five research papers (SCIE Indexed) and five are in pipeline in SCIE indexed journals and published one book chapter and four book chapters are in production with reputed publishers such as CRC Press Taylor and Francis Group, IGI Global, Springer etc. She is also working as reviewer in different SCIE indexed journals and international conferences held in NIT Arunachal Pradesh and IIT BHU Varanasi. She has done B.Tech. in Computer Science & Engineering from UPTU Lucknow India and M.Tech. in Computer Science & Engineering from APJAKTU Lucknow India and PhD from HBTU Kanpur India.

Carla Távora is a Professional Master Studies in Graduate Program in Media and Technology, State University of Sao Paulo, UNESP, Brasil. Ph.D. in progress in Media and Technology, Unesp State University of Sao Paulo, UNESP, Brasi

Index

A

Adolescent 70
Artificial Intelligence 14-15, 19-20, 26, 32, 36, 41-42, 74, 98, 125, 138, 168, 174, 242, 277

B

Brazilian legislation 254, 258
Brazilian population 254
Business Transformation Projects 189

C

ChatGPT 114, 124-126, 128-129, 133-141, 143
Complainants 65-69, 71-74
Components 3, 31, 50, 78, 103, 107-108, 125, 129-130, 178-179, 183-184, 187, 191-192, 204, 243, 245, 272
Cryptography 6, 40, 53-55, 168, 226
Cues 80-81, 85-87
Cyber Laws 268, 274, 276
Cyber Threats 21, 23, 25, 41, 43, 55, 95
Cybercrime 3, 33-34, 44, 66-74, 76-77, 80, 193, 222-224, 226, 229, 231, 234, 268-273, 275-280
Cybersecurity 1-5, 8-10, 13-15, 19-26, 31-36, 54, 86, 94-101, 103, 107-108, 112-113, 117, 119, 138, 153-154, 167-168, 172, 174-175, 177, 189, 191-193, 195, 201, 205, 221, 241-245, 249, 251, 268, 273, 276, 280

D

Damage Reparation 260-261
Data Science 43, 156
Deep Learning 41-42, 51-53, 138, 169, 189
Defendants 67, 69, 71, 74, 262
Development and Operations 191
Digital 3, 15, 20, 41, 47, 67, 69, 74, 98, 107-108, 127, 137, 140, 142, 157, 174-175, 189, 193-195, 204-205, 220, 223-224, 226, 228-229, 231-233, 254-255, 257, 259-262, 273, 276
Digital Bank 254, 259-262
Digital Forensics 204-205, 224, 228, 233
Discord 220, 227-228, 230-233
Distributed Denial of Service Attacks 167, 169

E

Education 3, 5, 21, 25, 33, 35-36, 42-43, 82-83, 86, 95, 100-101, 106-108, 127-128, 135-136, 138-139, 193, 222, 242, 269, 273
elderly people 253-254, 257
Emails 14, 22-23, 35, 44, 49, 77, 79, 81-88, 193, 273
Enterprise Architecture 179, 188-189
Eye-Tracker 86-88

F

Framework 9, 32-33, 36, 45-46, 53, 94-97, 100-101, 103-104, 107-108, 112, 114-115, 117, 119-120, 124, 129, 131, 134, 156, 170, 172, 177, 179-180, 184, 187-189, 204, 214, 223

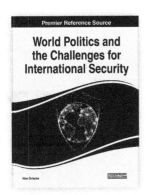

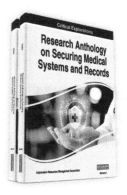

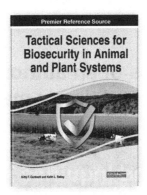

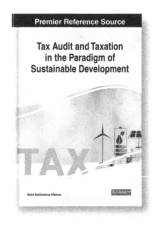

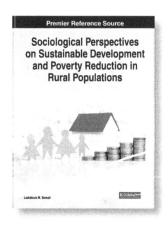

Printed in the United States
by Baker & Taylor Publisher Services